Rural Education
in Urbanized Nations

Other Titles in This Series

Evaluating Teachers and Administrators: A Performance Objectives Approach, George B. Redfern

Education in Rural America: A Reassessment of Conventional Wisdom, edited by Jonathan P. Sher

Also of Interest

The Family in Rural Society, edited by Raymond T. Coward and William M. Smith

Goodbye to Excellence: A Critical Look at Minimum Competency Testing, Mitchell B. Lazarus

The Transition of Youth to Adulthood: A Bridge Too Long, The National Commission on Youth, B. Frank Brown, Director

The Undergraduate Curriculum: A Guide to Innovation and Reform, Clifton F. Conrad

Found: Long-Term Gains from Early Intervention, edited by Bernard Brown

Legal Handbook for Educators, Patricia A. Hollander

Psychology and Education of Gifted Children, Philip Vernon, Georgina Adamson, and Dorothy Vernon

Politics in Rural America: People, Parties, and Policy, Frank M. Bryan

Poverty in Rural America: A Case Study, Janet M. Fitchen

Westview Special Studies in Education

Rural Education in Urbanized Nations:
Issues and Innovations
edited by Jonathan P. Sher

A reversal in rural-to-urban migration patterns is creating increasing interest in the quality of education in rural areas and in techniques for meeting educational needs in sparsely populated regions. Wholesale urbanization of rural schools generally is rejected as a potential solution: it is logistically inefficient; centralization and standardization are met with growing resistance; and conventional solutions to educational problems produce uneven results when applied to rural areas.

This book addresses the broad spectrum of rural education issues within OECD member countries. The authors identify innovative programs, policies, and strategies and point toward the more promising paths for rural school improvement. They also issue warnings about some of the blind alleys and dead ends that can be encountered. The major topics covered include delivery systems, in-school innovations, support mechanisms, and community-school linkages.

Jonathan P. Sher, author of *Education in Rural America: A Reassessment of Conventional Wisdom* (Westview Press, 1977), is the head of the Rural Programme, Centre for Educational Research and Innovation, of the Organisation for Economic Co-operation and Development in Paris, France. In addition, Dr. Sher is currently a visiting scholar at the school of education of the University of North Carolina in Chapel Hill.

Published in cooperation with the
Centre for Educational Research and Innovation,
Organisation for Economic Co-operation and Development,
Paris, France

Rural Education in Urbanized Nations: Issues and Innovations

edited by Jonathan P. Sher

An OECD/CERI Report

Westview Press / Boulder, Colorado

Westview Special Studies in Education

Copyright © 1981 by the Organisation for Economic Co-operation and Development

Published in 1981 in the United States of America by
   Westview Press, Inc.
   5500 Central Avenue
   Boulder, Colorado 80301
   Frederick A. Praeger, Publisher

Library of Congress Cataloging in Publication Data
Main entry under title:
Rural education in urbanized nations.
   (Westview special studies in education)
   "An OECD/CERI report."
   Includes bibliographical references.
   1. Education, Rural—Addresses, essays, lectures. 2. Correspondence schools and courses
—Addresses, essays, lectures. 3. Television in education—Addresses, essays, lectures. I. Sher,
Jonathan P. II. Centre for Educational Research and Innovation.
LC5146.R87   370.19'346   80-19083
ISBN 0-89158-964-3

Printed and bound in the United States of America

To my family:
especially Ada, Mom and Pop Sher,
and Matthew and Evelyn

If Blanche Dubois had had you behind her,
she wouldn't have had to rely on
the kindness of strangers.

Contents

PART 1
THE REEMERGENCE OF RURAL EDUCATION

PART 2
RURAL EDUCATION INNOVATIONS

DELIVERY AND SUPPORT SYSTEM INNOVATIONS

Tables and Figures

Preface

The information that appears in this volume was collected as part of the program of work for the OECD/CERI SPA project. Before introducing the book's contents, it may be useful to begin by unscrambling all these initials.

OECD is the Organisation for Economic Co-operation and Development. Although it was officially created in 1961, OECD can properly be seen as having started just after World War II. In fact, in its earlier incarnation, OECD was the agency directly responsible for administering the Marshall Plan for the economic recovery of Europe.

Currently, the Organisation is composed of twenty-four member national governments. Included are the following countries: Australia, Austria, Belgium, Canada, Denmark, Finland, France, Germany, Greece, Iceland, Ireland, Italy, Japan, Luxembourg, Netherlands, New Zealand, Norway, Portugal, Spain, Sweden, Switzerland, Turkey, United Kingdom, and the United States. Yugoslavia also participates in the work of OECD under a special arrangement.

OECD's basic missions are, first, to help member governments promote economic growth, employment, and improved standards of living; and second, to help promote a sound world economy through international cooperation. Under the direction of the OECD Council, the secretary general, and specialized committees, the Organisation is divided into a series of administrative directorates. In relation to this volume, the most important of these is the Directorate for Social Affairs, Manpower and Education.

Within this directorate is a research-oriented unit called the Centre for Educational Research and Innovation (CERI). Created in 1968, CERI operates under the supervision of an independent governing board (on which each member country holds one seat). CERI's basic mandate has been to promote cooperation among member countries in the field of educational research and innovation. Over the past twelve years, CERI has sponsored projects on a wide range of educational concerns including recurrent and continuing education, educational technology, curriculum development, in-service education and teacher training, the management of higher education, the education of handicapped adolescents, and early childhood education.[1]

In 1976, the CERI governing board authorized the creation of the Project on Basic Education and Teacher Support in Sparsely-Populated Areas, more commonly referred to as the SPA project. This project officially terminated at the end of 1978 after the final conference was held in Aurillac, France. Still, national-level follow-up conferences on SPA issues were held during 1979 in England, Finland, and Australia.

In addition, the CERI governing board approved a new project in May 1979, Education and Local Development, which was intended not only to carry forward the work begun under the auspices of the SPA project but also to complement the earlier emphasis on in-school innovations with a broader look at the roles (actual and potential) education plays in the overall development of the local communities being served.

The new CERI Education and Local Development (ELD) project is scheduled to operate until the end of 1981. Although ELD has an urban component, heavy emphasis will be accorded to the rural side in terms of both operational activities and supporting research. This "positive discrimination" in favor of the rural component is largely a function of the momentum built up through the SPA project.

Thus, this volume should be seen as a sort of midterm report. The intention is to provide a foundation of information and insights on education in the sparsely populated areas of a group of industrialized nations. However, there is still much work to be done both nationally and internationally before a complete understanding of rural schooling in urban societies can be claimed.

The hope is that this book can point out some of the more promising paths toward rural school improvement that have been discovered, as well as issue warnings about some of the blind alleys and dead ends encountered. If this volume stimulates readers not only to reconsider the direction of rural education activities in their own countries but also to keep in mind the lessons to be gained from the experience of other countries, it will have served its purpose well.

Jonathan P. Sher

Note

1. For further information about the work done by OECD's Centre for Educational Research and Innovation, see *The First Ten Years: 1968–1978* (Paris: OECD/CERI, 1978). Also distributed gratis is a brief newsletter appearing three times each year entitled *Innovation in Education: News from the OECD, Paris.* A list of publications available from the OECD as a whole (including education) can be requested from OECD Publications Office, 2, rue André-Pascal, 75775 Paris Cedex 16, France.

Acknowledgments

Although "rugged individualism" is a traditional characteristic of rural life, it is not an apt description of the process that led to this volume on rural education in a group of OECD member countries. Rather, this book is the result of a generous pooling of information, ideas, and experiences by everyone involved. Indeed, the level of commitment and the cooperative spirit evidenced by so many people was remarkable.

First and foremost I would like to express my gratitude to those individuals without whom this book (quite literally) could not have been completed—that is, the fifteen people responsible for the case studies and descriptive reports found herein. I would like to single out two members of this group for special praise: L. C. "Kim" Taylor, who initiated this OECD/CERI activity and very ably led it through the formative period, and R. S. "Bert" Johnston, whose guidance, encouragement, and assistance were invaluable throughout the life of the project.

My sincere appreciation also must be extended to those who prepared the background reports from which my own chapters were constructed, especially Stuart A. Rosenfeld (United States); Geoffrey Elsmore, Peter Boulter, and Barry Taylor (England); Andri Isaksson (Iceland); Bettina Laville, Jacqueline Bonjean, and Françoise Le Hénaff (France); Elgar Henry (New Zealand); Max Angus, Don Edgar, Ken Egan, and Greg Hancock (Australia); Karl Jan Solstad, Asle Høgmo, and Harald Jørgensen (Norway); Annika Andrae and Per-Erik Eriksson (Sweden); Reijo Laukkanen (Finland); and R. S. Johnston (Scotland).

Special thanks are also due to David Mossenson (Director-General of Education in Western Australia), Larry Oates, Max Angus, and Brian Courtney for their work in organizing an Australian national follow-up conference to the CERI SPA Project; to Geoffrey Elsmore, Peter Boulter, and John Banks for organizing a similar SPA follow-up conference in England; and to Pirkko Mela, Ukko Laurila, and Reijo Laukkanen for organizing the Finnish national SPA follow-up conference. The assistance and generosity of the French Ministry of Education (especially Jean Pachot, Bettina Laville, and

Jacqueline Bonjean) in organizing the final SPA conference in Aurillac, France, are gratefully acknowledged as well.

John Cornman and David Chewning of the National Rural Center deserve a great deal of credit for all the institutional support provided by NRC to this project. Needless to say, the many contributions made by my colleagues within OECD's Centre for Educational Research and Innovation were of enormous help. I would also like to applaud the splendid (and indefatigable) secretarial assistance of Ann Bonnel, Susan Williamson, and Judith Cummings.

J.P.S.

The Contributors

Max Angus is superintendent of the research branch of the Education Department of Western Australia.

Glen Diggins is senior education officer for the Isolated Students Matriculation Scheme in the Education Department of Western Australia.

Faith Dunne is associate professor of education at Dartmouth College (United States) and director of the National Study on Small Rural Schools.

Kathryn A. Hecht was associate professor of education at the Center for Cross-Cultural Studies, University of Alaska (United States), at the time this chapter was written and currently is an independent consultant in San Francisco, California (United States).

R. Hillen is the principal of the Chidley Centre in Western Australia.

R. S. Johnston is Her Majesty's Chief Inspector of Schools in Scotland (northern division).

Reijo Laukkanen is chief inspector in the Research and Development Bureau of the National Board of General Education (Finland).

Finlay MacLeod is deputy director of education for the Western Isles Islands Council (Scotland).

Hector McVeagh was principal of the New Zealand Correspondence School for many years and currently is an adviser to the New Zealand Department of Education.

Lauri Muhonen is director of school affairs for the municipality of Kuusamo, Finland.

John Murray was the director of the Bilingual Education Project at the time his chapter was written and currently is the assistant director of education (community) for the Western Isles Islands Council (Scotland).

Gail Armstrong Parks is the education director of the National Rural Center in Washington, D.C. (United States).

Jonathan P. Sher is head of the Rural Programme within the Centre for Educational Research and Innovation (CERI) of the Organisation for Economic Co-operation and Development (OECD) in Paris (France).

Karl Jan Solstad is professor of education at the Institute for Social Science, University of Tromsø (Norway).

L. C. Taylor was the original head of the OECD/CERI Project on Basic Education and Teacher Support in Sparsely-Populated Areas and currently is head of the Educational Programme Services for the Independent Broadcasting Authority (England).

Michael Williams is a staff member of the Western Australia Department of Education's research branch.

Part 1

The Reemergence
of Rural Education

Education in the Countryside: Establishing the Context

Jonathan P. Sher

The Bad News

Just as country roads have been routinely left off national maps, so too country schools have been routinely left off national education agendas. Of course, their absence from the map does not mean that the small country roads have disappeared. Similarly, the fact that most OECD (Organisation for Economic Co-operation and Development) nations have not put rural education on their list of priorities does not mean that country schools have ceased to exist.

Nevertheless, being left off the "map" did have an impact that was both negative and pervasive. In physical terms, far too many rural schools were allowed to fall into disrepair, and their material resources became more and more meager in comparison to metropolitan schools. In educational terms, rural-oriented curricula became the exception rather than the rule, and rural schools were encouraged (if not mandated) to imitate urban/suburban educational models.

Perceptions of and attitudes toward country schools (especially small ones) took a negative turn as well. Professionally, rural assignments were often viewed with disdain; they were seen as way stations where bright young educators had to put in their time before receiving choice assignments in the urban areas; as places for untrained teachers; or as dumping grounds for older educators who had either proved incompetent or fallen out of favor with their supervisors.

Politically, too, rural education fell into a measure of disrepute. Policymakers dealt with country schools largely in negative terms (when they gave them any consideration at all), instead of recognizing or building upon their capacity for excellence. In addition, the discovery that rural schools could be ignored, closed, or treated less than equitably without engendering serious political repercussions made the temptation to treat them this way enormous. The result, even if unintentional, was that national bureaucracies behaved as if quality education should not be wasted on children in sparsely populated areas and as if second-rate schooling was good enough for their rural constituents.

Understandably, all of this had a decidedly demoralizing effect on rural communities as a whole and placed special burdens on rural parents and students. People who were physically isolated by virtue of being rural often came to feel psychologically and politically isolated as well.

Faced with this situation, many rural parents became apathetic toward their children's schools. However, it was an apathy born of ambivalence rather than ignorance or disinterest. To them, education elicited mixed emotions. On the one hand, it was attractive because of both its intrinsic value and the economic opportunities it made available to successful students. On the other hand, education was repellent to the extent that it not only socialized rural children to equate "the good life" with urban areas, but also encouraged and equipped rural youth to leave their home communities permanently.

Thus, over many years, a powerful cycle of negative self-fulfilling prophecies about rural education became deeply entrenched in most OECD member countries. Low expectations led to inadequate attention and resources, which led to unsatisfactory conditions, which led to negative results, which led to lower expectations—and on and on the cycle went.

This rather harsh picture of modern rural schooling in the advanced societies is neither wholly accurate nor equally applicable to every OECD member country. To the extent that it implies that one can safely disregard either the many examples of rural educational excellence found in these countries or the wide divergence in how rural schools and rural policies have developed internationally, this description should be softened. However, pointing out the failure of national educational policies and practices to fully satisfy the needs of rural children and rural communities *is* accurate. Variation among countries has been a matter of degree rather than anything more fundamental.

To better understand this point, it might be useful to think about what a fundamentally different set of priorities and policies would look like. Imagine for a moment a developed nation which regarded its rural schools as its elite and as models to be envied and emulated by metropolitan schools. Imagine a system in which rural schools were the prime beneficiaries of educational research, the recipients of a steady stream of the nation's best educators, and the bastions of the education world's power, prestige, and resources.

In some countries (such as the United States) this elite sector can be found in the suburbs of major metropolitan areas. In other countries (such as France) deference is paid to the large urban centers. Yet no OECD country could (or would) claim that this elevated status had been conferred upon its rural schools.

The Good News

Up until the mid-1970s, the portrait painted thus far would have been broadly true for the OECD countries. However, it is quickly becoming outdated. In the past five years, a major shift in attitudes and policies toward rural education has occurred in many OECD nations. After decades of relative obscurity, issues surrounding the nature and provision of educational services in sparsely populated areas have reemerged and begun to occupy a prominent position on national education agendas.

While it would be overly dramatic to liken this reemergence to the phoenix rising from the ashes or the metamorphosis of a caterpillar into a butterfly, the change has been a significant one nearly everywhere and an almost startling one in several cases. Even in the midst of generally gloomy economic conditions and a tightening of governmental expenditures, the allocation of both human and financial resources in favor of rural education is rising. Some countries have already made substantial new investments in rural programs and/or rural research; others are planning to do so in the near future. Thus rural education as both a field of research and a sphere of governmental action is likely to grow in importance during the 1980s.

Perhaps the most appropriate analogy for this policy shift can be found in Hans Christian Andersen's famous children's story *The Ugly Duckling*. In this story a little bird who had been an outcast among a group of ducks turned out to be a beautiful swan rather than an ugly duckling. So too, policymakers and educators are discovering that rural education seems "ugly" only when compared to a vision of schooling quite remote from the realities of rural life. The growing awareness that rural education is a "swan" (or at least a distinctly different kind of duck) has not only allowed rural schools to be seen in a more positive light but also encouraged policymakers to adopt new and more appropriate ways of dealing with them.

All of this should not be taken to mean that the industrialized countries have suddenly decided that rural education is their top priority or that extravagant sums of money are being allocated to rural school improvement. Although desirable, commitments of this magnitude have not been made and are unlikely to be forthcoming. Rather, the point is that resources for rural efforts are increasing and country schools are now accorded a level of respectability within the education profession and visibility within the political arena which would have been unheard of even ten years ago.

Why is there now a policy shift in favor of rural education? As might be expected, the reasons are neither simple nor universal. Explanations vary considerably both within and among the OECD countries. Still, several circumstances of international relevance have fostered this renewed interest and support. These include demographic and economic changes; trends toward decentralization; dissatisfaction with traditional policies; renewed respect for rural models; and, perhaps most important, pressures for equal educational opportunity. Each of these influences will be discussed below.

Demographic and Economic Changes

The process of urbanization has been an extremely powerful one in the OECD nations. For a few countries, this trend became dominant early in the twentieth century. But for most nations, the big rural-to-urban population shift took place in the period from the end of World War II until 1975.

It was during this period that many OECD countries went from being predominantly rural countries (in terms of population distribution) to predominantly urban ones. For instance, in the years from 1950 to 1974, Finland went from having 32 percent of its population residing in urban areas to having 58 percent in cities. Switzerland and Greece both went from being 37 percent urban in 1950 to being 57 percent urban in 1975.[1] Similarly, Canada's urban population rose during these years from 52 percent to 76 percent, while Ireland jumped from being 42 percent urban to being 55 percent urban.[2] The most dramatic shift came in Sweden, where the urban share of the total population increased from 48 percent in 1950 to 84 percent in 1975.

Even in countries that retained a majority of their population in the countryside, the trend toward urbanization was apparent. For example, Portugal went from having 21 percent of its people located in urban zones in 1950 to having 29 percent of the population in such areas by 1975. Similarly, Norway's urban population expanded its percentage of the total from 32 percent to 45 percent during the same twenty-five-year period. Yugoslavia's urban zones more than doubled their share of the total population (from 19 percent in 1950 to 39 percent in 1975), but it remained a predominantly rural country.

And finally, OECD countries which already had the majority of their population residing in urban areas by 1950 saw this urban dominance solidify even further in the decades following World War II. For instance, the percentage of people classified as urban during these years went from 71 percent to 83 percent in New Zealand; 61 percent to 73 percent in the United

States;[3] 72 percent to 83 percent in both Iceland and the Federal Republic of Germany; 63 percent to 87 percent in Belgium; and 59 percent to 71 percent in France.

This notable urban growth was accompanied by (and, many would argue, spurred by) a fundamental shift in the wealthier OECD countries from labor-intensive agriculture to capital-intensive agriculture and from small family farms to much larger commercial farms.

Thus, the statistics on the percentage of the active population working in the agricultural sector reveal a sharp decline during the twenty-year period between 1950 and 1970.[4] For example, the percentage of people working in agriculture dropped from 33 percent to 14 percent in Austria; 47 percent to 21 percent in Finland; 21 percent to 10 percent in France; 23 percent to 8 percent in the Federal Republic of Germany; 42 percent to 17 percent in Italy; 50 percent to 25 percent in Spain; 21 percent to 8 percent in Sweden; and 17 percent to 8 percent in Switzerland. In the United States, the absolute levels of farm employment dropped rapidly from 9.9 million employed in 1950 to 4.4 million in 1976.[5]

Rapidly rising urban growth — much of which could be accounted for by relatively poor and undereducated rural migrants — placed great strains on the cities' resources and capacity to cope. Accordingly, many OECD countries gave (and continue to give) justifiable priority to urban problems and the delivery of urban public services (including education). In this circumstance, rural deprivation, although equally serious, *seemed* less pressing and national policymakers tended to focus primarily on the more politically (and literally) explosive problems of metropolitan regions.

Urbanization, industrialization, and the steep decline in both the absolute and relative number of people dependent upon agricultural (and other primary-sector) work all combined to foster the impression that rural life was fading away in the OECD nations. Aside from a strong, but narrowly focused, farm lobby, the rural population became politically invisible in many countries.

Policymakers increasingly behaved as if their rural constituencies either had already moved, or would soon all be moving, to the cities. Thus, there didn't seem too much impetus, or even much sense, in allocating all the time, energy, and resources necessary to significantly improve rural conditions.

The assumed demise of the rural sector was (and is) a dangerous misimpression. Fortunately, there is now a growing awareness among national governments that the demographic and economic assumptions which allowed rural problems to be ignored are no longer reasonable. Politicians and government officials throughout the OECD countries are beginning to understand that the anticipated "disappearance" of their rural population is not actually going to happen. Rural communities can empathize with the author Mark Twain, who was once compelled to remind his readers, "The reports of my death are greatly exaggerated."

How did this misimpression start? In part, it was the result of a misinterpretation of the meaning and impact of rural-to-urban migration trends. For example, there was confusion between a significant relative decline in the rural population (which did occur) and a significant absolute decline (which only rarely occurred). In other words, the fact that a smaller *proportion* of the national population lived in rural areas did not mean that the actual number of people living in rural areas had dropped dramatically.

Even in countries where the percentage of rural residents dropped noticeably between 1950 and 1975, the absolute number of rural people either declined only gradually or remained fairly stable.[6] For example, the rural population of Norway in 1950 was 2.22 million, and in 1974 it was still 2.20 million. Switzerland's rural population was 2.99 million in 1950 and 2.85 million in 1970. Similarly, the change in this period was only from 1.7 million to 1.4 million in Ireland; 13.8 million to 12.6 million in Yugoslavia; 17.6 million to 15.4 million in Spain; 17.7 million to 15 million in France; 4.8 million to 4.1 million in Greece; 13.7 million to 11.4 million in the Federal Republic of Germany; 27.9 million to 25.7 million in Italy; and 587,000 to 531,000 in New Zealand.

During the same period, there was even a group of OECD nations in which the number of rural residents grew larger.[7] The rural population of Austria went from 3.52 million in 1951 to 3.59 million in 1971. In Portugal there was an increase from 5.8 million to 6.3 million, and in Scotland the rural population rose from 1.47 million in 1951 to 1.57 million in 1974. The rest of the United Kingdom also registered more rural residents in the 1970s than in the 1950s.[8]

Further, some demographers are suggesting that the traditional flow of people from the countryside to the conurbations is slowing down considerably and, in certain cases, being offset by a new urban-to-rural migratory trend in the OECD countries. Although final confirmation of this hypothesis will have to wait until the early 1980s when new census data will be available from most countries, there appear to be solid grounds for asserting that the rural population will grow (or at least hold steady) during the foreseeable future.[9]

There are many reasons for this demographic change. In the countries of Southern Europe, there is a burgeoning return migration of rural workers from the cities of Western and Northern Europe. In Scandinavia, national governments have implemented a series of reasonably strong incentives for population redistribution. In parts of the United States, Canada, and Australia, natural resource and energy-related developments are spurring rural growth. In a host of OECD countries, the relocation of some industrial (and other economic) activity into the countryside, coupled with the saturation of urban labor markets, has made rural outmigration less attractive than in earlier years.[10]

Perhaps the clearest evidence of this new trend comes from the United States. Since 1970, rural America's population base has experienced a significant resurgence. As one of America's leading demographers, Calvin Beale, concluded, "The vast rural to urban migration of people that was the common pattern of U.S. population movement in the decades after World War II has been halted and, on balance, even reversed. . . . This decentralization trend is not confined to metropolitan sprawl. Very rural areas have increased their population more rapidly than metropolitan areas."[11] This reversal of population distribution patterns has gained momentum during the 1970s. President Carter's rural and small towns policy statement at the end of 1979 noted that rural areas were gaining population at a rate 40 percent higher than metropolitan areas.[12] Even though the farm population in the United States has continued to decline (and now represents less than 20 percent of the rural population), rural areas continue to attract a growing number of residents.[13]

The general implication of the demographic facts noted above is that policymakers in industrialized countries cannot simply write off the continuation, and continuing importance, of their rural constituencies. Seen in the aggregate the rural population of the industrialized countries is enormous. Even the most conservative estimates would place the OECD rural population well in excess of 220 million.[14]

In other words, the combined rural population of the twenty-four OECD member countries (plus Yugoslavia) is greater than the total population of the world's twenty-five largest metropolitan areas.[15] In fact, the OECD rural sector is roughly equal to the combined total population of France, Germany, Italy, and the United Kingdom.[16] Thus, it is both inaccurate and unconscionable for government policy to treat the rural sector as a marginal one.

The implication for education policy should be equally clear. If rural regions are able to retain a greater proportion of their indigenous population and attract a modicum of new residents, then the rural school population will remain as a significant education constituency in most OECD countries; will no longer be viewed as a declining education sector; and will have the political basis for seeking (and receiving) increased government attention and assistance.

Trends toward Decentralization

Beyond the realization that a sizable proportion of their nation's citizens will continue to live in sparsely populated areas, government officials in a variety of OECD countries have become interested in rural education as a result of the efforts to decentralize governmental responsibility. A great deal of political action in the past decade has been directed toward strenuously (and often successfully) asserting the rights of a particular region, locality, or minority group to control its own affairs more directly. For example, countries with a federal-state system, such as Australia, the United States, and the Federal Republic of Germany, have witnessed a reassertion of states' rights in general and of state control of education in particular. Yugoslavia remains extraordinarily dedicated to local and regional autonomy. Even such bastions of centralized power as France have moved toward giving greater decision-making powers to the regions and *départements*.[17]

The common feature here is a very positive attitude toward traditional local/regional characteristics and qualities, coupled with an aversion to any standardization or "homogenization" sought by central governments. Two factors link these decentralist trends with the heightened awareness of and attention to rural education.

First, they often have their roots in and draw a sizable proportion of their constituency from sparsely populated regions of the OECD member countries. This is particularly true of groups or movements representing distinctive cultural, religious, or racial groups with an historical attachment to rural areas. Second, the schools, for a host of social, historical, and political reasons, have often become the specific battleground used by decentralists to advance their cause. Curricular issues (including the use of special texts) are commonly a focal point, as is bilingualism.

As has become evident, it is difficult to limit the impact of this decentralist movement. Once unleashed, there is a tendency for what were traditionally regarded as strictly technical or professional issues to become politicized. For example, in recent years teacher qualifications, the use of standardized achievement tests, and school finance mechanisms have all become points of contention in the continuing debates about centralization versus decentralization and standardization versus local relevance.

Thus, it should come as no surprise that much of the Project on Basic Education and Teacher Support in Sparsely-Populated Areas reflects this tension within the countries themselves. The detailed reports in this volume on the Lofoten Islands Project in Northern Norway, the Bilingual Education Project in the Western Isles of Scotland, and the replacement of a single, state-operated school system in Alaska (United States) with more than twenty independent regional school systems all directly deal with the decentralization issue. Most of the other reports on rural innovations found in the volume reflect these concerns too, albeit more implicitly.

Dissatisfaction with Traditional Policies

Another important factor spurring policymakers to look seriously at rural education is a growing (and increasingly vocal) dissatisfaction with conventional solutions to the educational problems of sparsely populated areas. These strong reservations about the benefits of standard governmental responses to long-standing rural education problems are being expressed by a wide range of rural parents, local educators, community leaders, and government officials.

From an international perspective, one of the most fascinating features of this debate is a split within the OECD ranks about the nature both of the problems and of the most reasonable solutions. With the possible exception of the Federal Republic of Germany, the wealthier and more industrialized OECD countries are seriously questioning the value and utility of two widely implemented responses to rural problems: boarding schools and the consolidation or reorganization of small rural schools (i.e., merging them with other schools to form larger units). The debate about school closures and the supporting evidence (or lack thereof) will be examined in detail in Chapter 2 of this volume. Simultaneously, less industrialized OECD member countries (e.g., Portugal, Spain, Greece, and Turkey) are now pushing for precisely these same "reforms" as a new response to their rural problems. For example, a recent Spanish government report noted:

> Inequality of opportunity is still considerable in the rural areas in comparison with the provincial towns. . . . it may be that there will have to be *positive discrimination* in favor of the less privileged regions, provinces, localities, areas and centers. . . . as a result there has been a large scale transformation or abolition of rural schools with one (or only a few) teachers and the transfer of pupils (using school buses and, where appropriate, boarding facilities) to Regional Centers prepared or built for this purpose.[18]

As a recent government document made clear, the response in Turkey is very similar:

> Rural primary school graduates in rural areas had limited opportunities to continue their education at middle school level (now the second cycle of basic education). Another necessity is to lessen the existing inequality between rural and urban areas. . . .
>
> In rural areas and even in some villages the demand for middle schools was great. Although Turkey is undergoing a rapid urbanization process, most of

the population still lives in rural areas (64 per cent). In some regions the rural settlement units are scattered, which creates several problems in bringing to those places certain socio-economic services, and education as well. Different sorts of schools were needed to bring educational services to those places. . . .

The problems of villages with a population of under 250 and of villages which, although they have enough population, have not adequate schools and teachers, will be solved by means of central schools which will be established in the central villages. These 8-year basic education schools will be boarding or daily according to the conditions of the area.[19]

Although there is more than a little irony in the fact that one group of OECD countries is in the midst of fighting to adopt a set of reforms simultaneously being discarded by another group of OECD countries, the common thread is a rejection of the status quo. This dissatisfaction has, in effect, reintroduced the question of how best to meet the needs of children in sparsely populated areas and has forced policymakers to more critically rethink their past responses to this query.

Renewed Respect for Rural Educational Models

After years of being routinely assailed by leading educators and policymakers for being backward and inadequate, rural schools are beginning to receive a measure of praise for the qualities they do possess. This is not to suggest that their very real shortcomings have either ceased to exist or are now being overlooked. Rather the point is that within both the rural community and the education profession in OECD member countries there is a growing appreciation for what schools in sparsely populated areas *have* (as well as seeing what they lack) and an appreciation for where they *succeed* (as well as understanding where they fail).

Among the subjects of recent praise are such things as:

1. the role of the school as a primary source of community pride, identity, and stability in rural areas;
2. the informal, familial environment which exists in many (though by no means all) small rural schools;
3. the relative success of rural schools in teaching the so-called basics (after controlling for IQ and social class); and
4. the historic role of schools in sparsely populated areas as a natural laboratory for such "innovative" educational practices as individualized instruction, cross-age grouping, older students teaching younger students, using the community as a learning resource, and "mainstreaming" mildly handicapped children.

That rural schools should be treated with a measure of respect and that they often do have advantages as well as disadvantages is no longer a secret. As a report from New Zealand put it, "Certain fundamental advantages of the small rural schools are well-recognized. These include the close school and community relationships usually established and opportunities for the growth in children's values and attitudes considered desirable for their sound academic and personal development."[20]

The Gittins Report (a well-known investigation of primary education in Wales) included these remarks:

> One of the liveliest rural schools we have seen is a one-teacher school. Its work illustrated how the rural school can be like a family, with close and friendly relationships between children and teachers. Children can work as individuals or in small groups. If the school is prepared to allow the children to learn through activity, there can be a true integration of learning, within a completely flexible timetable. Environmental studies and science can begin at the doorstep of the school, in field, forest or mountainside. There can be lively discussion and easy movement from one area of study to another. The younger children can learn from the older, groups can be flexibly re-arranged for different aspects of work, and children can learn to live and work in a community.[21]

And finally, as Ray Barnhardt et al. noted in summing up recent American research in this field:

> A major study of the relative effects of big schools vs. small schools has indicated that small schools provide distinct advantages with regard to the potential depth and personal quality of learning experiences that can be obtained. In small schools, students were found to participate more, school meant more to them, they were more tolerant of others, they formed closer, more lasting relationships, they were more effective in group processes, they could communicate better, they were more productive, and they found their work more meaningful. Research also showed that small schools are more closely and integrally tied to the communities in which they operate and are, therefore, in a position to contribute more effectively to the development of student self-concept and sense of control, both of which are factors closely related to academic achievement.[22]

Equal Educational Opportunity

Because this volume will both explicitly and implicitly deal with the meaning and manifestations of "equal educational opportunity" in the context of rural school reform, little will be said about it here. However, it is fair to say that without the strong and enduring push for equality which has been at the root of nearly all educational reform in OECD countries, the current reemergence of rural education probably would not have occurred.

In part, the fact that the search for equality has led to a new focus on rurality was predictable, given the disproportionately high percentage of poor and other disadvantaged populations found in sparsely populated areas of most OECD countries. Yet this connection also springs from a more sophisticated understanding that inequality of educational opportunity occurs not only on the basis of income, class, race, and sex, but also on the basis of place of residence. Obviously, any continuing restrictions on educational equality (however defined) occurring simply as the result of where a child happens to live (be it the inner city or a remote rural settlement) belies any country's claim of having achieved genuine equality for all its children.

Evolution of the SPA Project

Thus far, this chapter has focused on the general context of rural education in the industrialized nations. The fact that the balance of governmental and professional opinion has shifted in favor of increased resources and attention for rural schools has also been noted. Further, the influences causing this policy shift have been explored.

Taken together, a profile of the setting for the CERI Project on Basic Education and Teacher Support in Sparsely-Populated Areas (SPA) begins to emerge. Interest in this kind of cooperative international project was already apparent at the time the CERI SPA activity was launched in 1976. However, the newly favorable predisposition toward rural education gained a good deal of strength and credibility during the three-year life of this project. In other words, what began as curiosity about schooling in remote locales ended in a firmer resolve among participating governments to actively work toward the improvement of rural education.

The project itself changed along the way, too. Consequently, before tackling the basic substantive issues raised by the SPA activity, it might prove useful to briefly trace the evolution of the project itself.

Originally, the SPA project was based on three rather straightforward assumptions:[23]

1. that students in sparsely populated areas deserve to receive educational opportunities equal to those available to their urban and suburban counterparts, but that, in most cases, genuine equality does not exist;
2. that the primary barriers to genuine equality are logistic and technical, i.e., the result of difficulties encountered in actually

delivering educational services to very small groups of children scattered across such remote areas; and

3. that, as a consequence of assumptions 1 and 2, the SPA project should focus on strategies for lessening the effects of the "abnormal" situation in which the most remote rural schools find themselves. In other words, the original intent was to promote equality of educational opportunity in SPA schools by making them as "normal" as circumstances would permit.

Once the SPA project became operational (in January 1976) an effort was made to identify member countries desirous of becoming active participants. Eventually, eleven countries joined—Australia (represented by Western Australia), Finland, France, Iceland, New Zealand, Norway, Portugal, Sweden, Switzerland, the United Kingdom (represented by both England and Scotland), and the United States.

Work on the project was carried out in three broad categories: secretariat (i.e., CERI staff) missions and research, country papers containing relevant background information on SPA education, and special reports on particularly interesting rural educational innovations within the participating nations.

Originally, it was hoped that each participating country would produce a rather extensive country paper which would provide all the necessary background information for an international comparison. Approximately half the participating governments were able to produce such a document. The remaining project members were not able to do so for a variety of reasons ranging from internal governmental problems to persistent difficulties in actually generating or locating relevant data.

After weighing the various alternatives, the secretariat decided that the best way to get the needed background information in the absence of a formal country paper was to submit a detailed series of questions to project members which could be answered relatively quickly and informally. This scheme was at least partially successful in that it did evoke the requisite responses from some of the member countries not submitting country papers. However, even after all the country papers and/or answers to the secretariat's list of SPA-related questions were complete, there were still obvious gaps in information and knowledge. Some of these gaps have now been filled, but others remain. Given this circumstance, it should not be surprising that one of the general recommendations emerging from this project (presented in Chapter 2) deals directly with the need for more concerted research and data collection efforts on rural education in OECD member countries.

Chapter 2 brings together the information garnered through the country papers, selected publications, and responses to the CERI SPA questionnaire. Some of the data come from 1977 or even earlier. However, most of the evidence cited in the first two chapters of this volume is from 1978-79 and represents the most recent information available.

The effort to produce a series of special reports on educational innovations in the rural regions of participating countries was notably more successful than the solicitation of formal country papers. The quality of these special reports reflects not only the intrinsic fascination of the innovations themselves, but also the dedication and seriousness brought to the task by the authors. The SPA reports constitute a unique body of knowledge about rural education in the developed countries.

The fact that so little has been published internationally (and even nationally in some cases) on these innovations is ironic, considering the voluminous literature on rural innovations in the Third World, and is a stark reminder of why the SPA project was needed at all.

As the SPA work progressed, the original ideas and definitions were refined. The general consensus among project participants was that the initial conception of the SPA effort was too limited to enable CERI to take full advantage of the expanding concern about rural affairs generally and rural education in particular. Thus the project activities were continually shaped and reshaped in response to changing realities and opportunities within the member countries. Three specific conceptual evolutions (involving constituency identification, the limits of "technical" solutions, and the meaning of equal educational opportunity in a rural context) warrant attention.

The first area given further thought by project participants involved the definition of the relevant constituency. Basically, the consensus was that the project should be expanded to encompass rural education as a whole, rather than keeping it to one specific rural subgroup (i.e., only the most remotely situated rural children). However, it was agreed that retaining the original age parameters of the SPA project (that is, students of compulsory school age) was appropriate. There were three central reasons behind this shift.

First, in conceptual terms, it was felt that the variations between "SPA schools" and "rural schools" were differences of degree, rather than indicators of two separate and distinct realities. For example, while it is certainly true that the remote SPA schools often have a very hard time recruiting teachers, locating appropriate curricula, and gaining effective access to specialized sources of assistance, these same difficulties are commonly shared (albeit to a somewhat lesser extent) by less remote rural schools. Second, in political terms, it was felt that splitting the rural constituency into various subgroups (like SPAs) was not the most productive strategy for exploiting the relatively favorable political environment in which rural schools exist today. It was further felt that maintaining a unified focus on rural schools would better serve the needs of interested government officials and policymakers. And third, in pragmatic terms, there were two difficulties with the more restrictive SPA concept: virtually no data (particularly at the national level) either existed or could readily be acquired which conformed to the SPA definition, and some of the most interesting and potentially useful innovations were occurring in rural areas which did not fit the SPA classification.

The second conceptual modification involved a refinement of the assumption that the technical and logistic problems of education provision lie at the heart of the SPA dilemma. There was full agreement that such problems were nearly always considerable and, in some cases, seemingly intractable. However, project participants repeatedly pointed out that most conventional strategies for overcoming these problems were hampered by an attempt to make remote rural schools resemble urban and suburban schools to the fullest possible extent. This attempt was criticized on the grounds that:

1. judging rural schools by urban criteria and standards virtually guarantees a negative assessment, even in situations where the rural schools are serving their students well on their own terms;
2. urging rural schools to adopt urban models of education may be counterproductive, not only because such models are inappropriate in the rural context but also because the urban models themselves may be seriously flawed; and
3. utilizing urban models often inhibits rural schools from creatively exploiting their own unique advantages. For example, many rural schools have given up individualized instruction in order to be more like "normal" classrooms. Similarly, participants noted the irony inherent in rural children studying science strictly by using old urban-designed texts while the huge natural laboratory surrounding them all too often went unnoticed and unused.

Nearly everyone agreed that rural schools need better curricular offerings and materials. However, coupled with this agreement was the warning that "better" has too often meant "more like metropolitan schools" instead of better in meeting the educational needs of rural children. Similarly, there was consensus regarding the need for better teachers in sparsely populated areas. Once again, though, participants made it clear that they meant "better" in the sense of being able to work more effectively in the rural circumstance, rather than the conventional notion of "more highly credentialed" or "urban trained."[24]

As Karl Jan Solstad more succinctly stated, "Schools in urban middle class areas have been viewed as being 'best' and so the same style of education has been implemented in remote rural areas. Yet, the result has been an increasingly 'remote' education; that is, an education remote from the world experienced by rural children."[25]

The third, and final, modification of the SPA project's conceptual framework involved a sharpening of the "equality of educational opportunity" argument. Basically, this was an outgrowth of the movement toward creating uniquely rural solutions to uniquely rural problems. In other words, participants in the SPA project drew a distinction between equality as meaning that every student should receive the *same* (in terms of specialized services, financial resources, curricular offerings, etc.) and equality as meaning that, within the constraint of available resources, students should receive the particular opportunities and specific services they need to fully realize whatever potential they may possess. It may be that, on occasion, equality demands different activities, services, and delivery systems rather than the unwavering pursuit of uniformity.

Pragmatically, the "uniform" notion of equality implies strong centralist policies while the local relevance model implies more of a decentralist thrust. With a few notable exceptions, the second concept of equality was clearly the more popular among SPA project participants.

This introduction has focused on the gradual metamorphosis of the SPA project. The project originally was intended to be an effort to locate innovative solutions to the logistic and technical problems associated with the delivery of educational services in very remote rural areas. This focus was retained, but supplemented by a broader attempt to understand the realities of rural education within the developed countries so that both the shortcomings and the positive qualities common to rural schools and rural students could be dealt with as effectively as possible.

In a fundamental sense, the evolution of the SPA project mirrored the attitudinal and policy shift toward rural education occurring in the OECD nations themselves. Rural schooling was no longer being viewed as a minor technical concern but rather as a field of increasing political and educational importance, and the SPA project reflected this change. As rural education reappeared on national education agendas, the shortage of comparative information on issues and innovations became painfully obvious. It was into this nearly uncharted territory that the SPA project ventured. The remainder of this volume presents the fruits of SPA's collaborative international effort.

Notes

1. The data on European countries are taken from Secretariat of the Economic Commission for Europe (SECE), *Labour Supply and Migration in Europe:*

Demographic Dimensions 1950-1975 and Prospects (New York: United Nations, 1979), Chapters 4, 5, and 6, and Appendix Table 4.1.

2. Canadian data from *Canada Handbook* (Ottawa: Statistics Canada Publishing Office, 1979).

3. New Zealand data from *New Zealand Official Yearbook* (Wellington: New Zealand Department of Statistics, 1977). American data from U.S. Bureau of the Census, *Statistical Abstract of the United States* (Washington, D. C.: U. S. Government Printing Office, 1979).

4. SECE, op. cit., Table 5.6. Also see Agriculture Directorate, *Review of Agricultural Policies* (Paris: Organisation for Economic Co-operation and Development, 1978).

5. U. S. Bureau of the Census, op. cit.

6. SECE, op. cit., Table 4.1.

7. Ibid.

8. Ibid. For England and Wales, the rural population rose from 8.4 million in 1951 to an estimated 10.9 million in 1973. However, the definition of *rural* is unusually liberal in England and Wales, and exact comparisons are difficult to make. Conversely, the country experiencing the most severe drop in its rural population (Sweden — from 3.7 million in 1950 to 1.5 million in 1970) adopted a more restrictive definition in 1960, and this may account for a sizable proportion of the rural population loss. Finally, it should be noted that a genuine "rural depopulation" did occur in particular regions of the OECD countries, such as the Mezzogiorno in Italy.

9. Many of the analyses which suggested that major rural depopulations would be widespread were predicated on continuing rapid economic growth, further concentration of industrial and service employment in urban areas, and continuing demand for rural migrants in urban labor markets. The economic slowdown and related problems since the mid-1970s have rendered each of these assumptions invalid.

10. The educational implications of changing patterns of rural economic development are very important, but they were not part of the OECD/SERI SPA project's program of work. However, the considerations are a major part of SPA's "daughter," the OECD/CERI project on education and local development.

11. Calvin L. Beale, *The Revival of Population Growth in Nonmetropolitan America* (Washington, D. C.: U. S. Government Printing office, 1975), p. 3.

12. President Carter's policy statement indicates that the trend Beale documented in the early 1970s continued throughout the rest of the decade. For further information, see The Carter Administration, *Small Community and Rural Development Policy* (Washington, D. C.: U. S. Government Printing Office, 1979).

13. Ibid. Also see U.S. Department of Agriculture, *Structural Issues in American Agriculture* (Washington, D. C.: U. S. Government Printing Office, 1979).

14. Most data from the early 1970s. Estimated nonurban populations in the twenty-four OECD countries (plus Yugoslavia) total approximately 234 million, lowered to 220 million to account for semiurban populations. Source is George E. Delury et al., *The World Almanac 1978* (New York: Newspaper Enterprise Association, 1978), pp. 511–595. Country estimates (in millions) are as follows: Australia 2.5; Austria 3.6; Belgium 1.3; Canada 5.7; Denmark 0.8; Finland 2.0; France 15.0; Germany 11.4; Greece 4.1; Ireland 1.4; Iceland 0.03; Italy 25.7; Japan 23.1; Luxem-

bourg 0.1; Netherlands 3.1; Norway 2.2; Portugal 6.3; Spain 15.4; Sweden 1.5; Switzerland 2.8; Turkey 24.2; United Kingdom 13.3; United States 54.9; and Yugoslavia 12.6.

15. Delury et al., op. cit., p. 602. Includes central cities and surrounding areas.

16. Ibid. Estimated 1976 total population for France is 53 million; Germany 61.5 million; Italy 56 million; and United Kingdom 56 million. Thus the total combined population is approximately 226.5 million.

17. For further information on the implementation of regional schemes in education, see *Education and Regional Development, Volumes I and II* (Paris: Organisation for Economic Co-operation and Development, 1979). Volume I is a general report summarizing the findings of the OECD Secretariat. Volume II is a collection of technical reports on education in a regional context from Australia, England, Finland, France, Italy, Norway, Sweden, Switzerland, United States, and Yugoslavia.

18. *Policies for Basic Education: Spain's National Statement* (Paris: Organisation for Economic Co-operation and Development, 1978), pp. 5 and 8.

19. *Policies for Basic Education: Turkey's National Statement* (Paris: Organisation for Economic Co-operation and Development, 1978), pp. 2 and 7.

20. Elgar E. Henry, *Aspects of Pre-School, Primary and Secondary Education in Sparsely-Populated Areas of New Zealand* (Paris: Centre for Educational Research and Innovation, OECD, 1978), p. 64.

21. *The Gittens Report: Primary Education in Wales* (London: Her Majesty's Stationery Office, 1968), p. 111.

22. Ray Barnhardt et al., *Small High School Programs for Rural Alaska, Volume I* (Fairbanks, Alaska: Center for Cross-Cultural Studies, University of Alaska, 1979), pp. 15–16.

23. For a fuller examination, see "Notes and Guidelines for Country Papers" (document code CERI/TS/76.02), published in 1976.

24. See the detailed discussion of this and related issues appearing in Chapter 2 of this volume.

25. Karl Jan Solstad, "The Curriculum Needs of Remote Areas" (Paper presented at the 1978 Highland Conference of the Scottish Educational Research Association).

Education in the Countryside: Overview of Conditions and Some Conclusions

Jonathan P. Sher

Think of a rural community. Think, for example, of families living in the Western Australian outback a hundred miles from their closest "neighbors" and perhaps twice that distance from the nearest town. Then, think of families living on the outskirts of a small village in rural England, within perhaps ten miles of half a dozen similar villages and certainly no more than a day's journey from London. Both are considered rural in their own national contexts, yet their differences would seem to outweigh their similarities.

The images conjured up by the word *rural* vary enormously from country to country (and often within countries as well). From reindeer-herding communities in Lapland to Appalachian coal mining communities in the United States; from remote farming villages in the Mediterranean countries where donkeys are still the most common form of transportation to chic ski resort areas in Switzerland frequented by the "jet set"; and from fishing settlements on the coast of Iceland to the château country in France, the range of conditions and communities which fall into the "rural" category is truly staggering.

Rural communities characterized by considerable wealth are by no means unknown, although rural regions tend to be among the poorest in each country (and some resemble their Third World counterparts more than the usual image of "advanced" countries). Some rural areas are the fastest-growing areas in their countries while others are experiencing steep declines. In some OECD countries, rural adult illiteracy is virtually nonexistent, while in others it is more commonplace than a secondary-level education.

Even at a statistical level, the diversity of "ruralness" is easily seen. Actually, most countries have either not been able, or have simply not bothered, to define rural areas at all. Rather, the common practice is to carefully define the urban (and semiurban) populations and consider any place left over to be rural.[1]

The most restrictive definitions of *rural* are found in the five Scandinavian countries, where the word is used to describe people living in the open countryside or in places having fewer than 200 to 300 residents.[2] Several countries, including France, Germany, Greece, Ireland, the Netherlands, New Zealand, the United States, and Yugoslavia, equate *rural* with the open countryside and places of fewer than 1,000 to 2,500 residents.[3] The next cluster of countries, including Austria and Belgium, use *rural* to refer to a place with fewer than 5,000 inhabitants. The most liberal definitions can be found in countries like Italy, Spain, Portugal, and Switzerland, which consider places of as many as 10,000 residents to still be rural.[4] And finally, a few countries like Australia and the United Kingdom tend to use socioeconomic and population density criteria rather than strictly numerical definitions.[5]

The obvious conclusion to be drawn here is that there is no single definition of *rural* or *sparsely populated* which is meaningful in an international context. Diversity is a central characteristic of rural communities both within and among participating countries. Given the enormous range of communities, people, and circumstances in the sparsely populated regions of OECD member countries, the precise meaning of ruralness has been, and will remain, rather elusive. We know, of course, that rural communities are characterized by small populations and low population density ratios. However, since *rural* and *sparsely populated* are relative terms, all population- and density-based definitions are suggestive rather than absolute. The point here is simply that ruralness, like beauty, lies in the eye of the beholder. Therefore, each country's conception of the meaning of *rural* or *sparsely populated* should be respected and attempts to impose a more global definition resisted.

There is another, equally important point to be made. The great diversity existing among rural communities and rural schools in the OECD countries makes it difficult (if not foolhardy) to issue sweeping generalizations. There was no attempt made within the SPA project to conduct formal cross-national comparisons or to construct elegant models attempting to reduce the real world to a series of equations. Indeed, there was a strong suspicion among secretariat members and country participants alike that an obsessive search for commonality was not only unlikely to succeed but also beside the point. Much of the fascination of this international study has come from paying close attention to the differences, paradoxes, and anomalies which exist in the experiences of the participating countries, rather than trying to pretend that they either do not exist at all or that they can be easily categorized and explained.

However, despite this caveat, one of the most pleasant surprises of the SPA project was the discovery of just how much commonality does exist among OECD countries in terms of rural education problems and policies. As an illustration, the participating countries were able to agree on a series of conclusions and findings about rural education. These conclusions are interspersed throughout this chapter and are summarized at the end.

The evidence leading to these conclusions has been clustered into three major areas, as follows: general characteristics of education in sparsely populated areas; rural school closures and the alternatives to closure; and rural teacher issues. The remainder of this chapter will be devoted to exploring each of these key areas of concern.

Characteristics of Education in Sparsely Populated Areas

Compulsory Education

All OECD countries have compulsory education laws, and in nearly all countries these laws are equally applicable to urban and rural children. The general trend has been one of expanding the length of compulsory education. For example, several Nordic countries have added an additional, ninth, year to their period of mandatory education. Similarly, several Southern European countries have started to require (and enforce) an eight-year cycle of compulsory education. At least nine years of education are required in the majority of OECD countries, but attendance for a longer period is customary in several nations.

Iceland is an interesting case in that both the number of years required and the length of the school year itself are traditionally shorter in rural areas than in the cities.[6] As Andri Isaksson noted, "In the past, children in rural areas sometimes began school at the age of nine or ten (instead of seven) and the school year was much shorter; sometimes only three months rather than the usual eight or nine months."[7] Even though there has been a major reduction in these disparities, it was nevertheless true that in 1977-78, 15 percent of Iceland's schools (all of them rural) operated for seven months or less compared to nine months in city schools.[8]

Iceland was not alone in this practice. Even where arrangements like this have not been formal or officially sanctioned, there has been a tradition of curtailing the rural school calendar in order to allow children to help their parents during harvest time and other peak periods of rural economic activity. This custom is waning but it still exists in many OECD countries, particularly for students at the upper end of compulsory education.

This raises another sensitive issue; that is, the number of rural children who do not receive all or any of their compulsory instruction. Very few countries publish data on children out of school. However, rural education experts in most countries acknowledge that this has been, and continues to be, a problem. Of course, much of the information on this topic is retrospective and inferred largely from statistics on the population of adult illiterates. Still, random pieces of current data are available. For example, a 1978 government report from Spain noted, "Basic General Education is compulsory. At the present time it can be said that it is of a genuinely compulsory character. The 5,473,468 pupils enrolled in the year 1975-1976 constitute practically the whole school-age population between 6 and 13 years."[9]

The obvious inference here is that until now attendance has not been "genuinely compulsory." Also, it should be noted that "practically the whole school-age population" implies that some students (even if only a tiny fraction) are *not* receiving instruction. This report went on to note that "every child, without exception, has access to a school place."[10] However, there is an important difference between a child "having access" to a school place and actually being there on a regular basis.

Although the problem of rural children not receiving their full compulsory education has been most prevalent in the poorer OECD countries, it is by no means limited to them. In the wealthier OECD countries, this phenomenon is most common in rural poverty areas; among agricultural migrants; and within rural minority and indigenous populations (i.e., Blacks, Native Americans, Same populations in Lapland, Maoris in New Zealand, or aborigines in Australia). It is suspected that many of these out-of-school children are "unlucky" to begin with; teenaged mothers, handicapped children, discipline problems, etc. Ironically, they may need the most help and end up getting the least.

One of the very few comprehensive, well-researched investigations ever undertaken in this area reveals the extent of the problem in one wealthy OECD country, the United States. This 1974 report, entitled *Children Out of School in America,* indicates that at least 5 percent of all rural school-aged children were not enrolled in any school (even though they all "had access" to one).[11] This represented a nonenrollment rate more than 50 percent higher than the comparable urban rate. As the report stated,

> Most Americans assume that all children go to school. This is not true. According to our analysis of 1970 U.S. Bureau of the Census data on nonenrollment, more than three quarters of a million children between the ages of 7 and 13 were not enrolled in school. . . . Of the ten states with the highest nonenrollment rates, almost all had substantial rural populations. Some rural states have more than seven per cent of their total school-age population (ages 7–17) out of school.[12]

It must be pointed out that some nations have already gone to extraordinary lengths to ensure that *every* child gets at least a basic education in practice as well as in theory. Scotland, for instance, has been extremely diligent about providing a teacher, if not a whole school, in even the most remote and trying circumstances. As a result, there are a considerable number of rural schools in Scotland with less than ten students enrolled.[13] When necessary, the Scottish authorities even have sent a teacher to a remote island to provide instruction to a single child.[14]

Other countries have dealt successfully with this problem by adopting innovative strategies to guarantee that rural children receive their full measure of compulsory education. Often this is done by drawing a distinction between compulsory *education* and compulsory *schooling*. For example, in a 1979 report entitled *Primary and Secondary Education in the Nordic Countries,* the authors pointed out,

> It was formerly the custom to talk of "compulsory school attendance" in the Nordic countries. However, this term is gradually giving way in national legislation on primary and lower-secondary education to the term "compulsory education.". . . "Compulsory education" as distinct from the term "compulsory school attendance" indicates that a child's education and upbringing can be secured by methods other than attendance at a publicly provided school. In other words, all children between certain ages are compelled to participate in education; the manner in which this duty is fulfilled can include alternatives other than public school attendance.[15]

Three of the special reports on rural innovations found later in this volume also focus on the provision of education to children for whom "normal" classroom instruction is not possible. These include the reports on Telescola in Portugal, the New Zealand Correspondence School, and the Isolated Students Matriculation Scheme in Western Australia.

Given the above information, the conclusion was drawn that although improvements have been made, there are still rural school-age children in poor countries and in the poverty areas of wealthy countries who are not receiving all their "compulsory" education. Attention must be given to this problem and appropriate actions must be taken by OECD governments to ensure that rural children actually receive all the education to which they are legally entitled.

Of course, an overwhelming majority of children in all OECD countries do receive a complete compulsory education. Further, this education is delivered to a very high percentage of students through schools rather than alternative means. Both these statements are as applicable to rural children as to urban ones.

However, rural schools are distinguishable from city schools in a number of important ways. They tend to be less specialized, less well equipped, and less bureaucratic than their urban counterparts. Phrased differently, rural schools tend to be more oriented toward teaching the "basics," more reliant on the particular qualities of individual teachers, and more familial and relaxed in their operating style than is true of comparable institutions in metropolitan regions.

Nevertheless, generalizations about rural schools must be approached with the same caution that accompanies generalizations about rural communities as a whole. Once again, diversity is the norm. Rural primary schools encompass everything from a poverty-stricken outpost with a single untrained teacher to a prosperous regional school with well-credentialed teachers for each grade level. This category includes schools in rapidly growing boom towns and schools in communities where declining enrollments have reduced the student ranks to nearly zero. Many rural schools would be considered excellent by any standard, while others are woefully inadequate and desperately in need of assistance. As a consequence, talking about rural primary schools as if they were all the same (nationally or internationally) would be a serious mistake.

Differing structures for the delivery of educational services inhibit cross-national comparisons as well. Several of the OECD countries, such as the United Kingdom, Switzerland, Canada, Australia, Germany, and the United States, entrust most of the responsibility for education to various state, regional, or local governmental bodies.[16] However, in most OECD nations, policymaking and decisionmaking responsibilities for educational matters are heavily centralized.

School Size

Despite these reservations, it is apparent that rural primary schools in the developed nations do share some fundamental characteristics. Perhaps the most important of these is that rural primary schools everywhere are significantly smaller than primary schools in the cities.

Rural schools in the industrialized countries tend to be quite small in absolute as well as relative terms. One- and two-teacher schools (i.e., schools with an enrollment of fewer than fifty students) are still commonplace. In fact, rural primary schools with three teachers and/or less than one hundred pupils are the norm rather than the exception.

For example, in Iceland rural primary schools have an average enrollment of about 50 pupils (compared to an average of 300 to 500 in Iceland's urban areas).[17] The smallest rural school had 3 students, and even the largest rural school in the country had only 150 pupils.

In New Zealand, rural primary schools are typically one- or two-teacher institutions serving between nine and sixty pupils. In 1977 there were 691 such schools (or roughly one-third of the nation's total). Of these, 248 were single-teacher units while the remaining 443 were two-teacher schools.[18]

Scotland, too, exhibited a similar distribution of schools. In 1977, 36 percent of *all* Scottish primary schools had fewer than one hundred students; 25 percent had fewer than fifty students; 12 percent had fewer than twenty-five students; and 57 schools (2 percent of the nation's total) had fewer than ten students.[19] Needless to say, the percentage of small schools in the predominantly rural regions of Scotland was higher still. For example, primary schools having twenty-five or fewer pupils accounted for 48 percent of all primary schools in Orkney; 34 percent in Shetland; 31 percent in the Borders region; 29 percent in the Highland region; and 25 percent in the Western Isles.[20]

In Western Australia, 67 of the 111 rural primary schools have an enrollment of fewer than one hundred students and more than 10 percent (i.e., 15 schools) have fewer than twenty-five students.[21] In addition, there are 33 nongovernmental (mostly Catholic) schools operating in sparsely populated areas. These schools have an average enrollment of fewer than one hundred in their primary education departments.[22]

The United States followed the pattern of having rural schools with much smaller enrollments than the metropolitan average. Depending on the state, U. S. nonmetropolitan schools enrolled 40 to 80 percent fewer students than metropolitan ones.[23] Yet, even though there are more than 1,100 one-teacher schools left in America, these constitute only about 3 percent of the nation's total number of nonmetropolitan schools.[24]

Countries also can be found at the other end of this continuum. For example, in 1978 Finland had 42 percent of the nation's schoolchildren attending two-teacher primary schools.[25] In fact, 70 percent of *all* Finnish primary students are enrolled in schools with three or fewer teachers.[26] Portugal, too, has an extraordinary percentage of its students in very small schools. As of 1978, 51 percent of all Portuguese children attended schools with only one classroom, and more than 80 percent are served by institutions no larger than two classrooms. In the rural areas of these two countries, it is very rare to find a school with more than three teachers.

Of all the OECD countries studied, France had by far the largest number of one-teacher schools.[27] In 1979, there were approximately 11,000 rural one-teacher schools in France, 95 percent of which had an enrollment of fewer than twenty-five pupils.[28] More than 1,300 of these schools had eight or fewer students, and several thousand had fewer than fifteen pupils enrolled.[29]

Needless to say, differences in school size produce differences in what can, and does, actually happen within the school. Many of these differences, and the ways in which countries have responded to them, will be dealt with later in this chapter. For the moment, two points should be remembered.

First, very small (i.e., one- or two-teacher) rural primary schools tend to magnify "normal" strengths and weaknesses rather than create wholly new ones. For example, the personal and professional characteristics of a particular teacher are important in any school. However, in very small rural schools these individual attributes absolutely make or break the quality of education received by the students.

In most metropolitan communities, the classroom teacher is only one influence among many outside the home. In isolated rural communities, the teacher is often the most important, and occasionally the only, interpreter of the "outside world" that exists beyond a child's own family. Thus, an excellent teacher in a small rural school can have an unusually strong and positive impact on students' lives, as well as on their education. Unfortunately, the impact of a poor teacher tends to be just as pronounced. With all the normal strengths and weaknesses thrown into sharp relief by virtue of their small scale, one- and two-teacher schools are not often seen as being "average," "mediocre," or "just like all the rest." Rather, these schools tend to elicit more extreme reactions. To borrow a line from a children's poem, when they're good, they're very very good; and when they're bad, they're horrid.

The other key point here is that, for better or worse, most of the very small rural schools in existence today will remain in existence for a long time to come. There has been a tendency in many OECD countries to treat small rural schools as temporary institutions. The danger in this assumption is twofold. First, it has an unsettling and demoralizing effect on the rural teachers, parents, and students concerned. Second, it encourages policymakers and administrators to refrain from making needed investments of time, money, and assistance.

Many small rural schools have been closed in the past thirty years, either by design or by default. Doubtless, more can, should, and will be closed (or will "close themselves" because of declining enrollments) in the next decade. Nonetheless, in the majority of the developed nations, the small rural schools in existence today are there neither frivolously nor because of artificially supportive policies. Instead, the bulk of these schools have stayed open because they are necessary and because the alternatives are onerous.

The evidence collected leads to the conclusion that no matter what general policies emerge from the school closure controversy (and even accounting for continued declining enrollments), there are a significant number of small rural schools which will remain in operation because there are no feasible alternatives to their continued existence. Therefore, it is hoped that governments will make every effort to both identify and assist these indispensible rural schools.

School Transportation

Questions about how rural children get to school and the difficulties encountered in transporting them were not a major part of the SPA project's agenda. Even so, some interesting facts surfaced. The information supports the conventional wisdom about rural school transportation: more children must travel much longer distances at much higher costs in rural areas than in cities. As a general rule, primary-level students are transported shorter distances than secondary-level students.

In Sweden, more than two-thirds of the rural students get to school by bus or taxi.[30] The national board of education has recommended that one-way journeys to school entail a ride of no more than forty-five minutes. This forty-five-minute limit was fairly common among all the OECD nations. On average, this guideline is followed carefully in Sweden, and mean travelling times even in sparsely populated areas are often well below the recommended limit. However, there is a significant minority of rural students who routinely have to exceed this guideline in order to attend classes. In some cases, students must endure journeys of three hours or more each day.[31] Moreover, it is not unusual for bad weather either to extend the normal travel time or to force students to miss school until the roads are clear again.

In the United States, as in most other OECD countries, better roads and modern vehicles have made school consolidations feasible. Longer travel time is a notable consequence. As a recent report noted,

> The catchment areas of rural schools, particularly in the wake of widespread consolidation are typically several times larger than in metropolitan places. In some regions of the country, it is common for a single rural school to draw its student body from an area of more than 50 square miles. Since relatively few rural students live within walking distance of their school and public transportation is all but nonexistent, many more rural students ride school buses (e.g. 75 per cent in predominantly rural West Virginia versus 46 per cent in mostly urban New Jersey) for longer distances over poorer roads. The cost implications are obvious. Thus, it is not surprising to discover that in 1974, a rural state like North Dakota spent $172 per pupil on transportation, whereas an urban state like Rhode Island spent only $85.[32]

Rural school transportation has also become an extensive enterprise in Western Australia, as the following makes clear:

> If there are eleven or more children living beyond a radius of 4.5 kilometres from the school, a school bus may be used. During 1976, in Western Australia 700 school buses conveyed 23,000 children more than 80,000 kilometres daily.

. . . the Education Department has, in effect, advised schools and bus contractors that no child should spend more than three hours on a bus each day. Nevertheless, there are instances of longer services operating, with some straight runs with secondary school children of up to 130 kilometres. These longer services are usually a result of approaches from parents who prefer their children travel the longer distance rather than arrange boarding away from home or correspondence education.[33]

One of the interesting aspects of the rural school transportation issue is all the variations which occur. Transportation is provided free nearly everywhere, when it is provided. For families living too far from established bus routes, yet still technically eligible for free transportation, a system of subsidies exists in many countries. Usually, parents are reimbursed for private automobile expenses incurred in bringing their children to school. In a few areas of the United States there is a "shoe allowance," designed to reimburse parents whose children have to walk a long distance to school or to a school bus stop. In the Western Isles of Scotland, there is even a family which receives a "hay allowance," as their children ride a long way to school by pony.

Most rural children, particularly at the secondary level, now travel to school by bus. The next most widely used method is private transportation (i.e., walking, bicycling, or private automobile). However, more exotic ways of getting to school in rural areas can also be found. Some children take taxis, some ride horses, some come by boat or train, and a few even ski to school (although there has not yet been a "wax allowance" offered).

This subject should not be treated whimsically. Real difficulties do exist. The costs of rural transportation have always been disproportionately high. Inflation and rising fuel costs have only exacerbated this problem. Overall, the school bus safety record has been remarkably good in the OECD nations, but accidents have occurred and are an ever-present concern.

A recent report from New Zealand said, "The logistics of getting children to and from country schools are a constant source of friction. Parents have also expressed unease at the early hour that some young children are picked up in the morning and the late hour they return home."[34] These concerns were echoed in a 1977 Scottish report, as follows:

> Some features of the current provision have created difficulties. For example, many people no longer regard it as reasonable to expect a child under 8 to walk 2 miles to school or one over 8 to walk 3 miles. Parents who live just within the statutory walking distance feel aggrieved that they receive no assistance with the cost of their children's transport while other children go free because they live just beyond the statutory walking distance. Parents are also worried about increasing traffic and other hazards encountered on the way to

and from school. Transport companies are also becoming increasingly reluctant to allow reduced fares for pupils. Various attempts have been made in recent years to work out an improved scheme acceptable to all parties but these have proved unsuccessful.[35]

Still, the most serious reservations about long journeys to school have to do with the effects on students. As a 1977 report from the United States said, "Recent research, conducted at the University of Oklahoma by Yao-Chi Tu and Luther Tweeten, shows that busing has an adverse impact on achievement, even when IQ and social class are controlled."[36]

Norwegian research on this topic focused on the physical and psychological effects of rural school transportation. Although not definitive, the findings indicated that a sizable proportion of rural children bused a long distance tended to be less physically fit; to experience more physical discomfort; and to agree with the statement "I dread the school journey almost every day" more than was true for students bused only a short distance.[37]

Creative solutions to the nagging problems of rural school transportation should be sought. Some promising innovations have already been undertaken. For instance, in one part of the western United States the school buses have been equipped with seven-channel audio tape decks and headphones (similar to those used on airlines), and the channels are programmed with work in a variety of subjects at several academic levels.

On the basis of the available evidence, it seems reasonable to conclude that rural school transportation services are being provided in a satisfactory manner, although new strategies for reducing journeys and using the travel time constructively should be pursued.

Boarding Schools

For some rural children (particularly at the secondary level), the distance from home to school is so great that daily journeys present an unreasonable hardship. As several of the special reports in this volume discuss in detail, more and more OECD countries are trying to solve this problem either through a variety of "distance learning" schemes (i.e., correspondence education and instructional radio-television) or by expanding the network of rural schools.

However, the traditional solution has been to provide living accommodations for students at or near the school. All OECD countries have sponsored boarding schools in the past and nearly all of them continue to do so. In fact, there is a trend among the poorer and less industrialized OECD nations toward significantly enlarging the number of rural students using boarding facilities. For example, the Turkish government recently stated, "Because of limited financial resources it is not possible to bring educational services to the very small rural settlement units (for example the villages with a population of less than 250). . . . The capacity of regional boarding schools will be increased and these schools will be free of charge."[38]

In the wealthier OECD countries, the use of boarding arrangements has declined sharply since the end of World War II. This decline was, of course, directly tied to improvements in transportation. Better roads and modern vehicles greatly extended the distances rural children could reasonably travel on a daily basis to and from school.

Technology, too, has played a role in making distance learning a reasonable alternative to regular school attendance. In the case of correspondence education, telephone communication between teacher and students and the widespread use of instructional tape recordings have improved the quality of the existing service. Other distance learning schemes, such as the Australian "Schools of the Air" or Portugal's Telescola, are entirely dependent on radio and television.

Today, the primary impetus for substituting other types of provision for boarding arrangements is neither technological nor even financial (boarding schools do, of course, often cost a good deal of money to run properly). Rather, the boarding alternative has diminished as a result of the expressed preference of rural parents to have their children live at home; the difficulties experienced by rural boarding students; and the heightened sensitivity of educators to the psychological/emotional effects of boarding arrangements.

For example, a report on education in a sparsely populated region of one Canadian province stated,

> In the matter of where high school should be attended there was much expression of unhappiness about pupils having to go away from home. This unhappiness had an inverse relationship to the grade. Greatest concern was expressed about young students having to go away, but it persisted in respect of higher grades.
>
> The catalogue of complaints and concerns related to boarding included the following:
>
> 1. Lack of supervision of the children; fear of developing bad habits or consorting with undesirable company;
> 2. Loneliness and homesickness, leading to poor performance, or dropping out;
> 3. Discrimination, or a sense thereof; a feeling of not really belonging; and
> 4. Lack of guidance and sympathetic understanding on the part of the schools.[39]

In Sweden, it has been noted,

Sometimes distances to school are so far that pupils (especially from the mountainous areas and the archipelago) have to be lodged in the central village. However, this is not very common now in Sweden because of negative attitudes toward boarding; not least among rural parents.[40]

Scotland, too, has noted problems in this area:

On the issue of hostel residence (boarding) the headmaster of one small rural secondary school spoke eloquently of the sense of displacement felt by a child on leaving his home community and of the irremediable loss of contact with the people among whom he had grown up. A hostel warden echoed the first speaker. It was interesting that both had experienced hostels as pupils, and even more interesting that they had come in not in the first, but in the fourth year of secondary education, from rural secondary schools where they had lived at home. Recent research undertaken by the Aberdeen College of Education also highlighted the difficulties facing school hostels in their efforts to balance their custodial role with their desire to practise and promote social education.[41]

Although atypical among OECD countries, the degree of serious boarding-related problems revealed by a major research study in Alaska (United States) stands as a warning against the indiscriminate use of the boarding alternative. The report deals with the effects of different boarding arrangements on Native Alaskan students coming from very small, isolated villages. The findings of this report were partially responsible for the decentralization of education and the creation of many new village-based secondary schools in rural Alaska (as described later in one of the SPA case studies).

As the author of the research report explained,

When I began this study 3 years ago, it was not my intention to show that boarding home programs and regional high schools were helping to destroy a generation of village children. Quite the contrary, I believed that the serious problems of rural secondary education away from home were due in large part to bad matches between particular types of village students and particular types of high schools. . . .

But as I saw what actually happened to the 1971-72 class of village students who entered the three representative high school programs studied, I was compelled to give up these initial views. In all of these programs, the majority of village children were developing serious social and emotional problems as a result of their high school experiences. Our follow-up study of graduates from these school programs suggested that in many cases, the school experience had left these students with a set of self-defeating ways for dealing with the world. . . .

Of the students studied, the high school experience led to school-related social and emotional problems in: seventy-six per cent of the students in the rural boarding home program; seventy-four per cent of the students in the boarding school; and fifty-eight per cent of the students in the urban boarding home program. In *village* ninth and tenth grade programs, only about 10 per cent of the students were reported by teachers to suffer from social and emotional problems, and these problems were rarely school-related. . . .

The majority of the students studied either dropped out of school and received no further education or else transferred from school to school in a nomadic pattern that can create identity problems. . . .

In addition, the supposed educational benefits of a large high school with a wide variety of courses and specialized teachers did not materialize for most village students.[42]

Fortunately, the other OECD countries have had considerably better experiences with boarding arrangements for rural pupils. Success in these programs is not accidental or easy to achieve. Over the years, many countries have been willing to allocate the extra time, money, and assistance necessary to ensure that boarding students get the best education and the most personal support which circumstances permit.

Perhaps a more common experience is that of France. There are currently very few boarding schools left in the country, both because of France's extensive network of very small rural schools and because of improvements in transportation. Nevertheless, there are still a few areas, such as in the mountainous and sparsely populated Massif Central region, in which boarding schools are occasionally necessary even for primary-level students. The following is an excerpt from a report by a French inspector of schools on one such institution. In it he has pointed out some of the typical strengths and weaknesses of boarding life:

The primary boarding school is sometimes a regrettable necessity but thanks to the determination of all concerned (administrators, teachers, supervisors and even pupils) it can become the lesser of two evils, or even a good thing for certain children who are under-privileged at home.

At an age when small children most need affection and are separated from their families, theirs could not be a happy life without the devoted care of all those responsible for them in the course of the day. This is an essential condition for the development of their personalities without serious emotional deprivation. This is fully understood by all the adults living in this little school and all help with the children's education—the director, manager, supervisors and domestic staff. Nor do the older pupils play a negligible role. The establishment has thus become a large family, where a cordial atmosphere prevails and life is pleasant. This, of course, was possible only because:

- the dimensions of the school and the numbers of pupils are small: 200 pupils in all; and
- everyone is permanently available to all, with no thought for timetables or maximum working hours.

Thanks to the boarding school the children receive normal schooling, which otherwise would have been impossible. The family atmosphere of the boarding school helps them to develop their personality and learn to live in a community, and even in some cases to find more affection in school than they would find in their somewhat undemonstrative families.

Although they do not appear to miss the daily presence of their parents, and in particular their mother, it may well be that in the long run this abnormal manner of living away from their families will leave some psychical mark.

Life at the primary boarding school is indeed a premature break with the family. On this account the boarding school, despite its merits, can only be regarded as a necessary evil.[43]

The important point is that boarding schools *can* offer advantages to their students which realistically cannot (or at least will not) be provided in the home community. These advantages range from access to specialized equipment and course offerings to greatly increased opportunities for social interaction and growth among children from isolated settings. In any case, the simple fact is that for a small contingent of students in the wealthier OECD countries and a larger number of students in less developed OECD countries, boarding school is the best available alternative.

Therefore, although educational arrangements allowing rural students to live at home are usually preferable (especially for primary students), boarding schools are occasionally necessary and can be an appropriate and satisfactory alternative for secondary students living long distances from the nearest school.

Noncompulsory Education

Although the CERI SPA project focused on the compulsory years of rural schooling, some data on both preschool and postcompulsory education issues surfaced. On the basis of the data, the diagnosis appears to be roughly the same at either end of the spectrum; that is, the current situation is not very good, but noticeable improvements have been, and are still being, made.

In preschool activities and in postcompulsory education, rural participation rates are significantly lower than urban ones throughout the OECD nations. Obviously, rural children cannot benefit from programs they do not take part in either by choice or because of a lack of effective access.

When one compares the prospects and performance of a rural youth having only eight or nine years of compulsory schooling with those of a metropolitan youth having had preschool and upper-secondary experiences, the fact that inequalities exist should come as no surprise. The irony is that rural children may need these extended opportunities as much, and probably more, than their urban and suburban counterparts.

At the preschool level, children in sparsely populated areas tend to have far fewer sources of intellectual stimulation and social interaction than metropolitan children. In fact, rural educators from several OECD countries tell anecdotes about children coming to school at age five, six, or seven from isolated farms or homesteads who could not (or would not) speak—not because of any physical handicaps but simply because they so rarely heard people talking in their home environments. Of course, children like this are quite exceptional, but less extreme versions of understimulated children are not rarities in rural schools.

Life in the open countryside, or on a remote island, or on top of a mountain all have advantages which should not be forgotten or denigrated. Nevertheless, children growing up far from any neighbors, friends, or the stimulations of town life may be in special need of the kind of social intercourse and developmental assistance which excellent early childhood education programs can provide.

Unfortunately, the evidence shows that these children are usually the last ones served by preschool programs and play groups rather than the first. For example, a 1975 study from New Zealand showed that even though more than 15 percent of the nation's children lived in rural areas, less than 2 percent of New Zealand's kindergarten programs were located in rural communities.[44] In fact, this study reported that while many rural communities were served by informal play centers, there were still more than 1,500 rural districts which had no preschools at all.[45]

New Zealand was by no means alone. A nine-nation study completed in 1975 concluded, "No country has yet coped adequately with providing organized child-care programmes in rural areas. . . . All countries reflect some geographical inequities and maldistributions with regard to the availability of organized child-care programmes. In particular, there is an imbalance between rural and urban areas."[46]

Similarly, a Council of Europe report argued that the rural disadvantage in terms of preschool education was the result of three "interlocking deficits":

1. Educational and social services [at the preschool level] are either missing, inadequate or poorly linked to the overall education network;
2. The differences between urban and rural socialization processes and motivational structures have rarely been investigated and taken into consideration; and

3. Alternative [preschool] educational programmes for rural districts have not been developed and tested sufficiently.[47]

The overall picture of rural preschool education is not a good one. However, this problem has finally been given some attention in the past four years and the situation is gradually improving. Although few countries have launched programs as large (and costly) as Head Start in the United States, interesting experiments are now being undertaken in most OECD countries.

In Switzerland, a training center has been set up in a mountainous area to recruit and prepare local people for a variety of rural early childhood education jobs. In parts of England, a wide network of rural play groups and other early childhood programs linked to primary schools is being organized.[48] In parts of the United States, television programs especially designed for young rural children have been developed and broadcast on a regular basis.[49] In the Nordic countries, a major series of preschool experiments in sparsely populated areas has been successfully launched.[50] And finally, in New Zealand, the government has been hard at work in the past few years to correct earlier deficiencies through

1. assistance to play groups;
2. encouragement of the use of primary school resources for preschool groups;
3. development of a mobile preschool service in suitable rural areas;
4. specially prepared preschool broadcasts on radio and television; and
5. preschool courses run by the New Zealand Correspondence School to guide mothers, to supply materials, and to supplement preschool broadcasts.[51]

Even given the incomplete data received, it seems reasonable to conclude that early childhood education is as important in rural areas as in urban ones, but at present preschool opportunities are not readily available in sparsely populated areas and rural provision remains inadequate.

It is considerably riskier to draw conclusions about postcompulsory education in rural areas based upon the information collected through the SPA project. This topic is both very important and frustratingly complex. Clearly, it is an area which merits much more in-depth research and analysis.

There is widespread agreement that fewer students in sparsely populated areas proceed immediately to postcompulsory schooling than students from metropolitan areas. For example, in Western Australia only 20 percent of the rural students complete the second year of postcompulsory schooling, whereas the figure for metropolitan students is 34 percent.[52]

In France, 54 percent of the rural pupils (as opposed to 41 percent of the urban ones) do not continue their state-sponsored education beyond the compulsory level.[53] Even when French rural students do take advantage of further education, a far greater percentage enroll in short-term practical training courses than their urban counterparts (33 percent versus 9 percent).[54]

In England, it is reported that the "staying on rate" beyond the period of compulsory schooling is notably lower among children from sparsely populated areas.[55] Further, rural students in England appear to have lower career aspirations than students in urban areas.[56]

This last point about lower aspirations is echoed by numerous other countries. As one government official put it, "There is some aspect of the rural environment — whether in home, school or community — which discourages young people from even attempting to continue their formal education to the higher levels necessary for advanced career development."[57]

To the extent that these lower aspirations and reduced school continuation rates are a matter of free choice, they are not a matter for governmental action. However, if these behavior patterns are not really voluntary, but rather the legacy of a second-rate education or of a lack of access to further opportunities, then governmental intervention becomes appropriate.

The fact that specialized education and training opportunities are not generally available in sparsely populated areas is readily conceded by policymakers in all the OECD countries. Some countries, such as Norway, have gone to extraordinary lengths to ensure a more equitable distribution (and decentralization) of facilities, resources, and opportunities than existed in earlier years.

However, no country could, or would, claim that its rural communities are all endowed with the same range of institutions and sources of assistance that exist in the metropolitan areas. After all, in the less-developed OECD countries, even universally accessible *basic* education is a comparatively new phenomenon.

Instead, government officials will point out that, in principle, qualified rural students have the same rights and access to postcompulsory schooling as students anywhere. However, as noted earlier, access in theory and access in practice can be very different. In order to make practical use of this access, rural students must be willing to endure hardships (such as moving away from home and/or regularly traveling long distances) which rarely are necessary for urban students. Not surprisingly, only the most tenacious and talented rural youth are able to turn their rights into realities.

Issues of the quality and appropriateness of postcompulsory education from a rural perspective will not be dealt with here, as they are beyond the scope of the CERI SPA investigation. Similarly, recommendations for overcoming these problems cannot be offered on the basis of the data collected.

It is hoped that governments will give the whole topic of noncompulsory education in sparsely populated areas more careful and sustained study than it has been accorded to date.[58]

On the basis of what is currently known, it seems reasonable to conclude that the provision of adequate postcompulsory educational opportunities in sparsely populated areas continues to be a major problem, and effective access to existing opportunities is too often denied to rural students.

Special Needs Populations

There is one other issue which merits attention here even though it lies outside the official mandate of the SPA project. In country after country, a strong impression emerges that while compulsory education in sparsely populated areas is satisfactory and sometimes quite good for average children, there are special groups of students whom it has failed with alarming frequency. These rural groups tend to fall into four broad categories: minority/indigenous populations; children from poverty families; handicapped children; and girls and young women. Naturally, all OECD countries do not share the same magnitude of problems here nor the same track record in dealing with them. However, at the aggregate level, children in these categories continue to be disproportionately underserved or badly served by the education system.[59]

The costs — personal, social, and economic — of past discrimination against racial, ethnic, and other minority groups found in sparsely populated areas of OECD countries have been enormous. The extent to which children from poor homes have been denigrated and "kept in their place" by rural education systems is a tragedy. The degree to which physically or mentally handicapped rural children have been shunned or conveniently forgotten in "advanced" nations is appalling. And finally, the way in which sex-role stereotyping and condescension have stunted the development and limited the accomplishments of rural girls and young women in nearly all the OECD nations is inexcusable.

The waste of human lives and the loss of all these potential human resources for the revitalization of rural communities are a long-standing disgrace. This has not been exclusively, or even primarily, a rural problem. However, rural education systems have often not done all they could do to effectively meet the special needs of these populations.

Fortunately, these problems are no longer "skeletons in the closet" of the OECD nations. There is an increasing tendency to directly confront these past failures and to develop more reasonable responses. Much hard work remains to be done; however, the steps taken in several OECD countries are far more than mere token gestures. They are serious attempts to diminish, if not solve, these problems and thus represent a laudable new era in governmental responses. Education agencies, too, are becoming involved. One such effort is the Disadvantaged Country Areas Program operated by the schools commission in Australia. Established in 1977 as an extension of the national Disadvantaged Schools Program, the Disadvantaged Country Areas Program funds and assists a fascinating range of rural innovations in six Australian states.[60]

Other countries (such as the United States with its "rural concentration" within the massive Title I program) have implemented similar activities. Special education for rural handicapped children has also received a big boost in the attention and resources allocated to it.[61]

Although significant strides have been made in recent years to improve the situation, one can still conclude that real equality of educational opportunity often does not exist for special needs populations in rural areas. Governments must push to ensure that special needs populations in rural areas are provided with the most appropriate and effective educational experiences possible. At the same time, education alone cannot be expected to solve all the serious problems of rural special needs groups. Ronald Fitzgerald's perceptive observation on Australia and on the work of the Disadvantaged Country Areas Program has broad applicability in other OECD countries as well:

> In considering the problem of rural disadvantage it should be emphasised that simply to set aside further resources for country schools will not be enough. The complex problems of our country communities are embedded in the prevailing economic and social fabric in Australia and to concentrate on any single aspect of rural disadvantage would be an inadequate response. . . . As a nation we have permitted the gradual destruction of our country communities and it is perhaps time that our society reappraised its attitude to them. The initiative of the Schools Commission in focusing on country education as an area of particular attention is to be welcomed but this will inevitably be inadequate unless economic problems are attacked at the same time.[62]

Is Small Beautiful? School Closures and the Alternatives

The Context

To close or not to close . . . that is the question most frequently raised in discussions about the current status and future prospects of rural schools. The closure of small rural schools is a complex and controversial issue in many OECD countries. This is perhaps not surprising in view of the potent mix of economic, technical, educational, psychological, and political factors which inevitably must be weighed and balanced by policymakers. Even in countries (or parts of countries) where a major wave of rural school closures is

not being actively considered, the strengths and weaknesses of rural education are being reassessed. In the current political environment, doing
nothing, i.e., maintaining the status quo, has become as much of a policy
decision as more active policies of school closure or school improvement.

There is a split here between the Mediterranean OECD countries and the
more industrialized countries. Although exceptions can certainly be found,
there is currently a tendency for the Mediterranean countries to favor school
consolidation strategies, whereas alternatives to consolidation are more actively sought in the non-Mediterranean countries.

Several explanations can be offered. First, the more urbanized countries
have actually experienced rural school closures and consolidations to a far
greater extent than the less urbanized countries. This has had two effects: (1)
nearly all the genuinely awful rural schools have been eliminated in the
more developed nations; and (2) claims about the alleged benefits and advantages of consolidation have been greatly tempered by the reality of consolidated schools which have not lived up to these claims.

Resource constraints also play an important role in explaining this split.
Even though governmental budgets are getting tighter and tighter, the
wealthier OECD countries still have enough trained teachers, strong enough
educational support systems, and enough material and financial resources to
make an extensive network of small but good rural schools plausible. By and
large, the poorer OECD countries do not.

There is a psychological/political dimension here as well. In the urbanized OECD nations, small schools (i.e., one- to three-teacher primary
schools or secondary schools with enrollments under one hundred) are not
the norm nationally, even if they are common in sparsely populated areas.
In these countries, national policymakers have traditionally equated abnor-
mality with inequality, and thus small rural schools looked very suspect.
However, as the political meaning of educational equality evolved from absolute uniformity to the ideal of equity (i.e., different responses based upon
different needs) the retention of "abnormal" rural schools seemed like less of
an affront to the goal of equality.

The less urbanized countries have tended to retain a more uniform interpretation of equality. This interpretation reduces the attractiveness of small
rural schools, but it is not their biggest problem in the view of policymakers.
Put simply, even though small rural schools are in fact the norm in these nations, they do not fit the vision held by national leaders and education
policymakers of what the norm should be. Whether this vision is "correct" is
beside the point. Politically, the replacement of small rural schools with
more "modern" institutions fits with, and has become part of, powerful
movements toward national "progress."

There is, of course, more than a little irony in the fact that the less urbanized countries are repeating the former pattern of the more urbanized countries by eliminating small rural schools at the same time that the more urbanized countries have started to look favorably upon such schools and have begun to implement strategies for their preservation and improvement. However, this may just be another example of the degree to which schools reflect the political and economic climate of their nation.

This section will examine the issues surrounding the future of small rural schools. It will encompass the economic aspects of rural education; concerns about the quality of education; the viability issue; and finally, the alternatives to closure.

A few background points should first be made. This view will only deal with small rural schools. In the OECD countries studied, large rural schools are a "nonissue" and are very rarely at risk of being discontinued (except when declining enrollments make them small schools again). As noted earlier, in an international context *small* is used to refer to rural primary schools with as many as three teachers and rural secondary schools with fewer than one hundred students enrolled.

It must be remembered, however, that considerable variations exist among the OECD nations as to the meaning of smallness. For example, in rural France or rural Portugal, a three-teacher primary school would not be considered particularly small. Conversely, a rural primary school in the United States having "only" one teacher per grade level would be considered relatively small.

It is not the purpose of this section to either condemn or defend small rural schools. The evidence gathered through the CERI SPA project offers little solace to extremists who either seek wholesale elimination of small rural schools or, alternatively, pretend that every one of these institutions merits being preserved. The profile which emerges is more ambivalent than polemic; strengths and weaknesses are equally evident, and the way the balance tips is more often a question of local circumstance than an application of global principles.

Nevertheless, as discussed in Chapter 1, the attitude toward small rural schools has become increasingly positive in recent years, particularly among the more urbanized OECD nations. The evidence presented reflects this attitudinal and policy shift. Accordingly, the overall assessment of these schools is considerably more favorable than a similar review would have been even ten years ago.

This generally positive tone is also a result of two biases in the data collected. The first is that far more information was available from the wealthier OECD countries than from the poorer ones where, presumably, the weaknesses of small rural schools are more glaring and the strengths more circumscribed. The second bias is that reliable "hard" data—on cost comparisons, on student achievement, on physical and material resources—were remarkably scarce. The reliable statistics which did exist often did not differentiate urban from rural schools nor small rural schools from large ones. Hard data could occasionally be found for particular rural schools or districts, but no consistent patterns existed, and even if they had, claims about representativeness would have been risky.

Whenever hard evidence is in short supply, informed opinions must be accorded greater than usual credence. Thus, much of the data gathered on small rural schools come from educators, policymakers, inspectors, and other professionals actively involved in rural education work. Accepting the views of these participants and observers as absolutely conclusive evidence would be almost as unwise as dismissing them out of hand. However, the fact that most of the points and conclusions presented below emerged over and over again in a range of countries confirms that these assessments are something more than coincidence or merely random impressions.

Economic Considerations

On the surface, it would appear that the economic arguments against rural schools are overwhelming. Not a single country providing information to the SPA project indicates that schools in sparsely populated areas cost less to operate than metropolitan schools.[63] Aside from some data showing that "distance education" could be delivered at a very reasonable cost, the available figures show rural school expenses to be disproportionately high.[64] In some cases the per-pupil cost differences were reasonably small, but more often they were said to be from 50 to 100 percent higher.[65]

The explanation is straightforward. Personnel costs are normally the largest single item in school budgets. Given statewide or, more commonly, nationwide salary scales and markedly lower pupil-to-teacher ratios in rural schools, per-pupil teacher costs are higher in rural schools.[66] Typically, per-pupil transportation costs are dramatically higher in rural areas, as are certain fixed costs like those for basic equipment, because there are fewer children among whom these expenses can be divided.[67] Thus, although absolute costs tend to be low, per-pupil costs tend to be significantly above average in sparsely populated areas.

Some illustrations might help make this clearer. In Greece, the national pupil-to-teacher ratio is 30 to 1. However, a recent government document points out that this 30:1 "average" is an illusion.[68] Rural schools will often have twenty or fewer students per teacher while urban schools will often have more than forty. Since the rural teacher with twenty students is paid the same as the urban teacher with forty students, the per-pupil teacher costs are about twice as high in the rural case.

In terms of transportation expenses, the difference can be astonishing. For example, recent evidence from Sweden indicates that in Stockholm the per-pupil transportation bill was 62 crowns, whereas in Ore, a sparsely populated region, the amount was 796 crowns per student.[69] Although this difference of nearly 1300 percent is extreme, a figure in the 200 to 500 percent range is not uncommon in many OECD countries.

Comparisons of expenses for materials yield much the same result. A film projector or a set of encyclopedias or a piano has the same price tag whether it is used in a rural or a metropolitan school. Yet, when this fixed price is divided among 200 pupils in a metropolitan school and among 50 pupils in a rural school, the per-pupil cost implications are obvious. Rural schools have generally kept their materials costs low, not through any economic advantage but rather by simply doing without material resources normally found in urban classes.

Thus, the oft-heard argument that schools in sparsely populated areas cost too much is simply fatuous. The question "Compared to what?" must constantly be borne in mind. For instance, compared to the cost of gathering enough children to have an urban-sized school in a remote rural area (via boarding arrangements or daily transportation), today's rural school tends to be a bargain.

Similarly, compared to what it would cost to provide exactly the same program, materials, and specialized services and resources routinely found in metropolitan schools to each existing rural school, the money actually spent in country schools begins to look miserly rather than profligate.

In practice, rural schools have been financially able to offer educational programs and services of at least reasonable breadth and quality by inaugurating such measures as

1. sharing resources (human, material, and financial) with other rural schools;
2. utilizing extensive parental assistance and in-kind contributions from the rural community;
3. hiring generalists at the secondary level who could perform multiple roles in the schools rather than hiring specialists;
4. promoting individualized instruction and independent study instead of extensive formal course offerings; and
5. simply doing without sophisticated equipment and expensive facilities.

The reality of high per-pupil expenditures in rural schools that offer adequate programs has not changed in recent years. Population sparsity ensures that rural districts will have relatively high per-pupil costs for transportation, specialized programs and services, administrative overhead, energy, equipment and materials, and the maintenance and construction of school facilities.

There are certain minimum fixed costs which any school must bear regardless of its enrollment level. Higher costs which are a consequence of sparsity must be regarded as one of the economic facts of rural life rather than as evidence of wastefulness or as expenses which can be erased by stricter expenditure controls.

Therefore, two conclusions can be drawn. First, the costs of delivering needed educational services in sparsely populated areas are inherently and inevitably higher than the costs of providing the same services in more densely populated areas. Second, rural schools have already reduced their costs, and can continue to do so, by sharing resources, and adopting other locally appropriate strategies.

One other facet of these urban-rural cost comparisons bears mentioning. Several OECD countries have indicated that rural populations tend to use considerably fewer public services than their urban counterparts. In part, this is the result of strong familial and community networks of voluntary assistance. However, an equally powerful explanation is that many public services are just not readily accessible to people in sparsely populated areas.

Viewed from the broader perspective of the total demands upon the public purse made by urban versus rural citizens, the situation looks different than when comparisons are limited to per-pupil expenditures. Even taking the high costs of rural schooling into account, the rural drain on public services is relatively low. Thus, rural communities, as one observer pointed out, "may feel entitled to their 'expensive' village school."[70]

Unfortunately, definitive cost comparisons within the rural sector are difficult to make. There is an abundance of anecdotal evidence and very little reliable systematic data available. The general impression is that the smaller the rural school is, the larger the per-pupil cost will be.

The reasoning behind this impression is basically the same as in urban-rural comparisons. Both common sense and the available statistics suggest that significant economies of scale can be achieved by enlarging the enrollment of small rural schools.[71] In short, it would seem that if small rural schools (particularly one- and two-teacher institutions) can be defended, it will not be on economic grounds. But in this debate there are always several important "howevers" to remember. What appears at first glance to be an open and shut economic case against small rural schools turns out to be far murkier and inconclusive.

Once again, the "Compared to what?" question looms large. Particularly for schools serving isolated or widely scattered families, alternatives to the existing small school (such as forcing primary-level children to board away from home or to travel for hours each day) are regarded as both too onerous and too expensive to be seriously considered. In these situations, strong diseconomies of scale outweigh any potential savings which could be achieved through school consolidation.

Abandoning the small school in favor of potentially less expensive distance learning strategies remains a possibility. But most OECD countries neither have the capability nor show any sign of wanting to develop it to implement first-rate schemes of this sort.

For genuinely remote and isolated areas, parents will argue, and educational administrators will usually concede, that the high costs of maintaining even a very small school are irrelevant. Just as physically and mentally handicapped children cost more to educate than "normal" children, so too a reasonable education in isolated (i.e., geographically "handicapped") areas will remain relatively more expensive.

Many small rural schools cannot claim this isolated status and could, in fact, easily be closed or merged with another school. In some countries, such as England, rural schools in this situation are very common. Nevertheless, "howevers" are frequently voiced here as well. There are two main economic justifications put forward for the continuation of small rural schools in nonisolated areas. Interestingly, both justifications transcend (or sidestep, depending on one's point of view) a strict accounting of direct costs.

The first argument is that there are hidden costs of school consolidation which must be taken into consideration even if the exact price tag remains elusive. For example, it is noted that the level of alienation often found among students in large schools has a significant personal, social, and economic cost attached. A recent government study from the United States indicating that vandalism increases as school and community size increases lends credence to this claim.[72]

At the end of a three-year investigation of very small rural primary schools in Wales, Roy Nash offered a cogent statement of this line of reasoning:

> In crude terms, rural children are expensive to educate. Even if all small primary schools were closed the costs would still be large, for the costs of transport have increased, are increasing and are likely to continue to increase. In many ways, however, rural children make few demands on local authority services. For example, almost none are in care, almost none are on probation, almost none take up the time of the child guidance service, few need expensive remedial education; they present, in fact, very few problems of this sort indeed. No one can be sure that if urban values and styles of life were introduced at an early age to country children — and busing does this as well as anything else — that this will continue to be true. Considered in this light the small rural schools may be a bargain.[73]

The second economic justification put forward for nonisolated small schools in rural areas is that they are essential to the economic development of rural regions. This line of thought is particularly prevalent in the Nordic countries. It has, in fact, been one of the guiding principles behind currently favorable small school policies in these countries. The strategy here is clear-cut. As part of a package of incentives to encourage balanced national growth, a decentralization of industry, and overall rural development, it is necessary to maintain a healthy and attractive infrastructure of community services — most prominently education. The absence of a good school in the community is thought to be a strong disincentive to families moving to rural areas. Thus, maintaining a strong network of well-equipped small rural schools (high costs and all) is increasingly being seen as a vital part of regional development policy.

To wrap up this discussion, it should be remembered that while there are many situations in which rural school consolidation could lead to a reduction in overall costs, this is far from universally true. As Ian Hind has warned, based on a detailed analysis of cost functions for rural primary schools in Australia,

> In Australia, most of the small schools that were established were in areas of relatively high population density such as the closely settled coastal dairying regions. Many of these schools are now closed, with the small schools remaining being in sparsely populated areas and/or located considerable distances from other schools. The possibility of economies being realized would thus, in present circumstances, appear rather limited.[14]

Similarly, a recent study of school consolidation in the United States pointed out,

> In communities having four ramshackle one-teacher schools with an average enrollment of less than ten pupils, all located within a ten square-mile area, school consolidation was probably an economically propitious strategy. However, in regions having four well-maintained, one-teacher schools with an average enrollment of twenty students, all spread out over a fifty square-mile area, school consolidation was probably devoid of any economic justification.[15]

Thus, local circumstance is the key determinant of the relative economic merits of either maintaining or closing small rural schools.

Quality Considerations

Important as the economic arguments may be, the continuing debate about the future of small rural schools in OECD countries cannot, and will not, be reduced to a duel between competing accountants. The real driving force behind this controversy is a hodgepodge of educational, political, and community-based issues which can be grouped under the rubric of "quality considerations."

As on the economic side, the level of reliable hard data about the quality of small rural schools is so low that making definitive pronouncements on the subject ranks somewhere between risky and foolish. This dilemma is compounded by the fact that small rural schools are so diverse, especially when viewed internationally, that one can find evidence to support nearly any characterization. Someone wishing to describe these institutions as ineffective, stifling, third rate, or worse will have little trouble finding schools that fully deserve such criticism. However, another person desirous of portraying small rural schools as innovative, high-performance, delightful places will have equal ease in justifying such a glowing assessment.

Neither person will be lying, nor will he or she be telling the whole truth. Comfortable stereotypes will have to be put aside before progress can be made toward understanding what is really happening with today's small rural schools. Only then will policymakers have the information and insight needed to formulate a sensible set of governmental interventions in this field.

That firm foundation of knowledge does not yet exist in all, or even most, of the OECD nations. Fortunately, the situation is rapidly improving. In the wake of the political reemergence of rural education (and, not coincidentally, the CERI SPA project) serious investigations and reappraisals have been launched. A few have already completed their work and others are well under way.

The information collected during the course of the SPA project is certainly better than the comparable data of five or ten years ago. Gaps still are evident. However, in a world in which the data are never all in, several OECD countries can take pride in what they have accomplished on both the research and action levels.

To begin at the most basic level, attention should be given to the physical characteristics of small rural schools. The places currently used as rural schools range from the ridiculous to the sublime — with a strong tendency toward the barely adequate. There is a correlation between national wealth and the quality of rural facilities, but it is not as strong as one might suspect.

Finland, for example, has worked hard and invested heavily in order to ensure that the quality of building and material resources in the countryside are not deficient even when compared to the cities. By contrast, in the United States, France, and a few other "rich" OECD nations, the physical quality of rural schools too often leaves much to be desired. Yet in most countries (including these two) there is a good deal of variation among localities. These differences are particularly apparent in countries having a system under which the local communities are largely responsible for the provision of their own supplies and the condition of their own facilities.

In areas having sufficient local resources, this decentralized responsibility encourages a level of motivation, interest, and pride which might not exist if everything was taken care of elsewhere. In these communities, the facilities normally are first rate and, even if they lack some of the more sophisticated scientific, technical, and athletic resources found in metropolitan areas, they are more than satisfactory for the demands placed upon them.

In poorer areas, the situation is more bleak. Outdoor toilets, crumbling facades, second-hand textbooks, improper heating, thirty-year-old maps (if any), and no play area worthy of the name are still well-known features of a very significant percentage of rural schools in the OECD countries. In some, the calendar is the only thing which is up to date. The grimness of "learning environments" like these has a detrimental impact on students and teachers alike. Parents too are adversely affected by this constant reminder of their poverty and inability even to provide their own children with the kind of school they would like them to have.

Local wealth is not the only determinant of the physical quality of small rural schools. The push for rural school closures and consolidations throughout the twentieth century has also made a negative contribution. This has manifested itself in two ways. First, implicit bargains have been struck between small rural schools and their authorities whereby the price of being allowed to remain open is that no major demands for renovations, extra materials, and so forth are made by the school. Any local complaints about bad conditions were immediately turned around and used as justifications for closure (as if poor quality or closure were the only two alternatives). Second, authorities have frequently treated small rural schools as temporary; for indeed their intention was to close them as expeditiously as possible. Accordingly, it struck administrators as being inappropriate and wasteful to renovate, improve, or even repair old rural schools which would soon be torn down. Sadly, some small rural schools in operation today have been treated as temporary since the end of World War II. Finally, though, some of these schools have been closed because they had been allowed to deteriorate to the point of being irreparable.

It should be noted that the following conclusion is not a plea for each rural school to have the full range of the latest gadgets and the most sophisticated equipment possible. First, this is impossible given existing financial constraints. Second, there is no evidence that proves the lasting educational worth of being blessed with an abundance of technological wonders. And third, to the extent that very expensive equipment *is* needed, it is most sensible for rural schools to band together, formally or informally, in order to share the costs and the benefits.

Rather, the plea here is for governments to ensure that all rural children are given the opportunity to attend a safe, adequately equipped, reasonably comfortable school that, at a minimum, does not detract from their education and, insofar as possible, enhances it.

Thus, the conclusion here is that although the general physical standard of rural schools is satisfactory in most OECD nations, there are still far too many rural schools in which a major upgrading of facilities and material resources is needed.

Since there is such a paucity of achievement data on rural students and since the data available is so often flawed, no statistically grounded conclusions on the performance of rural schools can be made here. There are bits and pieces of evidence that students in rural schools do as well as or even slightly better than urban students on basic literacy and mathematical tests. Other reports give the impression that rural student attainment is below average across the board, particularly in the less-developed OECD nations.

Neither result can be viewed as definitive, largely because it is unusual for achievement data to differentiate rural from urban students and even more unusual for reliable controls on IQ and on socioeconomic status to be utilized. As a consequence, it is virtually impossible to sort out the various influences contributing to performance.

If children from small rural schools in a certain region score lower (or higher) than their metropolitan counterparts, what exactly does that mean? Is it a function of their ruralness? A cultural bias in the test? Lower than average native intelligence? Inadequate instruction? School size? Bad luck? A poverty background? Perhaps some combination of all of these? The point is that crude comparisons of student achievement in urban versus rural schools are just that—crude.

As an illustration, the National Assessment of Educational Progress in the United States shows that the only group scoring lower (on the average) than children in relatively poor agricultural communities are children in impoverished urban areas.[76] Such data confirm that socioeconomic factors such as parents' income and education are powerful determinants of student achievement everywhere. They would also suggest that neither the specialization typical of big urban schools nor the coziness of small rural schools make a very great impact on the performance of their pupils when compared with more profound influences.

At a minimum, data like these make clear that "urbanness" and "ruralness" per se are very weak explanatory variables for fluctuations in student achievement. Consequently, there are strong grounds for suspecting that simply contrasting urban and rural data is both inappropriate and misleading. Comparing the performance of urban and rural schools may be like comparing the proverbial apples and oranges—only less fruitful.

Instead, it would seem more productive to compare and contrast the merits of different sizes and types of schools within the same rural milieu. Doing this should allow the differences in *schools* to come into sharper focus, while concomitantly reducing the impact of extraneous (or uncontrollable) influences.

Luckily, the intrinsic strengths and weaknesses of different kinds of rural schools have been observed (even if not as systematically as one might hope). These investigations yield virtually identical impressions from country to country.

First, it was felt that to the extent that school consolidation (i.e., the creation of larger units) has merits, its benefits flow predominantly toward upper primary and secondary-level students. Very little encouragement was given to school closures which would affect children of lower primary school age. There was a general feeling that the familial qualities, security, and quality of primary instruction in small rural schools was such that major benefits would not result from switching young children into larger schools outside their home communities.

For example, a classic study of the rural school consolidation issue from New Zealand made this often-expressed point very effectively:

> In the main, it would seem possible to provide very well for the educational needs of the younger children in the small country school. . . . One cannot but conclude that it is desirable to retain the local country schools for the younger children. There is, of course, room for improvement in many of the practices of the small school, but as far as the younger children are concerned such improvement can be brought about within the existing framework. . . . Eight and nine year olds can be well looked after in the little school and should be left there; they have more to lose than to gain by consolidation. The tens and elevens present a less clear-cut picture. These seem to be the borderline ages: they would gain something of social breadth in the larger school, but they would lose something of the homelike intimacy of the smaller. Taking into account the strain of bus travel and the length of the school day, particularly in the less populous areas, I think they too would be better left in the local school.[77]

Nash's rural study group in Wales came to a similar conclusion, as follows:

> The successes of the small schools studied are far more impressive than their failures. Their pupils are respected as people in their own right; their presence in the school is noticeably valued; and they attain a perfectly satisfactory standard in academic and in most non-academic areas of the curriculum. The relations between teachers and the parents are close, the school provides an emotional focus for the community and, in many cases, an actual meeting place. We believe that the school of one teacher plus nursery assistant with between

15–25 children is a viable and satisfactory type of school for the small rural community. Such a school could act as a nursery and infant school — accepting children as young as three years (perhaps on a part-time basis) while junior children might either remain in the school or transfer to a larger neighbouring school at the age of eight or nine.[78]

And finally, as the following excerpt from a report by one of Her Majesty's Inspectors of Schools on primary performance in one area of rural Scotland stated,

> Pupils are lively, knowledgeable and industrious and join, regardless of age, in art and craft activities, outdoor expeditions, and discussing and writing about subjects of common interest, all without detriment to progress in basic skills. There is no doubt that the atmosphere of intimacy among staff, pupils and parents which exists in the one- to four-teacher schools is a contributing factor in the success of those which have adopted these desirable approaches to primary education.[79]

However, the sense of approval widely felt toward young students remaining in small rural schools does not hold for older students. The advantages of a larger, more diversified setting are perceived to tip the balance in favor of larger rural schools once children are in the upper levels of primary education.

Thus, a major working group of school leaders in rural England came to the conclusion that while small primary schools were acceptable for small children, larger schools were needed for older pupils.[80] This sentiment was echoed in Switzerland, Ireland, Portugal, New Zealand, and other countries as well.

Given that the SPA work was limited to the years of compulsory schooling, an extended discussion of the merits of consolidation at the secondary levels will not be presented. However, there was general agreement about the value of schools sufficiently large to offer rural students a range of opportunities for their personal, vocational, and intellectual development. Further, it was felt that this range was difficult (although not impossible) to provide in very small units. Thus, while the investigation did not reveal any optimum size for a rural secondary school, there was general agreement that such schools needed to be significantly larger than rural primary schools in order to be effective.

Again, opinions varied as to the most advantageous size for rural primary schools. With few exceptions (most notably the United States) countries seemed to agree that it was not necessary to have larger than three-teacher schools in order to provide a good standard of education. Further, it was repeatedly stated that one and two teachers were capable of providing a perfectly reasonable primary education too, so long as good teacher quality and teacher support were maintained.

Thus, based on the available evidence, three related conclusions seem in order: (1) that the great majority of rural schools are providing at least an acceptable quality of education at the compulsory level; (2) that very small rural schools can be and often are effective in meeting the personal and educational needs of young students; and (3) that very small rural schools may not be as successful in serving their older pupils and therefore other types of provision should be made available, as necessary, to these students.

Before leaving this discussion on the comparative advantages of large and small rural schools and on the wisdom of school consolidation policies, it might be instructive to briefly review the experience of the United States in this area, although the U. S. situation is quite different from that of the other OECD countries.

One difference is that the United States has actually implemented policies of school closure and consolidation for a longer time and to a greater extent than any other OECD nation. For example, from 1930 until 1972, approximately 98 percent of the country's one-teacher schools were closed.[81] In absolute terms, this represented a drop from about 149,000 one-teacher schools in 1930 to 1,475 in 1972.[82] More important, the consolidation movement was not confined to the closure of one-teacher schools. During this same period, the total number of primary schools fell from 238,000 to 64,945.[83] Similarly, the total number of secondary schools went from 16,500 to 6,500 even though secondary-level enrollments tripled during the same period.[84] As a result, the average school enrollment in the United States is now 527, and even in nonmetropolitan areas the average number of students per school is 395.[85] Thus, rural school consolidation ranks as one of the most successfully *implemented* reforms in U. S. education history.

And yet, was it a success? Clearly, consolidation has been useful and beneficial in some rural communities. As a result of the consolidation movement, most of the grossly inadequate rural schools in the United States were closed, and schools which previously had very little in terms of specialized curricular offerings or sophisticated resources were able to upgrade their programs. Occasionally, consolidation even brought some cost savings and increased efficiency.

It is also clear, however, that in many situations consolidation's benefits were illusory. Many rural communities were forced to send their children long distances to attend consolidated schools which were no better than the community schools they replaced. In addition, consolidation occurred in thousands of communities where such a drastic reform was neither appropriate nor necessary. Often, the values of smallness were lost in the process of consolidation, and rural communities received little (educationally or economically) in return.

Today, it is interesting to note that in several American states there is still a push for further rural school consolidation. However, as is the case in a few other OECD countries, there is much stiffer political resistance. The main reason for this opposition is that, by now, consolidated rural schools are neither an untried novelty nor very popular among the intended beneficiaries.

A recent study of this topic, funded by the U. S. National Institute of Education, offered five conclusions which, if not directly relevant to all OECD countries, may be instructive nonetheless:

1. "Good" schools and "bad" schools (however defined) come in all sizes. Educational improvement and economic efficiency are the real challenges, and schools of every size could benefit from efforts in this direction. However, there is simply no basis for the belief that making a school bigger will automatically make it better.

2. After more than 30 years of experience with rural school consolidation, it is clear that consolidation has not lived up to the claims made by its supporters. By and large, the benefits have been exaggerated and the liabilities simply ignored.

3. While some schools and districts can benefit economically or educationally by consolidating, such places (at least in the U.S.) are a distinct minority and are becoming increasingly rare. In most cases, it is far more sensible to devise creative ways of bringing resources to children rather than forcing children to go long distances for these resources.

4. Any decision about consolidation involves trade-offs. To some individuals, getting what big schools can offer (e.g. more equipment and more specialists) is worth the costs (e.g. loss of a community institution, more transportation and reduced participation in school and extra-curricular activities). To other individuals, the benefits are not worth what must be given up to get them.

5. The decision to consolidate should not be made hastily or without careful consideration of its likely effects. Unlike most educational decisions (for example, the choice of textbooks), consolidation is almost irreversible. Once old schools have been closed, new ones built, and new buses and equipment purchased, it is very difficult to go back to the way things were, even if consolidation doesn't work out well.[86]

Alternatives to Consolidation

As mentioned above, political resistance to rural school consolidation has been growing in the United States. For instance, there is now a very active and successful citizens' organization called People United for Rural Education. This organization, based in the state of Iowa but with a national membership, has been fighting to both preserve and improve rural schools.

However, America is by no means the only country in which the political tide has started to turn against further school closures. For example, in England there is now a National Association for the Support of Small Schools. Political activism in England on this issue has been high. As Rick Rogers has reported,

> Given that there are so many alleged educational and economic disadvantages involved, it is surprising that so many parents, teachers and local communities actually want to keep their small school open. But parents are not stupid; they do not fight to ensure their children have a poor education. Some battle on to the point of barricading themselves inside a school threatened with closure; others attempt to run the school themselves.
> The fact is that the closure of small schools — urban and rural — is now being vehemently challenged because there are powerful arguments for their continuation and enhancement.[87]

Sweden, too, has experienced a reversal of policies on small schools. As Annika Andrae and Per-Erik Eriksson have pointed out,

> National policy has gone from favoring centralization (i.e. closing rural schools and busing the students) to favoring decentralization and the maintenance of small schools. This trend includes urban small schools as well as rural ones. In fact, the next step may be one of starting new small schools.
> It is possible that broader political changes in the composition of the Riksdag [Parliament] and the leading role of the former Agrarian Party in the new Government has caused this switch on policies. However, there are also very strong pressure groups in Sweden struggling for government decentralization, for rural improvements and for small rural schools.[88]

Although it is a much more limited example, the resistance of rural citizens in Portugal to the closure of their local Telescola "schools" fits into the broader pattern. As L. C. Taylor writes,

> In 1976, 128 villages were given the chance to choose the educational system they preferred. It was proposed that their Telescola "school" should be closed. Instead, special school buses would take the village children to nearby preparatory schools. The village authorities duly considered the offer: 20 failed to answer, 3 were in favor of the proposal and 105 were against it. Such resounding opposition had been unexpected.[89]

Finland also actively favors the maintenance of small schools. Reijo Laukkanen has described this change as follows:

> In the planning of the nation's school network, the Finnish authorities have
> had to choose between two alternatives: to take rural pupils long distances to
> big school units or to keep the schools as near as possible to the pupils' homes
> and to have many small school units. The latter strategy has been adopted as
> fully as possible in recent years. . . .
>
> An important reason for the policy favouring small rural schools has been
> the appreciation of a school's effect on the rural community. The task of the
> school in the sparsely populated areas is not restricted only to its educational
> function. The school is an important factor in the community's cultural and
> social life, and the services offered to, and by, the community decrease con-
> siderably with the closure of a small village school. For this reason, the local
> population in Finland wants to maintain its own schools and the activities
> relating to their educational function for as long as possible.[90]

Perhaps it is Norway which has actually gone the farthest in terms of institutionalizing policies favoring small rural schools. A 1978 government
report candidly discussed what has happened and why:

> The trend towards "consolidation" of school units was broken around 1970.
> This is partly explained by strong political opposition from small communities
> fearing the loss of their local school as an essential element in the life of the
> community. More important, however, has been the increasing reaction
> against professional ideas about the way a school should function.
>
> Such ideas emphasized the need for specialised teaching qualifications and,
> particularly in the youth school, separate grouping of pupils with different
> levels of ability. Such functional specialisation within the school inevitably led
> to professional pressure for larger school units, and the political acceptance of
> such ideas was the main factor behind the tendency towards increased school
> size in children's schools during the 1950s and 1960s.
>
> The breakdown of faith in such professional concepts of schooling, both at
> the political and professional level, is the main factor behind the abandon-
> ment of consolidation policies for children's schools, and the decline in unit
> size of youth schools. *This is clearly manifested in the decision by Parliament
> to make 450 pupils the maximum size of a compulsory school,* even if it covers
> all nine grades, and its indication that when permitted by population size,
> schools of 200–250 pupils may be the most desirable in our school organization.
>
> Such attitudes are reflected in the emphasis on the use of class teachers (as
> contrasted to specialised subject teachers) all the way up to the 9th grade, the
> indication of subjects as a basis for child-oriented and problem-oriented
> teaching, as well as the abandonment of organised streaming in the youth
> schools. Schools should not be seen as institutions managing educational
> technology, and following the principles of industrial division of labour. They
> should primarily be social milieus in which children can easily accommodate

and develop, in close personal contact with teachers they know well, and who are well integrated in the local community surrounding the school.

Such ideas are still controversial, and there are frequent reactions based on concern for traditional knowledge acquisition and "intellectual standards." Yet, there is no evidence that such standards have suffered by the shift in educational concepts dominating compulsory education in Norway.[91]

What all of these attitudinal and policy changes add up to is a new era in the relations between small rural schools and the education authorities in a group of OECD nations. If it can be sustained, this change means that aggressive programs of rural school closure will come to an end in these countries.

Some schools might still shut down as declining birth rates eliminate the pool of students in a particular district. The real difference will be that such schools will, in essence, close themselves—that is, they will close despite governmental policies rather than because of them.

Not closing small rural schools needlessly may well be a step in the right direction. However, if it is seen as a final step on the government's part rather than the first step, this new era may leave a legacy of more harm than good. It is not enough to simply keep schools open. Doing nothing, in most cases, is not an effective alternative to closure. Saving rural schools from the ax is no great kindness if they are then abandoned and left to starve.

As R. S. Johnston perceptively observes, "Small schools, particularly in remote areas, which merely survive—but remain cut-off from necessary resources and assistance—can hardly be viewed as dynamic institutions or as schools which are living up to their not inconsiderable potential. The conditions for success in these instances are very clear. Survival *must* be accompanied by active and appropriate *support*."[92] The inference here is that the most potent and lasting alternative to consolidation is the improvement of rural schools. In other words, if rural schools can be helped to more fully realize their potential, then the rationale for closing them becomes weaker and weaker.

Much of the rest of this volume is devoted to detailed examinations of some of the most promising rural education innovations being undertaken in the OECD countries. These SPA special reports reveal a number of fascinating roads to improvement.

In addition to the innovations reported on in depth here, there are a few other very useful alternatives which should be singled out for special attention. For example, in the sparsely populated Massif Central region of France, two experiments are under way which are designed to help make further consolidations unnecessary. One is the mobile resource center and the other is the linked-school strategy.[93]

The linked-school strategy was explicitly created to help very small rural schools experiencing declining enrollments to avoid closure. The basic idea is simple. A group of two to four schools in the same geographic area agree to form an alliance and to share all resources. However, the heart of the French linked-school strategy is to share students as well as learning resources. Thus, for example, on a rotating basis, one linked school will teach all the youngest children in a four-school catchment area, one will teach the six- to seven-year-olds, another will teach the eight- to nine-year-olds, and the fourth will teach the ten- to eleven-year-olds.

As of 1979, there were 1,764 schools throughout France active in this movement,[94] serving more than 180,000 pupils. This level of adoption is quite extraordinary and makes it the most successful new rural education strategy in France.

In practice, the linked schools have demonstrated a number of advantages over keeping tiny schools open but separate. It has helped to improve rural preschool education by designating one of the schools in each group as the preschool center and then developing (usually for the first time) a cohesive program for the provision of rural early childhood education. The scheme has also been a great help in reducing the isolation, both physical and psychological, which is often felt keenly by rural teachers and students alike. Of course, the educational benefit is that each school deals with only one age group and thus is able to focus fully on its students' specific educational needs.

Not surprisingly, the linked-school strategy has encountered some difficulties because of local rivalries, financial complexities, and logistic and climatic problems. However, the rapid growth of the scheme indicates that its assets outweigh its liabilities.

Another useful experiment under way in the Massif Central involves mobile resource centers. Once again, the idea is simple — an experienced teacher/*animateur* travels on a regular basis from school to school delivering much-needed learning resources and serving as an informal advisor for teachers working in isolated circumstances. Usually, the mobile resource center is matched with the most isolated and deprived schools. These are tiny institutions too remote to participate in a linked-school group.

The mobile resource center offers two services which have been enthusiastically received by local teachers: (1) an ample stock of films, tapes, slides, texts, and other learning materials to supplement and extend the classroom teacher's own efforts; and (2) a measure of peer support for the teacher and outside stimulation for the pupils.

Without this assistance or the ability to join in a linked-school arrangement, many of these small rural schools would be prime candidates for closure. With these two forms of support, the education offered has improved and the pressures for closure have diminished accordingly.

Two local education authorities in England are currently experimenting with alternatives to closure which resemble the French linked-school strategy. Cambridgeshire and Norfolk have begun experiments with a "cluster school" idea in their rural areas.[95] In the Norfolk cluster scheme, a group of as many as four small rural primary schools are administratively and programmatically joined under one head teacher. The village schools remain in operation, but only for the young students (ages four to eight). Older students (ages eight to eleven) all attend one of the cluster schools.

Similarly, the Cambridgeshire "federation" scheme brings together a group of existing small schools to share resources and plan cooperatively.[96] In this case, the consolidation which occurs is largely administrative. The village schools retain the full age range but teachers move from site to site and the children are occasionally bused for special events and joint activities. Two factors help facilitate this arrangement; a new minibus and the fact that the schools are very close together.

Other examples of supportive measures which serve as alternatives to closure abound in the OECD countries. In Sweden, the PANG project is an elaborate attempt to provide advanced instruction in decentralized rural schools through the creation of a highly individualized, nongraded learning environment.[97]

In Somerset, England, a public commitment to small rural schools (a pronounced departure from twenty-five years of centralist policy) has led to the establishment of a series of vital support mechanisms including assistance in curriculum development; specially tailored in-service training; deployment of specialist advisors in rural areas; and an expansion of rural-oriented teacher centers.[98]

In New Zealand, the government recently initiated the Rural Education Activities Programme,[99] intended to provide schools in sparsely populated areas with new teacher support mechanisms such as a corps of guidance/visiting teachers; liaison between existing schools; itinerant speech therapists; and specialist faculty members at the secondary level.

In the United States, a variety of alternatives have been tried, most prominently the creation of informal regional cooperatives to share costs, services, and experience and the development of more formal regional service centers run by state governments.[100]

In Australia there has been a push to inject modern technologies as a supplement to the capacities of local rural schools. Radio stations, video projects, and computer-related initiatives have all received funding through the Disadvantaged Country Area Program.[101] For example, ROCTAPUS (Really

Outstanding Colour Television About Practically Unlimited Subjects) is a fortnightly magazine-style television program provided to more than ten thousand students in the ten- to sixteen-year-old age group in the rural areas of the Australian state of Queensland.[102] ROCTAPUS puts isolated children in touch with the wider world. ROCTAPUS also makes use of local content and involves the audience as directly as possible in influencing the content of the programs.

And finally, in Finland, as well as a group of other OECD nations, experiments are under way to keep rural schools open by turning them into centers of activity for the whole community rather than limiting their use to school-age children.[103] The specific schemes vary considerably but often include integrating preschool programs into the regular school, providing health and social work services, and using spare capacity in existing facilities for community organizations and/or government offices.

All of the alternatives to closure mentioned above share a common trait, their focus on changing (or supporting or improving) small rural schools from the outside in. Perhaps, however, the most profound changes are those which come from the inside out.

It may be that the best defense against both closure *and* mere survival comes from taking a hard look at what a uniquely rural education consists of and then working to implement it so well that closure becomes a nonissue. In other words, heightened quality may be the best alternative of all.

What is a uniquely rural education? What kind of curriculum best serves the interests of rural students? Issues like these have been a constant undercurrent in the SPA project. Successfully coming to grips with these questions is not easy, but neither is it impossible.

The following excerpt is the result of one rural educator's work toward resolving some of the practical questions and theoretical problems inherent in constructing a quality rural education. This section of Tom Gjelten's booklet, *Schooling in Isolated Communities,* is reprinted in full (with the author's kind permission) not only because it was the most lucid statement about rural curriculum development available, but also because it captures so well the essence of this element of the SPA project's line of reasoning.

As background, it should be noted that this "model" of a rural curriculum grew out of Gjelten's experiences as a teaching principal on a small island off the coast of Maine in the United States. In 1978, there was one school on the island serving eighty-four children (from kindergarten through year 12) with a full-time instructional staff of eight. In this "remote and necessary" school, a "normal," metropolitan-style curriculum was simply not possible; hence the development of the local alternative described below.

EXCERPT FROM SCHOOLING IN ISOLATED COMMUNITIES

In the debate over the strengths and weaknesses of rural education, the most frequently mentioned problem in small schools is the difficulty of providing an adequate curriculum for students growing up in an increasingly complex world. It is in this area that schools are most vulnerable to suffering by comparison with urban schools.

It is obvious that small community schools (1) cannot employ teachers to teach exclusively in the field of their expertise; (2) cannot offer courses which require expensive equipment and special facilities; (3) cannot afford to keep all textbooks and other curricular materials constantly up to date; (4) cannot offer the wide variety of courses and opportunities for advanced study in a particular area which is available in large schools; and (5) cannot provide special curricular "tracks" for students with different career interests: college preparatory, vocational, or general.

Does this mean that small rural schools must inevitably suffer from these problems, that they never will be able to compete with urban schools in the area of curriculum? Proponents of consolidation would probably say yes. To those of us who believe that the small rural school can potentially be a better system than the large urban one, the answer is no. True, as long as rural schools emulate an urban model of education, rely on curriculum materials written for urban children, and seek to hire the same kind of teachers as urban schools seek, they probably will be second-rate. But rural schools do not need to fashion themselves after urban schools. They have their own model, with its own wonderful strengths. What's more, an urban school curriculum is not appropriate for the needs of rural students, coming from small communities rather than from cities. Rural schools' curricula are not fated to be inferior, as long as they take advantage of the rich resources of the rural community and relate directly to the experience of rural children. What would such a curriculum entail?

A curriculum suited to the unique needs of remote rural communities would probably include the following general features:

1. *A strong foundation in the teaching of basic skills and essential facts.* There are certain skills which children must learn to be able to function effectively as adults in today's world, regardless of where they come from and what they hope to become. Among these are:

speaking articulately	expressing creativity
listening attentively	being careful and accurate
thinking clearly	counting and using numbers
decoding written material (reading)	making computations
comprehending what is read or heard	solving problems using numbers and ideas

| writing effectively | coordinating physical movements |
| explaining | maintaining physical fitness |

There is also a general body of knowledge which all children need to learn, including facts about one's body and how it works, the natural environment and the relationship of its parts, and where things are in the world.

There is much more, of course, which must be learned, but beyond this minimum, it begins to vary with circumstance. At this basic level, rural schools do not suffer any handicaps in comparison with urban schools. Classic teaching methods and simple materials are usually sufficient to accomplish these goals. If anything, teachers in rural schools are perhaps in a better position to convey these skills. Children learn best in the kind of atmosphere which is characteristic of rural classrooms: warm and informal, with constant personal attention, in the company of familiar people, and close to home both physically and socially. Particularly during the elementary years, there should be constant attention to learning these skills and to establishing performance standards which insist upon their mastery.

2. *An emphasis on practical skills.* In all schools it is important to connect what is learned in school with what is done outside of school. I include this notion as a feature of a special rural curriculum for two reasons. First, practical knowledge is much more highly valued in traditional rural communities than abstract knowledge. For the school to be successful, its program must be consistent with local values, and should convey to students skills and knowledge useful to them in their own experience. Teachers in rural communities soon discover that they have a much easier time communicating material if there is an apparent reason for learning it: studying fractions while learning to use the ruler makes sense; doing it because it happens to be the next chapter in the textbook does not.

Second, rural curricula ought to have a highly practical orientation for the simple reason that it is much easier for rural schools to maintain it than it is for large urban schools. The proximity of the small rural school to the world outside the classroom is a natural advantage which should be exploited to its limit. Teachers in city schools separated from the outdoors by three flights of stairs and several bureaucratic forms are justifiably envious of the rural teacher who can lead her class out the back door of her classroom to the school playground bordering on a meadow, a stream, and several acres of woods. The ambitious city teacher can also provide enriching learning experiences outside the building, but problems of transportation and management are often discouraging. The rural teacher, on the other hand, can spontaneously follow up a lesson on measurement by having the students pace off the distance from the school to the Grange Hall down the road, using several units. People driving by will wave or stop for a friendly word, rather than lean on their horn and curse.

3. *Training in self-directed study and the development of initiative.* Students in large urban schools must learn how to manage the technology of language and science labs, and how to take notes and listen to lectures, because these are characteristics of large-group instruction. Students in rural areas must learn how to gather information on their own, work for extended periods without supervision, and take more responsibility for their own learning, because those are the skills which are necessary in a system where instruction is by necessity individualized. These skills are not learned automatically—they must be taught sequentially—and the rural curriculum must emphasize the learning of them in the same way it stresses the learning of other academic skills. This emphasis must begin in the early grades and continue into the upper grades, so that by the time a student enters high school, where the teachers are generalists and there is less technology to support learning than in other high schools, he or she will have already learned how to dig deeper into a subject independently.

4. *A focus on the community.* A strong rural curriculum involves teaching students about their community, through their community, and for their community. The school is in a position to teach students to appreciate the rich diversity of their community's human and natural resources. Just as it aims to teach them the national heritage, so, too, it must teach students the local heritage—or arrange for it to be taught, as in this case the teachers are often not the experts. The community is also an example and an experience through which one can learn lessons in language arts, social studies, science, crafts, art, and music.

The school in a small rural town must focus on the local world in its curriculum because it is committed to the community and its preservation. Many of the students attending the school will undoubtedly remain in the local community for the rest of their lives. For all those students, there needs to be built into the curriculum a preparation for that possibility. The school is a part of the community, and it has an obligation to serve it.

One of the ways it can best do this is to include in its program a component which, followed to its conclusion, makes students better equipped for the vocational and civic responsibilities of life in their hometown. Such a component would include considerable background in local history and culture, detailed knowledge of the position of the community in its political and economic relations with the rest of the region and nation, an understanding of the primary issues facing the community in the future, and the preparation of the student to assume a responsible role as an adult citizen.

5. *An orientation to familiarizing students with the outside world.* There is a need for an orientation to the outside world, just as there is a necessity of maintaining a local focus. Both themes have unique significance for rural

schools. In an isolated community, youths often develop a tenuous relationship with the larger world. They probably know a lot about other places, but their isolation from them has kept them from experiencing them directly. The result is a feeling of confusion and conflict that may complicate their own development into worldly-wise adults. The rural school's curriculum must include teaching about the larger world, and also provide a structure for experiences which help students to clarify their relationship with the outside world in their own lives. Until they become more familiar with places outside their own community, they will not be certain of the extent to which they are part of it, or the extent to which they are independent of it. It is increasingly important for rural students to be sophisticated about the world beyond their hometown. They can no longer automatically assume there will be a place for them somewhere in their community—the economic situations in many rural towns preclude that guarantee. And for those who do stay in their own town, knowing how to manage relations with people and institutions from outside the community is more necessary than ever before, as our society becomes increasingly complicated and centralized.

6. *Attention to the futures of the students.* Until recent years, schools have given little thought to the experiences facing youth after they leave school. There is a special need for rural schools to accept this responsibility, however, and make career development programs a fundamental theme in their curricula. Rural youths encounter unique dilemmas as they face prospects for their future, most notably the tension between their loyalty to family and community on the one hand, and their interest in the outside world on the other. The rural school curriculum must provide support for all the options facing youth, making each of them seem legitimate and possible. Students need to have experiences within the curriculum of the school which leave them with a sense of control over their future: a conviction that they are choosing among options with which they are familiar; the confidence to go ahead and choose; and the preparation to follow whatever choice they make to its conclusion.[104]

Based upon the preceding discussion of the school closure issue and the alternatives, three conclusions emerge: first, that rural school consolidations/closures are not necessarily the best strategy for improving rural education—local circumstance must be the key determinant of the educational merits of consolidation/closure; second, that an increasing number of countries are actively seeking ways of preserving and improving their small rural schools, rather than replacing them; and third, that effective alternatives to consolidation/closure do exist and can be expanded through new structural arrangements, support systems, and in-school innovations.

Teacher Issues

Thus far, attention has been paid to a variety of concerns about rural education: facilities, transportation, school size, student achievement, curricula, costs, national policies, demographic trends, school closure, alternatives to closure, special needs populations, and more. Nevertheless, no diagnosis of rural education can bypass the heart of the system — the teacher.

Neglecting teachers in an examination of rural education is like discussing rural health care and forgetting to mention the doctors, or discussing agriculture and ignoring the farmers. Delivery systems are important; support systems can be vital; and national policies often have a major impact. Yet, in the final analysis, somebody has to actually make the system *work*. In an overwhelming majority of cases, that somebody in rural education is the local teacher. Thus, the rural teacher can properly be viewed as the key to the quality of rural education.

The above statement elicits nearly universal agreement in principle. Unfortunately, OECD countries have too often belied in practice what they have preached in principle. As a consequence, there are still important issues surrounding rural teaching and rural teachers in virtually all the industrialized nations. The overall picture has improved in recent years, but it remains a less than rosy one. There is little reason for deep concern about rural teachers; on the other hand, there is even less reason for complacency.

This section will explore the issues in three clusters: teacher characteristics in sparsely populated areas; recruitment and retention problems; and support for rural teachers. One overriding point should be noted at the outset: this is yet another topic on which there are significant differences between the situations of the less-developed and the more-developed OECD countries. One group of countries (the United Kingdom, Germany, and the United States among them) is trying to come to grips with the problem of declining enrollments and highly qualified but "redundant" teachers. Simultaneously, another group of countries (Portugal, Turkey, and Greece among them) is experiencing such rapid rises in enrollment that their teaching supply is strained to the breaking point — and sometimes beyond it.

For example, Greece has recently passed a new law extending the period of compulsory education from six to nine years.[105] The 50 percent increase in the size and scope of the nation's basic education system has caused enormous new staffing requirements. The situation is much the same in Portugal, where enrollments in preparatory education (years 5 and 6) have rocketed from approximately 91,000 in 1969-70 to more than 220,000 in 1977-78.[106] In the same brief period, Portugal's demand for teachers at this level has gone from less than 3,000 to more than 18,000.[107]

This particular split in the ranks of OECD countries is merely the most dramatic example of the diversity among all the countries in terms of both the nature and the severity of problems related to rural teachers. Although some interesting patterns do emerge, no pretense of uniformity among countries is made and none should be inferred.

Teacher Characteristics

There once was a time when it was easy to distinguish rural teachers from urban ones in most OECD nations. The rural teacher was ill prepared, underpaid, overworked, and wholly isolated within the classroom and within the profession.

In one-room and other very small rural schools, the teacher was expected to be the janitor, the groundskeeper, the cook, the accountant, the administrator, the nurse, the social worker, the disciplinarian, the psychologist/counselor, and the "pillar of the community" — in addition, of course, to teaching the full range of subjects to the full range of students. The only thing more amazing than the demands placed upon the rural teacher is the fact that many of them succeeded in this role.

Today's rural teachers are better prepared, better paid, and usually less isolated than their predecessors. However, they are still expected to play most of the roles noted above without complaint. Rural teachers ordinarily perform a range of tasks which would seem extraordinary in any large metropolitan school. In short, while a rural teacher's life can be idyllic, it is rarely idle.

Viewed from the outside, the "rural teacher problem" is obvious. In theory, effective teaching in a small rural school requires the best talent available. In practice, the rural teacher's most common attribute has been availability rather than proven talent. That so many grew on the job and *became* talented is a tribute to the teachers themselves. It was not a result that education authorities had a right to expect, nor one that they had tried very hard to ensure.

Viewed from the inside, rural teaching is often an intense experience, personally and professionally. Under the right circumstances, it can be immensely enjoyable and rewarding work. Under less advantageous circumstances, it can be traumatic and frustrating. Rarely, though, is it "just a job" in the way that specialized positions can be in large metropolitan schools.

As noted earlier, the severity of problems related to rural teachers is diminishing in most developed nations. However, change is a slow process. The joke about last year's rural student being this year's rural teacher seems humorous in most countries, but in others it is no laughing matter. For example, in 1977 nearly 2 percent of Portugal's primary school teachers were under twenty years of age.[108]

This is not so unusual as it may seem at first glance. Almost everywhere, the age distribution of rural teachers is skewed at both ends; rural schools tend to have a disproportionately high number of very young and very old teachers. For example, in 1977 the Australian state of Queensland reported that 87.5 percent of their rural school staff were in their first or second year of teaching.[109] The comparable figure for urban schools was 19.6 percent. Conversely, in England some local education authorities indicate that "there is a significantly higher proportion of long-serving staff in rural areas."[110]

This is not a statistical fluke. Rather, it is the result of an attitude in the education profession toward rural schools (especially small ones) as reasonable places to begin or end one's career, but not as places to be during one's prime. At the individual level, there are numerous exceptions, but the general pattern still exists.

Although there is little statistical evidence, it would appear that rural teachers can be broadly classified into three groups. Other typologies exist as well, but the following three groups are recognizable (if simplistically described) types in many sparsely populated areas.[111]

1. *Homebodies* — individuals who grew up in the same (or very similar) rural areas in which they teach. The time they spent away from home for their training, and perhaps their practice probationary teaching, is often their only "outside" experience. Their general strength is their empathy with, understanding of, and commitment to the local community and its children. Their general weakness is a tendency not only to have somewhat parochial attitudes but also to lack a background of experiences and ideas upon which to draw in trying to improve the school. In professional terms, they run the gamut from poor to excellent. For the most part their teaching is solid and fairly competent, especially in the "basics." Because they have a deep personal commitment to the area, these individuals tend to settle in fairly quickly and do not seek promotions which would take them outside the community.

2. *Flashes in the pan* — individuals, usually quite young, who come to the rural school either involuntarily (it was all that was available, or they had no say in the assignment) or because they have decided that such a post is a useful stepping stone. Their basic trait is their mobility. Psychologically, they are often on their way up and out from the day they arrive. In terms of strengths, they are usually bright, innovative, energetic, and willing to shake up the status quo. On the negative side, they generally are not very sensitive to local customs and values, and they tend to be somewhat doctrinaire about whatever educational theory or method they prefer. Both of these faults stem from the self-imposed transience of their position. It takes patience and commitment to want, and be able, to understand the community and the children well enough to modify one's teaching to fit the

local needs. Unfortunately, patience and commitment are not characteristic of this group. At their best, they can inspire a lively environment and some useful innovations. However, they are usually gone before the innovations can become institutionalized and so the changes made fade away quickly.

3. *Transplants* — people from urban areas who now live in the countryside. Frequently, they come to the rural area either because their spouses have been reassigned to jobs nearby (branch offices of private firms, military installations, universities, decentralized factories, and / or government agencies) or because of a conscious rejection of the urban life-style. Their general strength is a wealth of experience and ideas picked up from other schools and communities. Their general weakness is an inability to adjust to and feel comfortable in the community and the school. This, in turn, sets up a degree of alienation all around. As with any transplant, there is the risk of rejection — by the community, the teacher or, occasionally, both at once. Professionally, transplants are often very good teachers with a special talent uncommon in the local area (for example, in the performing arts). Transplants tend to be the most extreme in terms of their impact. When there is a good match, the transplant often proves to be the best type of teacher in small rural situations, providing more continuity and sensitivity than the "flash in the pan" teacher and more breadth and open-mindedness than most "homebodies." When the match is not good, the likelihood of serious levels of antagonism and frustration, a bad situation for everyone concerned, is fairly strong.

In terms of credentials and qualifications, the once-great gap between urban and rural teachers has largely been closed. In some countries, such as Scotland, Sweden, and New Zealand, there are no fundamental differences between the qualifications of rural and urban teachers.[112]

However, much remains to be done in correcting the qualification problems which still exist in a great many OECD nations. In Portugal, nearly 25 percent of the preparatory education teachers had no degree or special qualification; the same proportion were fully certified; and most of the remainder had a university degree but no specific teaching qualifications.[113] This phenomenon was not limited to the less-developed OECD countries. France, for example, reports that many of its small primary schools in sparsely populated areas are staffed by inexperienced teachers and that there is a good deal of staff turnover.[114] Further, at the secondary education level, rural schools tend to have a large proportion of teachers with lower credentials than their urban counterparts.[115]

Iceland, too, provided statistics showing that whereas nearly all the urban teachers are fully qualified, approximately half the nation's rural teachers lacked comparable credentials.[116] Iceland was also one of the few countries in which men outnumbered women among rural primary school teachers.

Several countries, such as the United States and New Zealand, had a majority of males in head teacher and/or school principal roles in rural areas, but women were more numerous among classroom teachers.

Of course, how much preservice training teachers have had is not a foolproof predictor of their eventual performance in the classroom. Highly credentialed teachers can turn out to be mediocre, while uncredentialed ones sometimes prove absolutely first rate. Yet even if good training cannot make a person ill suited to teaching into a brilliant practitioner, it can still serve two useful functions: helping teachers having the right natural attributes to realize their full potential, and preparing potential teachers for the realities of the schools and communities in which they will be working after graduation.

This is the logical place in the chapter to discuss training programs for rural teachers. However, so few institutions in the OECD countries intentionally train teachers for rural service (or promote teaching strategies especially relevant to rural teaching, e.g., cross-age instruction, community education, outdoor/environmental studies, and experiential learning) that there is very little to be said. That is the problem. Training institutions usually provide teachers with general instruction on theories and methods of teaching and then proceed to various subject matter specialities. To the extent that special programs exist, they tend to operate only on the urban side. The fact that rural schools must accept teachers without specialized rural training puts them at a disadvantage they can ill afford.

This is not to suggest that teacher training should be rigidly divided into "urban," "suburban," and "rural" categories, as if there were no important commonalities. Nor is this an argument for effectively limiting teacher mobility. Rather, the point is that teachers from metropolitan areas who receive training in metropolitan institutions using metropolitan-oriented materials and methods which they test out during practice teaching experiences in metropolitan schools are not likely to be particularly well prepared for the special challenges and opportunities awaiting them in a small rural school.

The one bright spot in an otherwise bleak situation is that more teacher training institutions are beginning to take seriously their responsibilities toward the rural sector. Full-scale rural programs continue to be exceedingly rare, but it is not so unusual now for one or more rural-oriented courses to be offered. More important, there has been a marked increase in the number of institutions arranging for students to do their practice teaching in small rural schools. Such arrangements can be most helpful in raising the consciousness of prospective teachers about the problems and potentials of modern rural schools and in encouraging them to seek rural teaching posts after their trial periods.

As Ivan Muse has persuasively argued,

> Teachers who were trained or have taught in urban schools are often disappointed to discover that the job of rural teaching is more complicated than urban teaching and that living in a small community is not as personally satisfying (for many) as they had hoped it would be.
>
> One can't help but wonder how many beginning teachers fail or become discouraged with teaching because they were not adequately prepared for the unique teaching position in which they became employed—especially since a recent study found that future teachers who complete their practice teaching in a rural school will most likely want to teach in that area. This is true even though that job will include more personal contact with parents and community, more class preparations, and more assigned after-school activities. . . .
>
> The best rural teachers are the ones who are committed to community and rural life, who can adapt to unique situations, and who prefer teaching children rather than subjects.
>
> And the best teacher-training program—for all concerned—provides opportunities for future teachers to experience, early on, the values and rewards of both urban and rural teaching. Then they, while still *future* teachers, can decide in which kind of school and community they, both professionally and personally, are better suited to direct their careers.[117]

In terms of teacher characteristics, two conclusions can be drawn. First, although all countries have some very good rural teachers and a few countries have a high percentage of first-rate rural teachers, overall there are still significant urban-rural disparities in teacher quality and qualifications. Second, teacher training specifically tailored for rural service continues to be either inadequate or missing altogether.

Recruitment and Retention Problems

Encouraging the best available teachers to come to schools in sparsely populated areas and then making it attractive for them to remain there long enough to make a lasting, positive contribution to the school is a long-standing problem throughout the OECD world. Significant strides have been made in the past few years to alleviate this problem and more measures are in the planning stages. There is reason for optimism nearly everywhere. However, since many of the promising reforms here are of such recent vintage, it would be premature to state that recruitment and retention problems will no longer be major concerns. The available evidence suggests that getting and keeping competent individuals to teach the "three R's" in rural schools is largely a function of the "three C's": characteristics, conditions, and compensation. Each will be considered in turn.

Who can be attracted to come and stay at remote rural schools depends on who is in the pool of available teachers. This is a simple thought, but one with important implications. For example, if the current roster of teachers in a given country is heavily weighted toward urban-bred, urban-trained specialists, the likelihood of finding many candidates willing and able to teach in a remote two-teacher, all-ages primary school is rather low. Not surprisingly, the odds of finding someone good improve when the pool of teachers includes a fair percentage of generalist primary teachers raised in rural areas and hoping to return to them. In other words, the really important recruitment work may need to be done at the teacher training level. If active efforts were made to seek out and train rural people interested in becoming teachers in their own or other rural communities, much of the later recruitment problems would be eliminated.

This point has particular significance in relation to rural minority communities. No matter how well intentioned or technically competent, "outside" teachers having to overcome social, cultural, and language barriers as well as urban-rural ones are not normally as effective as well-trained teachers from the rural minority community itself.

Some countries, most notably Scotland, have both a tradition and a conscious policy of encouraging rural young people to become rural teachers. In the Western Isles of Scotland (a bilingual, Gaelic-English region) nearly 90 percent of all primary-level teachers are from the Isles themselves.[118] It should be emphasized that this does *not* mean compromising on the level of training or the quality of teachers.[119] In the Western Isles, the teachers are fully certified, and in the view of national authorities are at least as competent as teachers elsewhere in the nation. Thus, Scotland is blessed with a relatively low level of teacher recruitment and retention difficulties, partly by good luck but more by the careful recruitment of rural teachers at the preservice level.

Conditions of rural teaching are also an important factor here. It is just common sense that teachers will be attracted to certain kinds of schools and communities and will find others unappealing. Other things being equal, rural schools located in a scenic area, with a temperate climate, congenial community, good facilities, and easy access to shopping areas and recreational opportunities rarely encounter difficulties in staffing their schools. Conversely, it can be extremely difficult to secure teachers in rural communities characterized by harsh climates, decrepit facilities, very remote locations, severe poverty, and/or a bad reputation among other teachers. Put another way, finding qualified teachers willing to go to Hawaii or the French Riviera is not hard, but finding qualified candidates for schools in the hinterlands of Turkey or Lapland can be more problematic.

Some of these conditions simply "come with the territory" and remain beyond the control of government action. Others, such as poor facilities, may be possible to remedy in theory but not in practice (for example, because of limited funds). However, there is nearly always something that can be done to make an inherently difficult situation more tolerable. For example, while school authorities cannot change the reality of harsh winters in mountainous zones, they can ensure that the school is well heated and well insulated. Similarly, government policy cannot alter the fact that a certain school is located a hundred miles from the nearest town of any size, but it can provide teachers with the time and the means to make enough trips to alleviate some of the psychological effects of isolation.

When governments either cannot or will not relieve these conditions, the impact is as negative as it is predictable. For example, in explaining the creation of a rural boarding school in France, an inspector gave a glimpse of past conditions in the area:

> In winter the winds sweep across these lonely expanses dotted with hamlets, blocking the roads with snow-drifts, and isolating farms and villages sometimes for days. Snow conditions last from Christmas to Easter. It is an adventure to travel in this region when the storm wind known as the "Hécyre" is blowing. It led to the death of a postman last year, despite his knowledge of the country. . . .
> What is the use of a school here with only two or three pupils, and a supply teacher who is inadequately trained? Or when two or three teachers follow each other, *sometimes during the same year,* since young girls exiled in these snow-bound districts find it so hard to bear their cloistered existence that they often have to be sent back to towns to avoid a nervous breakdown?[120]

Although less dramatically stated, the following description implies that the situation is much the same in Norway:

> A shortage of qualified teachers and high teacher turnover have for many years been a problem of great concern for the school authorities in many remote areas, especially in the northern and some western parts of the country. The extremely small primary schools of only one or two multiage classes seem to be the worst hit. In many cases, the pupils and the parents have had to adjust to at least as many teachers as school years. . . . recent research indicates that there seems to be a relationship between *degree of isolation* of the school and its power to recruit teachers. In addition the data indicated that the staffing problems of the coastal schools of western and northern Norway not only are connected with the communication difficulties, but may also be partly due to the *hard climate* of these parts of the country.[121]

High teacher turnover is also a fact of life in rural Alaska (United States), where physical isolation and cultural conflicts make it difficult to provide coherent and consistent school programs: "At the present teacher turnover rate, most small high school students in rural Alaska will experience, on the average, two to three complete turnovers of teaching staff during a four-year high school career. In some one or two-teacher schools, it may even go as high as five or six turnovers."[122]

In order to sum up the effects of rural conditions on attracting and retaining teachers, the following excerpts from a 1979 study of teacher transfers in Western Australia make some widely applicable points:

> Some of the most important influences encouraging teachers to leave, like access to family and friends and isolation are difficult or impossible to change. Others, like the cost of living and facilities for further study, are more readily reduced. One feature of the results was the diversity of opinion over the factors that influence the length of time that teachers would be prepared to stay at the school. This suggests the importance of considering schools individually with regard to the factors which may affect teachers' willingness to remain for worthwhile periods of time, as well as attempting to match teachers with schools that best suit them.
>
> There was considerable agreement about factors that encourage teachers to stay. School facilities, staff relationships, the challenging nature of the job, climate and recreational facilities were commonly given favourable ratings.[123]

The third "C," after characteristics and conditions, is compensation. For many teachers (as for the rest of us) this factor is particularly important. Hence, it is not surprising that this is the area most governments have focused on in trying to improve rural recruitment and retention.

It must be emphasized at the outset that nearly all OECD countries have regional or, much more commonly, national salary standards and schedules. This means that, at a minimum, rural teachers are paid as much as equally qualified urban teachers in equivalent positions. Thus, the issue in most countries is not one of reducing salary disparities between city teachers and countryside teachers. Rather, the emphasis is on building a package of incentives to encourage qualified teachers to come and stay at remote schools they might otherwise shun.

Before taking a more detailed look at these incentives, some special factors should be pointed out. For instance, the absence of urban-rural salary disparities in nearly all countries does not mean that teachers are very well paid. In some countries teachers' salaries are quite reasonable; in others, they are not. In Greece, for example, C. Karmas has reminded us that

> One of the major problems of Greek education is the non-competitiveness of salaries. The salaries of pre-primary, primary and secondary school teachers are below those of other civil servants with the same qualifications. This fact

induces many graduates to view teaching as a "last resort" occupation. They seek employment in the education sector only after they have failed to secure a position in one of the other government sectors.[124]

Surprisingly, however, the financial position of rural teachers is most disadvantageous, in relative terms, in one of the wealthiest countries: the United States. This is the consequence of a school finance system in which local communities are largely responsible for their own education costs, including teacher salaries. Put simply, this means that relatively poor (or relatively miserly) communities are not competitive in the salaries they offer.

Even bearing in mind the diversity of the U.S. scene and the fact that many rural teachers are paid reasonably well, the aggregate national statistics from the 1970s do reveal some rather startling salary differences for teachers depending upon the location and type of school in which they work. For example, the average salary of a nonmetropolitan teacher was 24 percent lower than for a metropolitan teacher.[125] Similarly, teachers in predominantly rural counties earned 35 percent less than teachers in heavily urban counties.[126] In local education authorities serving fewer than 50 students (there were 2,053 such districts in 1972 out of 16,000 nationally), teachers received an annual salary 47 percent below that paid to teachers in local authorities enrolling more than 3,000 pupils.[127] And finally, it should be noted that neither differences in the qualifications of teachers nor in the rural cost of living can account for disparities of this magnitude.[128]

Clearly, people involved in rural teaching in the United States are not in it for the money. This raises a point of international relevance. Although the importance of monetary remuneration should not be minimized, it should be kept in mind that not all compensation is financial and that not all teachers select schools on the basis of salary. There are a myriad of noneconomic reasons why some teachers are attracted to rural schools. Five of these crop up with some regularity in the literature and in rural education forums: family ties; a sense of mission; easy access to natural and recreational resources; status within the community (if not within the profession); and considerations of quality of life. Teachers often have personal incentives such as these, which have little relationship to the government incentives offered.

Some nations, such as England, do not offer any formal incentives for teachers to come to rural schools.[129] Whether because of the personal incentives mentioned above or lack of other employment opportunities or a combination of the two, England has not usually had much trouble in hiring qualified rural teachers, and so formal incentives have been unnecessary.

This has not been the experience of most other OECD countries. Accordingly, packages of incentives have been created. Typically, these include salary supplements; other economic supplements (extra travel allowances, moving expenses to and from the school, housing allowances or free housing, etc.); accelerated career advancement opportunities; generous pupil-to-teacher ratios; and extra in-service education. These measures have generally proven to be satisfactory stimuli, although it cannot honestly be said that rural recruitment and retention problems have been eliminated as a result.

It is also interesting to observe that several countries have inaugurated policies too strong to be called incentives and yet which are directed toward the same end. For example, in New Zealand a period of rural service is mandatory in order for teachers to become eligible for promotion.[130] In Western Australia, rural service is expected of teachers. As Max Angus has explained,

> In general, teaching appointments in the metropolitan area are more popular than appointments to the country. Teachers, however, when they join the Education Department's permanent staff must undertake to teach anywhere in the State if so appointed. It is the usual practice for younger teachers, particularly those recently graduated from a teacher training institution, to receive a country appointment. However, after serving for approximately two or three years in a rural school these teachers are usually transferred to a metropolitan centre if they so wish. In other words, most teachers when they join the Education Department's teaching staff expect to undertake a period of country service early in their career.[131]

In order to fill senior teaching and administrative posts in country schools, Western Australia relies upon an extensive series of incentives rather than insisting that a particular person accept a particular assignment.[132]

Another scheme offered in several countries to secure needed staff in rural areas is the possibility for married couples to have dual appointments in the same community. Usually, this means a dual teaching appointment in the same rural school (assuming, of course, that both individuals are suitable and qualified). However, the combinations can be more exotic. For example, in the Highlands of Scotland dual appointments have been developed (and been filled) for a teacher and a clergyman; a sole-charge teacher and a ferryboat operator; and, interestingly, a primary school teacher and a gravedigger.

Because many countries share its policies (except for the promotion regulation), the following brief overview of New Zealand's incentive package for rural teachers has considerable international relevance as well:

> Most appointments to teaching positions in New Zealand primary schools are on a voluntary basis. The system operates nationally so that teachers may apply for a position in any part of the country. Salary scales are also uniform throughout New Zealand. Teaching positions of responsibility in country

schools are equated with their urban counterparts for salary purposes and additional incentives are built in to the system to try to ensure adequate staffing of the more remote schools. For a principal these include a salary equivalent to a senior teacher or deputy principal in a larger urban school, and in most small rural schools the provision of a school house at a low rental. Removal expenses are also paid to and from country positions.

Regulations have been introduced over the years to ensure staffing stability of country positions. A teacher, once appointed, must serve for at least a period of two years in the position. All teachers are expected to teach for at least two years in a position designated "country service" before a bar on their salary scale is removed.

Besides these incentives and regulations a teacher in a "very remote" school has the right of transfer to a less remote school after three years in his position and each year of service whilst in a "very remote" situation counts as one-and-a-half times the country service requirement.

There has never been a shortage of applicants for principals of sole-charge or two-teacher schools. Young male teachers have sought these positions to improve their salaries, to gain wider teaching experience, and to obtain low cost accommodation. One of the most impelling incentives, particularly for a man, has been the opportunity to gain administrative experience early before applying for the headship of a larger school. . . .

In spite of a current surplus of teachers in some areas of New Zealand it is still difficult to attract assistant teachers to the more remote small schools. Distance from larger centres and accommodation difficulties discourage young teachers from applying for these jobs. The problem is usually overcome by placing young teachers in their second and third years of service in the vacancies. Whilst this practice is not wholly desirable because of their limited teaching experience, support from the principal and advisers to rural schools is expected to ensure adequate teaching practice.

Where accommodation for assistant teachers is not available the positions of both the principal and the assistant may be classified as "dual appointments" and advertised specifically for married couples. This nearly always solves staffing problems.[133]

From the available evidence, it can be concluded that although there are still countries experiencing major difficulties, government incentives and the growing attractiveness of rural life have reduced the severity of the rural teacher recruitment and retention problem. Further, it can be concluded that new initiatives, such as explicitly recruiting rural-oriented candidates at the preservice training stage, have a significant potential for ensuring a continuing supply of qualified rural teachers.

Teacher Support

Since many of the SPA reports found in this volume describe innovative teacher support schemes in detail, the commentary here will be brief.

Once again, the level and quality of provision are improving, although much work remains to be done in most countries. Historically, rural teacher support schemes have suffered from two problems: first, they have often been superficial; and second, they have often been uncreative and/or inappropriate.

In-service education illustrates both these points. In many OECD countries, in-service education for rural teachers has usually meant that a large group of teachers are brought together for a day or two in order to be lectured at by university professors, government officials, or other experts. Normally, there is "not enough time" for the kind of intensive small group discussions of actual situations faced by the participating teachers which may be most needed. Moreover, the topics around which the sessions are organized tend to be so oriented to big schools that rural teachers often feel left out. All in all, the situation has been neither happy nor productive.

Fortunately, changes have been made in recent years which represent major steps forward. These reforms have been in two major directions. Residential in-service education opportunities for rural teachers have begun to be organized (1) for longer periods; (2) around topics relating to specific small school problems and strategies; and (3) with more of an emphasis on teachers and "experts" actively exchanging information and analyzing experiences rather than relying upon formal lectures. The other type of reform has been to implement *school-based* in-service education schemes which match an outside resource person and a local teacher on a regular basis to evaluate actual classroom practices and explore the possibilities for making any needed changes. Although exact measurements of the effectiveness of any type of in-service education are difficult to make, countries report that the satisfaction expressed by participants tends to be much greater using these new methods. Many OECD countries also maintain teams of school advisors and/or inspectors. Normally, these are subject specialists who visit the schools on an occasional basis and who are available to assist teachers requesting their help.

The problems associated with this teacher support mechanism usually are not a function of the quality of the advisors. In fact, they are often highly competent individuals who were very successful teachers in their own right. Rather, the deficiencies have been quantitative — there are rarely enough advisors available to effectively meet the needs of all the rural teachers. Contacts tend to be sporadic and short.

There is sometimes a problem in making the connection between advisors and the teachers most in need of their help. Advisors are on the road much of the time and not as readily accessible as they are supposed to be in theory. In addition, there is a real reluctance on the part of some rural teachers to call upon the advisors, either because they don't want to "bother" the advisors or because they don't want to expose their problems to the education authority which hires (and can fire) them.

Largely as a result of severe budgeting constraints in nearly all OECD countries, these problems continue to exist. However, some countries have been trying to reallocate existing resources in order to allow a needed expansion of their advisory services for teachers in sparsely populated areas.

Another mechanism used in almost all developed countries is a system of itinerant (travelling) specialist teachers. These are not advisors in a formal sense, for their basic assignment is to work on a regularly scheduled basis with the *children* in small rural schools. Depending on the country, these teachers offer instruction in a variety of subjects (e.g., art, science, foreign languages, and music). However, they very often serve as informal professional advisors for the rural classroom teacher, as well as providing a much-needed source of morale boosting and peer contact.

Beyond these common forms of teacher support, a group of countries is experimenting with more innovative strategies. "Distance learning" (via radio, television, correspondence, and even satellites) as a means of providing needed in-service education to teachers in remote areas has been tried with a fair degree of success.[134]

Rural teacher centers are also becoming a much-discussed innovation in this field. However, tight budgets have prevented the actual creation of very many such centers. The available (largely anecdotal) evidence confirms the value of this innovation, but it seems unlikely that the development of such centers will be widespread in the near future.

Although for both cultural and political reasons it has not become widespread, the practice of using community people and community institutions as an integral part of the rural school program has a great deal of potential.[135] Used properly, such schemes can have very positive impacts not only upon the children but also upon the teachers. In other words, the fuller integration of the rural school into its surrounding community promises to enhance the school program; reduce the isolation of rural teachers; and lessen the need for more sophisticated and expensive teacher support systems based outside the community.

Thus it can be concluded, first, that teacher support systems in sparsely populated areas are very much needed, but are not yet operating to the extent they should; and second, that there remains a need to develop and fully implement a series of reforms and/or innovations which will increase the effectiveness of rural teacher support systems.

Summary of Conclusions

Much was learned during the course of the CERI SPA project, but much still remains to be learned. One of the most encouraging results was a discernible increase in the interest and willingness of national governments to continue the search. This was accompanied by the commitment in more than a few countries to seek new directions for educational policy and practice in sparsely populated areas. All governments have made errors of omission and commission in the past concerning rural education. Without a doubt, demanding "more of the same" is not the answer to the pressing questions posed by rural education today. Thus, to the extent that countries are now willing and able to carefully examine and then embrace new directions for rural education, the future of rural schools can be a bright one.[136]

Many conclusions emerged from the work of the SPA project. Six general ones will be presented, followed by a concise listing of the specific issue-oriented conclusions drawn earlier in this analysis. It should be noted, first, that the order in which these conclusions are listed is essentially random and no ranking should be inferred; and second, that the degree to which any particular conclusion is applicable varies from country to country.

General Conclusions

Conclusion 1: The rural education sector will remain as a major constituency within the education system of most OECD countries.

> There are several trends and circumstances supporting this conclusion (which were discussed in some detail in Chapter 1). One should not lose sight of the fundamental reality that *millions* of children are dependent upon rural schools and rural delivery systems for their education during the compulsory years of schooling. By all indications, this fact will not change dramatically in the foreseeable future.

Conclusion 2: The current state of research, data collection, and information dissemination about rural education is not impressive and must be improved.

> In an age when people are concerned about "information overloads," the paucity of reliable information and research on rural education is genuinely startling. In too many countries, the most rudimentary data about rural schools, communities, students, and teachers is simply not known and/or available. Research, data collection, and information dissemination about rural education must all be expanded and upgraded if policymakers are to have the evidence they need to make informed choices for the future.

Conclusion 3: The linkages between schools and communities in sparsely populated areas should be expanded and the bonds between them strengthened.

Schools have been (and continue to be) absolutely vital as *community* institutions as well as educational ones in rural areas. Policies and reforms which restrict the linkages or weaken the bonds between the school and the community are highly counterproductive. In rural areas, the school needs the community to supplement and extend their efforts, and the community needs the school both as a source of community identity and a reinforcement of the community's child-rearing practices. This active interdependence between community and school is one of the key attributes of rural education. Reforms which sacrifice this relationship have a markedly detrimental effect on all parties concerned.

Conclusion 4: Reforms which intentionally or unwittingly serve to "urbanize" rural education are likely to have negative effects.

In case after case, it can be demonstrated that educational programs and curricula, reform strategies, and organizational arrangements originally designed for and utilized by school systems in metropolitan areas are inappropriate in rural settings and rarely replicated successfully by rural schools. There is a pressing need to develop rural schools which reflect and build upon the unique opportunities and natural advantages inherent to them and their communities.

Conclusion 5: Innovations in the content and delivery of rural educational services are both necessary and feasible.

For years, the prevailing wisdom in education has been that rural communities and rural schools are so conservative and resistant to change that developing and supporting innovative educational strategies and programs was hardly worth the effort. The SPA project, particularly through the ten special reports appearing in this volume, provided a powerful refutation of this bit of conventional wisdom. In fact, there is considerable evidence that rural communities (once convinced of the merits of the proposed innovation) are remarkably able to implement new ideas and can serve as splendid laboratories for educational innovation.

Conclusion 6: Little lasting and significant improvement of rural education will occur in the absence of explicit and appropriate governmental policies and assistance.

The primacy of local circumstance and the value of local initiative must, of course, be remembered and respected. Reform strategies which seek to circumvent local traditions, values, and capabilities rather than build on them are not likely to succeed. Still, it is equally apparent that rural schools have been, are, and doubtless will continue to be both dependent on governmental assistance and subject to governmental regulation and/or control. Thus, the willingness and ability of the OECD governments to exert leadership and act forcefully in ways which enhance and strengthen education within their sparsely populated areas will have a profound effect on the long-term development of rural children and rural communities.

Issue-oriented Conclusions

Conclusion 7: Although improvements have been made, there are still rural school-age children in poor countries and in the poverty areas of wealthy countries who are not receiving all their compulsory education.

Conclusion 8: No matter what general policies emerge from the school closure controversy (and even accounting for continued declining enrollments), there are a significant number of small rural schools which will remain in operation because there are no feasible alternatives to their continued existence.

Conclusion 9: Rural school transportation services are being provided in a satisfactory manner, although new strategies for both reducing journeys and using the travel time constructively should be pursued.

Conclusion 10: Although educational arrangements allowing rural students to live at home are usually preferable (especially for primary students), boarding schools are occasionally necessary and can be an appropriate and satisfactory alternative for secondary students living long distances from the nearest school.

Conclusion 11: Early childhood education is as important in rural areas as in urban ones, but at present, preschool opportunities are not readily available in sparsely populated areas and rural provision remains inadequate.

Conclusion 12: The provision of adequate postcompulsory educational opportunities in sparsely populated areas continues to be a major problem, and effective access to existing opportunities is too often denied to rural students.

Conclusion 13: Real equality of educational opportunity often does not exist for special needs populations in rural areas.

Conclusion 14: The costs of delivering needed educational services in sparsely populated areas are inherently and inevitably higher than the costs of providing the same services in more densely populated areas.

Conclusion 15: Rural schools have already reduced their costs, and can continue to do so, by sharing resources and adopting other locally appropriate strategies.

Conclusion 16: Local circumstance is the key determinant of the relative economic merits of either maintaining or closing small rural schools.

Conclusion 17: Although the general physical standard of rural schools is satisfactory in most OECD nations, there are still far too many rural schools in which a major upgrading of facilities and material resources is needed.

Conclusion 18: (1) The great majority of rural schools are providing at least an acceptable quality of education at the compulsory level; (2) very small rural schools can be and often are effective in meeting the personal and educational needs of young students; and (3) very small rural schools may not be as successful in serving their older pupils and therefore other types of provision should be made available as necessary to these students.

Conclusion 19: Rural school consolidations or closures are not necessarily the best strategy for improving rural education; local circumstance must be the key determinant of the educational merits of consolidation or closure.

Conclusion 20: An increasing number of countries are actively seeking ways of preserving and improving their small rural schools, rather than replacing them.

Conclusion 21: Effective alternatives to consolidation or closure do exist and can be expanded through new structural arrangements, support systems, and in-school innovations.

Conclusion 22: Although all countries have some very good rural teachers and a few countries have a high percentage of first-rate ones, overall there are still significant urban-rural disparities in teacher quality and qualifications.

Conclusion 23: Teacher training specifically tailored for rural service continues to be either inadequate or missing altogether.

Conclusion 24: Although there are still countries experiencing major difficulties, government incentives and the growing attractiveness of rural life have reduced the severity of the rural teacher recruitment and retention problem.

Conclusion 25: New initiatives, such as explicitly recruiting rural-oriented candidates at the preservice training stage, have significant potential for ensuring a continuing supply of qualified rural teachers.

Conclusion 26: Teacher support systems in sparsely populated areas are very much needed but are not yet operating to the extent they should.

Conclusion 27: There remains a need to develop and fully implement a series of reforms and/or innovations which will increase the effectiveness of rural teacher support systems.

Notes

1. For country-by-country definitions of *urban* and *rural* in Europe, see Secretariat of the Economic Commission for Europe, *Labour Supply and Migration in Europe: Demographic Dimensions 1950–1975 and Prospects* (New York: United Nations, 1979), Appendix Table 4.1. The pattern of using "residual definitions" of the rural population is common in the non-European OECD countries too.

2. Ibid.

3. Ibid. For New Zealand, see *New Zealand Official Yearbook* (Wellington: New Zealand Department of Statistics, 1977). For the United States, see U. S. Bureau of the Census, *Statistical Abstract of the United States, 1979* (Washington, D. C.: U. S. Government Printing Office, 1979).

4. Secretariat of the Economic Commission for Europe, op. cit.

5. For example, England uses the following population density criteria to identify community types:

Persons/Hectare	*Classification*
0.00–0.02	Virtually uninhabited
0.02–0.10	Very sparse
0.10–0.20	Sparse rural
0.20–1.50	Dense rural
1.50–25.00	Suburban
25.00–100.00	Urban
100.00 +	Dense urban

Taken from Geoffrey Elsmore et al., *Basic Education and Teacher Support in Sparsely Populated Areas of England* (Paris: Centre for Educational Research and Innovation, OECD, 1977).

6. Taken from Icelandic response to CERI SPA questionnaire prepared by Andri Isaksson in 1978. Also see Andri Isaksson and Atli Gudmundsson, *Menntum Og Bryggdapróun* [Rural education and development in Iceland] (Paris: Centre for Educational Research and Innovation, OECD, 1979).

7. Ibid., p. 9.

8. Ibid.

9. *Policies for Basic Education: Spain's National Statement* (Paris: Organisation for Economic Co-operation and Development, 1979), p. 4.

10. Ibid.

11. Marian Wright Edelman, Marylee Allen, Cindy Brown, Ann Rosewater et al., *Children Out of School in America* (Cambridge, Mass.: Children's Defense Fund, 1974).

12. Ibid., pp. 6 and 37.

13. R. S. Johnston, *Basic Education and Teacher Support in Sparsely-Populated Areas: Scottish Report* (Paris: Centre for Educational Research and Innovation, OECD, 1977).

14. Ibid.

15. The Secretariat for Nordic Cultural Cooperation, *Primary and Secondary Education in the Nordic Countries: A Comparative Study* (Copenhagen: Nordic Council of Ministers, 1979), p. 11.

16. Even within countries, the differences among delivery systems can be startling. For example, in America there is one state (Hawaii) which operates a single statewide school system and another state (Nebraska) which contains more than 1,300 independent school districts within its borders.

17. Isaksson, op. cit., p. 2.

18. Elgar E. Henry, *Aspects of Pre-School, Primary and Secondary Education in Sparsely-Populated Areas of New Zealand* (Paris: Centre for Educational Research and Innovation, OECD, 1978), p. 21.

19. Johnston, op. cit.

20. Ibid.

21. Sandra Brown, Michael Williams et al., *Educational Provision in Sparsely Populated Areas of Western Australia* (Perth, Western Australia: Department of Education, 1979), Table 3.1.

22. Ibid. It should be noted that there are also fifteen rural "district high schools" in Western Australia which offer instruction from preschool through year 10. These schools tend to have higher primary-level enrollment than the free-standing primary schools.

23. U.S. Bureau of the Census, *1972 Census of Governments: Volume 1, Governmental Organization* (Washington, D. C.: U.S. Government Printing Office, 1973). Also see U. S. Department of Health, Education and Welfare, National Center for Educational Statistics, *Statistics of Local Public School Systems: Pupils and Staff* (Washington, D. C.: U.S. Government Printing Office, 1975).

24. U.S. Bureau of the Census, *1972 Census of Governments*.

25. Reijo Laukkanen, *Basic Education and Teacher Support in Sparsely-Populated Areas: Finnish Report* (Paris: Centre for Educational Research and Innovation, OECD, 1978), p. 9.

26. Ibid.

27. It is possible that another OECD country, Turkey, has more one-teacher schools, but current data were not available.

28. Bettina Laville and Jacqueline Bonjean, "French Response to the CERI SPA Questionnaire," 1978.

29. Ibid.

30. Annika Andrae and Per-Erik Eriksson, "Swedish Response to the CERI SPA Questionnaire," 1978, pp. 8–11.

31. Ibid., p. 11.

32. Jonathan P. Sher, *Revitalizing Rural Education: A Legislator's Handbook* (Washington, D. C.: National Conference of State Legislatures, 1978), p. 22.

33. Brown, Williams et al., op. cit., p. 17.

34. Henry, op. cit., p. 26.

35. Johnston, op. cit., p. 4.

36. The research referred to is Yao-Chi Tu and Luther Tweeten, "The Impact of Busing on Student Achievement" in *Growth and Change*, Vol. 4, No. 4 (October 1973). The quote comes from Timothy Weaver, "Class Conflict in Rural Education: A Case Study of Preston County, Western Virginia" in Jonathan P. Sher, ed., *Education in Rural America: A Reassessment of Conventional Wisdom* (Boulder, Colo.: Westview Press, 1977), p. 181.

37. Karl Jan Solstad and Harald Jørgensen, *Basic Education and Teacher Support in Sparsely Populated Areas: Norwegian Report* (Paris: Centre for Educational Research and Innovation, OECD, 1978), p. 26.

38. *Policies for Basic Education: Turkey's National Statement* (Paris: Organisation for Economic Co-operation and Development, 1978), pp. 2 and 7.

39. Northland School Division Study Group, *Report to the Alberta Minister of Education* (Edmonton: Government of Alberta, 1975), pp. 52–53.

40. Andrae and Eriksson, op. cit., p. 8.

41. Johnston, op. cit., p. 45.

42. Judith Kleinfeld, *A Long Way From Home: Effects of Public High Schools on Village Children Away from Home* (Fairbanks: University of Alaska, 1973).

43. M. Pastre, *An Example of a Primary Boarding School in a Mountain Area: Allanche (Cantal)* (Paper presented at a conference on boarding schools in Vichy, France, 1973).

44. David Barney, *Who Gets to Pre-School?: The Availability of Pre-School Education in New Zealand* (Wellington: New Zealand Council for Educational Research, 1975).

45. Ibid.

46. A. J. Kahn and S. B. Kamerman, *Child-Care Programmes in 9 Countries: A Report Prepared for the OECD* (Washington, D. C.: U.S. Department of Health, Education and Welfare, 1975).

47. K. Schleicher, *The Use of Television in Pre-School Education in Sparsely-Populated Areas* (Strasbourg: Council of Europe, 1977), p. 36.

48. J. G. Owen, *The Planning of Alternative Pre-School Arrangements in an Area Where Few Pre-School Establishments Exist: Devon in the United Kingdom* (Strasbourg: Council of Europe, 1977).

49. The Appalachian Educational Laboratory has been particularly active in this

area. For further information, see Subcommittee on Health and Child Development, *Appalachian Child Development: A Report on Thirteen States* (Washington, D. C.: Appalachian Regional Commission, 1975).

50. The Nordic Cultural Secretariat, *Förskola i Glesbygd* [Preschools in sparsely populated areas] (Copenhagen: Nordic Council of Ministers, 1977).

51. Henry, op. cit., p. 14.

52. Max Angus et al., "Western Australian Response to CERI SPA Questionnaire," 1978. Angus noted that these figures have some built-in biases because of the number of country students boarding at metropolitan schools.

53. Laville and Bonjean, op. cit., p. 26.

54. Ibid.

55. Elsmore et al., op. cit.

56. Ibid.

57. Frank Fratoe, *Rural Education and Rural Labor Force in the Seventies* (Washington, D. C.: U. S. Department of Agriculture, 1978), p. 19.

58. It is anticipated that the CERI project on education and local development, created in mid-1979, will be able to tackle several of the key issues here.

59. See, for example, Ronald T. Fitzgerald, *Poverty and Education in Australia* (Canberra: Australian Government Publishing Service, 1976); New Zealand Planning Council, *He Mātāpuna: Some Maori Perspectives* (Wellington: New Zealand Planning Council, 1979); Doreen Goodman, *Educational Disadvantage: A Bibliography* (Canberra: Schools Commission, 1979); Ray Barnhardt et al., *Cross-Cultural Issues in Alaskan Education* (Fairbanks: University of Alaska, 1977); Canadian Council on Rural Development, *Regional Poverty and Change* (Ottawa: Canadian Council on Rural Development, 1976); Fratoe, op, cit.; and Edelman et al., op. cit.

60. Schools Commission, *Learning to Share: A Report on the Disadvantaged Country Areas Program for 1977* (Canberra: Schools Commission, 1978).

61. See, for instance, the special report on Western Australia's Chidley Centre found in Chapter 5 of this volume.

62. Ronald T. Fitzgerald, *Schools, Community and Work: Urban and Rural Aspects* (Canberra: Australian Government Publishing Service, 1978).

63. Two qualifications should be made here. First, under circumstances in which rural schools are either badly overcrowded and/or reliant upon an untrained, low-paid teacher (as occasionally happens in the less-developed OECD countries), the costs may be below those of normal metropolitan schools. However, this is not a common occurrence. Further, the actual education offered in such a situation is not at all equivalent to the urban norm even if the costs are roughly equal. Second, in countries without global salary scales for teachers (such as the United States), rural schools may pay so little that overall costs become approximately the same. Again, however, there are problems of comparability.

64. On distance learning expenditures, see the cost data presented in this volume's special reports on Telescola (Chapter 3) and the New Zealand Correspondence School (Chapter 7).

65. For example, see Isaksson, op. cit.; Johnston, op. cit.; Andrae and Eriksson,

op. cit.; Angus et al., op. cit.; Laville and Bonjean, op. cit.; and Solstad and Jørgensen, op. cit.

66. Ibid.

67. Ibid.

68. C. Karmas, *The Greek Educational System* (Athens: Center for Planning and Economic Research, 1978), p. 9.

69. Andrae and Eriksson, op. cit., pp. 33–34.

70. David Clark, *The Decline of Rural Services* (London: Standing Conference of Rural Community Councils, 1978).

71. Economy of scale — that is, the reduction of unit costs as size increases — is both a simple and much-abused concept. The primary problem with economy-of-scale arguments for school consolidation is that they tend to ignore or discount the reality of offsetting diseconomies of scale; that is, new or enlarged costs attributable to increased size of operations. For further information, see Jonathan P. Sher and Rachel B. Tompkins, *Economy, Efficiency and Equality: The Myths of Rural School and District Consolidation* (Washington, D. C.: National Institute of Education, 1977); and Ian W. Hind, "Estimates of Cost Functions for Primary Schools in Rural Areas," *Australian Journal of Agricultural Economics*, Vol. 21, No. 1 (April 1977).

72. National Institute of Education, *Violent Schools — Safe Schools* (Washington, D. C.: U. S. Government Printing Office, 1977). The degree to which studies like this are applicable depends in large measure on what kind of consolidation is being proposed. In situations where young children from small rural schools are suddenly shifted to large faraway regional or metropolitan schools, the risk of alienation and its attendant problems is rather high. Conversely, where consolidation only means a shift from a two-teacher school to a four-teacher school down the road a couple of miles, the risk of such trauma is slight.

73. R. Nash, M. Williams, and M. Evans, "The One-Teacher School," *British Journal of Educational Studies* (February 1976). The argument put forward by Nash et al. is reminiscent of the story about the old farmer who, after listening to a government official trying to promote consolidation on the basis that children could then be provided with a full-time school psychologist, remarked, "Maybe if we left the schools small, they wouldn't *need* a school psychologist."

74. Hind, op. cit., p. 24.

75. Sher and Tompkins, op. cit., p. 6.

76. Wayne H. Martin, *Student Achievement in Rural Schools: A View from the National Assessment Data* (Denver, Colo.: Education Commission of the States, 1979).

77. G. W. Parkyn, *The Consolidation of Rural Schools* (Wellington: New Zealand Council for Educational Research, 1952), pp. 139–141.

78. Nash et al., op. cit.

79. H. M. Inspector of Schools, *Education in Inverness-shire* (Edinburgh: Scottish Education Department, 1974), p. 22.

80. Peter Boulter et al., *Sparsely Populated Areas Project: Ambleside Conference Report* (London: Department of Education and Science, 1979).

81. National Center for Educational Statistics, *Digest of Educational Statistics*

(Washington, D. C.: U. S. Government Printing Office, 1974).

82. Ibid.

83. Ibid.

84. Ibid.

85. U. S. Bureau of the Census, *1972 Census of Governments.* Note that the averages given do not distinguish between primary and secondary schools. A more sophisticated presentation of the data would reveal average primary school enrollments to be somewhat lower and average secondary school enrollments to be somewhat higher.

86. Sher, *Revitalizing Rural Education,* pp. 17–18; also see Sher, ed., *Education in Rural America.*

87. Rick Rogers, *Schools Under Threat: A Handbook on Closures* (London: Advisory Centre for Education, 1979), p. 27. This booklet, which presents a detailed (if slightly controversial) account of the school closure issue in England, can be obtained from the Advisory Centre for Education, 18 Victoria Park Square, London E2, England.

88. Andrae and Eriksson, op. cit., pp. 36–37.

89. See Taylor's chapter on Telescola in this volume (Chapter 3).

90. Laukkanen, op. cit. Further information. appears in Laukkanen and Muhonen's chapter in this volume on Finnish rural education (Chapter 9).

91. *Policies for Basic Education: Norway's National Statement* (Paris: Organisation for Economic Co-operation and Development, 1978), pp. 6–7.

92. See Johnston's chapter on Scottish rural teacher support appearing in this volume (Chapter 4).

93. The description of these two innovations is excerpted from Jacqueline Bonjean and Bettina Laville, *Support Systems for Primary Schools in the Massif Central Region of France* (Paris: Center for Educational Research and Innovation, OECD, 1978), pp. 25–35.

94. Ibid., p. 33.

95. For further information, see Boulter et al., op. cit., Appendix 5; also see Rogers, op. cit., pp. 59–65, on these and other alternatives to closure in England. It should be noted, first, that the Norfolk and Cambridgeshire experiments are very new and small scale, and second, that other local education authorities in England also have similar arrangements under active consideration.

96. More detailed information on the Cambridgeshire federation can be found in *The London Times Educational Supplement* (September 22, 1978).

97. For a further description, see Annika Andrae, ed., *Non-Graded Instruction: Experience from the PANG Project* (Mölndal, Sweden: Univeristy of Göteborg, 1976).

98. Information taken from an unpublished paper submitted in 1978 to the SPA project by Barry Taylor entitled "Keeping Somerset's Small Rural Schools."

99. Henry, op. cit.

100. For further information, see Faith Dunne, "Choosing Smallness: An Examination of the Small School Experience in Rural America," in Sher, ed., op. cit., as well as Chapter 12 in this volume. Information on formal regional units can be found in *The Emerging Role of Regional Service Centers,* Proceedings of the Second Na-

tional Conference of the National Federation for the Improvement of Rural Education (Austin, Tex.: National Education Laboratory Publishers, 1974); and E. Robert Stephens, *Regional Education Service Centers* (Arlington, Va.: Educational Research Service, Inc., 1975).

101. School Commission, op. cit.

102. Ibid., p. 33.

103. Anita Stromberg, *The School: A Center for the Local Community* (Helsinki: Academy of Finland, Research Council for Technology, 1979). The Finnish effort is part of a Nordic project also involving Norway and Sweden.

104. Tom Gjelten, *Schooling in Isolated Communities* (North Haven, Maine: North Haven Project, 1978). Copies can be ordered from The North Haven Project, Box 123, Portland, Maine 04112, U.S.A.

105. Karmas, op. cit. The "new education system" in Greece was introduced in 1976, with full adoption scheduled for the 1980–81 school year.

106. *Policies for Basic Education: Portugal's National Statement* (Paris: Organisation for Economic Co-operation and Development, 1979), p. 31.

107. Ibid., p. 33.

108. Ibid., p. 3.

109. B. McGaw, R. S. Warry, P. J. Varley, and J. Alcoin, "Prospects for School Leavers," in *School Leavers: Choice and Opportunities* (Canberra: Australian Government Publishing Service, 1977).

110. Elsmore, et al., op. cit.

111. For instance, see Roy Nash, "Rethinking Rural Education," *Planet* (January 1978). Nash groups the head teachers of twenty-six Welsh country schools into five categories, as follows: (1) dedicated teachers—mature individuals in the same post for some years whose life revolves around the school; (2) ambitious teachers—young innovative teachers using the post as stepping-stone to larger schools; (3) established teachers—competent, if uninspired, individuals who focus on community responsibilities rather than the school program; (4) uninvolved teachers—bored and boring individuals whose real life is centered around personal pursuits away from the school and community; and (5) preretired teachers—very unimaginative individuals teaching the same things in the same ways, year after year.

112. Johnston, op. cit.; Andrae and Eriksson, op. cit.; and Henry, op. cit.

113. *Policies for Basic Education: Portugal's National Statement,* p. 34.

114. Laville and Bonjean, op. cit., pp. 17–19.

115. Ibid.

116. Isaksson, op. cit., p. 3.

117. Ivan D. Muse, "How Well Do We Prepare Teachers For Rural Schools?" *PTA Today* (December 1979); also see Ivan D. Muse, Robert J. Parsons, and Edward M. Hoppe, *A Study of Rural Teachers and the Rural Schools as Perceived by School Administrators, Teachers, Parents and Students* (Provo, Utah: College of Education, Brigham Young University, 1975).

118. Johnston, op. cit.

119. Ibid. Although there are some concerns about the insularity and possible parochialism of having such a high proportion of "homebodies," this is not felt to be a big problem either in the Western Isles or by the national authorities. Further,

there is no discrimination or avoidance of "outside" educators; indeed, the current director of education in the Western Isles is not a native of the area. Rather, the new emphasis on bilingual instruction and the availability of good candidates from the area serve as disincentives to a large influx of "transplants."

120. Pastre, op. cit., pp. 2–3.

121. Solstad and Jørgensen, op. cit., pp. 29 and 31.

122. Barnhardt et al., op. cit., pp. 54–55.

123. P. A. Deschamps, T. M. Beck et al., *Teacher Transfers,* Studies in Rural Education, Number 2 (Perth: Education Department of Western Australia, 1979), p. 23.

124. Karmas, op. cit., p. 7.

125. U. S. Bureau of the Census, *1972 Census of Governments, Vol. 3, No. 2 — Compendium of Public Employment* (Washington, D.C.: U.S. Government Printing Office, 1974), Table 9.

126. Ibid., Table 16.

127. Ibid., Table 22.

128. Sher, ed., op. cit., pp. 26–28.

129. Elsmore et al., op. cit.

130. Henry, op. cit.

131. Angus et al., op. cit., p. 19.

132. Ibid., pp. 21–23.

133. Henry, op. cit., pp. 27–29.

134. For example, see Hector McVeagh's chapter in this volume on teacher training provided through the New Zealand Correspondence School (Chapter 7). Also see Faith Dunne, op. cit., and Schools Commission, op. cit.

135. For an excellent example of work in this area, see Don Edgar, *Defining Rural Schools Disadvantage* (Melbourne: Victoria Country Education Project, 1979). Copies can be ordered from the Victoria Country Education Project, Nauru House, Collins Street, Melbourne 3000, Australia.

136. In fact, the Australian national follow-up conference to the SPA project, sponsored by the Education Department of Western Australia and OECD/CERI, was called "New Directions in Rural Education." For further information, see: D. Mossenson, et al., *New Directions in Rural Education: Conference Summary* (Perth: Education Department of Western Australia, 1979).

Part 2

Rural Education Innovations

Introduction

Jonathan P. Sher

As discussed in Chapter 1, one of the most useful outcomes of the CERI SPA project was a series of ten special reports on innovations in rural education. These reports (which constitute Chapters 3 through 12 of this volume) reinforce and extend the overview of rural education issues presented in Part 1. In addition, they serve as a powerful reminder of the fact that successful rural innovations *can* be created and "institutionalized."

The reports themselves can be divided into two general categories: *delivery and support system innovations* and *in-school innovations*. Although such a division is somewhat artificial and a little overlap is inevitable, these two categories highlight the central characteristics of the activities described.

Delivery and Support System Innovations

There are five special reports under the classification of delivery and support system innovations. The countries represented here are Portugal, Scotland, Australia, the United States, and New Zealand.

The *delivery system* reports are united by their focus on new (or improved) strategies for the provision of basic educational services in very remote rural communities. Obviously these efforts include a serious concern for the nature and content of the services provided. However, their special value as innovations lies in their ability to overcome the occasionally awesome technical and logistic problems of delivering *any* services to such a widely dispersed, geographically isolated constituency.

The common thread running through the reports on *support systems* is an emphasis on new strategies and programs for providing rural students, teachers, and school systems with the external resources and assistance they require. Rural schools, although often geographically isolated, should not have to exist in isolation from the best resources available in their region and nation. The reports here describe interesting attempts to provide rural schools with resources and assistance which are not available within the rural community itself.

The first report in the delivery and support system category was written by L. C. Taylor and is entitled "Schooling with Television in Rural Areas: Portugal's Telescola." This chapter details the experiences of the Telescola effort over the past thirteen years of operation. Basically, Telescola is the only well-established example in the OECD countries of an integrated learning system in which television plays a central instructional role, covering the full curriculum at the "first-cycle secondary" level (grades 5 and 6) and serving tens of thousands of rural children. Although recent political developments in Portugal have altered the original Telescola strategy, it remains a remarkable example of the use of advanced technologies to deliver basic educational services to remote rural populations. Three features of this innovation are particularly noteworthy:

1. its ability to transcend television's conventional role as an occasional supplement to "normal" school operations and to successfully use television as a primary medium of instruction;
2. its ability to effectively integrate the technological and human elements of the rural "reception posts" (i.e., schools) so that they become mutually supportive; and
3. its ability not only to provide rural students (in their own communities) with educational opportunities far beyond those previously available, but also to deliver these services at a cost far below that of traditionally organized educational programs in the towns and cities.

The second delivery and support system report comes from Scotland. The chapter, written by R. S. Johnston, is entitled "Beyond Mere Survival: Teacher Support in Scotland's Rural Schools." This report discusses the problems and characteristics of teachers working in the remote areas of rural Scotland (primarily the Highlands and islands) and describes the range of support services and assistance available to such teachers.

Basically, there are three sources of help available at present. The first source is the local (i.e., regional or island) education authority, which normally offers the services of specialist (subject matter) advisers, staff tutors, and visiting teachers to rural teachers throughout Scotland.

Assistance is also provided by several colleges of education, not only through relatively common mechanisms like residential in-service education programs but, more interestingly, through a new program of school-based teacher support. Because of this recent activity, rural teachers are now receiving intensive assistance from college faculty members, particularly in the creation of needed curricular materials.

A third source of assistance is available through Her Majesty's Inspectors of Schools, who offer guidance and advice not only to education authorities but also to individual teachers (primarily through the inspection process).

Taken together, these support mechanisms for rural teachers are rather impressive and may be one factor explaining the relative attractiveness of teaching posts in rural Scotland. Still, new mechanisms are now being developed to further enhance the support available to rural teachers. One of the new developments meriting special mention is a scheme which places faculty members from one of the colleges of education into sparsely populated areas for extended periods of time in order to enhance the school-based assistance previously noted.

The third report in this category is from Western Australia and is entitled "Putting the Outback into the Forefront: Education Innovations in Western Australia." In this chapter, the authors, Max Angus, Michael Williams, R. Hillen, and Glen Diggins, describe two distinct innovations. The first is the Isolated Students Matriculation Scheme and the second is the Chidley Education Centre.

The Isolated Students Matriculation Scheme (ISMS) was initiated in 1974 in response to the fact that correspondence education in Western Australia did not include the final two years of secondary-level schooling (years 11 and 12). As a result, rural children either had to leave their families and be boarded in an urban area or discontinue their formal education entirely. The ISMS was designed to be a real educational alternative available to rural youth desirous of both continuing their education and remaining in their home area.

Although the scheme essentially provides instruction by correspondence, it has certain distinctive features. First, it includes a comprehensive curriculum development unit, which has prepared the print and audiovisual materials used by students. Secondly, the scheme employs twelve senior teachers as tutors, who are in personal contact on a regular basis with students. Thirdly, teacher contact with students is reinforced through study camps, which are held twice annually, and through home visits by regional tutors three times each year.

Although it is still too early to judge all the effects of the ISMS, it has already earned a continuing place in the educational system of Western Australia. Its current efforts to both expand the available curricular offerings and explore the possibilities of utilizing microfiche and/or satellite communications to reach isolated students in a more effective manner bode well for the future of this effort.

The second half of this chapter focuses on the Chidley Education Centre. The Centre was created in 1976 to respond to the need for sophisticated assistance to rural children (and often their teachers and parents as well) who either have severe learning disabilities or other serious handicaps. The equipment, facilities, and specialized staff offer rural students with such problems a level of support and assistance quite beyond anything previously available to them. The Centre's program, although individualized, contains five basic steps: assessment and diagnosis, program development, implementation of learning strategies, transition to the local environment, and follow-up. Three features of the Chidley Centre are particularly noteworthy:

1. It is not intended to replace "normal" schooling in the home or community environment but rather to find out exactly how a particular child's problem can best be dealt with where he or she lives. Thus, children stay at the Centre for relatively short periods of time (usually three to six months) rather than permanently.
2. Extensive support is given to rural parents and to teachers in order to help them successfully follow up the work begun by the Centre staff.
3. The Centre's services are available at little or no cost to the parents.

The fourth special report in the delivery and support system category is entitled "The Educational Challenge in Rural Alaska: Era of Local Control." The author, Kathryn Hecht, focuses on the decentralization of rural education in Alaska in 1976 which resulted in the elimination of the state-operated system of rural schools and the creation of twenty-one new local education authorities.

There were two central forces behind the creation of these new Regional Educational Attendance Areas (REAA): first, a political struggle led by Alaska Natives (who make up 80 percent of Alaska's rural population) to gain greater community involvement in and control over the education of rural children in the state; and second, a series of court cases which established the right of rural children in Alaska to receive an education in or near their home communities, rather than having to be boarded in cities or even out of the state, as was the earlier practice.

These new rural education authorities are now fully operational. Obviously, at this stage of development, it is too early to assess all the consequences of the decentralization. However, two key items currently on the agenda of the REAAs involve not only an extensive revision of existing school curricula and practices, but also the creation of complete secondary-level educational programs in nearly one hundred remote communities which have never before offered secondary education.

The fifth and final delivery and support system special report, written by Hector McVeagh, is entitled "The New Zealand Correspondence School: A Pragmatic System for the Basic Schooling of Isolated Children." This chapter describes a major rural educational effort which has been in operation in New Zealand for nearly sixty years.

Normally, systems which have functioned for as long as the New Zealand

Correspondence School are not classified as innovations; but the school does represent an approach to rural education and a level of programmatic sophistication which would be considered innovative in nearly all the OECD countries.

As it stands today, the correspondence school provides basic educational services to nearly 13,000 rural students ranging from three-year-old children to adults. The primary medium of instruction is the printed assignment, sent from and returned to the central correspondence facility through the postal system. However, this basic form is heavily supplemented by tape recordings, radio broadcasts, visual materials, practical kits, telephone contact, visiting teachers, residential summer schools, local camps and seminars, and other arrangements designed to enhance the learning experiences of isolated students.

The results to date have been impressive — existing data indicate that correspondence school students are progressing at a rate comparable to their urban counterparts, and their success rate on the national examinations is at, or above, the national average.

Two other features merit special attention. One involves the extensive teacher support and training available to teachers in remote schools through the correspondence school. The other is the network of support and guidance available to parents of isolated students through the school.

In-School Innovations

The second group of special reports comes under the heading of in-school innovations. Once again, five reports are presented, including one each from Scotland, Finland, and Norway, and two from the United States.

All of these reports are united by their focus on strategies and programs to improve the quality and effectiveness of what actually happens in rural schools. At the same time, several of the chapters also deal with innovative school-community exchanges.

In the first report, "Sea Change in the Western Isles of Scotland: The Rise of Locally Relevant Bilingual Education," John Murray and Finlay MacLeod discuss a series of important rural innovations which have been implemented recently in this remote group of islands. The impetus for the innovations was a 1975 governmental reorganization in Scotland which made the Western Isles a discrete governmental unit for the first time in the modern era. Although several innovations have gotten under way, this report focuses on the work of the Bilingual Education Project (BEP).

BEP was created to help teachers develop curriculum models and materials in rural primary schools starting to employ both Gaelic and English as languages of instruction. Gaelic had always been the primary language of the home, church, and community in the Western Isles, but until BEP began, English was the language of the schools. Thus, one aim of the project was to bridge the traditional gap between school and community, at least in part, by bridging the language gap.

BEP has provided extensive in-service education to participating teachers and has worked in the communities to secure local assistance and acceptance. It also has played an instrumental role in the formation of a new Gaelic-language publishing company which produces curricular materials for the schools of the Western Isles.

The second report, by Reijo Laukkanen and Lauri Muhonen, is entitled "Finland's Small Schools and Combined Grades." This chapter gives an overview of rural education programs and innovations in Finland, with particular reference to the district of Kuusamo. Kuusamo is a very rural area located just below the Arctic Circle on the Russian border. In addition to being a microcosm of the problems and potentials of Finnish rural education, Kuusamo was also the site for a 1979 Finnish follow-up conference to the CERI SPA project.

Included in this report is a discussion of the Finnish policy of establishing local school units wherever possible. As might be expected this has meant that, particularly in rural areas, the schools tend to be quite small. In fact, nearly 70 percent of all Finnish primary schools have three or fewer teachers. Inevitably, some form of combined grade instruction had to be utilized. The report details some recent experiments in Finland involving different grade groupings, new classroom organization schemes, curricular modifications, and innovative teaching arrangements. Some of these experiments have proved successful enough to now be considered for long-term adoption by small rural schools throughout Finland. One particularly useful model in two- and three-teacher schools involves using upper-level students as auxiliary teachers in order to allow one of the regular teachers to work intensively on a continuing basis with students needing remedial instruction and/or specialized assistance.

The third special report in this category is entitled "Foxfire: Experiential Education in Rural America." Its author, Gail Armstrong Parks, reviews and analyzes the fourteen-year history of one of the most successful rural educational innovations in America.

The Foxfire project grew out of a secondary school language arts class in a remote Georgia school in the Appalachian region of the United States. The teacher who created it began with the idea of helping students learn about themselves, their community, and their cultural heritage by going out and collecting oral histories of the area and its traditions from parents, relatives, neighbors, and other local residents.

These histories (covering a wide range of subjects such as traditional arts and crafts, folk medicine, local history, and folk tales) were then transcribed, edited, and published as *The Foxfire Book*. The volume became a rather phenomenal commercial success, and over the following years several similar, equally successful books (again researched, written, and produced by rural students) were published. Other activities include a student-written quarterly journal (*Foxfire Magazine*), which currently has several thousand subscribers nationally, and a student-run record company which is recording local folk music and tales. The Foxfire notion of experiential education to enhance student learning and foster community involvement and pride has inspired the creation of approximately 150 similar projects across the United States.

The fourth report focuses on a Nordic rural innovation. It is entitled "Locally Relevant Curricula in Rural Norway: The Lofoten Islands Example." The author is Karl Jan Solstad. The Lofoten project was an innovative action research program carried out in seven comprehensive schools in the Lofoten region of northern Norway. Developed by a group of research workers from the University of Tromsø, the project operated from 1973 until 1979 in cooperation with school authorities at the local and regional levels and a number of teachers in the schools concerned.

The basic assumption was that rural communities can be strengthened by an educational system which reflects the local and regional situation—socially, culturally, and economically. Thus, this project was reviewed as an aspect of regional planning in general. Educationally, the central themes were curriculum development and school-community relations. The participating schools created new curricula and materials designed to expand their students' knowledge of the surrounding rural environment. This knowledge in turn became the basis for further efforts to help these rural students understand their place in the region, nation, and world.

Although the formal project terminated in 1979, the Lofoten initiative is an on-going process. It has already provided important insights about the ways in which rural schools can, and should, balance local and national educational priorities.

The final report in this category, "Reform and Resistance: Rural School Improvement Projects in the United States," was written by Faith Dunne. Unlike the other chapters, this one does not single out one or two communities or projects for detailed examination. Rather, it describes and explores the major attempts during the past twenty years to promote innovation in U. S. rural schools. Both local initiatives and major state, federal, and private programs are reviewed. Two contrasting models of rural school reform are discussed carefully: the "Import and Improve" model and the "Community-Based" model.

The issues dealt with in this report range from curriculum development to the use of teacher aides in rural classrooms, but the overarching concern is why some attempts at rural innovations succeed so well while others are just as notable in their failure.

One of the conclusions here warrants particular attention: grass-roots (locally initiated and controlled) improvement projects which build upon existing rural practices and values seem to have a greater success rate than better-funded government initiatives designed and controlled outside the rural community. Yet, in the final analysis, successful rural school reforms result more often from a sensitive and pragmatic blending of local and outside influences than from the rigid application of one specific change strategy.

DELIVERY AND
SUPPORT SYSTEM INNOVATIONS

3

Schooling with Television in Rural Areas: Portugal's Telescola

L. C. Taylor

Telescola is a system that provides televised lessons beamed to "reception posts," where teacher-monitors first receive and then "exploit" the broadcasts with their classes. This "exploitation" is based on specifically prepared teachers' guides and pupils' texts. The integrated broadcast/print/monitor system of Telescola covers the two years of the preparatory cycle of schooling. These two years along with the four years of the primary cycle compose the span of basic education in Portugal. In 1979, fourteen years after its foundation, Telescola delivered postprimary schooling, in all subjects in the official curriculum except physical education, to more than 50,000 children, principally in rural areas.

For so large, long-lived, and rare an example of the use of the newer technologies in education, Telescola is surprisingly little known. The standard work "New Educational Media in Action," exhaustively compiled under UNESCO sponsorship, listed all the major instructional broadcasting systems around the globe, including many whose hopes of permanence seemed (and have proved) slight indeed, yet nowhere was Telescola mentioned. Nor is more than a passing mention to be found in other publications.

The descriptive and factual matter in this account follows, in a much abbreviated form, *An Evaluative Review of Telescola, with Recommendations,* produced in January 1977. The review was conducted jointly by a working party set up by the Portuguese Ministry of Education and Scientific Research and by the OECD (Technical Cooperation Service and Centre for Educational Research and Innovation). At certain specified points in this text, at a time of continued rapid change, features of Telescola have been described in their prerevolutionary rather than their current form, wherever, at the time of writing, the restoration of something similar to the earlier form seems imminent.

What accounts for this strange neglect? Politics, in part. In the days of Salazar and Caetano, Portugal was outcast from many international organizations, its achievements less noticed than its shortcomings. Misunderstanding also contributed. Western educators have ample evidence of television in schools, and, especially at postprimary levels, know it to be peripheral. Telescola is easily mistaken at first for "educational television," that familiar expedient for adding sauce to enrich from time to time the solid but often unpalatable ingredients of learning; or for "supplementary instructional television," used occasionally to deal with particular topics. It is altogether unexpected that out of Portugal should have emerged the only well-established example in Europe of an integrated learning system, covering the full curriculum at the "first-cycle secondary" level and involving tens of thousands of children, in which television plays a central instructional role.

The Development of Telescola

By the 1960s in Portugal the four grades of primary education had become compulsory and universal (i.e., extending to more than 95 percent of the population). Meanwhile, postprimary education slowly spread in the countryside; usually two additional complementary grades of schooling were tacked on to existing primary schools. The difference in academic quality between grades 5 and 6 in specialized town schools and in rural primary schools was marked and unsatisfactory.

Faced with this inequality, the ministry of education authorized its newly formed Institute for the Technology of Education to create broadcasts for grades 5 and 6. Such broadcasts, prepared and delivered by specialists, linked to specially prepared texts for children and including suggestions for follow-up activities by teacher-monitors, were intended to ease the new burdens on rural primary schools.

When broadcasts commenced in 1965, Telescola's "unified course" (combining the fifth- and sixth-grade curricula) was something of a leap into the dark. No one could tell whether television-based schooling as planned for Portugal would prove viable, either pedagogically or technically. Such a radical innovation could be licensed initially by the ministry of education only as "experimental"—which explains why the original recipients were located solely in private reception posts. Later the system, and most posts, became "official" as Telescola proved effective.

In 1968 the government rearranged the structure of schooling, establishing a "preparatory cycle" between the primary and secondary cycles. Grades 5 and 6 were to become compulsory. Telescola became a recognized part of the provision of compulsory schooling. Its unified course was re-

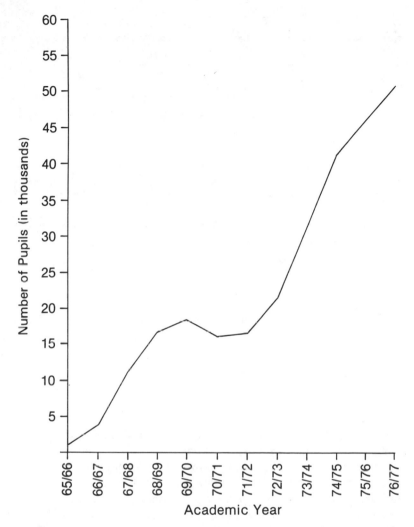

FIGURE 1 Ciclo Preparatorio TV (CPTV): Growth of the System.

named *Ciclo Preparatorio TV* (CPTV) and its subsequent growth, after a
pause for readjustment, was rapid (see Figure 1).

The policy of introducing a compulsory and more uniform curriculum for
the preparatory cycle (i.e., grades 5 and 6) into the Portuguese educational
system was consistent with the long-standing trend toward the unification of
schooling in Portugal. Through both the construction of new facilities for
preparatory schooling in urbanized areas and substitution of Telescola for

Table 1

GROWTH OF PREPARATORY CYCLE SCHOOLING IN PORTUGAL,
1972-1977

Type of Schooling	Number of Pupils (1972-73)	Number of Pupils (1976-77)
Preparatory cycle in "normal" classrooms	144,142	231,443
Preparatory cycle via Telescola	21,757	50,500
Complementary cycle (all forms)	47,930	10,782

the complementary cycle in the remoter regions, the Portuguese government hoped to come closer to realizing the principle of equal educational opportunities for all children, and to reducing the perceived disparities between town and country. Table 1 reveals the progress in achieving these goals.

In the 1980s the complementary cycle is likely to be eliminated altogether from Portuguese education. Coupled with this change will be the continued expansion of preparatory cycle schooling (including both the direct teaching and Telescola variety) as the school population actually brought back into compulsory preparatory education approaches the theoretical maximum.

How Telescola Works

For the most part, Telescola viewing groups were, and are, located in rural primary schools and consist of rural schoolchildren. There are, however, exceptions to this expected pattern which warrant special mention. For example, in the early years of Telescola, adults composed about 10 percent of the constituency for fifth- and sixth-grade broadcasts. Furthermore, school classrooms (even loosely defined) were not the exclusive location of Telescola viewing groups. Other sites included ships, factories, and prisons. The proportion of adults served by Telescola has declined over the years — the result of both lowered demand among adults (the accumulated demand having by now been largely met) and heightened demand from children (the priority population). It should be noted, too, that a surprisingly large number of Telescola posts were begun in suburban areas and have persisted, sometimes because new preparatory schools are crowded, sometimes because the local people prefer their viewing post.

Given Telescola's status as a rather unusual and successful delivery system for rural education, it is important to understand the precise ways in which it was organized and operated. The receiving end of the system will be discussed first, followed by a description of the arrangements for the creation, control, and support of Telescola's services.

Reception Posts

Various "collectivities" (normally villages) and certain individuals can apply for a license, annually renewed, to establish a reception post. A book of regulations issued by the Portuguese government lays down certain specific requirements that all reception posts must meet. Chief among them are the following:

1. *Minimum number.* There should be a minimum of seven pupils in each grade, i.e., a total not less than fourteen. However, smaller posts are certainly not unknown.
2. *Space.* There should be a minimum of two classrooms each able to seat twenty or more pupils, plus cloakrooms and other necessary facilities.
3. *Equipment.* The requirements include desks, blackboard, cupboard, workbench, and tools; science demonstration materials; and a television set with a 49-cm. screen. (Posts having no access to electricity are provided with a Honda generator.)
4. *Supervision.* At least one suitably qualified monitor must be appointed per class. One of these acts as "manager."
5. *Administration.* The regulations detail procedures for matriculation, daily registration, graduation, reporting to the central authority, operating the state system of subsidies for poorer pupils, and so forth.
6. *Pedagogic requirements.* For example, broadcasts must be viewed on a regular basis, all required tests and exams must be taken and pupils graded, specified training courses for monitors must be attended, and so on.

Initially many private posts were set up and managed outside the public educational system. Some still exist. In private posts, while Telescola meets the costs of producing and transmitting the programs and of supervising and controlling the system as a whole, the local manager is responsible for reception costs. To meet such costs, pupils in a private post can be charged a monthly fee for attendance, the maximum being fixed by the ministry of education. Sometimes a post, although private, has been housed in the local primary school; in that event, the manager is required to reserve 25 percent of places, free of charge, for the poorer local children. Subsidies are available to assist needy families with fees or other educational charges.

Beginning in 1970, the ministry started converting reception posts used primarily for schoolchildren into "official" posts, sometimes subsidizing the remaining private posts where the number of children was uneconomically small. By 1975-76, only thirty-five private posts remained. Except for adult "collectives," the latter category is likely to disappear before long. The shift from private to official posts is shown in Figure 2, which also shows the total number of Telescola classes. Incidentally, the number of classes provides a measure of the system's growth as significant as the total number of pupils

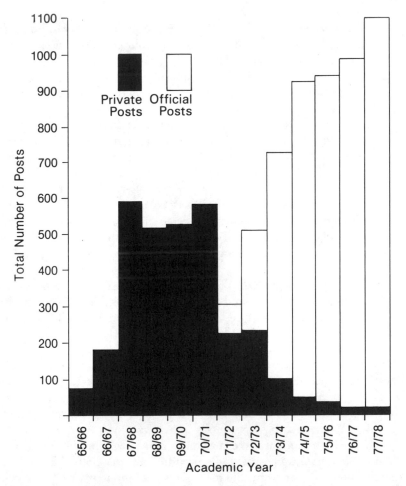

FIGURE 2 Number of Private and Official Reception Posts for Telescola, 1965–1978.

shown in Figure 1. The establishment of Telescola classes in a small and remote village may add little to the total tally of pupils, but it contributes usefully to the generalization of educational opportunity — a matter less of numbers than of equity.

Access and Attendance

The normal rules governing attendance at school apply officially also to Telescola: attendance is compulsory up to the age of fourteen. In practice, in country districts compulsory attendance beyond the primary stage is enforced with discretion, and not at all if a pupil has a journey to a Telescola post of more than three kilometers each way. Voluntary attendance, of course, extends much further. At the extreme, one hears about determined children who walk twelve kilometers daily to a post, and of a small group arriving from an outlying hamlet with an adult escort because the snow had made wolves a hazard. Attendance at posts is normally, of course, less dramatic, sometimes involving no more adventure than dodging traffic on the roads. Special school bus routes for Telescola students can be established, but in practice few such routes exist.

Actual attendance is extraordinarily regular at Telescola posts. Education beyond the primary stage in the rural areas of Portugal is still considered to be something of an exception and a privilege. In addition, pupils in village posts lack the cover of anonymity which, in the larger urban schools, sometimes allows a student's absence to pass unnoticed or uninvestigated.

Telescola lessons continue with unremitting regularity. For example, in 1975, during the worst confusions of the revolutionary period, the preparatory schools started the school year several weeks late and suffered numerous disruptions. In contrast, Telescola maintained its precise, unbroken schedule. The main hindrance to attendance is the agricultural cycle: a Telescola assistant (i.e. an inspector) cited the case of one of his posts in which during the olive harvest the normal number of seventeen pupils dwindled to four. With a proper sense of priorities (and of reality) he had decided to take no action.

Broadcast Content and Format

For Telescola students, school is in session Monday through Friday afternoons for approximately five hours a day. The basic format is of a twenty-minute broadcast immediately followed by a thirty-minute period of "exploitation" led by the monitor. On Wednesday afternoons, there are special broadcasts (sports, cultural events, and documentaries) followed by time left to the discretion of the monitor, used generally for sports, local field trips, project activities, or other more creative exercises.

The essential style of Telescola broadcast lessons is a presentation by a single teacher—for the most part, Telescola employs "talking heads." Although liberal use may be made of illustrative material, acted inserts, etc., the TV teacher aims to establish an atmosphere analogous to that of a classroom, and frequently addresses the class directly. He poses direct questions—in which case, if the classroom monitor points to a particular child in the class, he or she answers; if not, the whole class does so. Some TV teachers seem particularly successful at establishing a rapport with pupils across the air and become popular figures with the children.

After each broadcast, the monitor begins the period of exploitation. Armed with the suggestions contained in the notes for each lesson in the monitors' "Bulletin of Orientation," he asks questions designed to emphasize essential points in the lesson. The pupils then apply what they have learned by completing the exercises set out in their worksheets. Lessons are meant to be completed within the framework of the timetable. Homework is unusual. The monitors' bulletin discourages homework of a bookish sort, confining its suggestions to practical or creative exercises, such as planting and observing a seed, or measuring the milk produced by a cow or goat, noting specified features in the environment, and the like. Of course, some monitors assign more traditional forms of homework when they think it necessary.

The Role of the Monitors and Assistants

Frequently one hears the authorities responsible for Telescola insist that it is a system of teaching *with* television, not *by* television. They emphasize especially the importance of the teacher-monitor. Such an assertion has some political color. Teachers in Portugal, as elsewhere, view television as a doubtful ally.

The monitor's place in the teaching sequence contains some ambiguities, largely revolving around the degree of freedom he or she has, or should have, in the exploitation phase of the lesson. The monitor's dominance is undisputed, however, in that part of the learning process which depends upon a good working relationship between teacher and pupil. Because the monitor needs to expend less time and energy than does the classroom teacher in preparing formal lessons, he or she has an enhanced capacity to devote close attention to the needs of individual children. Furthermore, while preparatory-level teachers in normal "direct teaching" schools are specialists assigned to teach five or six different classes of children each day, monitors teach only one or two classes. Telescola monitors get to know each child in a number of different contexts. As a consequence, the monitor-pupil relationship tends to be closer than that found in regular preparatory schools.

In 1965, when Telescola began, care was taken to establish effective local supervision of the reception posts. The officials appointed were called "teacher-assistants" ("assistants" for short). The word "inspector" was deliberately avoided. "Assistant" implied a less authoritarian relationship between a supervisory official and a teacher than that conjured up by "inspector."

In practice, the Telescola assistants combine many of the functions normally associated with three different types of educators: inspectors, advisors, and field-based administrators. Thus, one finds assistants regularly performing such duties as the planning and creation of new Telescola posts; site evaluation and monitoring (a minimum of six visits per year are made to each post); coordination and distribution of needed equipment, materials, and supplies; advising teachers on curricular and other pedagogical issues; administration of government subsidies and other financial matters; administration of student examinations; and arbitration of local Telescola-related disputes.

Clearly, the role of the assistant, while personally demanding, is vital to the successful functioning of the Telescola system. Although the relationship between assistants and monitors cannot precisely be called collegial, it certainly seems far removed from traditional inspectoral relationships. The quality of this relationship depends critically upon the assistant having a manageable constituency of posts in terms of number and distance, as well as upon the assistant's personal and professional attributes. In 1974-75 there were thirty-five assistants serving 916 Telescola posts, with each assistant having between 25 and 40 posts to look after. The last figure clearly approaches the practical limit for the relationship intended.

Pupil Assessment

From the start of Telescola, a determined effort was directed toward establishing a standard throughout the system, against which the progress of pupils in the scattered reception posts could be checked, and such that the general public would know that any final certificate Telescola might award had more than merely local standing.

The instrument for this process of validation was a battery of tests that had achieved, by 1974, considerable complexity and finesse. With "liberation," in April of that year, examinations throughout the educational system either disappeared or took on strange local and democratic forms which required in those who took notice of the results a certain willing suspension of disbelief. The first constitutional government, elected in July 1976, restored much of the traditional rigor of examinations, but the elaborate assessment mechanisms developed before the revolution, and subsequently disrupted, could not be suddenly revived. The description that follows of Telescola examination arrangements is consequently not current in every detail. It is a description of the prerevolutionary system, some parts of which, but by no means all, are likely to be reconstituted in time.

1. *Objective tests.* Examinations were held three times a year, primarily utilizing multiple choice questions. These examinations were developed, corrected, and evaluated at Telescola headquarters.
2. *Complementary tests.* Designed to accompany the objective tests and to provide opportunities for more open-ended questioning, these examinations were developed by Telescola but graded by the local monitors according to marking instructions supplied.
3. *Monitors' grades.* In addition to the tests, monitors gave each pupil a grade reflecting their general view of the pupil's accomplishments through the use of a twenty-point scale. In certain subjects, such as art, the monitor's grade was the only form of pupil assessment.
4. *Oral tests.* In both Portuguese and French, pupils were required to respond to questions on tape once a year. These oral examinations were administered by the assistants.
5. *Concluding examinations.* At the end of grade 6, pupils took a special final examination. This test utilized both multiple-choice and open-ended questions and was significantly more extensive and exacting than earlier tests. Accordingly, the results of this exam were the primary determinant of whether a pupil received his or her Telescola diploma.

These tests were the basis of grade 5 promotion and grade 6 certification. The failure or repetition rate in Telescola in 1974-75 was about 7 percent at both levels. In "direct teaching" preparatory schools during the same years there was a 15 percent repetition rate at grade 5 and nearly 20 percent at grade 6. Critics of Telescola argued that its tests were too easy. They claimed that the style of examining (in which multiple-choice testing played a leading role) emphasized the simplest kind of question and answer, and was better suited to knowledge of fact than to the application of thought. In practice, the low repetition rate seems also to have reflected deliberate policy. The authorities judged that a repeated year in the circumstances of Telescola caused considerable practical problems and was seldom profitable. They adjusted the exam "pass level" accordingly, thus reducing repetition to the minimum compatible with contemporary teacher and parent expectations, and with the maintenance of a sense of achievement among the pupils.

Telescola's centrally controlled testing differed sharply from the practices of the normal school system in both frequency and objectivity. In regular Portuguese schools, the award of a grade to each pupil was the only form of public testing before the final exam. It reflected a total impression, rather than scores on specific tests, and was entirely at the discretion of each individual teacher. In Telescola, regular testing was part of an apparatus of close control that characterized the original system and that persists, even if in an attenuated form.

Practical Matters

We do not propose here to detail the "housekeeping" aspects of Telescola. Records kept for each post and each pupil; controlled dispensing of thousands of small items of expenditure; and a miscellany of elements, each with its proper timing, make up the complex flow chart of annual operations. Such minutiae make unilluminating reading and do not interest policymakers or educators.

However, we need to remember that the whole pedagogic enterprise of Telescola depends upon the faithful and exact execution of such routine, designed with unusual foresight at the very start of Telescola in 1965. This level of administration survived the trauma of revolution remarkably well; the "organs" of Telescola continued their automatic functioning even after its "head" (in the form of the central Telescola staff) had been cut off. By 1977, however, there were signs of rigor mortis setting in — the late arrival, the wrong arrival, sometimes the nonarrival of print materials and supplies, and the like. At the point when things started going wrong, the importance of routine housekeeping in Telescola was doubtless properly appreciated.

Housekeeping takes on added complications for Telescola on the islands — the Azores, Madeira, and São Tomé. Their distance from the mainland means that transmission must be local, and their generally mountainous configuration means that transmission cannot always be "open" and direct. On São Tomé, cable transmission is widely used by Telescola; on volcanic Madeira and some of the Azores, video cassettes. The Madeira installation is believed to be the world's largest video cassette operation in regular educational use. The broadcasts on original matrices are flown weekly from the mainland and are there transferred onto video cassettes, an operation requiring considerable care and checking to ensure consistent, good-quality registration. A regular "milk run" ensures that old cassettes are collected and new cassettes delivered at every listening post on the island twice a week.

Operations at Telescola Headquarters

In the aftermath of the revolution virtually all the TV teachers at Telescola were dismissed. The creation of new broadcasts was limited to social studies; for the rest, recordings of past programs filled the gap. Prerevolutionary staffing levels provide perhaps a better picture of Telescola running normally and of its scale of operations.

In 1974, then, the staff inhabiting the headquarters buildings consisted of the following: the director of Telescola; two directors of courses (one for CPTV, one for the primary-level "Radio Scolaire"); twenty-seven teachers preparing broadcast lessons; three teacher-producers; twenty-four technical assistants (graphics, documentation, etc.); ten administrative staff; and forty-one "auxiliaries" (secretarial, filing, cleaning, heating, canteen, driving, etc.).

Most Telescola broadcasts were developed by headquarters-based subject-matter teams of three or four teachers. Usually, one team member was assigned responsibility (including on-air presentation) for grade 5 and one for grade 6, with the extra(s) acting as collaborator(s) to both of them—the roles within the team being rotated. Since 1976, as new teams have been established each has had an additional member to help with evaluation and with liaison with assistants and monitors.

Having both to create and to present several broadcasts a week under technically exacting conditions might seem occupation enough for the small team of TV teachers in each subject. Their tasks extend further, however, to include preparing a wide range of supportive learning materials (guides for monitors, student worksheets, etc.) and test materials.

If this sounds like an exhausting schedule, so it should, for such it was and is. Of course, with time TV teachers acquire a labor-saving familiarity with their task (by 1974 some TV teachers had nine years' experience and every team included well-seasoned members, a few of whom returned with the 1976 restoration). Furthermore, provided the curriculum remains reasonably stable, some of the better broadcasts from previous years can be reused. As for the tests, a battery of validated questions has been accumulated from which a selection can be made, a few new questions being added from time to time. Yet even when such shortcuts are taken into account, the burden carried by Telescola's TV teachers and technical services will amaze anyone familiar with the less economical and less hectic way broadcasts are prepared elsewhere.

The Superstructure

No part of the Telescola system suffered so much from the revolution as its parent and governing body, the Institute for the Technology of Education (ITE). At one time its extinction seemed likely. It was moved from its building to a small set of offices above a cafe, its functions and action trimmed to match its new space. After July 1976 it returned to its original building, but the restoration of a dismantled technical service has inevitably been slow, especially because of strong employment protection regulations that inhibit personnel changes.

ITE's supervisory functions over Telescola include the following:

1. *General policy control.* ITE lays down the framework within which the director of Telescola and his staff work.
2. *Budgetary control.* Although Telescola itself necessarily keeps detailed records of expenditures, overall financial control, budgeting, and accounting are the responsibility of ITE (in consultation, of course, with Telescola's director).
3. *Appointment of staff.* Telescola's principal administrative staff members (e.g., the director) are appointed by ITE. So are the TV teachers and the assistants — normally by open competitive examination. Managers of posts and monitors are licensed by ITE, after due checking by the local assistant.
4. *Establishment of posts.* The setting up and the closing of reception posts is carried out by ITE acting on the advice of the school-mapping section at the Ministry of Education's Planning Bureau.
5. *Equipment.* The supply and maintenance of technical equipment at reception posts is managed by ITE.
6. *Pupil subsidies.* The various subsidies (general educational subsidy, books, transport) available to Portuguese families from the government's budget are decided on and administered, in the case of pupils at Telescola reception posts, by ITE (acting on the local advice of managers and assistants).
7. *Training.* ITE is responsible for the training courses given annually.
8. *The assistants.* We have examined the many different ways in which assistants supervise the functioning of reception posts and intervene when help is called for or when things go wrong. The assistants send reports both to Telescola headquarters and the ITE, but in most particulars act as the arm of ITE extended into the detailed operations of Telescola in the field.
9. *Pupil assessment.* The routines of testing and assessment are now carried out by Telescola headquarters and the teacher-monitors, whereas in prerevolutionary centrist days they were more directly managed by ITE. However, ITE retains overall responsibility for the maintenance of standards.
10. *Technical facilities.* Certain technical facilities (for filmmaking, still photography, illustration search, etc.) used by ITE for its educational operations at various levels and centered in Lisbon are at the disposal of the Telescola staff in preparing their programs.

Understanding the Telescola Experience

Evaluating educational innovations and experiments has always been complicated, even in the best of circumstances. In the unusual circumstances that have surrounded Telescola, making valid judgments and sensible generalizations is very tricky indeed. After all, this is not only a sweeping technical organizational and educational innovation, but also one which, in a brief fourteen-year history, has had to endure a national revolution and several rapid governmental turnovers across the political spectrum. An extra measure of caution is needed, then, in drawing any conclusions from the Telescola experience. All the same, given the relative paucity of major innovations in rural education, one can ill afford to overlook reforms such as Telescola that directly confront the thorny problems of delivering reasonable educational services to widely dispersed, and often isolated, rural children.

Perhaps the fairest and most accurate way to assess Telescola is first to separate out a series of objective criteria (such as costs, student achievement, and technical feasibility) on which to base judgments, and then to present the more subjective reactions of a variety of interested parties (central authorities, teacher unions, and rural constituents). It is hoped that this dual approach will equip readers with a broad enough range of information and opinion to understand Telescola's significance both to Portuguese education and to rural education in general.

Cost Data

Costing is necessarily retrospective. The most recent school year with which the 1977 review of Telescola could deal securely was 1974-75; later cost figures are still provisional. In normal times any one of two successive years will display much the same costs as the other, but in Portugal 1974-75 was the last year in which the "classical" prerevolutionary system persisted. The year 1975-76 was marked by radical reform, rapid inflation in salaries, and compensatory economies in other parts of the system. The differences between the two years were such that those who devised the costing study felt bound to attempt an analysis of both years.

Table 2 summarizes the results. The acronym CPTV refers to Telescola; CPES refers to the parallel grades in conventional Portuguese preparatory schools. A comparison of different sorts of schooling, each operating an accounting procedure and using line items evolved to suit its particular requirement, raises numerous technical difficulties. However, the technicalities need not detain us here. We should simply note that the best possible approximations and computations reveal that both in 1974-75 and in 1975-76 it cost slightly over two and one-half times more to educate a child in a normal preparatory school than in a Telescola reception post.

Table 2

SUMMARY OF UNIT COSTS OF TELESCOLA (CPTV) COMPARED TO CONVENTIONAL
"DIRECT TEACHING" PREPARATORY SCHOOLS (CPES) 1974-75 AND 1975-76 (IN ESCUDOS AND 1974-75 PRICES)

| | School Year 1974-75 | | | | School Year 1975-76(a) | | | | |
| | CPTV | | CPES | | CPTV | | | CPES | |
	No. of Units	Cost	No. of Units	Cost	No. of Units	Actual Operating Cost	Normal Operating Cost	No. of Units	Cost
Total cost		275,942 $\times 10^3$		3,115,829 $\times 10^3$		332,543 $\times 10^3$	345,711 $\times 10^3$		3,466,327 $\times 10^3$
Per receiving post	850 (b)	324,638			937	354,902	368,955		
Per class	2,070 (b)	133,305	6,906	451,177	2,276	145,109	151,894	8,064	429,826
Per pupil	39,000	7,075	171,640 (c)	18,153	46,838	7,100	7,381	206,910 (c)	16,753
Per hour of transmission (d)	688.5	400,787			684	486,174	505,425		
Per hour of class	790 (e)	349,293	818 (f)	3,809,082	835 (e)	398,255	414,025	818 (f)	4,237,564
Per pupil-hour	30,810,000	8.96	140,401,520	22.19	39,109,730	8.50	8.84	169,252,380	20.48

Notes: (a) 1975-76 prices converted to 1974-75 prices by being deflated 18 percent.
(b) Statistics adjusted for corrections made by teacher assistants.
(c) Regular day students only. 1975-76 figure based on provisional count.
(d) Based on number of hours contracted with Portuguese National Television.
(e) Number of school days in CPTV school year times five hours per day.
(f) Based on dividing CPES' 180 school days into 32 weeks and 4 days (counting Saturdays as half days) and multiplying by 25 hours per week.

The use of television in schools normally means an addition to costs: how is it that Telescola works out so much cheaper? In part, the answer lies in the fact that most school television is an extra, designed to provide enrichment within the normal teaching system. Telescola, on the contrary, is a direct alternative to that system — it is "instructional" rather than "educational" television. Other factors are important in explaining the economies. For example, Telescola is normally housed in a primary school. Grades 1 through 4 (primary) are taught in the mornings and grades 5 and 6 (Telescola) use the same classrooms in the afternoon. Such double use of buildings does not apply in the conventional circumstance of specially constructed preparatory schools. However, a rerun of costs to eliminate the effect of the difference in building costs still left conventional schooling more than twice as expensive as Telescola.

By far the largest single item in unit running cost for schooling is the salary bill for teaching and ancillary staff. In 1974-75, Telescola monitors were usually primary school teachers. Having taught grades 1 through 4 in the morning, they were paid extra to monitor grades 5 and 6 in the afternoon. In 1975-76, such double employment began to be phased out and full-time monitors were appointed in increasing numbers. Under either arrangement, monitors were routinely paid an average of 10 to 15 percent less than their counterparts in conventional preparatory schools. However, the key cause of cost differentials is to be found in the staffing patterns. In the Portuguese educational system, a conventional preparatory school having twelve classes of fifth- and sixth-grade students would be entitled to thirty staff members (i.e., specialist teachers and auxiliary and administrative personnel). In Telescola posts, each class rates the equivalent of one full-time teacher. Any twelve classes in the total system would rate only twelve professional staff. The cost saving in Telescola is obvious, even though Telescola classes (on average) are smaller than conventional ones (18.8 as against 24.9 in 1974-75).

What Telescola chiefly illustrates is that a television-based system can be substantially less expensive than a direct teaching system at the secondary school level, wherever schools are organized on the basis of specialist subject teachers rather than class teachers. The saving will tend to be most marked in rural areas (where the secondary school is likely to be small) and in countries in which secondary teachers are trained in narrow and exclusive specialties rather than qualified to teach a sufficiently wide span of subjects to allow an economical use of staff.

Student Achievement

Arrangements for an evaluation of pupils' performance in Telescola, as against those in normal schools, were not made when broadcasts began in

1965. The originators were understandably too busy with the intricate problems of starting and then rapidly expanding a new and hazardous enterprise to be bothered with comparative evaluation. What evaluation existed naturally tended to be formative, designed to improve the system rather than to provide some summative comparison with another system. Furthermore, Telescola students neither followed quite the same syllabuses nor completed the same sort of examinations as their urban counterparts. A "scientific" basis for comparison was clearly lacking.

Opinions on comparative school performance are, as one might expect, rather mixed. Some seventh-grade teachers in conventional schools contend that the standard of achievement among the Telescola students coming into their classes is comparatively low. Supporters of Telescola contend this view reflects urban and pedagogic biases. Rural children display rural patterns of speech and behavior, and have to adapt both to a new milieu and to a different method and routine of teaching. Tests at the *end* of the grade 7 year have shown ex-Telescola children doing rather better than average. Telescola's critics discount the result by declaring that the sample is skewed—only the brighter and more ambitious children from Telescola figure disproportionately among those who continue into the seventh grade.

Plainly, while we know that Telescola is cheaper, we have no means yet of knowing how much worse or better, on average, it is than direct teaching in terms of pupil performance. The problems of making any convincing comparison are daunting indeed. Besides, such a comparison, whatever the result, misses the more important point that Telescola, even if it were proved somewhat worse in terms of academic performance, may still be better than the real alternatives available to Portuguese rural children—such as schooling a very long bus ride away, or boarding.

Success as a Technical and Educational Innovation

Telescola's achievement in having brought first-cycle secondary schooling into the remotest rural areas is truly remarkable. Other countries faced with a similar need would find numerous details in the system worth their attention. Telescola before the revolution had reached a high peak of administrative and technical efficiency, much of which remains, and more of which will doubtless be recovered in time.

There is no question that Telescola opened up rural and remote areas of Portugal to postprimary schooling with a rapidity otherwise inconceivable, by finding a way to use primary school buildings and primary school teachers for first-cycle secondary purposes. Over and above this technical and administrative feat, Telescola successfully implemented a number of specific innovations, including:

1. establishing a "unified" or "comprehensive" curriculum for grades 5 and 6 (direct teaching schools used differentiated curricula);
2. combining traditional means of instruction and instructional television ("to arrive at teaching *with* television, not *by* television");
3. adopting coeducation;
4. introducing modern mathematics and more modern methods in certain other subject-disciplines, notably French, music, art, and crafts;
5. developing the role of assistants with advisory functions differing from those normally associated with the inspectorate of that period;
6. providing special texts for pupils (later worksheets) geared to the broadcasts;
7. developing the use of other means of distribution where open broadcasting was not feasible — by landlines in São Tomé, and by video cassettes in Madeira and the Azores; and
8. creating the role of and providing ongoing support for Telescola monitors. Telescola thereby provided valuable in-service education for those rural primary school teachers in Portugal who also served as monitors.

Telescola After the 1974 Revolution

Telescola deserves credit, then, on several counts. It is economical; well managed; technically advanced; able to adopt and successfully integrate a variety of innovations, possibly beneficial, but at least not detrimental to student achievement; and able to deliver a needed service not previously available. After ten years of experience, by 1974-75 Telescola had proved that it could successfully carry out the functions and services assigned to it.

Yet, in the aftermath of the 1974 revolution, fundamental questions about Telescola were raised. The emphasis shifted from concern about what Telescola *could* accomplish to a rethinking of whether a technologically based educational delivery system such as Telescola *should* exist at all. The political context and professional implications of Telescola became the focal point for the intense debates, reforms, and reformed reforms which followed. Currently, most (though not all) of the original Telescola model has been reinstated. Still, the issues raised and actions occurring between 1974 and 1977 contain lessons well worth exploring, even if only briefly.

Put simplistically (the issues are discussed more fully in the 1977 evaluative review), the political battles around Telescola pitted two key groups against each other. On the one hand, leftist leaders and teachers' unions sought the dismantling and/or radical reform of Telescola. On the other hand, an eclectic group of educators, Telescola employees, and, more important, rural parents and community leaders argued for the system's continuation.

Broadly, Telescola's opponents and critics felt that the TV teachers at headquarters should no longer control the learning process (by their lessons, the related texts, and the examinations). Instead, the teacher-monitor should act much more like a conventional teacher, and much less like a monitor. The broadcasts would constitute merely one among many resources that the teacher might elect to use. The reformers argued that Telescola was employing a simplistic model of learning — far too regimented and over-programed. In their view, neither monitors nor pupils had enough room for personal initiative; they could not modify sufficiently what was taught by the television teachers. Everyone had to march at a pace set by a drummer far away. Basically, they argued, the children in Telescola were receiving instruction, not education.

Since the reformers intended the Telescola monitor to play a more central teaching role, the part-time primary school teachers were to be replaced by full-time and suitably trained teachers. Double employment should end except where unavoidable as an interim measure, pending the arrival of full-time staff. Similarly, the apparatus of central control over the monitors should be weakened. For example, all the assistants were dismissed, and grading by monitors replaced objective, computer-marked testing. Even so, Telescola's critics regarded such measures as merely palliative. Telescola's preparatory cycle was (in the view of critics) inherently second-best and second-rate; an unfair discrimination inflicted upon rural people. Wherever possible, reception posts should immediately be closed down and children taken by bus to existing preparatory schools. Plans would be made to ensure that before long, preparatory schooling by direct teaching would become available to all children in Portugal. Telescola's CPTV courses would then end, and Telescola's facilities would be devoted to some better use.

This critique reflects attitudes common in many reforms of the revolutionary period — for example, a hostility to institutions marked by the high degree of centralization and central control typical in the Portuguese state as it then was, and a desire to increase the power of workers as organized into employment unions. In addition, however, the critique of Telescola embodied an antagonism among those teachers who perceived in Telescola's use of monitors an affront to their professional status and advancement. After all, a monitor had to conform not merely to a set curriculum, but to broadcasts that controlled the content and the pace of the lesson, hour by hour. The monitor was further bound to the lessons by suggestions for appropriate exploitation, by worksheets that had to be completed by the pupils, by frequent externally devised tests processed by computer, and by visits of locally based and unusually active assistants. Worse, subjects that "should" be taught by graduate specialists had been handled in Telescola by generalists—initially, indeed, by primary school teachers. The television set had taken over the archetypical function of the specialist, that quintessential act of the teacher—the illuminating exposition of knowledge to the expectant class.

It should occasion no surprise, then, that preparatory and secondary teachers—as trained subject specialists—found Telescola not only wrong but professionally threatening as a model for postprimary schooling. At a time when established authority faltered, established institutions dissolved, and syndicalism became dominant, a determined effort was mounted to make Telescola approximate much more closely, both in pedagogic style and administrative structure, to the norms of direct teaching. The reforms ultimately failed, however, for reasons much more fundamental than the turmoil of the times.

Rebuilding Telescola

Throughout the period of radical reform, as noted earlier, a major force working for the survival of Telescola was the rural constituency being served by it. We will discuss their reasons for taking this position shortly. Yet, it is important to note that among those arguing for the continuance of Telescola were to be found educators and administrators with no vested interest in the system.

Beyond the simple recognition that Telescola worked, these educators argued that the reformers' notions of providing more normal schooling opportunities in rural areas ignored critical facts about the geographic barriers to such provisions as well as the shortage of necessary human and financial resources. In many parts of the country, the transportation of children to centers large enough to sustain a preparatory school is hopelessly uneconomical and sometimes physically impractical. Telescola's defenders readily concede that teaching by television and monitor is in many important respects less satisfactory than conventional teaching. If one considers the *ideal* values inherent in each system, Telescola is certainly second-best—that is, if it is compared with a preparatory school staffed by excellent teachers and equipped with modern facilities. However, the real situation in Portugal, in all its detailed complexity, is remote from such absolutes. As Table 3 indicates, Portugal is very short of teachers qualified in a "scientific" knowledge of their chosen discipline, and there are even fewer fully qualified teachers (i.e., with both "scientific" and pedagogic training). Inevitably the rural and remote areas suffer when qualified teachers are in short supply. Those available are often attracted to the urban centers, and

Table 3

QUALIFICATIONS OF PORTUGUESE TEACHERS, 1976 (IN PERCENTAGES)

Level of Qualification	Primary	Preparatory	Secondary
Fully qualified ("scientific" plus "pedagogic" training)	100	20	26
"Scientific" qualification only		45	43
Neither of the above		35	31

their presence there seems justified by the principle of the greatest good being done for the greatest number.

The radical reformers and teachers' unions assumed that rural parents and students would welcome the opportunity to escape Telescola and attend a regular preparatory school. Thus, in 1976, 128 villages were given the chance to choose the educational system they preferred. It was proposed that their reception post should be closed. Instead, special school buses would take the village children to nearby preparatory schools. The village authorities duly considered the offer: 20 failed to answer, 3 were in favor of the proposal, and 105 were against it. Plainly this resounding opposition was unexpected, or the offer would not have seemed worth making.

Any attempt to explain the villages' response in the absence of extensive sampling must remain at the level of reasonable supposition. Certainly, though, reasons for the predilection for Telescola abound. Dr. Fernando Rocha, the director of Telescola during the period of radical reform, suggested the following:

1. Pupils at a local Telescola post are often from poor families. "They have meals at home and go to school on foot." Attending a regular school means they have "to participate in the expense of bussing (60 escudos a month) and to eat outside the home."

2. The parents of Telescola pupils "also need help and education from the teacher, who sees them, and 'educates' them." Such a relationship with the home is feasible with Telescola because the monitor is locally accessible and locally known. A teacher in a distant preparatory school can rarely achieve such a relationship with village parents.

3. The pupil attending a Telescola post is available in the morning to help around the home with the younger children, or to work on the smallholding or in the family workshop. A pupil from a village attending a CPES school has to attend school throughout the day. What time remains is further invaded by travel and homework. He can make no substantial contribu-

tion to a family economy which may be precarious.

From discussions with monitors and others connected with Telescola, we would add two further points to those Dr. Rocha makes:

4. The Telescola reception post offers children and parents a familiar experience. In scale and style it is similar to the primary school. Even though it utilizes an advanced technology, the actual teaching format (i.e., "talking head") is very traditional. In the past the monitor was usually the local primary teacher, working overtime. The monitor deals with at most two classes, made up of relatively few children whom he or she gets to know well. In a conventional preparatory school, the location, the style, and the scale all differ markedly from a village child's previous experience. Since the teachers specialize in only one or two subject-disciplines, they teach several different classes and do not focus to the same degree upon a few individuals. The situation is altogether less familial.

5. Village children in many parts of Portugal are sharply distinguished from town children. Until they have adjusted to the more sophisticated patterns of behavior of the town their position can be awkward. In any case, such adjustment to town norms often displeases village parents, who generally regard the towns (particularly in the period of turmoil following the revolution) as centers of contagion spreading permissive behavior.

The gap between the urban and rural styles of life is more marked in Portugal than in most Western countries. It does much to explain the polarization of attitudes toward Telescola. The recent political history of Portugal, which witnessed a gradual replacement of extreme leftists by moderates and finally the election of a constitutional government in 1976, included many vivid illustrations of the rejection in rural areas of what was certainly the more vocal opinion in the capital and other urban areas. The conflict had no such dramatic expression in education as it had in politics, but it can be traced, we believe, in rural resistance to "obvious" improvements—such as the proposed substitution of conventional schooling a bus ride away for "second-rate" Telescola instruction near home.

The Future of Telescola

As the fourteen-year history of this innovation amply illustrates, the acceptance and maintenance of particular educational models and delivery systems rests as much on political, social, and professional considerations as it does on more technical assessments of performance and capabilities. Thus, as long as the political situation in Portugal remains somewhat unstable, it would be imprudent to state absolutely that Telescola will (or will not) survive.

Assuming, however, that Telescola does continue to exist (a reasonably likely prospect), there remains the need to upgrade its current level of service. In part, this means reinstating some of the elements of the original system which were discontinued in the wake of the revolution. Yet, at a more fundamental level, there is need to acknowledge the validity of some of the criticisms aimed at Telescola and to adjust accordingly.

One of the more far-reaching proposals arising from the 1977 review of Telescola envisages a mixture, or rather a juxtaposition, of Telescola's instructional television and of direct teaching. The suggestion is that the teacher-monitors should continue to act as monitors, regularly using instructional television as a requirement, with regard to certain subjects; but act as teachers, occasionally using educational television as a resource if they so wish, in other subjects. There are certain "technical" subjects, such as mathematics, physical sciences, foreign languages, music, and art, for which instructional television seems necessary because rural areas, for the foreseeable future, are likely to be short of adequate facilities and qualified staff. Other subjects, however (which form a reasonably homogeneous group for teacher-training purposes), such as Portuguese language and literature, history and geography, "morals," and studies of the environment, suffer from no such shortages. These are the subjects having particularly rich opportunities for flexible learning strategies—discussion, project work, and the like—which are best left to a teacher's initiative and discretion. These are the subjects, moreover, in which the encouragement of local and individual variety may be most essential.

Telescola was originally created to supply remote places with a completely self-contained and uniform system as an alternative to conventional schooling. For the future such an "either-or" perspective may, with advantage, give way to a "both-and" view. A mixture would provide teacher-monitors and children alike with more varied opportunities and more room for flexibility and local initiative.

The wealthier Western democracies committed themselves to generalized first-cycle secondary education before television was sufficiently familiar or developed to offer the basis for any credible alternative to conventional schooling. Wholesale busing or boarding were the strategies adopted for delivering village children to the place of schooling. When television came to be used, it fitted the established habit best as an embellishment, as enrichment. The curiosity of the Portuguese situation is not only that an effective instructional television system has been created, but also that, as a result, many rural and even suburban communities have actually been given a choice between two different styles of secondary schooling.

One is more intimate, local, and in some respects restricted; the other more "institutional" and distant, if more ample. Since successive governments have promised not to close down Telescola listening posts against local wishes, the choice has been a genuine if complex one. Rarely has such a direct choice between "normal" and technologically based rural education systems been offered in the OECD countries. Would other rural people, given the choice, show a similar preference for a Telescola-type system rather than the more conventional style of education in rural areas? Idle speculation, perhaps — but the Portuguese experience should encourage those countries not yet committed to large units and wholesale busing to think long and hard about possible adaptations of the Telescola model. As for Telescola itself, one must hope that this rare innovation will not only continue, but also be provided with the resources and encouragement necessary for its further development.

4

Beyond Mere Survival: Teacher Support in Scotland's Rural Schools

R. S. Johnston

In Scotland, as in the United Kingdom as a whole, the closure of small schools has become an important educational and political issue. More than that, the continued existence of small schools has become a *passionate* issue in the minds of supporters and doubters alike. These passions have often generated more heat than light. There has also been an unfortunate tendency for blanket assertions to obliterate a careful, case-by-case weighing of available evidence in the debate about school closures. No doubt some administrators, properly concerned about declining enrollments, financial constraints, and the quality of education, will argue for further closures of certain small schools. There is also little doubt that some parents and communities, properly concerned about the integrity of their community and the quality of education, will advance increasingly sophisticated and convincing arguments for saving certain small schools.[1]

This tension could be regarded as a constructive one—an illustration of a healthy system of checks and balances—were it not for one factor. Put simply, the danger is that far too often the debate has been reduced to the question of mere survival. There is a great temptation among both parents and administrators to behave as if the decision to keep a given small school open marks the end of the necessary action and discussion about its future. This temptation must be strenuously resisted. Small schools, particularly in

This chapter could not have been written without the help, which was always most willingly given, of many people. Among those to whom tribute must be paid are members of staff in Aberdeen, Craigie, and Dundee Colleges of Education, and the director of education and his advisors in the Highland region. Inevitably, some selection of material from the many particular illustrations of teacher support submitted was necessary. This statement of appreciation applies equally to those whose work is not precisely mentioned.

remote areas, which merely survive, but remain cut off from necessary resources and assistance, can hardly be viewed as dynamic institutions or as schools which are living up to their not inconsiderable potential. The condition for success in these instances is very clear—survival must be accompanied by active and appropriate support.

Support for small rural schools should include a variety of measures. These might range from renovating and properly equipping older schools to devising strategies which enable isolated rural children to have at least occasional access to some of the specialized facilities and services generally available to their urban counterparts. However, given the paramount importance of individual teachers in small rural schools, the most pressing need is for teacher support.

This need has by no means gone unrecognized in Scotland. Accordingly, this chapter will document some of the strategies widely employed to provide teacher support in sparsely populated areas. Special attention will be given to current Scottish innovations in the delivery of support services. In order to better understand the context in which these innovations occur, some basic background information on the Scottish education system and Scottish teachers will be provided.

The Scottish Education System

The public education service is a partnership of national and regional governments (see Figure 1). A distinctive feature is the devolution of power to regional authorities and their schools. Central government does not run any schools; nor does it engage teachers; nor does it prescribe curricula. However, it does determine the amount of money to be spent on educational buildings by education authorities, and the secretary of state gives guidance on staffing, the curriculum, and teaching methods. Education authorities are required to ensure that there is adequate and efficient provision of school education for children in their areas. They must also ensure that the facilities accord with schemes prepared by the authorities and approved by the secretary of state. Education authorities are responsible for the construction of educational buildings, the employment of teachers and education advisors, and the provision of equipment and materials.

In Scotland, as in the rest of the United Kingdom, compulsory schooling begins at age five and ends at age sixteen. Public schools (not to be confused with public schools in the English sense) include nursery (ages three through five), primary (five through eleven), and secondary (twelve through fifteen and sixteen plus) institutions which are operated by education authorities and supported by public finances. Most of these are nondenominational and coeducational; some are Roman Catholic schools. The public schools form

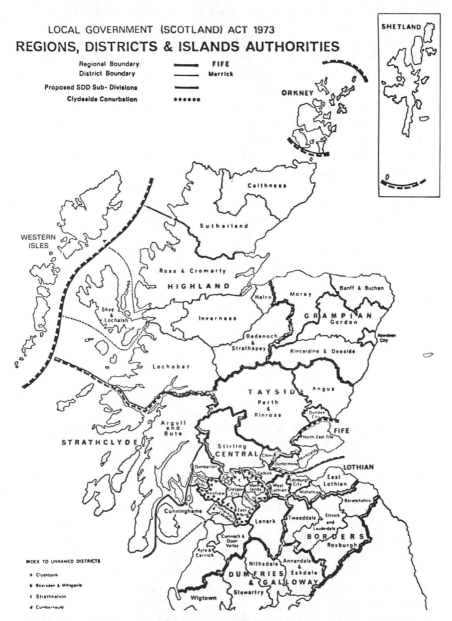

LOCAL GOVERNMENT (SCOTLAND) ACT 1973

REGIONS, DISTRICTS & ISLANDS AUTHORITIES

Regional Boundary   **FIFE**
District Boundary   Merrick
Proposed SDD Sub- Divisions
Clydeside Conurbation   ●●●●●●

FIGURE 1 Map of Regional Education Authorities in Scotland.

by far the largest part of the school system, taking in about 95 percent of the pupils. Education in the sparsely populated areas of Scotland is almost entirely in the public sector.

Students may continue their education beyond age sixteen on a voluntary basis. Scotland, like many other countries, utilizes a system of national examinations at the secondary level. There is a wide variety of educational opportunities of both an academic and technical nature available beyond the compulsory schooling stage. Still, it is not always possible for students from remote areas to continue living at home full time throughout their secondary schooling experience. Accordingly, provision of long-distance transportation, boarding, and other necessary arrangements have been organized by the education authorities.

Although Scotland is a relatively small country in physical terms, its terrain, climate, and population distribution combine to create extensive problems of remoteness and inaccessibility. Therefore, a considerable number of small rural schools is accepted as a necessary and inevitable feature of Scottish education. For example, there are currently 600 primary schools (or 24 percent of the total number) which enroll fewer than 50 students; 300 (12 percent) which enroll fewer than 25 students; and 57 schools (2 percent) with fewer than 10 pupils. Similarly, 45 (10 percent) of Scotland's secondary schools have fewer than 100 pupils.

Teaching in Rural Scotland

The secretary of state prescribes the requirements for entry to teacher training, on the advice of the General Teaching Council for Scotland. All teachers in primary and secondary schools are required to hold a teaching qualification awarded by a college of education and to be registered with the General Teaching Council. The normal route to teaching in a secondary school is by a one-year postgraduate course of professional training at a college of education subsequent to a three- or four-year degree course at a university. The normal route to teaching in a primary school is by a three-year course of professional training at a college of education. After initial entry to the profession, all teachers have a probationary period of two years; their registration with the General Teaching Council is dependent upon satisfactory reports by the head teacher of the school(s) in which they serve. The professional training and qualifications of Scottish teachers have, therefore, a national framework; those of teachers in rural areas are entirely comparable with those of their colleagues in other areas, and there is no technical impediment to the movement of teachers to and from and within rural areas.

Salary scales for teachers are also national. Special additions to these scales are available to teachers in certain rural areas. A "remote areas allowance" (offered at two levels, depending on degree of the school's inaccessibility) is payable to teachers on the basis of the length and difficulty of the route they have to use from the school to the nearest recognized center of population. There is also a "distant islands allowance." This was introduced in 1945 to compensate for the relatively higher costs on such islands of items like fuel, for the distance from shopping centers, and for the lack of public transportation.

Education authorities in rural areas meet the cost of travel to interviews for teaching posts, assist teachers with moving expenses when they begin employment, provide car allowances for itinerant teachers and members of their advisory support service, and regularly meet the traveling expenses and subsistence of teachers who attend in-service training courses in various parts of the country. In recent years, financial constraints have obliged the authorities to be more selective in granting assistance for in-service training.

As of 1979, the national pupil-to-teacher ratio in primary schools was 20.3:1. These calculations include the head teacher but exclude teachers of remedial education and visiting teachers of special aspects of primary education such as art, music, and physical education. The ratios in the rural areas were better than the national average (e.g., Shetland 16.7:1; Orkney 17.2:1; Western Isles 17:1; and Highland 19.1:1).

Staffing standards in primary schools are calculated so that in a school with a traditional, one-teacher/one-year stage organization the average class size does not exceed thirty. The standards apply, however, to small schools thus:

Pupils	Teachers
1–19	1
20–49	2
50–75	3
76–100	4

In 1979, the national pupil-to-teacher ratio in secondary schools was 14.4:1. The ratios in the rural areas were again better than the national average (e.g., Shetland 13.2:1; Orkney 13:1; Western Isles 12.1:1; and Highland 14:1). Staffing standards in secondary schools are related to complements recommended by the secretary of state, and to a national pupil-to-teacher standard of 15:1.

Differing regional circumstances are recognized, and more favorable ratios obtain in smaller schools, with consequent benefit for rural areas. Teachers in the rural schools are apt to be deployed in a more versatile role than their urban colleagues. In the small primary schools, teachers are responsible for groups including pupils of different ages and varying abilities. The Scottish secondary teacher is trained, and normally deployed, as a subject specialist. In small rural schools, however, teachers may have to teach more than one subject—e.g., English and French, mathematics and science—or combine secondary and primary teaching. There is concern in some of the more remote areas that the supply of teachers able and prepared to fulfill this versatile role may diminish.

Traditionally, a high proportion of the teachers in sparsely populated areas of Scotland are born and bred in those areas and, after their professional training, decide to return. This has been especially true of primary schools. In the Western Isles and Orkney, for example, the proportion of primary school teachers with their roots in the local area is still more than 40 percent. The proportions are less in areas such as the Easter Ross part of the Highland region, where industrial growth required a rapid influx of teachers. The proportion of "local teachers" is approximately the same in secondary schools. For example, in the Western Isles and certain parts of the Highland region it is about 50 percent.

One feature of staffing in the rural areas is the high proportion of married women who are head teachers of small primary schools. These home-produced teachers represent a core of stability and cultural affinity. Particularly in the small townships of the rural areas, they create a ready pool of talent—able to fill in for absent teachers or act as part-time specialists. They also enhance any distinctiveness in local language, whether it be a forthright, declared policy of bilingualism as in the Western Isles (Gaelic-English), or the less formal, but still assiduous, respect for a dialect as in Shetland.

In addition to the native core, certain teachers are attracted to the rural areas either for short spells or for good. Some are young teachers who wish to strike out early in their career, give the rural area their service for a few years, and then return to the urban environment. Some are husband-and-wife teams who make a joint contribution to the rural community; e.g., the head teacher wife and the ferryman husband, or the head teacher wife and the gravedigger husband. On occasion, the "incomer" is clearer about his discontent with the urban area than he is about his affinity with the rural area, and does not stay long. But, over the years, the appointing authorities have developed skills which enable them to assess applicants shrewdly.

Teacher Support in Rural Scotland

Whatever the circumstances in a particular small rural school, and whatever the characteristics of the teacher(s) working in it, an important common denominator is the need, and desire, for outside contact and assistance. Rural isolation is more than a mere physical phenomenon. Rather, it often carries with it significant feelings of professional and personal isolation. Thus, Scottish teacher support is designed to offer not only technical assistance, but also a degree of personal interaction and collegiality.

The remainder of this chapter describes a range of existing teacher support efforts and offers some concrete examples of how they actually operate. In discussing these systems and sources of support, attention is paid first to the regional and island authorities; next to three colleges of education; and finally to Her Majesty's Inspectors of Schools. To give as broad a view as space permits, the description of the colleges of education includes examples of their work, both with rural primary school teachers and with specialist teachers of geography in secondary schools.

Three points can be made about the evidence presented here. First, the quality of support provided by the regional and island authorities, the colleges of education, and the inspectors of schools depends upon the quality of their planned interrelationship. Second, most of the illustrations of actual support given relate to environmental education. There is always a hope that, without being parochial or neglecting the study of other environments and other peoples, schools in rural areas will make the most of their environmental setting. Finally, this chapter is written at a most interesting stage of development of support for teachers in sparsely populated areas. On the one hand, general financial constraints have prevented the regional authorities from expanding their advisory services and in-service training of teachers. On the other hand, the falling birth rate, dwindling school rolls, and waning demand for teachers are making it possible for the colleges of education to switch some of their resources from the preservice training of teachers to more sustained support of teachers in service. The sparsely populated areas stand to gain a great deal from this shift in emphasis.

Teacher Support by Regional and Island Authorities

Responsibility for the provision of education in the rural areas, as elsewhere in Scotland, lies with the regional and/or island authorities. The principal means of teacher support provided by the regions are specialist advisors, staff tutors, and visiting teachers. The extent and modes of deployment of advisors and tutors vary from region to region, but their consistent responsibilities are to visit schools; promote curriculum development directly and through working parties; assist new and young teachers; advise on educational resources; assess the need for, and provide, in-service training; and maintain links with colleges.

Some advisors in primary education have responsibility for development at particular stages or in particular aspects of the curriculum. Thus, the Western Isles authority, which is responsible for education in some sixty primary and fifteen secondary schools scattered over a very remote territory, employs full-time advisors in primary education, Gaelic, technical education, home economics, music, and art. In addition, a director and three teachers work full-time on the development of bilingual education. In Shetland there is a full-time advisor in music and a part-time advisor in physical education; the latter combines his duties of advisor with the post of head of the physical education department of the largest secondary school in the islands.

The pattern of deployment of advisors in rural areas maintains the traditional emphasis on the practical and aesthetic subjects. This tradition recognizes that support is very necessary for secondary school teachers in minimally staffed subject areas like art and technical education. At the same time, the employment of general advisors in primary education is a more modern development in recognition of the fundamental changes of philosophy and methodology which have taken place in Scottish primary schools over the past fifteen years.

The work of an advisor in a rural area is demanding, and effectiveness is directly related to the frequency with which he or she can sustain contact with schools, building up personal and professional relationships, confirming diagnoses, and analyzing needs. Between 1972 and 1975, before the severe financial constraints, there was very vigorous support for teachers in much of rural Scotland.

For example, the advisors in primary education, in conjunction with staff from Aberdeen College of Education and Her Majesty's Inspectors of Schools, maintained a program of study and in-service training for teachers in the Highland region. Over two and one-half years the same group of thirty teachers met six times for short conferences. These were held during the teachers' normal working week, lasted for two days, were residential (in accommodations as congenial and as conveniently located as possible), were related to an overall theme such as the development of reading or environmental studies, and endeavored to relate the study to practical work. Resources, teaching methods, and assessment of pupil progress were among the main concerns.

The teachers in the group represented nearly every facet of primary education and most were chosen because the chances of their translating these studies into action were rated high. Later, it was decided that certain head teachers should join the group because their understanding of the aims of the in-service program, their support for the individual teachers in the study group, and their influence on school policy and practice were of critical importance. The results of this effort included not only changes in the participants' classroom work, but also a series of guidelines for similar in-service activities in the future. Not surprisingly, follow-up liaison between tutors and schools helps to reinforce and "institutionalize" new insights and practices.

The financial constraints of recent years have inhibited the development of the advisory services and reduced the momentum of the 1972–1975 period. In the Highland region, for example, with 227 primary schools in its territory of 9,700 square miles, the number of advisors and tutors in primary education has been reduced to one principal advisor, one advisor, and two staff tutors. In the face of cutbacks, the Highland advisors and tutors have made support to the smaller rural schools a priority. This priority status has been granted because the isolation, and heavy professional burden, of rural teachers in small primary schools with pupils covering the age range five through twelve is understood and taken seriously.

The advisors have managed to sustain an ongoing series of one-day in-service courses and conferences for teachers in rural areas. Among the themes for these short courses in recent years have been language development, environmental studies, remedial education, preschool education, and curriculum in the small school. Advisors and tutors have also endeavored to gather teachers from small schools, usually in the second half of an afternoon, to review work undertaken as a result of the one-day conference. Examples of pupils' work are brought to these meetings, displayed, and discussed. On some occasions teachers have come together in the evening to discuss common problems. Advisors and tutors also attend meetings of parents to discuss modern teaching approaches and other educational topics of interest.

Of course, the advisor system is not the only teacher support strategy employed by regional education authorities in Scotland. For instance, the Highland region (in which less than 4 percent of the nation's population is scattered over about 33 percent of the land mass of Scotland) has adopted a highly decentralized management structure for education. There are five divisional educational officers stationed at strategic points and responsible for the day-to-day administration of a group of schools. The support role of the divisional education officer has still to find full definition. However, it is already evident that in the course of an officer's typical visit discussion may range over individual pupils with learning difficulties, population trends (the movement of one family can be significant), supplies, transportation, and property maintenance. The teachers have welcomed the opportunity to discuss problems, major and minor, which affect the school and community.

In addition, many regions deploy a corps of itinerant or visiting staff to give support to teachers in particular aspects of the primary school curriculum such as art, music (including instrumental instruction for pupils), and physical education and in subjects of the secondary curriculum where either the work load in individual schools does not justify a full-time appointment or requires a part-time teacher in addition to the complement of full-time staff. These peripatetic teachers are valuable not just for their particular expertise, but also because they provide an extra source of support for rural teachers and an additional adult with whom the rural students can interact.

Teacher Support by Colleges of Education

Preservice and in-service training for teachers is provided in ten colleges of education located in different parts of Scotland. Students from rural areas seeking to become teachers may apply to any college for training, and efforts are made to allow students to take part of their teaching practice in rural schools. Active teachers may attend in-service courses at the colleges during vacation periods or, with the support of their regional authorities, during the school term. The residential courses, some of which deal specifically with the organization and curriculum of rural primary schools, are valuable opportunities for teachers from sparsely populated areas to mix with colleagues from other locations.

Financial constraints have, however, reduced the support for college-based in-service courses from regional authorities, not least those in sparsely populated areas. At present the momentum in favor of school-based support (i.e., with college staff actually deployed in the sparsely populated areas) is increasing. School-based support requires careful nurturing. Teachers will profit from courses if the purpose is clearly known in advance, the topic acknowledged to be important, the emphasis of the course practical, and the outcome specific.

To provide support that meets those reasonable, but demanding, criteria requires accurate analysis of needs and efficient communication among the regional authorities, their schools, and the colleges. For several years, in-service courses have been planned to include individual follow-up visits in schools during which teacher and tutor could discuss the implementation of work done in the college. This interchange after the classroom experience was of value to rural teachers because it afforded the opportunity to focus attention on their particular problems.

School-based activities, however, have the advantage of offering an opportunity for teacher and tutor together to seek solutions to problems as they arise and to evaluate all aspects of the work as it progresses. The present expansion of school-based support in the more remote areas by the colleges could not have been carried out so easily or effectively without the groundwork of earlier years. In the sparsely populated areas there is a certain conservatism, of the best sort, which manifests itself as a desire to know what the people and institutions involved are really like before a commitment is made to any new ideas or programs.

Examples of Support by Aberdeen College of Education for Rural Primary School Teachers

Aberdeen College of Education is the most northerly of the colleges and over the years has given support to teachers in the sparsely populated, widely scattered, and often remote Highland and island areas of north and northwest Scotland. Advantage has been taken of declining enrollments in the preservice training programs to make staff and other resources available for more systematic school-based support.

The head teacher of Shieldaig primary school in the Highland region believed that in the curriculum of West Highland schools more attention should be paid to the cultural background, history, geography, and ecology of the area. She had already arranged for an exhibition of George Washington Wilson's photographs (showing crofting [farm] life in the 1880s) to be sent to the Shieldaig school by the Aberdeen University Library in June 1978. Her wish was that the school-based in-service activity (in April 1978) would set in motion a project on nineteenth-century Highland life which would continue until the arrival of the Wilson exhibition.

Because of the distance from the college, planning was done by telephone conversation and exchange of letters. The project involved the college tutor, the head teacher, and sixteen pupils at four stages of primary education at Shieldaig school for the whole of one school week. Each day the tutor talked to the pupils about an aspect of nineteenth-century Highland life — crofting life, the Clearances, emigration, and the Crofters' War. The aim was to start the pupils thinking and talking about the life led by their nineteenth-century predecessors. To stimulate them, a considerable range of materials was used — slides (specially made by the college's teaching aids department) of nineteenth-century Highland life; selected and edited source extracts relating to Shieldaig and other parts of the Highlands; and tapes of two radio programs, "From Scotland's Past."

The greater part of each day was then devoted to follow-up work, jointly planned and supervised by the head teacher and tutor, and taking the form of art work, model making, and imaginative writing. Part of one day was devoted to fieldwork — a visit to a ruined settlement one mile along the coast from the school. There was also discussion of the work to be done by the pupils on this topic during the following weeks. And finally, ideas were developed to overcome problems surrounding the availability of materials and the handling of several age groups in the same class (two perpetual concerns of small schools in remote areas). As a result of this activity, more and more teachers in this region have expressed an interest in local history and in using the physical, social, and cultural environment of the school as tools for learning with their students.

Still, many teachers in the sparsely populated areas are far removed from large libraries and other resource centers and so find it difficult to produce their own materials. Moreover, most commercial textbooks and materials deal with environments very different from those found in the Highlands and islands. The college is, therefore, producing a tape-slide sequence of source extracts describing conditions in the words of those who were there (crofters, factors, landowners, ministers), selected and edited to suit today's primary pupils, as well as background information for teachers and some suggestions on the use of these materials in the classroom.

Another example of Aberdeen College's support can be seen in the case of the primary department of Portree High School on the island of Skye. The school's specific request was for assistance in planning a language arts program. A preliminary visit was made by the college tutor soon after the initial contact with Portree's primary department. At first, the discussion during the preliminary visit centered on the availability of reading material within the school and the ways in which it was used in each of the classes. Later, however, consideration was given to the aims of an overall language program.

The skills the child should acquire as his reading ability matures were considered, and it was decided to concentrate on the skills involved in reading factual material for information. Reference and information books, magazines, and brochures introduced to the classroom by the teacher and the children themselves were studied and discussed. *The Reader's Digest Book of the Road,* the *AA Handbook,* the telephone directory, several guidebooks, holiday brochures, and transportation timetables were among the resources used in a unit on living in Skye. Similarly, cookbooks, favorite recipes, magazines, and geography books were used in a unit on food. The children quickly came to realize that different kinds of books give different insights and information. Two of the teachers developed and extended the work by opening a class "book shop." The third teacher replanned her project work so that children could practice the newly acquired skills.

As a result of the work during the week, the tutor was invited to return to the school for a further week to introduce a unit of work on the development of comprehension skills and written expression. It was decided that the focal point for this study should be a group of novels. The selected titles were *On the Banks of Plum Creek* (Laura Ingalls Wilder); *Viking's Dawn* (Henry Treece); and *The Children of Greene Knowe* (Lucy Boston). One of the teachers wrote to the tutor in these terms:

> My Vikings are *still* going strong. Our item for the concert will be a Gaelic song about a longship on a voyage from the Isle of Man north to Islay. It's a simple enough song, even if it is a Gaelic, but we are constructing a longship in sections (just a facade) which they will stand and hold and, underneath it, will hang cloth painted like the sea to hide their feet.
>
> The song has 20 men in the boat and the King's son (or chief's own son) steering, and that means that only six girls will be extra. They are going to be seamaidens and will hold a very large polystyrene island and slide slowly along behind the boat to give the impression of it moving. That's the theory anyway!
>
> We are in the throes of getting everybody kitted out in Viking dress. They will never rest now until that is all settled. As usual, the idea grows. In class everyone has chosen a Viking name, a weapon, and a name for the weapon like Skullsplitter, Deathkiss and someone — Kevin, typically — the Kiss of Life!!
>
> We got some good writing but I simply have not had time to collect it for you. One boy did not like the ending of *Viking's Dawn* and rewrote it to end happily — three close jotter pages. We have worked our way right through Henry Treece's trilogy. I thought they would be sick of Vikings long before this but not a bit of it. Our Vikings have been to Ireland, Gibraltar, Miklagard and back through Russia and are now on the whale's way across to America via Greenland to learn the ways of Eskimos and Red Indians.

During these activities the assistant head teacher of Portree was involved (after school hours) in all discussions. The plan now is to introduce all staff to new strategies for curriculum development.

Beginning in the 1978-79 school year, a further development of significance was introduced by Aberdeen College to add both quality and weight to school-based support for teachers in rural primary schools. Three college tutors were assigned for at least one year to particular sparsely populated areas: one to Shetland, one to Orkney, and one to the Highland region. In consultation with the local education authorities, each tutor gives support to a nominated group of schools, alternating two or three weeks of work in the field with similar periods in the college throughout the year. It is hoped that this more sustained deployment will create closer personal and professional relationships between tutors and schools, enable precise assessment of teachers' needs to be made, and promote sustained development. The tutors are expected to involve themselves in all aspects of the primary school curriculum, but they remain free to ask for assistance from colleagues on the college staff who have specialized knowledge and experience. It is recognized that this mode of deployment of the tutors will make heavy demands on them, and the rhythm of field and college attachment requires continuing evaluation.

The Aberdeen College experiment could be very important for the future overall support of teachers in sparsely populated areas and for a range of other matters such as college–education authority liaison and recruitment of college staff. If successful, this arrangement could prove to be a useful model both within the United Kingdom and elsewhere.

Examples of Support Provided by Craigie College of Education for Rural Primary School Teachers

The Dumfries and Galloway region is essentially a rural area with a coastal plain along the Solway Firth and three extensive valleys separated from the rest of Scotland by hills and high moorland. Only three towns have more than 400 inhabitants. Two-thirds of the schools have fewer than 100 pupils. Craigie College of Education, in Ayr, is a modern college lying approximately fifty miles from both Dumfries and Stranraer, the main centers of population, and has reasonably good road links to almost all parts of the region. The main purpose of Craigie College is to train primary school teachers. Four aspects of primary education in which Craigie has provided support for the region's rural schools are reading, social studies, science, and music. Each area will be described in turn.

The Craigie reading project has been aimed at smaller schools, and forty of them have been involved (with four schools in each project group). The teachers were given the opportunity, under guidance, to examine the work they were doing and to discuss it. For example, teachers kept a diary of their language work. This record was analyzed by the college tutors and discussed with the teachers. It was then possible to discuss in depth particular aspects of the reading program: comprehension, study skills, reading for pleasure. The final stage was to work out a reading program for each school, first for a term, then for a year. College staff were able to help teachers relate reading materials and teaching techniques to an overall reading program. To allow concentrated discussion by teachers, children were released for four afternoons in each group of schools. Teachers also visited the college reading center.

The Craigie social studies project was specifically designed for teachers who could not attend college-based courses. It was recognized that primary teachers want, above all, concise, up-to-date resource knowledge to build up their confidence. They are also prepared to develop an interest in methodology but usually only after this has a defined relationship with a specific topic and content.

Seventeen booklets, many on topics suggested by teachers themselves, were prepared over a three-and-one-half-year period. These vary in subject matter, in methods of treatment, and in extent of detail. One booklet, *Solway Ports and Shipping in the Past,* contains a considerable amount of local information, quotations from original sources, and suggestions on further sources and work which primary schools can undertake (e.g., locating gravestones carrying data on seamen; inn and hotel signs; or street and house names). On the other hand, *Using the Fifty Inch Plan* is partly a self-instruction booklet for teachers to allow them to familiarize themselves with a large-scale map; a short final section deals with using the plan with children in the school. Demand for these booklets has been such that they are to be published and made generally available. The authors of this scheme have deliberately set out to provide basic support materials for teachers. They are quite clear about the limitations of their exercise and acknowledge that it is only one part of total teacher support.

Teacher support in science grew in part from the success of the social studies booklets. One of the Craigie lecturers had devised a kit with science materials for primary pupils to use requiring minimum intervention by the teacher. The belief was that teachers could become more confident in presenting science to primary school children if it could be demonstrated that their pupils were capable of undertaking work on topics in which the teacher was not particularly knowledgeable. Since the small rural schools might not be able to acquire the complete kit for themselves, it was decided that some of the original development materials would be made available to the schools. The scheme has potential, but it has become clear that when a subject as unfamiliar as science is being introduced, direct teacher-tutor dialogue is important.

A research project identified the music-related needs of the small schools, and the Craigie music department has begun a fairly long-term in-service development effort based upon practical music making. A college lecturer is working with staff and younger pupils in one of the larger schools. Teachers from other rural schools are brought to the school in order to observe and take part in the work which has been done. Those interested are then supported in carrying out similar activities in their own schools. One of the difficulties, however, is that small schools often lack the necessary instruments. The college music department has proposed, therefore, to set up a music resource center.

Examples of Support for Rural
Secondary School Geography Teachers

In Scotland, the subject of geography has recently undergone great changes in curriculum, methodology, and resources. Teachers felt a need to meet, discuss, and work on all the new courses. In the sparsely populated areas, the problem was more acute because of the isolation of individual schools. To meet this need the Aberdeen College geography department used the Highland city of Inverness (100 miles from the college) as a base for short in-service courses. In this way, firm contact was established with almost all the geography teachers of the Highland region and representatives of those from the islands. This contact was extended in 1975 by short courses in Orkney and Shetland and further visits to remote areas to introduce the new curricula for the early years of secondary education. Meetings were arranged which brought together teachers from the small rural secondary schools and their specialist colleagues from the larger schools. Because of the good informal and professional relationships established here, the geography department of the college is now developing school-based support.

In order to determine teacher interest and publicize the new service, the Aberdeen geography department sent a personally addressed question-and-answer document to every principal, or sole geography teacher, in all secondary schools throughout northern Scotland. This document explained precisely what school-based in-service activities could mean for them. The letter made very clear that the procedure for applying was through the local education authority. When college staff go to a school, it is always with the full knowledge of the regional authority.

When the formal request from the school reaches the college, the geography department does its best to send the most suitable person (based on the specific request, knowledge of the local area, and individual links with the teacher). Whoever takes on the assignment contacts the school and teacher directly and arranges to make a preliminary visit to gain a full appreciation of the context. This visit is generally for a day and is relatively expensive, but the contact is essential.

The essence of school-based in-service activities is that the teacher pinpoints the topic, has a hand in determining the aims and objectives, and commits himself to a joint effort with the college lecturer. After the preliminary visit, the college assembles resources, drafts schemes, or makes whatever preparation is appropriate. The tutor travels to the school on an agreed date and sets to work with the teacher(s) for a period of some days. There can be difficulties with accommodations, especially in small schools, but a store, a corner of the library, or some other such space is always found.

In some cases the work being developed is tested either in the classroom or in fieldwork. The return to Aberdeen does not mark the end of the commitment. There are various items that need completing and these are dispatched to the school in due course. Already there are indications of a continuing, open relationship being established in which the teacher, having worked with the tutor, feels he can write from time to time to discuss further points or raise quite new topics. The hope is that by such informal contact geography teachers in the more remote schools can maintain a link with a college specialist who has a considerable range of contacts with other schools and other bodies engaged in curriculum development.

School-based support promises to build teachers' confidence in developing curriculum by their own efforts for their specific needs. In the sparsely inhabited areas—though not only there—teachers sometimes expect, and regret, that all curriculum development and new syllabuses will be handed down to them from a distant "establishment"—often ill defined—which they are not able to influence.

The Aberdeen approach is illustrated by work with a small combined primary-secondary school, Leurbost, in the Western Isles. Leurbost requested help to develop a study of the local environment. As it happened, the college tutor was a specialist with a knowledge of fieldwork techniques, historical geography, and geology, and had studied Gaelic at evening classes in Aberdeen. The tutor used part of a holiday to make a reconnaissance of the area to gain a reasonably comprehensive background on the landscape. A photographic record of the area around the school was made.

At the beginning of the school term a visit was paid to the school for detailed discussion. The project was envisaged as continuing over several years to build up a picture of the area based on information gathered directly from pupils at school and from other local sources. The school specifically sought help in presenting material cartographically and in fieldwork techniques.

The school-based support extended over one week, and comprised the production of an outline syllabus; visits with the teacher and pupils to appreciate the potential of the immediate area; and techniques of fieldwork, sketching, and mapping. A large-scale map was made of a croft visited. The influence of physical factors on land use and of physical environment in relation to settlement were shown by mapping a typical croft of the Leurbost stretch of coast. The effects of climate on many aspects of the Leurbost environment, past and present, were also investigated with the pupils.

Although the project was largely a success, one of the practical problems was the limited time available for extended discussion with teachers. Ways of overcoming this drawback, given the unfavorable budgetary situation throughout Scotland, are the subject of continuing discussion.

Teacher Support through Correspondence Courses: One Example

To help teachers respond to curriculum changes, a course titled "Management of a Geography Department" was offered by Dundee College of Education. The course originally required attendance at the college. However, the enrollment was six, far below the number required to operate a workshop course successfully. Although it was known that teachers wanted this course, it had also become clear that a traditional campus-based course would not be able to meet the demand.

Could the course be taken to the teachers by sending it through the mail? What difference would it make to enrollment if it could be provided in this way? A letter of explanation of the course was sent to school geography departments outlining the proposed five workshop exercises and offering a choice of method of participation. The five themes were the role of the head of department; timetabling and staff management; induction of new teachers; courses and resources; and assessment of materials and pupil performance. The study methods offered were individual; school-based group (i.e., momentum coming from a group of teachers); or school-based in-service (i.e., momentum coming from visits to school by college staff).

The estimate of need for the course was confirmed when, under the new proposals, the enrollment reached seventy-six. The majority of teachers chose to do the exercises individually; six schools wished to operate school groups; and three schools asked for school-based in-service. Not surprisingly, many of the teachers who chose (or perhaps felt compelled) to operate as individuals were those in small rural schools.

The design of the course was greatly altered to suit the new form of presentation. The final design comprised a memorandum to the head of the Dundee geography department from the head teacher requesting information on a particular topic; guidelines for action produced by the college's head of department; and a return communication from the head of department to the head teacher. Each exercise was sent out fortnightly. Teachers were happy doing the course in their own time and commented, "the course did not commit teachers to *x* nights in the College during some very inclement weather, and allowed freedom to complete assignments at times suited to their other commitments"; "the topic was presented in such a way that each idea had to be carefully analysed before responding, and unformulated or woolly thoughts were disposed of." This type of course allowed the teacher to tackle work when time was available. Teachers in isolated situations, with no direct and easy contact with advisors or colleges, had finally found a means of getting some of the help they desired.

The experience of providing a correspondence-based in-service course has demonstrated a number of things. The aims must be explicit, guidelines must be concise yet detailed, reference resources available should be listed, technical terms must be explained and understood, and the questions must be precise and clear. Perhaps most important of all, the time allowed for the completion of each exercise and subsequent response from the college must be reasonable. Introductory and follow-up meetings with the course members as a group would be beneficial. Much is demanded of the organizers in preparation time, correction time, and the collating of responses. Secretarial assistance is essential.

As a result of its experience in this course, the Dundee College geography department is planning a pilot whole-session course, "Preparation and Assessment of Structured Materials for the Geography Classroom," which if successful will be offered by other colleges of education in Scotland as a correspondence course for teachers in their areas. This course anticipates an increased emphasis in Scotland on school-based syllabuses and assessment.

Teacher Support by Her Majesty's Inspectors of Schools

Scottish education is provided by national and local government in partnership. As noted earlier, central government does not manage schools, nor engage teachers, nor prescribe curricula. The responsibility for the provision of education rests with the regional education authorities. However, the secretary of state, directly and through a national consultative committee, gives guidance to the regions on staffing, the development and balance of the curriculum, organization of courses, and teaching methods.

HM Inspectors of Schools are appointed by Her Majesty on the recommendation of the secretary of state. They have the right to enter schools and one of their principal functions, through the evidence which they gather from their inspections, is to advise the secretary of state on a wide spectrum of education issues. Their advice is also regularly available to regional authorities and individual schools.

Changes which the regions propose to make in their schemes of educational provision (for example, proposals to close a small school) require the approval of the secretary of state. Evidence of consultation with parents is insisted upon. In reaching his decisions the secretary of state has the advice of HM Inspectors of Schools. As a result of their advice, certain conditions may be stipulated. For example, a condition of the approval of the reorganization of secondary education in the Western Isles a few years ago was that the island council should set up a curriculum control group to harmonize courses and review staffing in the various small secondary schools so that the curriculum in each school would be sufficiently broad and comparable.

To give coherence to their policies for rural areas, to perform their roles in the field and maintain links with other national and international activities, there is a committee of HM Inspectors of Schools for sparsely populated areas under the chairmanship of the chief inspector of the northern division.

Each year the management plan of the inspectors includes the inspection of schools in sparsely populated areas. For the purpose of inspection Scotland is split into three territorial divisions: north, west, east. Most HM Inspectors of Schools are stationed so as to facilitate inspection of the sparsely populated areas and liaison with the regional and island authorities. For example, there are bases in Inverness (northwest), Aberdeen (northeast), Galashiels (southeast), and Dumfries and Ayr (southwest).

One of the inspectors based at Inverness has a special responsibility for Gaelic, and two of the inspectors based in Inverness speak Gaelic. Much of the inspection of schools in the sparsely populated territories is carried out by area surveys. This allows inspectors to take local circumstances into account; to form a comprehensive view of the quality of accommodation, resources, and teacher support provided by the regions; to consider liaison between schools and communities; and to assess transition from one stage of education to another (e.g., primary-secondary). Between 1971 and 1977 reports by inspectors on education in all the pre-1975 education authority areas were published; these included the sparsely populated areas.[2] Among the territories further inspected since then have been Shetland, part of Orkney, the Caithness and Lochaber districts of Highland, and the island of Skye.

The most direct support by HM Inspectors of Schools to teachers is through the detailed discussions which take place during and after inspection. The work of the school is debated with the head teacher and senior staff. In the case of very remote schools, for example small schools on isolated islands, the inspector establishes by telephone or letter whether there are any particular matters of organization or curriculum which teachers wish to discuss so that he may render the greatest help. Discussions between inspectors and teachers are full and frank. They manage to be so partly because inspectors are not responsible for any assessment of individual teachers which affects initial certification as a teacher, promotion, or salary.

Inspectors follow up their area and school inspections with the regional director of education and his advisors. At this more strategic level, the particular needs of the schools and the areas are analyzed, and ways in which these needs may be met are considered. For example, recent inspections of primary schools in part of the Highland region indicated particular uncertainties in the approaches to mathematics with the youngest pupils, and the region is now cooperating with Aberdeen College of Education to provide school-based support in that part of the curriculum.

Again, the analysis of needs may lead to the formation of working parties and development groups. For example, at the time of writing, the Highland region in collaboration with HM Inspectors of Schools has established working parties in science, mathematics, and the social subjects of the secondary school curriculum. Teachers in these working parties are being selected so that the different geographical areas and the different types of schools can be effectively represented.

In Tayside, inspectors have investigated various modes of deploying support personnel for art, music, and physical education, and have presented a comparative analysis to the region, enabling them to retain the best features at a time of financial constraint. Other issues which arise from inspection include the use of facilities and resources, deployment of support staff, and links between primary and secondary schools.

Inspectors also have close links with the colleges of education which provide preservice and in-service training for teachers and are financed by the Scottish education department. The chief inspector of each territorial division, in conjunction with a centrally based chief inspector who has overall responsibility for teacher training, promotes liaison between the colleges and the regional authorities, and helps national and regional committees for in-service training to establish priorities for courses and conferences. Specialist inspectors have direct liaison with particular departments in the colleges.

The development of school-based support for teachers and the deployment of college staff as field tutors outlined above have been specifically encouraged by HM Inspectors, as is shown by this extract from a contribution by the chairman of the committee on education in sparsely populated areas to a meeting of the northern area coordinating committee for in-service training:

> My concern is with the quality of liaison between the College and the Authorities; in-service training is a major expression of the quality of co-operation.
> What do I see?
> One college; five education Authorities—Grampian, Highland, Shetland, Orkney, Western Isles. Four Authorities out of the five with limited resources of their own for giving support to teachers. Much of the territory at a considerable distance from the college. And much of that territory is remote and sparsely populated. The sum of these features, for many teachers, is ISOLATION. These teachers deserve the opportunity for in-service training; for them, it may have to take less conventional forms. Those who teach in primary schools, responsible as they are for the total curriculum and for total relationships with children, have very great needs. The certainty of so much attention to secondary schools must not obscure the needs of primary education.
> What more do I want to see?
> An even better joint college-authority means of analysing in-service needs. An even more effective joint college-authority assessment of priorities. A measure of positive discrimination in favour of the more remote schools and areas. A recognition that school-based in-service training has very many advantages, and is there to stay. A planned relation of school-based to college-based training. A brief word about some of these, with an attempt to show that they are inter-related:
> We do not often achieve a patient, close analysis of needs. Without in any

way under-rating our present endeavours I think that they are often, in good faith, made on behalf of teachers rather than by teachers. Some years ago, in a different part of the country, and in a particular group of primary schools, it was established to my satisfaction that an accurate analysis of the teachers' needs required above all that there be a sustained relationship and contact between the teachers and those who were drawing together the needs. The teachers themselves did not claim to know their own greatest needs at the first time of asking.

Headteachers, too, acknowledged the need for help from people with a comparative experience of schools. Some education authority advisers meet all these criteria, but I remind you that at present there are few of them operating in large parts of the territories we have in mind. Because they are few, their duties tend to be thinly and miscellaneously spread and they are not always able to maintain that continuity of relationship with schools which I aver is the necessary basis for the accurate analysis of needs.

It is possible that, selectively, some of the best equipped members of the college staff could, with the agreement of education authorities, be deployed so as to help in the analysis and confirmation of needs. The major way in which the in-service training needs of teachers would then be met would be by the school-based mode. These efforts can only be successful when what is being done and where is fully agreed with the education authorities.

I encourage the formulation of an overall plan of priorities, not just year by year, probably over a longer period, which is jointly agreed between colleges and authorities. As school-based training develops, only such a plan will make sense of increased demands year by year from all the authorities. Not all needs will be able to be met in any one year. There must also be evaluations, in which teachers participate and to which they indisputably assent.

There are important consequences of this view. There are implications for the type of appointment made to the college of education and the type of work they do; there should be prospects of joint arrangements between authorities and colleges for employing staff of promise on short, flexible contracts; above all there is the implication that headteachers, heads of department, and promoted staff generally must develop a responsible democratic analysis of the needs of individual teachers for in-service training.

There is much more to be said. But I asked you to accept limitations. My predominant theme is that in the north, north-east and north-west of Scotland we have not just a particular opportunity but an inescapable obligation to promote in-service training for teachers who work at a distance from ready resources.

Notes

1. One of the ironies of the "small school problem" in Scotland is that it is becoming an urban as well as a rural concern. In fact, the most rapidly declining

enrollments and the greatest staffing problems have occurred in the largest urban areas. Thus, the most intense political and educational controversies surrounding school closures in the 1980s may not take place in the countryside, but rather in the cities.

2. These reports are available through HM Stationery Office. *Education in Sutherland* (1974), *Inverness* (1974), and *Argyll* (1972) are of particular interest.

5

Putting the Outback into the Forefront: Education Innovations in Western Australia

Max Angus, Michael Williams, R. Hillen, and Glen Diggins

I

RURAL EDUCATION IN WESTERN AUSTRALIA

Western Australia is by far the largest state of the commonwealth of Australia, occupying 2.5 million square kilometers, an area approximately the same as Western Europe. In contrast to its vast size, its population is a mere 1.2 million people. Moreover, a demographic sketch of Western Australia shows that almost 90 percent of this population is concentrated within 400 kilometers of Perth, the capital city (see Figure 1). The remaining 180,000 people thus occupy almost 90 percent of the state's area. In this sparsely populated 90 percent of the land mass, the average population density is less than one person per 10 square kilometers. Some areas, of course, have much lower population densities. The shire of Sandstone, for example, has an average of one person to every 400 square kilometers.

Thus, Western Australia's vast expanse, small population, and uneven distribution of people combine to make provision of community services, including education, a difficult and expensive undertaking. Not unexpectedly, therefore, education in sparsely populated areas is a topic of great interest and relevance in this state.

This chapter will briefly describe the educational provisions specifically designed to accommodate the special needs of people in sparsely populated areas. Included here are such items as school transportation, boarding, the Western Australian Correspondence School, and the Schools of the Air.

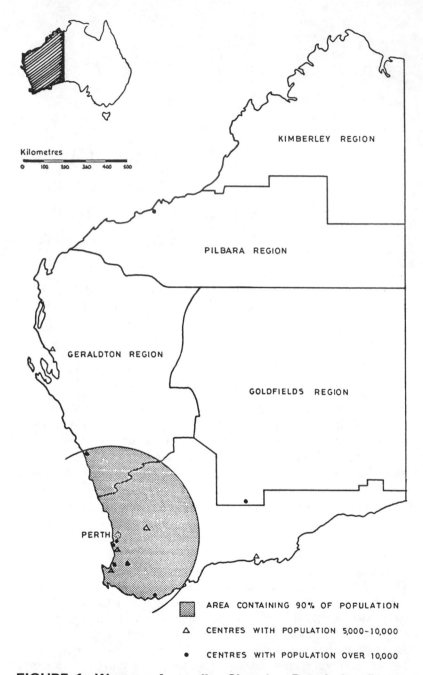

Kilometres

0   100   200   300   400   500

KIMBERLEY REGION

PILBARA REGION

GERALDTON REGION

GOLDFIELDS REGION

PERTH

AREA CONTAINING 90% OF POPULATION

△   CENTRES WITH POPULATION 5,000-10,000

●   CENTRES WITH POPULATION OVER 10,000

FIGURE 1 Western Australia, Showing Population Distribution in Relation to Educational Regions in Sparsely Populated Areas.

However, the second and greater part of this chapter will be devoted to a more detailed examination of two very recent (and very promising) rural education innovations. The first is the Isolated Students Matriculation Scheme, which enables students living in remote areas to complete their year 11 and 12 studies at home, rather than having to either stop their schooling or accept a boarding arrangement. The second innovation is the Chidley Education Centre, which was created to diagnose and remedy special learning difficulties for rural children lacking access to such assistance in their home areas.

Overview of Educational Problems and Provisions

In an area as large as the sparsely populated area of Western Australia, it is not surprising that there exist diverse groupings of people with different patterns of settlement and life-style. Each group presents to educators its own set of needs and problems, and thus educational provisions for each group tend to differ.

For instance, the Kimberley region comprises mainly stations (ranches) and mission settlements plus small iron ore mine sites. Its major towns are commercial and administrative by nature. The Pilbara region, on the other hand, has seen a rapid influx of population since the 1960s to service a rapidly growing mining industry. Thus, in addition to established administrative and agricultural townships, the Pilbara has been characterized by mushrooming new ports and mining towns. By contrast, the Eastern Goldfields, with its nickel and gold mining industry, is suffering serious depletion of population, with only the few older established administrative towns maintaining their population.

Thus, it is appropriate to distinguish three categories of inhabitants of these sparsely populated areas, namely:

1. isolated families living on stations (ranches) and farms, or on settlements such as construction camps or fishing bases;
2. residents of towns and settlements; and
3. minority ethnic communities (predominantly aborigines).

For purposes of this chapter, emphasis will be given to children in the first of these categories. This is not to imply that the educational problems of children in the other two categories are any less pressing or important. Rather, each merit the kind of full separate treatment which cannot be given here. In addition, the two innovations highlighted in this report are of particular (although by no means exclusive) relevance to the families of the first category. For these families, isolation is a pervasive feature of life. The following quote from a talk by a parent in this situation illustrates this point.

> Our property is 800 kilometres from Perth, 290 kilometres from Meekatharra, 144 kilometres from the nearest town (if you could call it that), and 64 kilometres from the nearest neighbour. We have no television and no telephone. On the Meekatharra radio network . . . most homesteads are at least 60 kilometres apart, and the distances from Meekatharra range up to 800 kilometres. Some children are as far again from Meekatharra as they are from Perth. Of course, being 60 kilometres from your nearest neighbour does not mean that you are 60 kilometres from a child of your own age or sex. In some instances, though very few, there is more than one family with children of comparable ages living on the same station. Our children are very lucky in this respect. On "Mileura," our home, there are nine children under nine. During the school holidays there are at least fourteen, often more, under twelve. About half are Aboriginal and they all play together. It is marvellous that there are so many, but it is the exception rather than rule in our part of the world. More often, children have to rely on their brothers and sisters for company, and large families seem to be decreasing as fast as boarding fees (for private schools in Perth) go up. You would, of course, realise that when contending with distances of this nature, week-end social activities are rare, so even other adults are seldom seen on regular basis.

As this passage indicates, outside the towns, families tend to be separated by large tracts of arid, uninviting country, divided into pastoral properties which provide an often less than secure living. Isolation from other families, from towns, and from most services is a fact of life for these people. Moreover, despite the uncertainty of commodity prices, poor seasons, and a gradual decline in the nontown rural population, this isolated life-style is expected to continue in Western Australia. Thus, educational provision for isolated children, either in small groups or individually, is of paramount interest and concern to educators.

Not surprisingly, the mere fact of the huge distances separating these people produces many problems which must be considered and overcome by educators. Factors such as the disproportionate cost of providing educational facilities and the difficulty of staffing are important. Similarly, the life-styles and experiences of these children create difficulties of relevancy of educational material. Special provision of educational services is clearly called for in circumstances such as those noted above. Efforts made by the Western Australia Department of Education in this direction will now be examined.

School Transportation Services

If there are 11 or more children living beyond a radius of 4.5

kilometers from the school, a school bus may be used. During 1976 in Western Australia, 700 school buses conveyed 23,000 children more than 80,000 kilometers daily. The service is fully subsidized by the education department and hence there is no fee for travel on the bus.

Parents of children who require transportation submit to the education department a statement outlining their requirements. The application is submitted through a local school bus advisory committee with parent, local government, and school staff membership. It is usually the principal of the school who administers the school bus service and is responsible for discipline on the buses.

A number of factors are taken into account when establishing a bus route. These include length of the route, the number of children under nine years of age, total number of children to be carried on the bus, condition of the road, and the impact of the new service on existing bus services. For instance, rather than stipulate a maximum length of a bus route in terms of distance travelled, the education department has in effect advised schools and bus contractors that no child should spend more than three hours on a bus each day. Nevertheless, there are instances of longer services operating, with some straight runs with secondary school children of up to 130 kilometers. These longer services are usually a result of approaches from parents who prefer that their children travel the longer distance rather than board away from home or use correspondence education.

School bus routes may be altered when extra children arrive in a district or when children leave the school. Deviations may be granted when children live more than 2.5 kilometers from an existing bus service. However, the interests of individual children and the cost involved in providing an additional service must be carefully weighed against the consequences of increased travelling time for the bus users.

In addition to these bus services, the education department provides a conveyance allowance to parents who must use private means to convey their children to and from school or to the existing bus route.

Facilities for Boarding away from Home

Due to the lack of secondary schools in sparsely populated areas, some children board away from home during the school term. In addition to independent boarding schools, most of which are in Perth, students can stay in hostels organized by the education department.

As Figure 2 shows, there were sixteen hostels, two established in Perth and the others in country towns. All but two are controlled by the Country High Schools Hostel Authority. They are run by local committees which, as a result of authority policy, enjoy a high degree of autonomy in staff recruitment, salaries, and conditions. Nevertheless, parents and the committee can

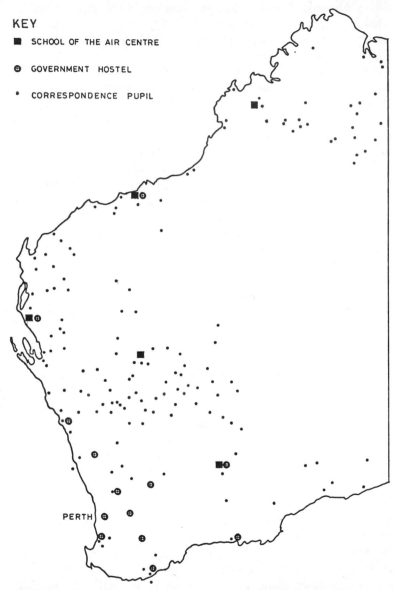

FIGURE 2 Western Australia, Showing Position of Hostels, Schools of the Air, and Correspondence School Pupils.

approach the authority with their problems. A warden or supervisor directs activities of ancillary staff, administers the hostel, and provides for the welfare of students.

Most hostels are coeducational, with girls and boys able to mix socially and in recreational activities. Hostels generally have facilities for sports and hobbies and organize programs of socials, dances, and outings. Students are supervised for study on most evenings and it is not unusual for teachers from the local high school to undertake the supervision.

Hostel fees vary from $A975 to $A1,395 per year and are subject to revision by the education department. The federal government offers assistance to parents of children who do not have reasonable access to a government school providing suitable courses. This assistance takes the form of a boarding allowance of up to $A500 per child annually, regardless of family income, supplemented by additional allowances of up to $A450, inversely related to the parents' incomes. Special grants of up to $A550 may be made in cases of extreme economic hardship. In addition, the state government offers parents a further $A150 per child annually.

Recently there has been a trend toward decreased hostel enrollments. At present, a little less than 80 percent of the 1,400 hostel places have been filled. Apart from the decline in some rural incomes since the early 1970s and continued increase of hostel fees, a number of factors help account for this drop in hostel enrollments. These include:

1. improved school bus services;
2. the preference of some parents to supervise their children at home (this option may have become more attractive to parents or senior students since the establishment of the Isolated Students Matriculation Scheme);
3. the decision by some older students to work on their parents' farming properties at a time when labor is relatively expensive; and
4. the construction of new high schools in towns in the Pilbara and the Goldfields.

Although parents who live beyond the range of school bus services may decide to send their children away to school, few do so until the children are old enough to attend a secondary school. The majority of isolated children study at home until they have finished the equivalent of year 7, and even subsequent to this, many undertake secondary studies at home. The Western Australian Correspondence School provides courses from years 1 to 10 for students who do not have access to schools, while five Schools of the Air enable two-way radio communication between teachers and isolated students to complement the correspondence courses.

Western Australian Correspondence School

The Western Australian Correspondence School was founded in 1918, when the first group of outback children began to receive correspondence lessons. Enrollments rose from less than 100 in the first year to a peak of 2,162 in 1933. Subsequently, enrollments fell steadily due to the consolidation of schools, improved transportation services, and more generous government financial assistance for parents who sent their children away to school. The last two decades have brought a levelling out of enrollments, annual numbers being between 400 and 600 primary students and approximately 100 secondary students. The distribution of students throughout the state is shown in Figure 2.

The Western Australian Correspondence School primary courses include reading, spelling, English, writing, mathematics, social studies, art, and religious studies. Secondary school courses, all approved by the board of secondary education, are English, mathematics, social studies, and science (the core subjects) and art, health education, bookkeeping, and commerce.

Lesson sheets and other printed material are divided into twenty sets of work, which students are required to complete and forward for marking every two weeks. These lesson sheets incorporate suggestions from parents and teachers. Most textbooks are written by the staff of the education department's curriculum branch and are issued free to students. In addition to written materials, students now work with audio cassettes, slides and filmstrips, and video equipment, enabling the development of a greater range of skills.

Supervision of students' work is an important element of correspondence education. One in six isolated families employs a governess for this purpose, although financial constraints typically prevent parents from employing supervisory help. Thus, most correspondence students are supervised by their mothers. Some parents find supervision of correspondence lessons quite demanding due to lack of training, other work pressures, and the emotional bonds between parent and child.

Prompt return of marked lessons to students from the correspondence school is an essential part of the learning process but one which is fraught with difficulties. Dependence on mail deliveries makes the arrangement susceptible to unexpected disruptions. For instance, some mail is lost in transit, necessitating duplication of work. In some parts of the Kimberleys and Pilbara, there are no mail services at all and residents receive mail only when they travel to the nearest town, which may be 300 kilometers away.

Western Australian Correspondence School staff are selected on the basis of their interest in correspondence education and their ability to relate to isolated children in a correspondence teaching program. Appointments are for relatively short terms (up to two years) to ensure that staff have had recent, relevant classroom experience. Many of the fifty-four professional staff are engaged in course revision and development, with particular emphasis on the preparation of useful, attractive materials.

Correspondence education has a necessary and continuing role in Western Australian education. While it is unlikely that significant growth will occur in this state's isolated rural population in the foreseeable future, it is equally improbable that the children of the scattered ranchers, miners, roadworkers, and hunters who compose the correspondence school's clientele will decline greatly in number.

The Schools of the Air

Schools of the Air are small units located in regional towns. They are classed as primary schools and are staffed by one or two teachers. They provide direct communication, through a two-way radio system, between 55 percent of families with children in correspondence courses and their correspondence school teacher. Their location is indicated on Figure 2.

The main functions of the Schools of the Air are to develop and supplement the correspondence courses in each subject area and to provide experiences in areas not covered by the established courses. In addition, assistance is given to supervisors in such aspects of their task as teaching techniques, daily lesson plans, and assignment completion.

Only primary students may enroll in these schools. Groups of five to ten pupils from each year level have a half-hour lesson each day, during which time they may listen and talk to their teacher and to each other. This enables more rapid feedback than the mail system and children gain a group identity. In addition, parents' queries, oral reports, and examination of selected students may occur.

There are many schemes aimed at extending the quality of service provided by the Schools of the Air. For instance, to assist families in providing transmitters, cheaper sets licensed only for Schools of the Air are available. Alternatively, families may apply to join a transceiver leasing scheme.

Another useful adjunct to the Schools of the Air is the itinerant teacher. This teacher, by visits to isolated children and their families, can provide on-the-spot assistance to pupils which supplements both correspondence school mail and School of the Air broadcasts. Additionally, the principals or teachers in charge of the Schools of the Air have been given in-service experience in the use of audiovisual aids and tape-recorded materials with the correspondence sets so that, in turn, parents could be helped to gain experience in the use of such aids. Also, to encourage teachers to apply for the position of teacher in charge, the status of the schools has recently been upgraded.

In addition to School of the Air broadcasts, many isolated children listen to the Correspondence Schools of the Air and other school programs, which are broadcast by the Australian Broadcasting Commission. Although reception problems are encountered in some areas and a few families do not have radios, a wide coverage of the state has been achieved with these programs.

II

THE ISOLATED STUDENTS MATRICULATION SCHEME

Background

Australia's education system is divided into four stages: a preprimary year, optional for five-year-olds; seven primary years, known as years 1 to 7; five secondary years, comprising years 8 to 12; and a postsecondary or tertiary stage. Attendance at school is compulsory from the beginning of the year in which a child turns six until the end of the year in which he turns fifteen. Thus, a child usually proceeds to at least year 10, and somewhat more than half of the year 10 students proceed to year 11. In addition, technical and further education is available for students who have completed their compulsory schooling but elect not to proceed to year 11.

On completion of year 10, students receive an achievement certificate based on school assessments and awarded by a central body, the board of secondary education. The only external examinations are held at the end of year 12, and are intended to determine the eligibility of students to enter tertiary institutions. These are Western Australia's Tertiary Admissions Examinations (TAE). Over half of year 12 students proceed to postsecondary education. Year 12 students also receive a certificate of secondary education which is based on a combination of TAE results and school assessments. Like the achievement certificate, it is awarded by the board of secondary education.

Although education is a state government responsibility, a dual system of government and nongovernment schools has developed. Of Western Australia's 400,000 students, 80 percent attend government schools, which are free, secular, and open to all. The majority of nongovernment schools are Roman Catholic, and all receive financial assistance from the state and federal governments. The education department of Western Australia operates government schools and provides extensive support services at both the central and regional levels.

More than 600 schools are maintained by the education department, and one-quarter of these have a secondary component. Secondary schools are mainly confined to towns of more than 500 people, but primary schools have been established in even the smallest pockets of settlement. In larger centers, high schools and senior high schools enroll students in years 8 to 10 and 8 to 12, respectively. District high schools are located in smaller country towns, and consist of a combined primary and lower secondary school, usually admitting students up to year 10. Rarely does the secondary student enrollment in a district high school exceed 150.

The Isolated Schools Matriculation Project was established in 1974 by the education department of Western Australia as part of an initiative to increase the range of educational opportunities available to rural residents. The major aim of the project was to develop modern correspondence courses for rural matriculation students—students studying for the examinations which permit entry into tertiary institutions. Acknowledgment of the project's importance was given at the federal level by the schools commission, which supplemented the state's allocation of funds to the project during 1974 and 1975 and again in 1977 through 1979. Six highly qualified and experienced teachers were appointed to begin the preparation of courses for matriculation students in sparsely populated areas. The project evolved into the Isolated Students Matriculation Scheme.

This scheme was to develop and evaluate curriculum materials, including student guides, that would enable students to master matriculation level subjects without immediate access to continuing specialized teacher support. It was recognized that the scheme must include an effective structure for dispatching course materials and returning student work. Tutorial support for students with learning difficulties was also necessary. It was expected that the enrollments would consist of two categories of students who wished to pursue their matriculation studies while living at home. There would be those who lived near a district high school and who therefore had access to resources such as the school library. However, the school would not be able to offer matriculation instruction for reasons of economy. The second group would consist of truly isolated students who lived on farms and in tiny communities and who thus had no access to secondary schools near their homes.

A group of subjects that would satisfy matriculation requirements as well as varied interests was chosen for development. However, the subjects also had to be practically viable under correspondence conditions. For example, the practical problems of providing extensive and complicated laboratory equipment to a small number of students prevented the inclusion of the physical sciences, although the biological sciences could be represented. For these reasons, English, history, economics, human biology, two mathematics courses, technical drawing, and art were included in the scheme.

Students in small rural towns and on pastoral properties, with few peers of comparable age, have special social needs. For these students to be educated in the fullest sense it is important that they associate with peers and acquire social skills such as cooperating, mixing, and learning to be leaders and followers as various situations demand. In order to meet these needs, it was proposed that students integrate with their peers at residential camps and on other occasions.

Students were to be assisted to acquire study habits for each subject that would enable them to work without supervision. Attention would be given to this need in a student's course by tutors and other staff engaged in the scheme.

It was believed that the scheme would have a profound effect on secondary education in Western Australia, since it constitutes an alternative route to matriculation. In the longer term, the scheme could also provide options for schools in larger centers which have so few students wishing to study a particular subject that conventional instruction is not possible. The scheme makes individualized study by senior students a realistic prospect.

Organization of the Scheme

Since the establishment of the Isolated Students Matriculation Scheme (ISMS) in 1974, a program for producing curriculum materials and providing learning support has been developed. In this section, the organization as it existed in 1979 is described with only limited reference to the changes which have occurred.

ISMS operates as a special school attached to the head office of the education department. It is funded by the state government with minor contributions from the federal government through the Joint Country Disadvantaged Schools Programme. More than $A500,000 was allocated from the state budget in the 1978-79 financial year for recurrent expenditure, supplemented by a further $A7,500 from the federal program.

Throughout 1974 and 1975, the scheme was directed by the superintendent of the research branch of the education department. Weekly meetings were held to discuss progress, make recommendations, and develop ISMS policy. An education officer of the research branch was appointed to look after such specific management areas as access to typists, obtaining research materials, purchase of resources and equipment, and liaison between the scheme and other branches of the education department. Since the beginning of 1976, the scheme has been managed by a senior education officer who was selected from the original staff team. Staff are employed by the education department and are classified as education officers, tutors, or ancillary staff. The 1979 staff comprises three education officers, seventeen tutors and four ancillary staff.

Education officers undertake course development work under the control of the curriculum branch of the education department. They are senior teachers selected by senior education department officers with respon-

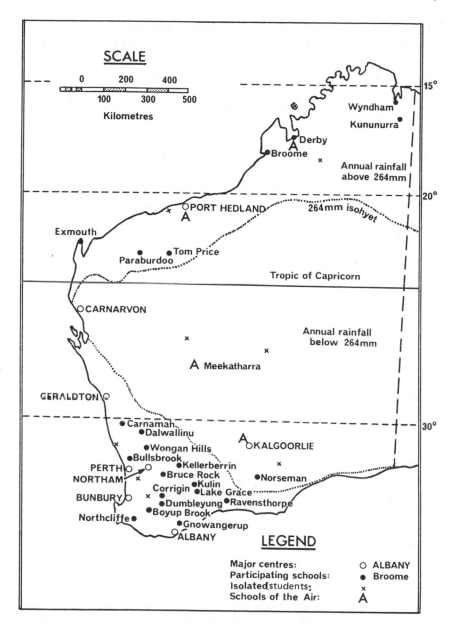

FIGURE 3 Map of Western Australia, Indicating the Location of Students Participating in the Isolated Students Matriculation Scheme in 1979.

sibilities in various subjects on the basis of their qualifications, experience, and writing skills. Two or three years is the usual term of appointment for an education officer. During this time, the officer is involved in writing and producing course materials and in course evaluation.

Tutors are qualified teachers appointed to support students enrolled in the scheme. They correct student work and correspond with individual students taking a particular subject. It is their responsibility to monitor students' progress and to provide encouragement. Tutors also contribute significantly to course evaluation and revision since they have the most contact with students.

Some tutors accept the additional role of regional tutor, taking responsibility for the overall progress of students within one of eight geographical regions of Western Australia. A regional tutor has an important part to play in the social, as well as academic, development of ISMS students. This person not only monitors the general progress of students but also arranges contact between students, parents, and teachers in a region.

Each tutor specializes in one subject area and supervises all students taking that subject at either the year 11 or year 12 level. Selection of tutors for the scheme is the subject superintendent's prerogative. Tutors are expected to demonstrate a commitment to rural education, teaching skill, patience, and a sense of humor. They, like education officers, are usually appointed for two or three years.

Ancillary staff includes typists, a teacher aide, and a clerical assistant, all of whom are instrumental in the efficient routine operation of the organization. In addition to typing, the ancillary staff maintains the stock of curriculum materials, keeps records, dispatches mail, and undertakes general clerical duties.

The ISMS staff is located at a government primary school in Perth, where vacant classrooms have been converted into offices and other facilities. A dispatch and typists' room, a storeroom and recording room, and a student classroom are included. The students' room contains art, science, and drawing facilities as well as carrels for quiet study. As many as five students can use the facility at once.

The Scheme in Practice

The Isolated Students Matriculation Scheme has entailed both the development of curriculum materials and the subsequent implementation of courses. At present, materials for economics, biology, and physical science are being developed by the scheme's three education officers, but work on other subjects has concluded, apart from minor revision by tutors. Major aspects of the scheme are outlined below.

Curriculum Development

A common matriculation syllabus exists for each subject studied at the year 11 and 12 levels in Western Australia. The main problem in curriculum development, then, was to prepare or adapt materials which would enable students working in isolation to meet the requirements of existing syllabi.

Examination of existing correspondence material was undertaken in the second half of 1974. During this period, the original project team also familiarized themselves with recent developments in audiovisual learning techniques. Areas of the state in which the scheme was likely to operate were visited by the team, so that problems caused by isolation could be anticipated. The results of these investigations guided the team in the production and use of learning materials.

Printed materials form the basis of ISMS learning materials. Subjects are developed around existing textbooks, which are purchased by students and supplemented by printed ISMS material. Material to compensate for sections of the syllabus not covered satisfactorily in texts is developed by the education officers.

A looseleaf format is used so that revision can be undertaken easily. Students are provided with binders in which to store their materials. Printing is carried out on small offset machines, with color being achieved either through black ink on colored paper or colored ink on white or colored paper. Printing runs are sufficient for two years' needs. Printed materials, including binders, are retained by the students.

It was recognized that the production of printed and audiovisual materials required extensive quality control. The publications and audiovisual branches of the education department were involved through their respective superintendents. Subject superintendents personally contributed to the exercise by examining materials and suggesting improvements. Advisory staff of the curriculum branch also assisted in the development of audiovisual materials in certain subjects.

Audiovisual materials include audio cassettes, filmstrips, and slides. Each student is loaned a cassette recorder, a set of headphones, and a slide/filmstrip viewer. The extent to which use is made of these materials varies from subject to subject. Both audio and audiovisual teaching materials have been developed, and other materials are provided for enrichment or motivation. Where suitable, reasonably priced, commercially produced material exists, it is incorporated into the scheme.

Although prerecorded cassettes have been effective generally, students have suggested some ways in which they are inferior to printed materials. One complaint is that students require uninterrupted time to play through a cassette, whereas one may skim through a book at one's own pace. Also, a student cannot easily highlight important points on a cassette or readily turn from one section to another and back again. The student is controlled by this medium to a greater extent than by print.

Experimentation was carried out to determine the extent to which the cassette could be used for communications. It was found that students could use cassettes effectively to record messages to their tutors, and, in so doing, enhance personal contact.

After use by students, teaching cassettes are returned and erased. Each cassette then has a new program recorded onto it. In this way, each cassette is used three or more times a year. Voices used on the recordings include those of the writer, other teachers, or guests. Professional announcers also have been used.

Filmstrips or slides are prepared by the audiovisual branch of the educational department, which also provides photographers when needed. The artists of the publications branch are available for art work.

Course Implementation

Information about enrollment in ISMS is sent through the schools (including the correspondence school) in the October preceding a particular year. Local newspapers carry advertisements for the scheme. As in any school, student enrollments are accepted throughout the year, although most occur before the beginning of the school year in February.

Any student who has completed year 10 and who does not have reasonable access to a senior high school is eligible for enrollment. It is recommended that students who enroll have at least average year 10 grades. Those applicants with lower grades will be counselled by ISMS staff to consider carefully the possibility that they might not have the capacity to matriculate; but, if they wish to enroll, they may do so.

Almost three-quarters of the 150 students enrolled with ISMS in 1979 have access to a district high school. Twenty-two district high schools are participating in the scheme and have made library and study facilities available. Regional tutors maintain liaison with district high school principals to clarify the relationship between the ISMS students and the schools. Students are expected to exercise discretion and responsibility, since they are not supervised or directed by the school staffs.

Students come from a variety of home backgrounds. Some families are financially destitute, while others could afford to send their children to boarding school if they chose. In some instances, the home situation might constitute an obstacle to study, as in the case of two students who do not have electric lights in their isolated homestead.

The group contains a substantial proportion of older students (23 out of 150). Like their younger counterparts, these students have opted to study five matriculation subjects over a period of two years. Students are sometimes advised to extend this to three years by ISMS staff.

One may speculate why more than 80 percent of the scheme's students are female. Perhaps one factor is that parents are still more inclined to send their sons rather than their daughters away to boarding school. An associated factor may be that girls are more likely than boys to remain at home beyond the school-leaving age, despite the difficulties that young, single females are experiencing in obtaining employment. Among the group there is also a proportion of unmarried mothers, five in 1979. Without a scheme of this type, matriculation studies might be impossible for them.

Approximately 25 to 30 percent of the students withdraw by the end of their year 11 course. However, few withdrawals occur among year 12 students.

An orientation camp is held during the first ten days of the school year for year 11 students and new year 12 students. All students are brought to Perth, at no expense to themselves, and accommodated in residential facilities provided by the education department. During this camp, many activities are undertaken. For example,

1. Students are introduced to the working operation of the scheme. Roles of tutors and regional tutors, arrangements for dispatch and return of materials, personal schedule guidance, and the use and maintenance of audiovisual equipment are all explained.
2. Students are familiarized with the content and presentation of each subject area and given guidance concerning final course selection.
3. Students start work on the first units of the subjects they have selected. Textbooks may be purchased through the scheme bookshop. Year 12 students who do not attend camp receive a program of work before school begins. Additional forms of support are presently under consideration.
4. Students get to know their tutors, regional tutor, and the support staff in a live-in situation. All staff spend time overnight at the camps and, as a general rule, are on first-name terms with the students. This policy has assisted in the establishment of sound working relationships between students and tutors.
5. Students get to know each other through carefully designed recreational programs carried out by specialist staff of the physical education branch of the education department.

Once the school year has begun, students send work back to their tutors regularly. Units of study vary in duration from three to ten weeks, depending on the subject. However, work is expected at least once per fortnight and preferably once a week. Postage costs both ways are met by the scheme.

The task of the tutor is to support the student in using the learning materials. For example, additional explanation, either written or recorded on an individual basis, is provided. Of course, the tutor also assesses and records student progress. Usually, student work is corrected and dispatched from the ISMS center within forty-eight hours, although the mail services determine how long it takes for students to receive the processed work.

The learning materials are backed up by collections of reference materials lodged in the libraries of the twenty-two district high schools participating in the scheme. Each collection comprises some 300 reference books and 60 items of audiovisual material, which are available to ISMS students who are affiliated with the district high school. In the case of students remote from these centers, tutors send a suitable range of reference materials with each new study unit.

Places of work vary. Students who live in a locality served by a district high school have access to the resources of the school and some do all their daytime work there. Schools have been generous in their support to students. Schedules have been arranged so that access to laboratory and art facilities is available. Staff have taken a great interest in the progress of students and have frequently been able to solve areas of difficulty. Librarians have been of special help in maintaining the reference material that is housed in the school library. The support and interest of principals has been crucial in district high schools; without it the scheme might not be successful in these localities.

Arrangements vary from student to student and school to school. However, students inevitably do much of their work at home. The typical pattern for ISMS students in district high schools is three days at home and two at school. Of course, students in more remote areas have no choice and must do all their work at home.

A vital part of the scheme is the maintenance of communication between student and tutor. Written communications are employed, but there has also been a significant development in the use of the spoken word. Audio cassettes are exchanged between student and tutor and have opened up fresh avenues for communication. The use of cassettes enables students to request specific assistance and have difficulties explained. The cassettes have been found to be of great value to staff and students alike.

However, neither the written nor cassette communications can solve immediate pressing problems. The telephone is often used by those students with access to it. Principals of district high schools have been generous in allowing students to use the school telephone to assist their progress. Students at home with a connected service may telephone a problem to

ISMS headquarters and receive a return call from their tutors. In this way, student expenses are kept to a minimum.

In March, three weeks after the completion of the orientation camp, students are visited by their regional tutor. The purpose of this visit is twofold. First, tutors discuss progress with students and parents in their home environments. If such visits cannot be undertaken because of the distance involved or time available, some central meeting point is arranged. All students are involved, since this visit is seen as an essential form of support. Second, tutors have discussions with district high school staff, where appropriate, to see that school-student relationships are progressing satisfactorily. During this time, new staff members are also given the opportunity to visit country regions within driving range of Perth so that they can meet students undertaking ISMS courses of study.

The regional tutor is a vital link between the ISMS organization and the student, since he is the person a student approaches regarding course or career advice. He may not be able to help directly, but will know who to approach to get the required assistance.

In May (during the usual two-week school holiday period) a ten-day camp is held for year 12 students. This camp provides an opportunity for concentrated study, when specific difficulties that students might have encountered can be identified and remedied. The camp is also used for career guidance. Visits to tertiary institutions, banks, hospitals, and other places of interest are part of the scheme's career guidance program.

For many year 12 students, this is the first time they have had personal contact with tutors new to the staff. The experience of day-by-day personal attention is valuable, serving both to stimulate students and to provide practical assistance.

The ISMS working year is divided into two semesters. The first semester ends on June 30, and during the final week of the semester all students take examinations. These examinations are part of the scheme's assessment program, the other part being based on the quality of work submitted, throughout the year. A detailed first semester report is received by each student in the first two weeks of July. This report indicates progress and standards of work submitted as well as results in the examinations.

In the third week of July, regional tutors undertake another series of visits to the students within their regions. This visit is similar to the March visit, but reports are also discussed. Overall progress is discussed with students, parents, and, where applicable, district high school principals.

A ten-day camp for year 11 students is run during the first two weeks of August, which is the beginning of spring. This camp has a chiefly practical orientation, where activities beyond the scope of correspondence can be undertaken. For example, biology excursions are carried out and students experience the learning benefits of group discussions. The camp is also a time for renewal of acquaintances — tutor with student and student with student. The motivation value of these days spent together is enormous.

Student visits to ISMS headquarters in Perth may take place at any time of the year and usually extend over one week. The visits give students a further opportunity to overcome difficulties or receive career advice through personal contact with their tutors. A room has been set up at ISMS headquarters where visiting students can work during the day. Normally, students stay with relatives or friends living in Perth, thus reducing expenses. Transportation costs are reimbursed by the government. Regional tutors arrange student visits to the ISMS center.

Early in October, a set of examinations is held for year 12 students. These cover the entire syllabus for each subject, and are seen as a final practice for the Tertiary Admissions Examinations in late November.

In early November, the regional tutors again visit their students. The purpose of this visit is threefold. (1) The tutors give final advice to the year 12 students regarding their Tertiary Admissions Examinations. (2) They provide moral support to year 11 students, who have a tendency at this time of the year to have doubts about the purposes and benefits of their work. This is a difficult time for young people and often they resist the advice and support of their parents. The regional tutor contact, therefore, can be of great benefit. (3) The tutors also interview prospective students and their parents in order to explain the scheme and offer advice on course selection.

Tertiary Admissions Examinations for year 12 students usually commence around November 20. ISMS examinations for year 11 students are conducted at about this time too.

Outcomes of the Scheme

Examination Results

The Isolated Students Matriculation Scheme prepares students for the Tertiary Admissions Examination (TAE). Although increasing numbers of mature-age students are enrolling, there are no plans to divert the scheme from its original purpose at this stage. While it is to be hoped that students will gain self-esteem and social confidence, the main indicator of the scheme's success is academic achievement.

However, it must be recognized that ISMS students constitute a group that differs considerably from the population of students undertaking matriculation studies in schools. In addition to the distinctive home backgrounds of the scheme's students, there are differences in academic preparation. Most of the ISMS group obtained only average year 10 results, although a few were outstanding. By contrast, students who proceed to year 12 in high schools tend to have had above-average results in year 10.

At the time of writing, two groups of students have completed years 11 and 12 and have taken the TAE. The overall performance of these groups has been satisfactory. For example, in 1977 six of the twenty-one students who took the examinations were accepted for tertiary studies, including primary teaching, computer programming, public administration, Asian studies, and psychology. In 1978, of the twenty-five students who took the examinations, at least seven were accepted into tertiary institutions, one student was tied for seventh in the state in the history examinations, and another tied for ninth in the art examination. The progress of these people will be followed with interest, because it is believed that the abilities for individual study developed through ISMS should be of great benefit in tertiary studies.

Student and Parental Evaluation

Throughout the two full years of operation, parents and students have been encouraged to contribute to the development of the scheme. Many letters have been received. Comments have generally been laudatory. For example:

> We [the parents] have nothing but praise for the Scheme to date, and of the dedication of the teachers involved. The personal interest and aid they give is a great encouragement to the students.
>
> It is quite apparent that together with your skill, you have put in much of yourselves by way of your time and encouragement to ensure the best results and opportunity for students.

Suggestions for improvement have also been made:

> We wonder, however, if it would not be a good thing if the students were called upon, say once a month or at least twice a term, by one or some of their tutors—I am inclined to think they are still rather young.
>
> I feel it may help if progress reports were sent to students indicating all other students' progress (comparison). This could be done every month or so and may encourage those who are behind to speed up a bit.

At the end of 1977 and 1978, evaluation questionnaires were sent to all year 12 students. The questionnaires contained fifty items, covering the entire range of the scheme as set out in the foregoing section "The Scheme in

Practice." The following are samples of students' responses:

What social benefits did you experience at camps?

We were able to get to know both tutors and other students, and we learned to speak out about our feelings and the problems we faced in the course. The tutors listened.

. . . meet other students, saw how they looked at life and school, and attitudes towards living in general.

It joined us together; tutors and students.

Did you receive enough staff support?

Whenever we needed help all we had to do was to ask for it and it was provided.

I received a tremendous amount of support from all the tutors. It was this support that helped me to continue with my work. . . .

If we wanted it, it was always there. We were never neglected.

Parents were also asked to comment. Their responses were more general:

We were very pleased with the ISMS course. It allowed _____ to further her education in a home environment—which she wanted—without the hassle of finding during-the-week accommodation. She thoroughly enjoyed the course and we also felt very involved in it. The tutors were great—always helpful and encouraging; treating students as individuals, questions and queries never being a bother to them.

I was satisfied with all aspects of the course and felt _____ applied herself well and the tutors gave their all. I feel the financial assistance given was generous. Despite the TAE results (which were worse than expected), _____'s knowledge greatly increased. Finally, having _____ at home for those important two years while she matured that much was rewarding to us.

I am very pleased that _____ has done these two years with ISMS, it certainly hasn't been two wasted years. I used to worry and think of all the things she was missing out on by not going to boarding school, but the way they have gained knowledge by this method the students are going to remember all they have learnt much longer than by going to an ordinary school.

The only thing that I think might improve the course is when you have your camp in May for the year 12 students you could get a good guidance officer to come and talk to them and provide all the literature about careers.

We appreciate very much what the Scheme has done for _____ over the past two years, I wish it was only the beginning and not the finish.

The responses of both students and parents were generally in favor of the scheme as it operates at present. It was hoped that the questionnaire would point to areas of weakness, but critical comments were rare.

Problems with the Scheme

The scheme has been developed as a worthwhile alternative to traditional upper secondary school education. The features described earlier constitute an extensive framework within which students can receive the instruction and support necessary for success. Despite the scheme's provisions, the nature and conditions of study give rise to some problems which affect isolated students more acutely than their counterparts in secondary schools. Some of these problems are discussed below.

Student Motivation

Motivation in all forms of education is important, and particularly so in correspondence education. Camps, visits, frequent communication, and other measures all help, but without personal drive students are unlikely to have success. Students who enroll should want to succeed.

Social Development

Students working by themselves or in small groups are severely handicapped socially. The social interaction experienced at camps is good for all students, but those students attending large schools daily have an obvious advantage in this regard.

Career Opportunities

Country children throughout Australia generally have less knowledge of available careers than their city peers. The smaller communities covered by ISMS are particularly disadvantaged in this respect. Although the scheme offers career assistance, opportunities for gaining firsthand knowledge are insufficient. This is an area urgently requiring attention.

Nature of ISMS

Not all students complete year 10 with the background of potential for successful matriculation study. Because only matriculation courses have been developed so far, some students find themselves attempting study at a level somewhat beyond their capacity. Nonmatriculation subjects, more suited to this type of student, are now being offered by senior high schools. Extending the range of ISMS subjects to include certain of these nonmatriculation subjects might be beneficial. However, such an extension would significantly alter the accepted function of the scheme and would require a deliberate policy change.

Science

As explained earlier, the physical science area was avoided in the initial subject development and only biological science subjects were prepared. This has led to an imbalance in the range of subjects available. Furthermore, because of the experimental nature of the subject, biology was initially limited to district high school areas. Although all students may now do biology, this means that the only science that students working in total isolation can elect to study is biology.

Revision of the science course is now being undertaken, with the aim of making it widely available to all interested students. A new matriculation subject, called physical science, is being developed by the curriculum branch for secondary schools to provide students with an alternative to physics and chemistry. It is also being adapted for use by ISMS. These initiatives should lead to increased attention by students to the science area in the near future.

Mail Service

All school correspondence operations are limited by the efficiency of their dispatch and retrieval organization. Once material has arrived at its destination, work can proceed, but the period between dispatch and delivery is lost time. Because of the distances involved and, often, weather conditions, delivery of mail to every doorstep is impossible. Delays affect the learning process because, although students can be supplied well in advance with work to be done, the delay of tutor support can often prevent progress.

Possible Future Developments in ISMS

There are many developments in technology which will ultimately affect ISMS. Some of these are discussed below.

Microfiche

The use of microfiche could revolutionize the format of presentation of printed and other visual material. Readers are light and unsophisticated, leading to the benefit that a whole year's course could be dispatched in a small package. The microfiche system may be a significant medium for course presentation if users become familiar with its potential.

Satellite Communications

Advances in communication as a result of satellite networks will have an enormous effect on outback Australia. A task force is currently hearing evidence throughout the country and will make recommendations to the federal government. Should an Australia-wide network be set up, allowing two-way conversations between centrally located tutors and isolated students, the educational benefits for ISMS would be immense. In any case, such systems will undoubtedly affect the way courses are presented.

Local Tutoring

Future technological developments can easily be seen to provide greater flexibility in the presentation of learning materials, but they will require new structures for supporting isolated students. One obvious avenue of development in the support mechanism is the involvement of local specialists as tutors. Such on-the-spot experts would be of great benefit to students, not only because problems could be solved quickly and personally, but also because the education would involve the local community. Identifying suitable people where they exist and developing such arrangements will be a challenge for the future.

Conclusion

The five years of development of the ISMS have been rewarding to all those involved, not only because of the new skills acquired and the sense of achievement felt in seeing one's efforts transformed into printed pages, photographs, or cassette recordings, but particularly because of the close involvement with students. Staff members consider that correspondence teachers tutoring one person at a time have more opportunity to relate personally to their students than do classroom teachers. It is rewarding to be able to give so much of one's self and one's knowledge.

The following guidelines for prospective developers of similar programs emerge from the experience of the ISMS staff:

1. A balanced choice of subjects should be selected for initial preparation.
2. Talented course writers are needed. These people need to be practically oriented.
3. Media should not be too sophisticated for the clientele.
4. An extensive support mechanism should be developed along with course materials. No matter how good the learning materials are, the tutors will still do a large proportion of the teaching.
5. Camps and other opportunities for personal interaction between student and tutor are essential.

6. Where local schools exist, access to their facilities should be arranged. Additional resources provided on site are an advantage.

7. The development of a comprehensive career guidance program to complement the learning program is essential.

III

THE CHIDLEY EDUCATION CENTRE

Background

The Chidley Education Centre is a unique educational innovation in Australia. Since its opening in 1976, it has offered a residential service to children from remote country areas who experience learning difficulties.

The education of children living in isolated locations poses special problems. Of particular importance is the provision of remedial and psychological services to such children. Even in large schools, with specialists in remedial education on the staff, and with access to guidance officers and school psychologists, the diagnosis and remediation of learning difficulties taxes both resources and the classroom teachers. For children in small remote schools, and for children living at home and working on correspondence lessons, problems of diagnosis and remediation are even more acute.

Very often the factors which underlie a learning disability are many and complex. Diagnosis may require sophisticated testing and examination and is very time-consuming. The development of special remediation programs usually requires a full appreciation of the child's learning disabilities, and the necessary resources may not be available even within larger metropolitan schools. There is a growing awareness that these difficulties must be detected and attended to as early as possible in the development of the child. Failure to respond quickly may seriously impair the child's future educational and social attainments.

At present, for financial and logistic reasons, most specialized diagnostic and remediation services are located in the metropolitan area of Perth and, in some instances, in larger country centers. It has been the pattern that children in small country communities and remote areas who suffer from some form of physical or educational handicap must travel, in many cases considerable distances, in order to receive diagnosis and educational assistance. Because the diagnosis and development of individualized remediation programs is complex and time-consuming, parents have been required to stay in Perth, sometimes for extended periods. The Chidley Education Centre has been developed in order to meet the needs of these children and parents.

Structure of the Chidley Education Centre

The Chidley site is located in the Perth suburb of Mosman Park, sixteen kilometers from the city center. Some educators favored a larger country town, closer to the communities that the facility would serve. However, two significant arguments in favor of the Perth location were the proximity to major medical, psychological, education, and other essential services, and an awareness that a more remote location would have made more difficult the recruitment of specialized staff. A further factor is that the students who attend Chidley come from all parts of the state, with the result that a location other than Perth would be less central for many students.

The Centre has been designed and built to avoid the traditional demarcation between home and school. Living and working accommodations have been carefully integrated. The Centre provides residential, remedial, and general educational facilities for a maximum of forty students. In the residential section, there are two cottages which each have a housemother and two live-in staff. Each cottage houses twenty students, five to a divided room.

The involvement of parents is seen as an important function of the Centre. Parents are encouraged to visit at some point during the child's stay. Four units are provided for parents who wish to accompany their children or who wish to participate in the program. Three parents can be accommodated per unit. The cost to the parent for full board is $A5.00 daily, and $A2.50 for each accompanying child. Financial assistance is available on application to the minister of education for those parents who are unable to meet the cost fully.

The remedial section consists basically of a multidisciplinary assessment center, which includes facilities for remedial, psychological, social, and special therapy services. The administration center is located in this section.

The educational complex has been designed along open-plan lines, including spaces of varying size and function, individual study carrels, a library-resource center, seminar rooms, conference rooms, and other specialized facilities. Staff claim that the open design reflects the sense of space with which country children are familiar. It also gives a child who is angry or frustrated by failure the opportunity to walk away to avoid a confrontation and the loss of face. In another part of the Centre there is a hall-gymnasium which can be used as a dining hall, an enclosed swimming pool, and an industrial kitchen.

Staffing

Chidley Centre's professional staff consists of a principal, a psychologist, and seven teachers, one of whom is a physical education specialist. All have had training in special education.

A large support staff is required to effectively manage the operations of the Centre. There are two housemothers, who work from when the children rise at 7:00 a.m. until 9:30 a.m., when lessons begin, and from 3:30 p.m. until 9:00 p.m., the children's bedtime. These women both have had experience as foster mothers, and they stay overnight in quarters above the children's bedrooms to be on call when required. Houseparents and support staff are not necessarily professionally trained. Thus, some children, especially those with behavioral problems, cannot be served adequately within the boarding facilities. These children are referred elsewhere.

Four trainee teachers spend twenty-four hours per fortnight on supervisory duties in return for a single-bedroom furnished apartment and meals. There are also six part-time staff who carry out supervision, mainly on weekends, bringing the total supervisory staff to twelve—a bare minimum in the view of the professional staff.

Each member of the professional and supervisory staff (except the principal, housemother, and psychologist) takes one or two children as their special charges. In this way, each child has a "guardian" in the Centre who acts to some degree as a surrogate parent. The guardians write to parents to reassure them, and keep up contact with children for a time after they leave the Centre. As well, a laundress, contract cook, gardener, maintenance worker, and six cleaners are employed by the Centre. In all, Chidley Centre is staffed by thirty-four professional and support staff.

The Children

One hundred and seventy-eight children attended Chidley in 1976-77. Table 1 indicates the percentage of students originating from each category of primary school and each region of the state. The categories refer to the student enrollment of the school. Schools with more than 300 students are designated class I, those with 100 to 299 are designated class II, those with 26 to 99, class III, and those with 25 students or fewer, class IV. Primary schools with fewer than 100 students are likely to have mixed grades of students (e.g., year 3, 4, and 5 students may be combined to form one class).

The figures in Table 1 provoke some speculation about the nature and consequences of isolation. For example, although 42 percent of Chidley's students came from schools with enrollments of 300 or more, a majority of this group were from the north of the state. In the north, distances between schools of that size are likely to be great, sometimes in excess of 300 kilometers. Despite the fact that these students attended large schools, they lived in relatively small towns that were quite isolated from other population centers. Under these circumstances, access to remedial facilities is extremely difficult.

Table 1

DISTRIBUTION OF CHIDLEY CENTRE STUDENTS, 1976-77,
BY REGION AND SCHOOL SIZE (IN PERCENTAGES)

| Region | Category of School | | | | | | Regional Totals |
	I	II	III	IV	Corres- pondence	Non-Govt.	
Metropolitan	0.6	-	-	-	-	-	0.6
South-West	6.8	6.3	4.0	-	-	1.7	18.8
Wheat-belt	7.4	6.3	4.5	2.3	-	1.2	21.7
Goldfields	1.7	1.2	1.7	-	-	0.6	5.1
Murchison	0.6	-	2.8	-	4.0	-	7.4
North-West	22.3	5.7	4.6	-	1.2	0.6	34.3
Kimberley	2.9	6.8	1.2	0.5	0.6	-	12.0
Total	42.3	26.3	18.8	2.8	5.7	4.1	100.0

Further south, in the southwest and wheat belt regions that lie within 500 kilometers of Perth, provision of resources to assist children with major learning difficulties is still an enormous problem. Again, geographical factors account for this, since in these areas towns, although more numerous, are nevertheless scattered at considerable distances from one another. Unlike northern towns, which tend to be mining or port settlements, many southern towns are small but service a larger, scattered population in surrounding farm districts. The schools in the south may have no greater access to special education resources than the isolated schools of the northwest.

To date, relatively few aboriginal students have been referred to the Centre. Approximately 5 percent of the Centre's enrollments during 1976-77 were aboriginal. Staff have reported a high success rate in overcoming the learning difficulties experienced by this group. This has been attributed in part to the support these children received from parents and local schools.

It may be that so few aboriginal students with learning difficulties are referred because some principals consider that the necessary parental support is not present. Although all aboriginal students referred to the Centre have been admitted, it is apparent that, in some cases, much more support is needed when the child returns home. For instance, one such student attended five different schools in the six months following his three-month stay at Chidley. The follow-up procedures in cases such as this become problematic.

The Program

The Chidley Centre admits students as vacancies arise, so that there is a continuous flow of children in and out of the Centre throughout the year. There are seldom more than five new intakes in a week, except at the beginning of a school term (February, May, and September), when as many as ten may be accepted. All students, therefore, enter an already established social situation, and are buoyed up to some extent by the happy and settled atmosphere. The "experienced" students generally are very sensitive to the newcomers' feelings of homesickness, and help to alleviate the pain of adjustment. A child usually stays at Chidley for three to six months.

Homesickness, perhaps surprisingly, is not a major problem. Typically, the younger students exhibit the symptoms of homesickness in the first week and then settle in rapidly, while the older students tend to be confident initially but occasionally suffer a subsequent bout of depression. In almost three years, only three children have been sent home because they were unable to bear being away from their parents.

Once a child has been at Chidley for two or three weeks, he begins a program which, though individualized, contains five basic steps: assessment and diagnosis, program development, implementation of learning strategies, transition before departure, and follow-up. The delay prior to the program is deliberate, since it enables behavior patterns to become established. It also allows the child to see the doctor and psychologist in a nonthreatening light and to form bonds of familiarity with the teacher.

After the settling-in period, a date is set for a conference between staff and the child's parents, when discussion of his learning difficulties occurs. Parents are invited to stay at the Centre in the assessment week which precedes the conference. During this week, the child is examined by a doctor, who arranges referrals to specialists if necessary, and talks with the child's parents if they are present. Intensive psychological and educational assessments are made during the first four days. All the teaching staff are trained in educational diagnosis and test interpretation. The Centre affords a nearly ideal situation in which to thoroughly assess students. Each teacher takes a group of six or seven students, including one who is new to the Centre. While the other students work on established programs, the teacher can concentrate on diagnostic work for the new student.

The room in which the conferences occur is equipped with closed-circuit television units and a videotape machine. These enable the child's reactions in testing situations (which have been monitored and recorded during the assessment week) to be studied. All staff can view a particular case together and share expertise as well. Similarly, by using the video, the staff can demonstrate to the parents where the difficulty lies. Several of the testing rooms are equipped with one-way mirrors, behind which are situated observation rooms to permit further study by teachers and parents of the child.

The conference at the end of the assessment week pieces together the observations of the various members to ascertain the nature of the learning difficulty. Teaching strategies are discussed, and an indication is given of the probable duration of the child's stay. If the parents are not able to attend, a report is sent to them to obtain their approval and support. The child's school principal also receives a report and is invited to send a teacher to visit the Centre during the last two weeks of the child's program.

Following the week of assessment and diagnosis, the child's teacher prepares a program of learning which the child will undertake at Chidley. Staff monitor the child's progress at all stages, through informal discussions and formal conferences.

Tours to the city, to the beach resorts, and to the zoo are just a few of the aspects of the substantial enrichment program at Chidley. Provided within the Centre are a fully equipped gymnasium and a swimming pool to ensure that the children's recreation time is spent enjoyably, while also assisting them to improve body coordination and to learn various physical skills. The Centre's physical education teacher has devised, and supervises, a structured recreation program. The pool is especially useful to children with physical handicaps.

Children may leave on weekends if they have relations or friends of the family in the metropolitan area. Teachers invite those without city relations to spend at least one weekend at their homes, and regularly take children on weekend excursions.

Parents are welcome to stay at the Centre at any time while their child is there. Usually, though, the parents are only involved in the assessment procedures and in occasional informal visits. Staff encourage parents to include themselves in the remediation process and consider that involvement can obviate feelings of guilt the parents may have for their child's "failure." For some who are diffident about helping their child, it can be encouraging to see that they can be competent with other children at the Centre. Consequently, they then find it easier to teach their own child.

Some parents may be invited to the Centre during the child's stay for specific purposes. For instance, in one interesting case a child had been participating in correspondence school, and his mother had been an important support. There was a need for his mother to learn some new teaching skills before the boy returned home. She was persuaded to teach her son in the Centre's observation room, and staff devised some new, helpful strategies she could use at home. The boy's correspondence school teacher also took part in the program. Other situations in which parents have been asked to return include cases when children have been ill, and some cases when a child's behavior has been inconsistent. Parents provide emotional support to the children and, often, valuable advice to the staff under these circumstances.

Until 1978, the child was returned to his local school with a program "package," which consisted of a detailed four-week program and the initial psychological and educational assessment and support materials. It was hoped that by the end of the month the child's teacher would continue the individualized program himself. However, this approach to follow-up was unsuccessful for various reasons. In a few instances, the package was not used at all, while less than 5 percent of schools returned to Chidley detailed reports about children's progress. Furthermore, children were being assimilated into normal class work instead of continuing with an individualized program. Some teachers reacted unfavorably to the advice; others worked conscientiously with the program package but found it difficult to implement.

Recently a different approach has been adopted, entailing two major changes. Students now experience a transition period prior to their departure from the Centre in which they work with the sorts of resources that are likely to be used in their own schools. In essence, they are weaned off the sophisticated and ample resources of the Centre. The second change is that the child's teacher and, if possible, his principal are invited to Chidley to participate in the transition phase. This has had a number of benefits. Teachers have worked with the Centre's staff, parents have been able to discuss their children openly with the teachers, and the individual children have seen their teachers showing special interest in them.

Chidley's staff are optimistic that the increased contact with local schools will pay dividends. However, the better support obtained in this way will need to be balanced against the additional expense of providing replacement teachers and transport costs for the local teachers.

The recent appointment of an itinerant guidance officer to provide a liaison with small schools and children working through correspondence schools is likely to strengthen the follow-up available in the most isolated areas. It is also to be expected that the number of referrals from such areas will rise. The growth of regional resource centers with advisory teachers competent in the area of remedial teaching should, in the long term, similarly strengthen follow-up procedures.

Developments and Problems

The main problem identified in the operation of the Chidley Education Centre has been the difficulty of ensuring adequate follow-up once a child returns home. Local teachers often have not had the expertise or the time to take the special needs of the ex-Chidley child into account. Similarly, the high turnover in staffing of rural schools is a problem in that follow-up programs may be disrupted when the child's teacher is transferred from the region. However, the involvement of local teachers and principals mentioned in the previous section represents a significant development to improve follow-up. It remains to be seen whether the initial promise of this development reaches fruition in the classroom.

Other problems occur in that parents, too, have sometimes lacked the confidence to work with the child as recommended. In a few cases, the domestic situation itself seems to have been a major factor in the child's learning difficulties. However, a majority of parents now are staying at Chidley for at least a part of the time that their children are there. Usually four or five parents are present in any week, with the result that approximately 70 percent of children have had their parents with them at some stage. An increase in this figure is unlikely because of accommodation limits.

A related development now under review is to shorten the child's initial stay, return him to school for as much as a year, and bring him back for a further period of assessment and diagnosis. This would enable the Chidley Centre to monitor the progress of the child over a much longer time than is presently possible. Staff would then be in a position to gauge the longer-term effects of their work.

Perhaps the most promising development is the greater communication between various agencies in the country and metropolitan areas, which will lessen the "isolation" of Chidley. Thus, increasingly, Chidley is being seen as an adjunct to school, with the school and the parents taking a greater responsibility for the necessary remediation.

6

The Educational Challenge in Rural Alaska: Era of Local Control

Kathryn A. Hecht

This chapter focuses on the recent decentralization of education in rural Alaska. It begins by introducing the reader to Alaska's unique geographic, economic, and social features. The evolution of the educational system in rural Alaska is then traced from the Russian era through the advent in 1976 of twenty-one rural Alaskan regional school districts. These Regional Educational Attendance Areas (REAAs) provide the first experience with local control of education for many of Alaska's rural Native residents. Local control had long been sought as a way to improve the quality of education while making it more responsive to rural needs and village life-styles. The problems encountered in implementing the REAAs are described and documented from a recent report by the Center for Cross-Cultural Studies. Finally, the issues now emerging from these recent changes are identified and discussed.

Alaska and Its Peoples

When Alaska is described to people who have not visited it, the most frequently used word is *unique*. Numerous factors intertwine to make Alaska an exciting, rapidly changing, diverse, and complex place. Although it is the largest U.S. state in area, equal to one-fifth of the contiguous forty-eight states (Figure 1), Alaska competes with Montana for the smallest population in the nation. Alaska's current population is estimated to be approximately 400,000, less than one person per square mile.[1] Over half the population lives in or near one of the two largest cities, Anchorage and Fairbanks. The rest live in hundreds of small towns and villages scattered over an immense area.

FIGURE 1 Alaska's Area Compared with That of the Contiguous Forty-Eight States.

Alaska's landscape ranges from rugged mountains to flowery tundra to rain forests. The climate varies from the extreme winter cold of the north to the milder rainy weather of the southeast, and 90°F summer temperatures are not infrequent in the interior.

Surface transportation is limited, so the population relies on air and water travel to traverse the state. Alaska is the only state with a capital city (Juneau) that can be reached solely by plane or boat. Outside of the major cities and highway towns, air service is the only means of transportation other than locally used roads, boats, snowmobiles, and dogsleds. Villages in rural Alaska are often not only small but also isolated.

Modern conveniences, including communications and other services, frequently are limited or totally lacking in rural areas. Despite satellite technology and recent demonstrations with both village phones and television, there are still many places without such services available on a regular, home-use basis.

Alaska's location further contributes to its uniqueness. As can be seen on Figure 2, Alaska shares no common boundaries with the rest of the United States. From another perspective, it is a member of the circumpolar community. If one were to view Alaska from above the North Pole, one would see it as illustrated in Figure 3. Culturally, racially, and linguistically, Alaska's original inhabitants are closer to these northern neighbors than to the

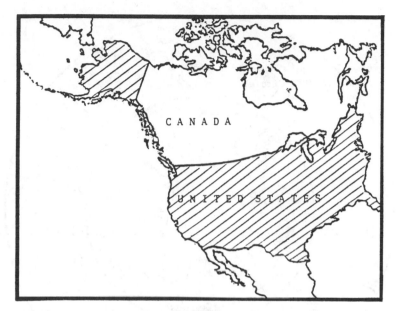

FIGURE 2   Alaska Shares No Common Boundaries with the Rest of the United States.

peoples of their own nation. Alaska's distance from the other states, and its large size and small population, result in a cost of living estimated to be 15 to 40 percent higher than that of the other forty-nine states.[2] The cost of living is highest in the rural areas both because of shipping expenses and the low volume of goods traded. Construction costs also are highest in the rural areas. It is estimated that construction of a school costs twice as much in the bush (the local name for rural, isolated Alaska) as in Anchorage.

In natural resources, Alaska's importance to the nation probably is greater than any other state's at this time in U.S. history. Alaska's best-known resource was gold until the first large commercial oil discovery in 1957. Following that, the trans-Alaska oil pipeline was constructed, extending from Alaska's northernmost border to a southern port at Valdez. Planning has now begun for a natural gas pipeline that will cross Alaska and Canada, culminating in the delivery of natural gas to the continental United States. It is expected that the state of Alaska, a territory which twenty years ago could barely meet a minimal budget, will have a large budget surplus before 1985, including an estimated $1.5 billion yearly income from oil and gas revenues.[3] Unlike most other sparsely populated areas of the world, Alaska will have almost unlimited funds to carry out whatever programs are deemed important.

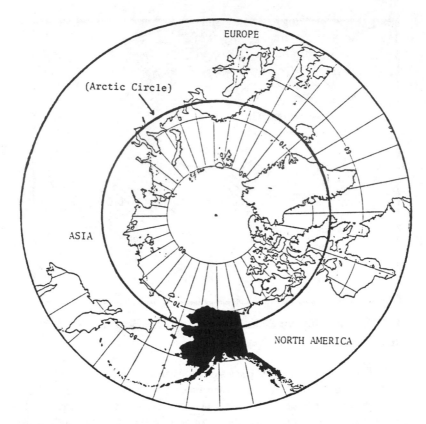

FIGURE 3 Alaska as a Member of the Circumpolar Community.

The Alaska Native Population

Perhaps what makes Alaska truly unique, and most important to our topic of rural education, is its Native population. The term *Alaska Native* has been used for many years in government reports to refer to the three distinct racial/cultural groups, Aleuts, Eskimos, and Indians, who have lived in Alaska for thousands of years. The term was given preference by those three groups in the Alaska Native Claims Settlement Act of 1971.

Although Natives represent only 18 percent (approximately 60,000) of the total Alaskan population, they compose 80 percent of the rural population. Alaska Natives differ from the non-Native Alaskans in income, education, and other social indicators. They hold fewer skilled jobs and are more often unemployed. According to the 1970 census, 40 percent of rural Native families had an income below $5,000. Even allowing for subsistence (hunting, fishing, and trapping) income, rural Native families earned only half as much as urban Natives and only one-third of the income of non-Natives. Rural adult Natives attained a median of six years of school compared to twelve years for non-Native Alaskans, both urban and rural. Seventeen percent of rural Native adults had no formal education at all, as opposed to less than 1 percent of non-Natives living in urban or rural areas.[4]

In discussing the contemporary Native scene, the importance of the Alaska Native Claims Settlement Act cannot be overestimated. In 1884 Congress agreed that Alaska Natives would not be disturbed in their use of land they occupied or claimed.[5] That agreement finally was fulfilled in 1971, in a settlement which included 40 million acres of land and almost $1 billion, to be administered through thirteen regional corporations controlled exclusively by Natives. Native corporations currently are trying hard to find the delicate balance between the need to make a profit and the preservation and extension of the Native way of life.

Perhaps because of the climate and the geographic isolation of the villages, Alaska Native culture has not been completely assimilated into Western culture. The Natives who live in the rural areas retain the older ways more than do those living in the towns and cities. For years the Native people in rural areas were not economically dependent on others. They maintained a cooperative existence and traditional values which many still strongly defend despite the changing society around them. A majority of Natives still rely on subsistence activities for half or more of their food. In a recent report, three-fourths of those interviewed in small and medium-sized villages said hunting and fishing were the aspects of village life they liked best. However, the needs and appetites for those things which can be bought with money have caused many Natives to take part-time jobs and increased their dependence on the majority society. Most Natives seem to prefer maintaining some aspects of the old culture and fitting their life-style into a modern society, thereby preserving the best of both.

A survey of Alaska Native expectations for education provides further evidence of the desire to maintain one's culture and yet integrate into the majority society. Of all adults questioned, 83 percent wanted both English and Native languages as languages of instruction in school. Eighty percent of the respondents believed that most children in their communities should at least complete high school, although only 65 percent believed they will. Nine percent thought most children should complete college; only 1 percent thought they would.[6] Although most Native adults have a limited education, they generally have high aspirations for their children—but they do not necessarily believe those aspirations will be fulfilled.

Alaska is frequently excluded from many programs and policies because of its separation from the contiguous forty-eight states and because of its distinctive characteristics. In educational research, Alaska's situation is often considered too unique to be of general applicability elsewhere. For example, a National Institute of Education study on rural school improvement efforts explicitly excluded Alaska, Hawaii, the Trust territories, and federally sponsored Indian schools. A letter from the director of this study noted that Alaska was one of "those situations in rural America where cultural/social and geographical conditions are sufficiently unique to require very different approaches to improving education."[7] How Alaska's system of rural education has evolved is discussed next.

An Evolving Educational System: Historical Perspective

Russian Period (1783 to 1867)

The colonization of Alaska began in 1783 as part of the expansion of the Russian fur industry. At that time, it is estimated that the original inhabitants, the Alaska Natives, numbered 74,000. Three types of Russian-sponsored schools were established: company schools for training Russian employees, government schools for Russian children, and mission schools for Alaska Natives and those of mixed blood. Russian schooling in Alaska continued even after the territory was purchased by the United States, the last Russian school in Alaska not closing until 1916.[8]

Early U.S. Period (1867 to 1900)

The United States purchased Alaska from Russia in 1867 for $7.2 million. Between 1867 and 1884, U.S. rule involved negligible activity. Congress even failed to establish any form of civil government until 1884, when it finally passed the First Organic Act. This act is noted in education history for having charged the secretary of the interior with making "needful and proper provision for the education of the children of school age in the Territory of Alaska, without preference to race."[9] The secretary did establish some schools, mostly by contracting with church and mission groups to run them. However, the amount of money appropriated by Congress was very limited. By 1900, it was estimated that less than 10 percent of all school-age children were in school. One hundred fifty villages simply had no schools.[10]

Emergence of the Dual System (1900 to 1917)

Under pressure from the non-Native population, who arrived in Alaska during the gold rush of the late 1800s, Congress provided for locally controlled schools in incorporated towns (those with an organized government) in 1900, and in unincorporated rural areas in 1905. These schools were to be established for "white children and children of mixed blood who lead a civilized life," while education of Eskimos and Indians in Alaska was to remain under the secretary of the interior.[11]

This was the beginning of what now is known as the dual system. The term refers to the division of authority between schools administered by the state of Alaska and those administered by the federal government. The system was dual in a racist sense: federal schools were established for Native children, and separate schools were established for all non-Native children. Non-Native parents elected their own local school boards, but no such control mechanism existed for parents of Native children in federal schools.[12]

The Second Organic Act in 1912 recognized Alaska as a U.S. territory. In 1917, Congress empowered the territorial legislature to "establish and maintain schools for white and colored children and children of mixed blood who lead a civilized life."[13] Later in 1917, the territory established the Department of Education, with jurisdiction over all schools in the territory except those for Natives, which were to be maintained under federal control. The dual system was reaffirmed by the new territorial government. Although no longer racially oriented, the dual organizational structure of education remains in existence today, with federal and state schools both having educational responsibilities in Alaska.

Territorial Period (1917 to 1959)

The territorial policy of the 1920s was that "the highest good of both races . . . seems to require separate schools for at least a few decades." This was based on the belief that the mingling of races would cause friction, that Native children's attendance would be sporadic, and that Native children would be unable to conform to Western standards of health and sanitation.

Despite this official policy, the dual system continued more in the sense of federal/state administration than of Native/non-Native segregation. In the rural areas, economy increasingly dictated that villages contain either a territorial or a federal school, but both. Separate school systems existed, but seldom in the same village. By 1934, one-third of the Native schoolchildren were being educated in nonfederal schools, and by the time Alaska became a state in 1959, territorial schools served more Native students than did the federal schools. Although Alaska Natives attended territorial schools, no significant number of non-Natives ever attended federal schools.

During the 1930s, legislation did away with the school boards for the territorial rural schools, and these schools came under the territorial board of education. This can be considered the beginning of a tripartite system: (1) the territorial board allowed local control of education in the organized areas; (2) conversely, it made all decisions for territorial schools in the rural areas; and (3) the U.S. Department of the Interior continued to operate federal schools exclusively for Native students.

Although the number of Natives attending territorial schools was substantial, the curriculum of these schools did not reflect the diversity of students attending. The federal schools did at times recognize the special needs of Native students, but the policy was never consistent.[14] After World War II, planning for amalgamation of the federal and state school systems began. In 1950 the Bureau of Indian Affairs (Department of the Interior) reached an agreement with the territorial government on the transfer of federally run Native schools to territorial control, including a provision for transitional funding. By 1954, forty-nine schools had been transferred, but the process was halted because of territorial concern over the cost of taking on additional schools.[15] After 1945, there appeared to be growing agreement that keeping the races apart was no longer appropriate. The question was how to plan and implement the transfer, the key point of controversy being financial responsibility. This issue is still under debate.

Since Statehood (1959 to 1979)

Alaska became the forty-ninth state in 1959. The Alaska Constitution says the state is to "establish and maintain a system of public schools open to all children of the state." In 1962 the Bureau of Indian Affairs (BIA) and state authorities again reached agreement on transferring federal schools into a single state system. Twenty-eight more schools were transferred to the state by 1970; few have been transferred since then, and forty-four remain in the BIA system.

During this period a more unified Native voice, with increasing political influence, began to be heard on educational interests. Native concerns included the need for programs specifically designed for rural, mostly Native schools, and an end to the practice of sending children from their home communities to distant schools. The potential power of the Native coalition is best demonstrated by the passage in 1971 of the Alaska Native Claims Settlement Act. The settlement appeared to give Native peoples confidence in using the political/legal system, as well as the experience needed for other Native advocacy efforts.

In response to increased attention to rural education, the state of Alaska in 1970 placed all rural schools in unorganized areas under the Alaska State-Operated School System (ASOSS). This new state agency operated independently of the Department of Education, which had been operating the schools. Local advisory boards were established, but all decisionmaking power was maintained by ASOSS, under a governing board appointed by the governor. With rural schools under a separate state agency, the three-part system became more formalized.

SB 35 and the REAAs. The creation of ASOSS did not satisfy demands for local control. Recognizing the need for another solution, the commissioner of education requested that the Center for Northern Educational Research (CNER) identify alternative means for delivering rural educational services. [This research institute within the University of Alaska has since changed its name to the Center for Cross-Cultural Studies. — Author] The end result of CNER's recommendations was an Alaska state law that in July 1976 replaced ASOSS with Regional Educational Attendance Areas (REAAs).[16] Senate Bill 35 (SB 35) for the first time gave Native village residents the right to elect their own regional school boards. Although SB 35 created twenty-one regional entities which differ in several respects from school districts in the boroughs and cities, they too are regulated by the state Department of Education and treated similarly to other school districts.[17] This move toward local control of rural education is a major event in Alaskan education. Its impact will be considered in detail below.

It is not a coincidence that the advent of the new regional school districts occurred at the same time as a precedent-setting state policy for small rural high schools. A lawsuit was instituted by a group of rural parents against the state, contending that their children were entitled to secondary education in their home community. In 1976 the state agreed to provide a high school in each community that has an elementary school.[18] These events illustrate the growing importance of ethnicity and the political influence of Native people in controlling their own destinies, including the education of their children.

Despite SB 35 and consolidation of the state system, a dual system survives. There are still federally run schools for Native children in Alaska. The transfer of schools has been further complicated by the federal Indian Self-Determination Act, which gives Alaska Natives at the community level the right to choose among state, federal, or Indian-controlled systems.[19] Most local villages with BIA schools appear to be waiting to see how successful the REAAs are. Therefore, the dual system can be expected to continue for some time.

The passage of SB 35 led to the division of all areas outside of organized boroughs and cities into twenty-one regional school districts called Regional Education Attendance Areas (REAAs). Residents of the new regional districts elected their first school boards and took over the new school districts in July 1976, one year after SB 35 was passed. It was the first opportunity for Native residents, the majority in most REAAs, to exercise direct influence over the formal education of their children. The REAAs provide elementary and secondary education for 11,000 pupils, 70 percent of whom are Native.[20]

The law allowed only a one-year transition period before the new boards became official, so most boards were made up of people who were not only newly elected, but also inexperienced. Although the REAA boards are elected by local residents, REAAs are large in geographic area and most include many widely scattered, small communities. The law attempted to assure that the voice of each village would be heard by setting up community school committees advisory to the REAA boards.

Local control. The movement for local control that led to SB 35 and the formation of the REAAs was of a grass-roots nature. Change was not imposed from above but demanded from below. How important the concept of gaining local control was to this movement is essential to an understanding and assessment of the new districts. Unlike countries where control of the educational program is nationally centralized or where professionals exercise considerable local autonomy, the U.S. philosophy considers parents and the local community the best judges of the direction of children's education. Education governed by elected lay boards is a long-established tradition. In settling governance disputes, the U.S. Supreme Court continues to recognize the importance of local control of education. In 1974 , the chief justice said, "No single tradition in public education is more deeply rooted than local control over the operation of schools; local autonomy has long been thought essential both to the maintenance of community concern and support for public schools and to quality of educational process."[21]

From studying the events that led up to the passage of SB 35, it is clear that local control was desired chiefly as a means to improve the quality of education for rural Native children. Without such control there was no way to effect change; with control closer to home vested in members of the community, change would be possible. The changes the rural Natives hoped to bring about reflected a resurgence of interest in the Native heritage coupled with growing feelings that the school curriculum should reflect community culture and life-style. A report prepared for the 1974 Alaska legislature cited the strong support among Native rural spokespersons for local control, quality education, and schooling sensitive to the life-style(s) of the rural Native community.[22] The effectiveness of the rural school districts in meeting these desires and other needs of rural Alaskan education is discussed in the following two sections.

The REAAs in Their First Year:
Problems of Implementation

The passage of SB 35 and the creation of the REAAs can be viewed as the culmination of a long struggle to gain local control of education. It was also the beginning of a new era of education in rural Alaska in which local control offers the opportunity to provide quality education as defined by the residents of the rural communities. However, the achievement of the means—local control—does not necessarily assure the desired end—quality education responsive to local needs.

The author of this chapter was principal investigator for the CNER study *New School Districts in Rural Alaska: A Report on the REAAs After One Year.* This section draws heavily from it.[23] The report was the only attempt to systematically collect and disseminate information about the first year of the new rural districts in Alaska. Even this effort was severely hampered by limited funding, which curtailed the amount of fieldwork possible. The report offers no conclusions about the REAAs after their first year of operation, but does provide a source of information, a variety of opinions, and some clear directions for further study.

In reality there are twenty-one emerging systems, each influenced by a different set of cultural, economic, and geographic conditions. Local control was intended to allow educational developments to adapt to these diverse situations. Therefore, the experiences of each REAA were expected to be unique in at least some areas. Indeed, if the intent is met, each district should develop in a different manner. One REAA superintendent, addressing his peers on the successes and failures of the first year of the REAAs, discussed difficulties in evaluating the new districts: "There was such a dynamic environment at the time. There were so many variables operating. It was not just the fact that we were going into a brand new school district, but at the same time we were asked to create new high school facilities, we were asked for bilingual programs. . . . The whole thing occurred in such a dynamic movement of activity. It is hard to say what would have happened had it not all taken place at one time."[24]

The task of decentralization, of creating a new school district, is in itself an enormous undertaking. Furthermore, in these rural areas residents have less than the average amount of formal education and no experience in running their own schools (having long been told that it was not their role). The new boards were obligated to establish educational policies and programs and were also confronted with many special problems, including planning for the new high schools, complying with court-mandated bilingual/ bicultural programs, and negotiating for BIA school transfers. A Native consultant to the CNER study noted, "And, if that were not enough, all these new tasks were expected to result in a higher quality of education."[25]

In decentralizing control and delivery of education to the most remote, rural areas of the state, Alaska went against the national trend of consolidating smaller districts into larger ones. From a strict logistical viewpoint, decentralization seems a far more complex process than centralization, since creating a host of new units where none previously existed is more difficult than the reverse. Given the myriad tasks facing the new district administrators and boards, it is not surprising that most of the discussions in the first year centered on problems of implementation.

Transition Year

The transition year, 1975-76, mainly was taken up with drawing the district boundaries, deciding upon the number and allocation of board seats in each district, and holding elections for both regional district boards and community school committees. Only a few months of the transition year remained after these tasks were completed. One of the final tasks, and perhaps the most critical, was to hire superintendents and other administrative and teaching staff.

Whether a longer transition time would have been better is difficult to say, since all districts operated on the same time line. One observer of the REAA transitional year predicted that the rapidity of the change might be the very thing that would impede real change.

> Perhaps the most remarkable aspect of the legislation is the rapidity with which it had to be implemented. The shape of Alaskan education always has depended on the legislative will of the federal and state governments. But never has such radical change been required so quickly. The irony is that because change must occur so suddenly, many things which ought to change will remain the same. The new REAA boards scurried to be functioning by the July 1, 1976, deadline. Some had to retain mediocre ASOSS administrators because time did not permit their replacement. Under these circumstances, little substantive improvement in local school management is predictable.[26]

Decentralization brought decisionmaking to regional and community levels where few had experienced the formalities and complexities of Western governmental procedures. Most villages have no local government beyond village councils. Native cultures involve different decisionmaking processes dependent on respect for elders and in which consensus is often not reached through a public process.

Setting a perspective for reviewing the progress of the new districts, Darnell reminded us that change requires understanding on the part of all those affected. He observed, "Innovations are generally seen as having a greater chance to succeed the more members of the organization affected by the innovation understand what is being changed. In this regard REAAs are experiencing difficulty. Neither sustained nor adequate efforts to educate rural residents in implications of the passage of SB 35 have been undertaken."[27]

Supporting Darnell's concern that a broad-based understanding is necessary to effect change is a superintendent's comment about the difficulty of convincing people that change was really taking place: "We had the problem of convincing the district that we *were* a local school district and convincing the teachers. I don't know that everybody really, really understands that at the present time — that we are a local school district and that we have local control."[28]

The people who seemed to express the most concern about the speed of transition and lack of preparation time were the administrators, who had to locate and establish new offices, hire and train support staff, purchase equipment and supplies, set up a budgeting system, and cope with last-minute teacher recruitment. One superintendent said, "We inherited a 7 million dollar a year business without any proper administrative foundation."[29]

Perhaps what is most surprising in the reactions to the hurried changeover from one to twenty-one systems is that those who were least prepared, the local people, seemed to accept the situation. Note the comments of the Native consultant who developed a case study on the REAA: "People did not view the transference of educational responsibility from the State to themselves as being a problem worthy of any particular concern. Rather, people simply accepted the responsibility and got on with business. Instead of hearing about how difficult the job was, what was heard was praise or criticism concerning some particular aspect of the job and how it was all going."[30]

REAA School Boards:
Elections, Functions, and Perceptions

The first REAA elections placed 147 people on the twenty-one new boards and subsequently 450 people on the community school committees. Given the small populations of the communities making up each regional district, plus the recent proliferation of boards and committees required by various federally funded programs as well as those necessary to carry out activities of the Native Claims Settlement Act, some have questioned whether there is an adequate pool of available persons. "The limits of participatory democracy in rural Alaska are being tested. How many people in a village of 50, 100, or even 2,000 people have the interest, abilities, and time to serve as an unpaid board or committee member?"[31] Many REAA board members serve on other boards and committees, a situation that can easily lead to conflict of time and interests.

The election process itself has come into serious question during the first year. It is seen at very least as cumbersome in remote rural areas and at worst, alien and insensitive to local culture: "I think as far as the election goes, the timing is really bad. When the time came for the people to sign up, these people were out there hunting, so come time for the election, there were people running unopposed because others didn't meet the deadline to run for these seats."[32]

How the boards function has been studied by a review of the REAA board meeting minutes for the first year. Inouye noted that public attendance at a majority of board meetings was high, particularly among those boards which chose to rotate their meetings among different communities within the district.[33] However, problems of distance, transportation, and weather often made it impossible to meet outside the larger towns. Frequently just getting a board together was costly and difficult to arrange.

Although it is said that the one-year transition went far better than might have been expected and that REAA boards readily accepted their responsibilities, others have questioned whether the frequently inexperienced board members are too dependent on their administrators. Some have criticized the boards for neglecting policy and program development and interfering in matters usually considered administrative, especially personnel matters. However, the question of the proper role of the board may be more a manifestation of cultural differences than experience. One of the prime motivating factors in the local control movement was to obtain teachers more sensitive to the village culture, so it is not surprising that Native board members considered their role and involvement in personnel matters an appropriate route toward improving education.

After a year of experience, those REAA members who responded to the CNER survey were unanimous in feeling the time spent was worthwhile. What they liked best about being on the board was participating in a challenging opportunity to improve education.[34] Perhaps the most revealing comments about what it was like to be an REAA board member the first year came in response to the question, "What advice would you give a new REAA board member?" The responses indicated the great amount of time and work rural residents willingly gave to get the new districts started:

> Be prepared to work hard. It is not an easy job. Expect a lot of travel.

> Be prepared to spend extensive time in studying and considering information in areas you may not be familiar with (i.e., finance, legislation, etc.) and be willing to make decisions at times that seem to go against what the vocal public might want because you have more information to base that decision on.

> Be well aware of the tasks involved, the time required, and come with improving education as your sole goal.[35]

Conflicts and Concerns

Although most REAA boards accomplished much of their business with a minimum of conflicts, there were numerous signs of discontent in some REAAs as well as concerns that seemed common to many of the new districts. Also, not all communities have been totally satisfied with their new board members, and there have been successful recall elections in two districts, a highly unusual event even among the established districts in the state.

One area of concern in many of the new districts that received considerable attention in the CNER report is the conflict between teachers and the REAA boards and/or community. The evidence of conflict includes high teacher turnover and several lawsuits. The issue as discussed in the CNER report seems to revolve around whether village teachers' life-styles outside the classroom are an educational or personal concern.

In a small, isolated community, social and classroom relationships are not easily separated. Teachers must live in the communities in which they teach because distance and the complete absence of roads preclude any other option. Having to adapt their life-styles to those of a culturally different community and its social standards is seen as an unnecessary hardship by those who feel they have already given up much and proved their dedication in moving to the village. From the viewpoint of the teachers' organization, teachers should be judged on their professional skills but permitted to live their personal lives with the same civil liberties one could expect anywhere in the country.[36] However, REAA boards generally feel teachers should act as role models both in and out of school.

Not all communities or teachers in the REAA districts experienced this conflict. Some seem to have had just the opposite experience. Responsibility for decisionmaking at the local level was said to have improved communication between the community and the teachers; with more community involvement, parents and teachers work better together toward shared educational goals.

Local Control and Quality

After one year of operation, how successful were the regional districts in meeting rural people's expectations for local control? Do the local people feel control is improving the quality of education? In questioning residents of one REAA about why they had considered it necessary to have local control of education, Goodwin found diverse opinions, but an underlying sense of agreement about the cultural relevance of education and the need for quality:

> Within the rural community there is a substantial regard for the quality of education. Although this regard for educational quality is left somewhat unarticulated, it is fairly easy to see that the concern for quality has been an impor-

tant motivating factor in obtaining local control. Consider, for example, that many respondents felt that local control was necessary so as to provide for community input in the selection of teachers and administrators. That is, many people felt that if the community could control the hiring of, for instance, teachers, "education would get better."[37]

Once the REAAs were functioning, local control seldom seemed to be directly discussed. However, when superintendents and school board members were asked the most positive features of the new REAA system, local control heavily dominated the responses. This school board member's answer was typical: "I think it was a step in the right direction to permit local control. Local people should be able to set their own priorities for educating their own children."[38] Overall, a sense of pride in running their own affairs was obvious. The implicit link to local relevance is made by the same respondent: "By designing our own district we are now able to provide students with an education system based on their needs and not the teachers' or bureaucrats'."[39]

Community school committees (CSCs) were most frequently mentioned among those aspects of the new system in need of change. They are the most local aspect of the REAA system (one in each community with a school) but are only advisory. In some villages, CSCs seemed to effectively communicate both within the village and between the village and the regional districts. In others, the committee members seemed to be inactive and very uncertain about their role. Most of the CSC members responding had not received any training. About half said they lacked guidelines from the REAA on how the CSCs should operate. Despite these difficulties, almost all agreed that the committees should be continued. Reasons given described CSCs as vehicles to meet local needs by providing input to teachers and the school program as well as a check on regional (REAA) power: "The CSC is needed to insure that the REAA school administration and staff are responsive to the desires of the local community residents in such areas as curriculum, student rights and responsibilities, professional standards for staff, and student discipline."[40]

At the other end of the governance structure, there continue to be differences of opinion as to level of control and/or assistance the state should exert over the regional school districts. A recent report notes, "There is less state control on the new REAAs than with the former State-Operated School system. He [the commissioner of education] said that every effort would be made to allow flexibility at the local level, and will treat the small rural school districts no differently than Anchorage, Fairbanks, Juneau or Nome."[41] The commissioner followed this philosophy and provided no special program of services in support of the new districts, although specific requests for technical assistance were generally met, as is the practice for all districts. One noticeable change was that the state board of education, recognizing its newly enlarged constituency, began to schedule some board meetings outside the major cities.

However, now that the rural areas no longer came under a special agency and were being treated no differently than other districts, some rural residents appeared to feel their special interests were being neglected. An attempt was made to increase rural input through a bill introduced in the state legislature (SB 124) that would have altered the membership of the state board of education in favor of increased rural (REAA) representation. (The bill did not pass.)

Is local control, in concept or practice, understood by the residents of the new districts? There is good reason to suspect that understanding is less than it should be for local control to be effective: "Let's not forget that the concept of local control is very foreign to the rural areas and for us to assume they know what it means—I think it's dangerous. . . . If we don't educate people to let them know what local control is, what they can do with it, what responsibility they have—then there's going to be some misunderstanding."[42]

Although there obviously are problems implementing local control, the REAA system is in place and operating smoothly for the most part, given its newness and the enormity of the job. Quality of education still is the foremost concern of those striving to make the new system work. Most participants in and observers of the new districts agree that it is too early to make judgments, although they are optimistic about the REAAs and their potential to provide quality education.

REAA superintendents saw the REAA experience with local control as a positive step that brings problems and their solutions closer to home and that will help rural residents understand the change process. It also was seen as increasing expectations as well as opportunities for locally determined quality education in the future.

> SB 35 is allowing some rural residents who were previously unfamiliar with "why" things were as they were to understand and realize the immense difficulty any change causes. . . . SB 35 gives rural residents increased *hope* for better schools.[43]

> The educational programs have a great opportunity for improvement. . . . we can tailor our particular district's efforts towards the local needs of that district rather than looking at it from state-wide perspective. We can really have an opportunity to build in some quality, try some different things. If it doesn't work we can easily get rid of it and try something else.[44]

Further supporting these positive outlooks, Goodwin found a high degree of awareness and self-criticism in the rural community as well as a sense of optimism. He concluded, "The rural community seems to be too critical of itself. However, this is a healthy environment for change. In the opinion of the author, the dissidence and criticism along with the optimism and awareness cannot help but result in an educational system far better for the children than it has been in the past."[45]

Emerging Issues: The Rural Challenge

Now that the REAAs have completed their second year of operation, more substantive educational issues have emerged. These issues are not necessarily new to rural education, in Alaska or elsewhere, but the creation of the REAAs plus the state's commitment to provide local high schools in every community has brought to bear both increased attention and resources. Alaska's rural settings, the multicultural population, and the substantial and growing monetary resources to serve a relatively small population suggest Alaska as a favorable location for rural educators to study these issues and their solutions.

In this final section, the author briefly highlights the issues and solutions as she perceives them. When available, references are provided for the reader who wishes further information. For projects described which now are in progress, the reader is urged to correspond directly with the agency cited for up-to-date information.

Local Control

How local does local control need to be? Do advisory community school committees (CSCs) bring regional school governance close enough to home? Should they be strengthened, or are they unnecessary? From the CNER study of the first year of REAAs, it appears clear that in many communities the CSCs were felt necessary to provide local input to the school and advice to the regional board. Despite the fact that some administrators see the CSCs as an unnecessary burden, it is doubtful that the concept of local control through regional districts will work without them. What appears necessary to make the CSC concept effective is provision for guidelines within each REAA on the role of the CSCs, their responsibilities, and how they are to relate to the regional board and to local and regional administrators. [In April 1979 the legislature repealed the requirements about CSCs. Each REAA is now free to decide not only the selection and organizational procedures for CSCs, but also whether these local committees will exist at all. — Author]

According to the Alaska State Department of Education, "new materials are being developed to educate the CSC members about themselves and about other parts of the state's educational system."[46] If the CSCs survive and prove effective, they could provide the degree of localism desired for each community's school, as well as local input and some relief to the REAA board from its excessive duties.

Finance

REAAs receive 100 percent of their basic need funding from the state, based upon the Public School Foundation Program formula. City and borough districts are also funded through the same formula, based upon the same state finance program and its basic need definition, but they usually add to this amount from local tax revenues. Since REAAs are not organized units of local government, and therefore have no taxing power, SB 35 allowed them extra funds per student above the formula equal to the average local tax revenue per average daily membership of city and borough districts. All districts utilize state and federal categorical funds in addition to sources mentioned above. Has this method of 100 percent state financing for REAAs provided sufficient resources? Have REAAs been responsible in handling funds that they do not have to raise from within their own communities?

One hundred percent state funding of local districts occurs nowhere else in the United States. (Hawaii has full state funding but does not have comparable local districts.) Increased state funding has been required by the courts in several states to equalize funding available to local districts, but many educators have expressed fears that with state funding, local control would diminish. One member of the Alaska State Board of Education "thought that everyone across the country was watching to see how much control the state is going to have over these emerging districts because they are 100% funded. She expressed hope that it can be done with a minimum amount."[47]

Despite the inexperience of the new REAA boards, and budgets based on insufficient facts and past records, only one REAA required supplemental funding the first year. In program matters, there were few charges of state interference. Most of these related to established federal and state regulations with which all districts must comply. However, the level of funding was not necessarily considered adequate. CNER conducted a study of school finance in Alaska. Part of that study included a report on regional workshops where people were able to discuss their financial concerns.[48] According to the study director, the verdict on the adequacy of financial support has not yet been given:

> This examination of the financing of REAAs in their first year of operation
> has only partially answered the question of whether the resources available to

REAAs were adequate to support the programs desired by local REAA boards. The discretion of local boards was certainly controlled by the amount of funds available, and it will be in future years given continuation of the current funding method. Any answer to the adequacy of funding would require an intensive examination of the quality and cost of local programs. With the possibility of substantial state revenues available for education in the future, REAAs might consider documenting the costs of necessary local programs and seeking funds for them rather than having their programs controlled by the set amounts of revenues provided under current funding schemes. If the students of rural Alaska are to be afforded an opportunity to education equal to those students in other districts, the manner of financial support is a concern that deserves continuing attention.[49]

James Conant, in an article entitled "Why full state funding needn't kill the power of local school boards,"[50] says that his concept of full state funding was never intended to do away with school boards or to diminish local control. In his plan, local boards would submit an educational plan in terms of manpower needs which would then be translated into dollars by the state staff. The REAAs, as an example of the application of 100 percent state financing along with local program control, deserve to be further analyzed to test the reality of such plans.

Training Needs: Boards, Administrators, and Teachers

Necessary training is discussed by board members, administrators, and teachers. Each group thinks the others need to learn more about individual roles and to increase their abilities to act effectively. Regional and community boards do need to better understand the federal and state regulations by which they must abide, but beyond that they should be encouraged to evolve new educational philosophies and methods. As one Native educator commented, "I hope that anyone who talks about board training is not really going to go out and put those people in some category—'this is the way it is done in the Establishment, and that's the reason why you ought to do it.' "[51] Rural Native residents are new to educational control; they want to be allowed to make their own mistakes and learn from them. All community members, not just those currently serving on school boards, need to further their understanding of the REAA system, or else the pool of knowledgeable citizens will remain limited.

Others have suggested that the need for REAA board training has been overstated and that administrators need to be trained to work with the boards. Training suggestions have ranged from increasing the crosscultural awareness of administrators to reeducating them to the benefits of community involvement.

Perhaps the most constructive attention has been directed toward teacher training needs in all stages of preparation, certification, orientation, and in-service. At the undergraduate level, for eight years the University of Alaska's Alaska Rural Teacher Training Program/Cross-Cultural Education Development Program has been training teachers for rural schools through a field-delivered, crosscultural approach. Although considered highly successful, the program is expensive and limited in size. Therefore, the REAAs will have to depend on teachers without specialized rural Alaskan training for some time.

A task force recently studied state teacher certification requirements and considered recommending to the state board of education that it adopt a two-step certification process. Completion of a four-year, approved teacher training program anywhere in the United States would entitle one to an "initial" certificate to teach in Alaska for two years, but a "standard" or permanent certificate would require that the teacher take Alaska-related training, including crosscultural studies.[52] Changing the certification requirements to allow nontraditional access to the profession by working up the career ladder as a teacher aide also would be permitted through recently introduced legislation.[53] Since many village residents are employed as aides, this change could provide a significant increase in the number of Native teachers already well experienced in rural classrooms.

Orientation and in-service programs often are discussed. Currently these are provided most frequently on an individual district basis. One district has cooperated with the Department of Education in issuing a booklet of teachers' personal comments on their experiences called *It Happens When We Get There: Conversations With Teachers in Alaskan Villages.*[54]

Much remains to be done. A variety of training needs must be met, the processes evaluated, and information disseminated so others will benefit. Rather than discussing training needs in an accusatory way, everyone concerned with education will need to cooperate so that all may learn.

Improved Curriculum and Programs

REAAs are increasingly turning their attention to improving current educational offerings and creating new ones, particularly for the many new village high schools. This work is being accomplished by varying combinations of regional and community boards, parents, teachers, administrators, specialists, and outside consultants. Concerns are both to expand the range of subject matter, especially incorporating cultural aspects and career options, and to experiment with new methods and techniques, including expanding the school into the community and beyond it through exchange and travel programs.

Two University of Alaska projects are developing programs for the small rural high schools. A product of one project, *Village High Schools: Some Education Strategies to Help Meet Developmental Needs of Rural Youth,*[55] focuses on the importance of educational environments outside the traditional high school classroom including work experience, student exchange, and travel study programs. The authors stress that the conventional high school is an unsuitable model for rural Alaska and discuss advantages of the smaller high school. The report describes a number of successful rural Alaska programs, as well as analyzing and integrating program types into a planning framework. The second study, now in progress, is the Small High School project, coordinated through the university's School of Education (Fairbanks). This project has placed graduate assistants in participating communities to begin to identify critical variables that go into effective high school programs. A preliminary report is available.[56]

Several districts have publicized their innovations. For example, the Northwest Arctic School District is developing an educational program which has as its goal the integration of crosscultural concepts in all subjects and grades. District representatives presented their program to the First Congress of Education in Canada.[57] Another REAA, Iditarod Area, has tried a variety of regionally and locally introduced changes. Regionally, the REAA has introduced self-paced core curriculum materials for secondary students, materials specifically designed for rural Alaska. While centralizing some aspects of the curriculum, the REAA has localized school scheduling, allowing each community to choose the schedule that best fits its living pattern.[58]

Integrating education into the local community and its culture, as well as preparing students to confidently choose among a variety of options outside the community if they wish, is the most difficult challenge faced by the new rural districts. The ingenuity already being shown by several of the REAAs in providing quality high school education to rural students, using resources both within and outside the local community, merits further study and dissemination.

Shared Resources and New Technology

Related to developing new and better-quality rural programs is the need to increase the amount and type of resources available to both teachers and students. Small schools will not have the range of subject-matter teachers who are available in larger city schools, nor will small schools have well-stocked laboratories, libraries, audiovisual centers, or specialists nearby. Furthermore, inadequate phone and mail services have meant teachers may wait a month or more for a response to a simple request. What is being done to provide supplemental course materials for students and resources for teachers? How is technology being employed?

SB 35 recognized that the new school districts would need decentralized resource services but that the cost of a well-supplied and staffed resource center in each REAA would be prohibitive. Consequently, the concept of regional resource centers was included in the legislation. Roles suggested for the centers included provision of fiscal services, instructional support, staff development, and board training for member districts. Unfortunately, the legislature delayed funding the centers and the effectiveness of their operation is unknown at this time.

Experimenting with nontraditional delivery, the Alaska Department of Education has developed a five-year plan to carry communications and instruction via satellite. The project, called Educational Telecommunications for Alaska, will include design, testing, and delivery via satellite of electronic mail service, computer help to schools, phone lines, and radio for instruction and nationwide access to educational resources. In 1978, the electronic mail system went into effect in ten districts, the education department, and several other sites, and was used to meet administrative communication needs. "Mail Box" has put the districts in daily touch with the department, resource centers, and each other, helping to overcome mail delays and telephone problems. The other parts of the system were planned as of 1978 and will be implemented in future years. Good small rural schools are by no means unknown, but modern technology and the wealth of instructional resources now available provide opportunities for quality education previously unobtainable.

Conclusion

Central to all the above issues is the need to learn more about the developing REAAs and to provide a method whereby REAAs can share that information and learn to work cooperatively. A coordinated evaluation and dissemination process to support the new districts does not yet exist. Decentralization, done in this case by creating twenty-one locally controlled districts to replace one state agency, was a political solution to answer the demands of rural residents. The challenge now facing Alaska's rural citizens is one of turning their political victories into solid educational accomplishments. The REAAs provide the framework for more responsive rural education. However, realizing this potential for improvement in a reasonably efficient and economic manner requires the close cooperation and continuing dedication of all parties concerned.

One hundred and twelve years have passed since Alaska was purchased from Russia by the United States, and twenty years since Alaska became a state, but only three since delivery of educational services in rural Alaska was decentralized among 21 regional school districts. Control of rural education by elected school boards has provided the first opportunity for Native parents, the majority of rural residents, to shape the education received by their children. Despite limited time and the complexity of the task, the Regional Educational Attendance Areas *are* operational. Given Alaska's multicultural society, wealth of resources, and commitment to rural education, there is cause to be optimistic about the legacy of the current era of local control.

Notes

1. John Hanrahan and Peter Gruenstein, *Lost Frontier: The Marketing of Alaska* (New York: W. W. Norton, 1977), pp. 1–3.

2. *Facts About Alaska: The Alaska Almanac* (Anchorage: Alaska Northwest Publishing, 1977), p. 33.

3. Hanrahan and Gruenstein, *Lost Frontier*, p. 195.

4. Facts in this paragraph are from *2(c) Report: Federal Programs and Alaska Natives. Task I—An Analysis of Alaska Natives' Wellbeing* (Portland, Ore.: U.S. Department of the Interior, 1975).

5. Alaska Native Foundation, *Alaska Natives: A Status Report* (Anchorage: Alaska Native Foundation, 1977), p. 1.

6. Survey findings in this and the above paragraph are from *2(c) Report: Federal Programs and Alaska Natives. Task III—A Survey of Natives' Views.*

7. Letter from Paul Nachtigal (Project Director, Rural Education Project, Education Commission for the States, Denver, Colo.) to CNER, February 14, 1978.

8. Don Dafoe, *The Governance, Organization, and Financing of Education for Alaska Natives* (Fairbanks: University of Alaska, Center for Northern Educational Research), pp. 8–9. Report submitted to NIE.

9. David Getches, *Law and Alaska Native Education* (Fairbanks: University of Alaska, Center for Northern Educational Research, 1977), p. 3. ERIC Number ED 148 155.

10. Dafoe, *Governance, Organization, and Financing*, p. 12.

11. Getches, *Law and Alaska Native Education*, p. 4.

12. William Marsh, *North to the Future* (Juneau: Alaska Department of Education, 1967), p. 23.

13. Getches, *Law and Alaska Native Education*, p. 4.

14. Material in this and the above paragraphs on the territorial period is drawn from Frank Darnell, "Historical Review and Perspective," in Katherine Hecht and Ronald Inouye, eds., *New School Districts in Rural Alaska: A Report on the REAAs After One Year* (Fairbanks: University of Alaska, Center for Northern Educational Research, 1978), pp. 16–19. ERIC Number ED 151 942.

15. All figures on transfer of BIA schools are from Bureau of Indian Affairs, *Alaska Native Needs Assessment in Education, Project Anna. Part II. Alaska Native Education, An Historical Perspective* (Juneau: U.S. Government Printing Office, 1974), p. 177. Number 679/253/106.

16. Frank Darnell, Katherine Hecht, and James Orvik, *Prehigher Education in*

the Unorganized Borough: Analysis and Recommendations (Fairbanks: Univeristy of Alaska, Center for Northern Educational Research, 1974). Not all the CNER recommendations were followed in drafting SB 35. CNER recommended granting local control of education through gradual transition to units of local government, but SB 35 called for setting up special regional units for educational services that were not a part of the borough and city government structure.

17. For a discussion of how the regional districts differ from city and borough districts in Alaska, see P. Poland, "SB 35 and Regional Government," in Hecht and Inouye, eds., *New School Districts*.

18. Getches, *Law and Alaska Native Education*, pp. 25–26. For background on the harmful effects of sending children outside the home community for schooling, see Judith Kleinfeld, *A Long Way From Home: Effects of Public High Schools on Village Children Away from Home* (Fairbanks: University of Alaska, Center for Northern Educational Research and Institute of Social, Economic and Government Research, 1973). ERIC Number ED 087 581.

19. Dafoe, *Governance, Organization, and Financing*, p. 43.

20. Figures supplied by Alaska Department of Education ("Enrollment by Ethnic Group, First Quarter, 1977-78").

21. Betsy Levin and Philip Moise, "School Desegregation Litigation in the Seventies," *Law and Contemporary Problems* 39 (Winter 1975):112.

22. Darnell, Hecht, and Orvik, *Prehigher Education in the Unorganized Borough*.

23. Hecht and Inouye, eds., *New School Districts*.

24. Ibid., p. 85.

25. P. Goodwin, "Community Perspectives of a REAA: A Case Study Emphasizing Cultural Implications," in Hecht and Inouye, eds., *New School Districts*, p. 102.

26. Getches, *Law and Alaska Native Education*, pp. 28–29.

27. Frank Darnell, "Historical Review and Perspective," in Hecht and Inouye, eds., *New School Districts*, p. 28.

28. Hecht and Inouye, eds., *New School Districts*, p. 85.

29. M. Halloran, "Independence Brings Problems, Triumphs," in Hecht and Inouye, eds., *New School Districts*, p. 166.

30. Goodwin, "Community Perspectives," in Hecht and Inouye, eds., *New School Districts*, p. 102.

31. Getches, *Law and Alaska Native Education*, p. 31.

32. Hecht and Inouye, eds., *New School Districts*, p. 197.

33. Ibid., pp. 58–59.

34. Ibid., p. 51.

35. Ibid., p. 53.

36. J. Alter, "A Teacher Perspective on Decentralization," in ibid.

37. Goodwin, "Community Perspectives," in ibid., p. 91.

38. Hecht and Inouye, eds., *New School Districts*, p. 44.

39. Ibid., p. 47.

40. S. Horton, "Survey of Alaska Community School Committees," in ibid., p. 112.

41. Hecht and Inouye, eds., *New School Districts,* p. 79 (as reported in the Minutes of the Alaska State Board of Education, September, 1976).

42. Ibid., p. 184.

43. Ibid., p. 44.

44. Ibid., p. 87.

45. Goodwin, "Community Perspectives," in ibid., p. 102.

46. Harry Gamble, "School Committees Growing Says Official," *Alaska Education News,* April 1978, p. 2.

47. Hecht and Inouye, eds., *New School Districts,* p. 79 (Minutes of the Alaska State Board of Education, May, 1976).

48. Anne Just and E. Dean Coon, *Summary of Findings, Alaska School Finance Study Workshops, October–November 1976* (Fairbanks: University of Alaska, Center for Northern Educational Research, 1977). ERIC Number ED 151 942.

49. E. D. Coon, "Financing the REAAs," in Hecht and Inouye, eds., *New School Districts,* p. 135.

50. James Conant, "Why full state funding needn't kill the powers of local school boards," *The American School Board Journal* 165 (April 1978):40–42.

51. Hecht and Inouye, eds., *New School Districts,* p. 185.

52. The Task Force on Certification reported to the Alaska State Board of Education at its June 1978 meeting. However, its recommendations were not accepted and the Department of Education was charged to draft revisions to the certification requirements.

53. House Bill 945 and Senate Bill 606. This law was not enacted during the 1978 session.

54. David Beers, *It Happens When We Get There: Conversations With Teachers in Alaskan Villages* (Juneau: Alaska Department of Education, 1978).

55. Judith Kleinfeld and Franklin Berry, *Village High Schools: Some Educational Strategies to Help Meet Developmental Needs of Rural Youth.* ISER Occasional Paper No. 13 (Fairbanks: University of Alaska, Institute of Social and Economic Research, 1978).

56. Ray Barnhardt et al., *Small High School Programs for Rural Alaska, A Preliminary Report of the Small High Schools Project* (Fairbanks: University of Alaska, Center for Cross-Cultural Studies, 1978).

57. Margie Bauman, "Northwest Takes Bilingual Innovations Abroad," *Tundra Times* (Fairbanks), May 10, 1978, p. 4.

58. Mary Halloran, "Iditarod Faces its Own Kinds of Challenges," *Alaska Education News,* May 1978, p. 5.

Additional References

Alaska Telecommunications Program. "Educational Telecommunications for Alaska." Juneau: Alaska Department of Education and the Northwest Regional Educational Laboratory, 1977.

Arnold, Robert, et al. *Alaska Native Land Claims*. Anchorage: Alaska Native Foundation, 1976.

Barnhardt, Ray (editor). *Cross-Cultural Issues in Alaskan Education*. Fairbanks: University of Alaska, Center for Northern Educational Research, 1977. ERIC Number ED 141 951.

Coles, Robert. *Children of Crisis, vol. 4, Eskimos, Chicanos, Indians*. Boston: Little, Brown, 1977.

Coon, E. Dean; Just, Anne; and Waddell, Jerry. *School Finance in Alaska Report No. 1: An Overview of Current Issues, Sources and Distribution of Funds for Public Elementary and Secondary Education*. Fairbanks: University of Alaska, Center for Northern Educational Research, 1976. ERIC Number ED 131 528.

The Cross-Cultural Education Development Program Report, 1975. Fairbanks: University of Alaska (School of Education), 1975.

Darnell, Frank (editor). *Education in the North: Selected Papers of the First International Conference on Cross-Cultural Education in the Circumpolar Nations and Related Articles*. Fairbanks: University of Alaska, Center for Northern Educational Research, in cooperation with the Arctic Institute of North America, Montreal, 1972.

Jenness, Diamond. *Eskimo Administration: I. Alaska*. Technical Paper No. 10. Montreal: Arctic Institute of North America, 1962.

Kleinfeld, Judith, and Berry, Franklin. *Village High Schools: Some Educational Strategies to Help Meet Developmental Needs of Rural Youth*. ISER Occasional Paper No. 13. Fairbanks: University of Alaska, Institute of Social and Economic Research, 1978.

Marsh, William. *North to the Future*. Juneau: Alaska Department of Education, 1967.

Orvik, James, and Barnhardt, Ray (editors). *Cultural Influences in Alaska Native Education*. Fairbanks: University of Alaska, Center for Northern Educational Research, 1974. ERIC Number 097 159.

Peratrovich, Robert, Jr. *Source Book on Alaska*. Juneau: Alaska Department of Education, 1971.

Tobeluk v. Lind. No. 72-2450, Alaska Superior Court, Third Judicial District, Agreement of Settlement. September 1976.

7

The New Zealand Correspondence School: A Pragmatic System for the Basic Schooling of Isolated Children

Hector E. McVeagh

Introduction[1]

By world standards New Zealand's population is small; only three million in a country approximately the size of the British Isles. It is therefore a country with a comparatively scattered population and could be described as sparsely populated.

New Zealand is long and narrow, more than 2,000 kilometers from north to south. It is made up of two main islands, with many smaller islands off the coast. A mountainous country with many high peaks and valleys, it has a long coastline of over 8,000 kilometers. There are still many places in New Zealand which could be described as remote.

The majority of New Zealand's population is of European, mainly British, origin. There is a minority of the indigenous Maori (Polynesian) people, the approximate proportions being 90 percent European and 10 percent Maori. The New Zealanders are therefore a fairly homogeneous people; almost without exception they speak English as their first language. For most purposes we can say that instruction in the institutions of learning is in English.

This is not to say that Maori is a dead language. It is still very much alive. In certain areas of New Zealand it is spoken every day by Maori people, and it is widely used on ceremonial occasions. There has recently been renewed interest in the preservation of Maori language and culture. There is a growing realization of the great value of a bicultural society, and this means a bilingual one. The New Zealand Correspondence School is playing a prominent part in the teaching of Maori. It is one of the most popular subjects, in which there are more than a thousand students. However, it is taught as a language of itself and is not the medium through which other subjects are taught.

New Zealand's national education system is based on the 1877 Education Act of Parliament. The purpose of this act was to establish a national network of free, compulsory (from ages six through fifteen), and secular primary schools. A commitment to equal educational opportunity for urban and rural children alike was the underlying principle of both the 1877 act and subsequent educational reforms. For example, a statement made by the minister of education in 1939 has served not only as a reaffirmation of the 1877 act, but also as a fundamental (and often quoted) principle of New Zealand's education system today. He declared, "Every person, whatever his level of academic ability, whether he be rich or poor, whether he live in town or country, has a right, as a citizen, to a free education of the kind for which he is best fitted and to the fullest extent of his power."

Ensuring equality of educational opportunity has not been an easy task, especially in sparsely populated areas. The traditional way of reaching rural children at the primary school level has been to create an extensive system of one- or two-teacher schools throughout the countryside. Although several hundred of these schools have been closed during the past fifty years (primarily because of rural depopulation), they continue to constitute a valuable and respected sector of the New Zealand school system. The fact that nearly 700 of these small rural schools (i.e., approximately one-third of all public primary schools) remain in operation today is a tribute to their endurance and a reminder of their importance.

Overview of the Correspondence School

Despite the wide distribution of small rural schools there has always been a small, but significant, group of children living in areas too remote to make regular school attendance possible. Until the 1920s, these children had few attractive options. A few were able to attend boarding schools. Some were taught individually by their parents. Unfortunately, many completely missed the chance to have any formal education.

In response to these needs, the New Zealand Correspondence School was created in 1922 to provide an education at the primary school level for children living in remote areas. In 1929 courses at the secondary level were added. In the following years more courses were added, more services were provided, and the correspondence school (located in Wellington) grew rapidly to become one of the biggest educational institutions in the country, and an important branch of the New Zealand educational system.

Most schools in New Zealand are controlled by a local board of governors or education board which is responsible for education within its own district. The correspondence school, however, is a national school whose activities cover the whole of the country, and it is controlled directly by the head office of the national department of education.

In addition to providing full educational services to a core group of very rural primary and secondary students, the correspondence school also provides its benefits to children who are unable to attend school regularly because of ill health. During the nearly sixty years of its existence, the correspondence school has greatly expanded both its program and its clientele to include the following:

1. preschool children (ages three through five) who are unable to regularly attend an officially recognized kindergarten, play center, or preschool class of a primary school;
2. handicapped children (both intellectually and physically handicapped), who are provided with special courses;
3. specially gifted children who require extension programs;
4. adults of all ages who wish to complete or continue their education, including adult illiterates or semiliterates who, for one reason or another, have never learned to read or write satisfactorily;
5. new settlers, i.e., immigrants with non–English language backgrounds who wish to learn English;
6. teachers (a) who have not completed their basic training; (b) who are fully qualified but have been out of active teaching for more than two years and are required to undergo revision courses; and (c) who are fully qualified and in the teaching service, who wish to advance in the profession and therefore take courses to improve their background qualifications and extend their professional knowledge; and
7. the pupils of other small rural schools needing instruction in subjects (for example, science) in which the local teacher lacks the necessary knowledge.

When the correspondence school opened in 1922, there were about one hundred primary pupils working under the supervision of one teacher. Since this modest beginning, both the enrollment and the staff have steadily increased. As Figure 1 and Tables 1 and 2 indicate, the correspondence school "community" comprises approximately 13,000 students and a total staff of more than 300. It is by far the largest school in New Zealand. Its activities are national in scope, and it has many contacts with other schools and educational institutions both in New Zealand and abroad.

The principal of the school is responsible to the director-general of education, through the assistant director-general, for the conduct of the school. Inspections are conducted regularly by school inspectors. Two liaison inspectors have responsibility for maintaining contact with the school, one at the primary and the other at the secondary level. The teachers take part in refresher courses and generally participate in professional matters with teachers of other schools.

TABLE 1

ENROLLMENT IN NEW ZEALAND CORRESPONDENCE SCHOOL,
BY CLASSIFICATION, 1978

Classification	Enrollment
Preschool pupils (ages 3-5)	204
Primary pupils	690
Home Training (Seriously handicapped)	297
Individual Programme Section (requiring special programmes)	
mainly remedial: Primary	124
Secondary	72
Adult	485
Full-time Secondary Pupils	668
Part-time Adult Students	6,558
Pupils from Other Schools	1,526
Teachers Studying for Diploma in Teaching and Service	
Increment Courses	1,372
Teachers Studying for Trained Teachers' Certificate	205
Teachers Studying for Teaching Intellectually Handicapped	
Children Certificate	52
Retraining of Teachers Course	500

The Standing Committee on the Correspondence School operates in the head office of the department of education. It meets regularly under the chairman (the assistant director-general of education). The committee consists of senior departmental officers on both the professional and administration sides, elected representatives from the staff of the correspondence school, and the principal of the school. This committee is of great importance, as it considers all matters connected with the correspondence school and its development. Because the members of the committee are in senior executive positions, they are able to ensure that its recommendations are carried out.

Organization and Finance

The school is organized into four major divisions:

1. *Primary School* is mainly for full-time primary-level pupils, ages three through twelve-plus. The Primary School is divided into the following sections: preschool (ages three and four); junior school (ages five through seven); middle and upper school (ages eight through twelve-plus); home training (seriously handicapped children); and individual program (children with specific learning difficulties).
2. *Secondary Division* is for school-age pupils thirteen through eighteen

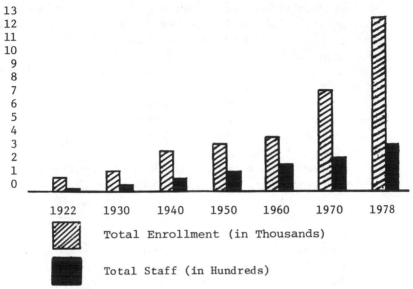

FIGURE 1 Growth of the New Zealand Correspondence School, 1922-1978.

TABLE 2

STAFF OF THE NEW ZEALAND CORRESPONDENCE SCHOOL,
BY FUNCTION, 1978

Function	Number
Chief Administrators	(5)
Principal	1
Associate Principal	1
Deputy Principals	3
Teachers	(264)
Preschool	8
Primary	47
Secondary	196
Resident	5
Advanced Teacher Studies	8
Administrative/Support Staff	(54)
Clerks	33
Typists	7
Storemen	6
Librarians	6
Illustrators	2

and for adults who want to continue their education. The Secondary Division is divided into the following groups: Avon (Form 3 and mathematics/science); Crescent (Form 4 and social studies, history, geography, and commerce); Hobson (Forms 5 through 7 and languages and music); Mansfield (Forms 5 through 7 and home economics and crafts; also pupils with special problems); the part-time adult student group; and the secondary schools group. (The names used for the groups have no particular significance except to describe where present groupings are located; they are simply a convenient method of distinguishing between groups.)

3. *The Advanced Studies for Teachers Division* conducts courses for teachers in cooperation with teacher training colleges.

4. *The Administration Division* provides backup support for the teaching groups.

The correspondence school is financed by an annual budget allocated from the government treasury through the department of education. The principal makes an annual application for funds to carry out the school activities, which are divided into certain categories. The most expensive items are (in descending order) salaries (paid directly by the department of education); post office charges; printing and stationery; traveling costs; resident courses; textbooks and library books; equipment; and general expenses, e.g., maintenance of buildings, electricity, local taxes, etc.

As the correspondence school is a nonprofit organization and part of New Zealand's free educational service, there are only minimal costs to parents of school-age children, and very modest fees for adult part-time students and for teachers. There is no charge to the parents for tuition; teaching materials (assignments, notes, etc.); postage; textbooks (loaned free of charge); and science, woodworking, and other kits with equipment (loaned free of charge).

Other expenses are subsidized by the government, such as the residential schools (parents pay approximately one-quarter of the fee, and travel is free); travel to other school activities (subsidized on a fifty-fifty basis); and school camps (the government pays for the camp itself, while parents make a contribution toward food and travel). The principal has at his disposal certain funds from donations and endowments which he can use to assist the children of needy parents. The general rule is that no children should be denied the opportunity of attending residential schools, camps, and the like because of their parents' financial circumstances.

As in other schools throughout New Zealand, parents are expected to purchase some items of equipment, e.g., exercise books, writing pads, pencils, pens, mathematical equipment, dressmaking materials, etc. Basically, however, the school provides a complete and free education for its school-age pupils.

The Correspondence School Program

Obviously, special procedures have had to be designed, tested, and modified over the years in order to ensure that as comprehensive a set of books, materials, and other instructional aids as possible are made available on a regular basis to the school's pupils. Years of experience have enabled the school to develop a relatively sophisticated process for assessing the learning needs and abilities of each child and for delivering an appropriate array of educational materials and services.

Not surprisingly, the heart of the correspondence school method is the printed assignment sent to and from the pupils through the mail. Each assignment contains two weeks' work for the student and is sent in specially constructed canvas or plastic bags. The school produces all its own assignments in all subjects at all levels. They are planned and written by teachers, illustrated and typed by the staff of the school, and presented ready for printing to the government printer. The printing itself is done by the New Zealand government printer on contract. The majority of the courses are printed by the offset process. Other printing requirements for the school, the various forms, books, magazines, and circulars, are also done by the government printer. The school does not run its own printing establishment, as the government printing office is located close to the school and can provide a complete service for all the school's needs.

Still, the necessity of supplying supplementary materials remains clear. Besides textbooks, library books are also sent from the school to its secondary-level students. In addition, the county library service mobile vans provide extra reading books for primary school children.

Isolated rural children, like children everywhere, want and need more than these printed materials. Therefore, the correspondence school has striven to provide other forms of stimulation and contact. For example, tape recordings are sent for courses in language, music, and several other subjects. Tapes (as will be discussed later) are also used as a medium of direct communication between the school's pupils and staff.

Increasing use is being made of visual materials throughout the school's curriculum. Color slides, photographs, and other such resources are now routinely sent along with the more formal instructional materials. For the pre-school students (and some older handicapped pupils), the school provides three-dimensional materials like toys, puzzles, and games on loan. And finally, students taking courses in arts and crafts, science, and woodworking are sent a variety of practical kits containing tools, experiments, and other more specialized materials which one could not expect to find in the home.

Beyond the provision of the resources mentioned above, the correspondence school places great emphasis on making possible the maximum number of live and direct contacts between students and their teachers. By definition, a correspondence-based school cannot begin to provide the same level of personal student-teacher interaction taken for granted in conventional schools. As a consequence, there is a conscious attempt to make up in quality and intensity what may be missing in terms of the number of teacher-student contacts.

There are several methods for achieving this end. Weekend seminars are occasionally organized for the more senior students and their teachers. Students and their families are also encouraged to visit the school's headquarters in Wellington to establish (or renew) contacts with teachers and other staff. A special program each year affords an opportunity for students to work directly with their teachers while their parents participate in the annual conference of the correspondence school Parents' Association.

Telephone contact (where possible) has also become an important avenue for home-school communication. Full-time school pupils or their parents may phone teachers collect when they feel such a call is justified. Teachers may call their students on the same basis. The usual situation justifying a special toll call is one in which the parent or child feels he needs counseling which can be more readily and quickly done person-to-person on the telephone, or in which the pupil is in danger of running out of work, or on any occasion where the school may have made a mistake and sent the wrong lessons. Teachers telephone new pupils to establish the exact course and to make an early personal contact.

Although no restriction has been placed on parents as to the number of calls they may make, our experience is that the use is not excessive. The telephone is used mostly as a method of prompt reassurance. It is a lifeline for troubled parents or pupils. This service has only recently been introduced and it is regarded as being of great value, particularly by the teachers, but also by the parents and pupils.

This is by no means all the contact provided. Indeed, two other methods—the resident and visiting teacher program and the audio media program—have proven to be most useful strategies. Each will be briefly described below.

Resident and Visiting Teachers

To a considerable extent, the isolation of the family and child can be dispelled through the visits of the resident teachers. At the moment there are five resident teachers, based in the Auckland area, the Waikato, east coast of the North Island, Marlborough-Nelson, and Otago-Southland. It is hoped that a sixth one will shortly be appointed to serve the Canterbury area. The resident teacher's role in making home visits is vital, particularly in the Primary Division. He meets the family, makes friends with the pupil, and finds out about his main interests and hobbies. He can evaluate the capabilities of the pupil and size up his potential. The resident teacher can also report on the level of work accomplished and on any difficulties being experienced. In a typical year, the five resident teachers together visit more than 700 homes. More than half of the homes are visited twice during the year. One-third of the school families are visited only once by the resident teacher, but approximately 10 percent enjoy three visits per year.

In those districts without a resident teacher, the school endeavors to send out a teacher from Wellington during the first term, so that every full-time pupil should be visited at least once a year. During 1977, six visiting teachers made journeys to outlying areas. One parent wrote a special note of praise for the visiting teacher: "We found her very understanding indeed, and she quickly became a family friend. A number of good things have happened since her visit, and we really appreciate the follow-up she has done."

Finally, it must be remembered that although it is the school's aim to have every pupil visited at least once a year, this cannot apply to those children who live overseas. They do not have the support or link that this service supplies, and must carry on as best they can. Perhaps the most isolated family we heard of was one in Nepal. One of the parents wrote: "We are 150 miles from Katmandu which takes ten days' walk to reach or 45 minutes by plane if there is one. Mail comes twice a week, but in the monsoon season from June to September, it is brought by runner from Katmandu every two or three weeks. Consequently, return of marked work is greatly delayed." How welcome a visit from a resident teacher would be to this family!

Audio Media

The correspondence school uses extensive audio backup to the printed assignment lessons. The school's audio program takes two basic forms: radio broadcasts and tape recordings.

The correspondence school broadcasts every morning of the school year for twenty minutes over a medium-wave network of Radio New Zealand. The program features the correspondence school's own teachers. In theory every part of New Zealand is covered by this program, although there are some localities in which reception is difficult. For students in these areas and those overseas who also are unable to hear the broadcast, the school arranges for cassette tapes to be made of the broadcasts, and these are mailed to pupils.

The broadcasts follow a regular pattern, and a program is issued with the handbook which is sent to all pupils at the beginning of the school year. Regular broadcasts include:

1. school assembly (held by the principal every two weeks, when special information is given on school events, current affairs, and matters of general interest);
2. junior program (assembly-type program for young pupils and their mothers);
3. music (primary and secondary level);
4. languages (English, French, Maori, and German);
5. speech training and poetry;
6. special groups (e.g., home training); and
7. secondary-level science and social studies.

The aim of the broadcasts is to enliven and extend the material in the printed lessons, but perhaps even more than this, to maintain a regular, direct, and aural contact between the school and the homes, the teachers and their pupils. Every school day starts at 9:00 a.m. with a broadcast direct from the teachers of the correspondence school.

In addition to the correspondence school's program, another is broadcast by Radio New Zealand in cooperation with the department of education. These "broadcasts to schools" are presented at different times of the day, but correspondence school children receive a program for the broadcasts and may listen to them when they are relevant to their own studies. Below is a fairly typical Radio New Zealand educational broadcast schedule:

Daily	9:25–9:45	Preschool "Join In"
Mondays	1:20–1:35	The World Today
	1:35–1:50	Story Time—Junior School
	1:50–2:00	Be Swift to Hear
Tuesdays	1:20–1:40	Tales and Legends
	1:40–2:00	Working with Music
Wednesdays	1:20–1:40	Family of Man
	1:40–2:00	Let's Make Music
Thursdays	1:20–1:30	The World Today
	1:30–1:45	Springboard
	1:45–2:00	Music and Movement—Junior School
Fridays	1:20–1:30	Comment
	1:30–1:50	Social Studies
	1:50–2:00	Listening Time—Junior School

In addition to the radio broadcasts, the correspondence school has developed (mainly over the past five years) its own system of tape recordings.

Originally these recordings were made to provide aural and oral work in languages. They were soon extended to music, and then to other subjects. They are now used to supplement the printed assignments in many subjects. Tape recordings are also used at the preschool and junior school level for story time; for the children to record their reading and return it to their teachers; and for direct contact between teacher and pupil. Although the school provides tape recordings in both reel-to-reel and cassette form, by far the majority of tapes are now sent on cassettes, and most students own cassette tape recorders. If a student does not have a recorder, the school will lend him one free of charge.

The growth rate for this service has been astronomical. In 1972, only 75 students received tape recordings from the school. Within five years, the number of regular users leaped to approximately 2,150. During the year each student may receive as many as 10 cassettes. This means that more than 20,000 cassettes are in use at present. These have been duplicated from master copies made by teachers at the school. At present the number of master copies in use comes to 350. This number will be increased to more than 500 in the coming year.

Social Contact

The relative lack of contact with teachers is not the only difference between correspondence school students and their counterparts in conventional schools. Peer contact also tends to be a relative rarity among children living in a remote rural areas, and social skills can suffer as a result. The school places great value, therefore, on facilitating social contact among students. The programs in this area will be briefly described.

One of the most important initiatives is the residential summer school. This is a full coeducational boarding school held for one month (November to December) on the campus of Massey University at Palmerston North, 150 kilometers north of Wellington. School-age children, aged ten to thirteen, are invited to spend one month with teachers from the correspondence school in a very broad educational, cultural, and social experience. With the staff of the school, a complete boarding school is established on the campus of the university.

Another popular program is the school camp. The resident and visiting teachers arrange camps for students of all ages in their own local areas, usually at a youth camp or other camp site. The camps are of a week's duration, and teachers from the school join in the program. Some parents go to the camps as well and have the chance of learning more modern educational methods. Parents assist in the actual running of the camps.

"School Weeks" and "School Days" are also organized on a regular basis. In the School Weeks program, various host schools invite correspondence school children to spend a week there. Children participate in the activities of the school to which they are attached. These activities are intended to extend beyond formal lessons and include drama programs, road safety instruction, visits to the local museum, swimming lessons, etc.

Throughout the country there are local parent-teacher groups organized by the resident teacher and the parents. They hold regular day-long meetings — School Days — at a local center. Teachers from the school often join in the activities. While the children are busy with their teachers, parents hold meetings — discussions on the children's work with other teachers, sometimes with specialized teachers brought in for the occasion. As the following comment from a rural parent points out, these School Days do more than enhance social contact for the children: "As a new mother, I felt completely lost and very unsure of my ability to teach my children. It was only by making the effort to go to a School Day I'd heard about, that I realised that here was a group of families all feeling pretty much as we did. By joining together, they were actively doing something to lessen the feelings of isolation both mental and physical."

Teaching and Teacher Support

Teaching at the correspondence school is carried out almost exclusively by full-time teachers employed at the school. Very little use is made of external part-time tutors except in the Advanced Studies for Teachers Division. Some adult students are taught by part-time tutors, but in the main, the teaching is done by the permanent full-time staff of the school. The correspondence school has developed a tradition of friendly, helpful, positive teaching on a one-to-one basis. Teachers are urged to treat every student as an individual, to write a personal letter with every returned assignment, and to encourage and generally promote the welfare of the students.

Teaching positions at the correspondence school are gained competitively in exactly the same manner as in all New Zealand state schools. Vacancies are advertised through the official "Education Gazette" and the rules of appointment to the state schools apply equally to the correspondence school. The school has built up a very well qualified staff.

The school is aware of the dangers of accepting teachers who have been unsatisfactory in the classroom. The policy of appointment is that pupils of the correspondence school need as good teachers as pupils elsewhere do. Although the teaching is done at a distance, it can be very personal and individualized. The experience of the correspondence school is that the importance of the teacher cannot be overstressed.

Because of the particular importance of the individual teacher, both in the correspondence school and in the network of small rural schools of New Zealand, teacher support has come to be a vital part of the school's overall program. This support takes many forms, the most prominent of which are dealt with below, but a central feature is the flexible, tailored approach offered.

In some sparsely populated districts of New Zealand there are not enough children to form a school qualifying for a fully certified teacher. In some regions the local education board is prepared to appoint an uncertified teacher to conduct a small school of as many as nine pupils. In this case, the education board will permit children to be placed fully on the correspondence school roll even though they actually attend a small local school.

In these schools the children have the advantage of some supervision and of working together on subjects in which group activity is desirable — music, drama, physical education, and art, for example. At the same time, they have the benefit of correspondence lessons and instruction, particularly in the basic subjects. They also have the advantage of being able to participate in the activities of correspondence students. In other words, they qualify for the school camps, residential school, etc. In addition, the school is visited by the resident and visiting teachers, who give the local inexperienced and uncertified teachers advice and guidance.

The correspondence school has for many years also offered a backup service to secondary schools throughout New Zealand. There are several reasons behind the creation of this service. Many of the smaller country schools are unable to offer a wide variety of subjects or to cope with teaching them at senior levels. The correspondence school is therefore available to ensure that children in the smaller schools in country areas have subject options comparable to those available in the larger centers.

The correspondence school will enroll and teach children whose own school suffers a sudden teaching shortage. This may be a temporary measure, but it ensures continuity of instruction. In addition, the correspondence school has large specialized departments, e.g., music and languages, and can offer these subjects at the highest level. Sometimes these levels are not available at local schools.

The correspondence school also provides resources to assist inexperienced and underqualified teachers. In certain circumstances these teachers may themselves enroll as adult students and follow the correspondence school courses. On other occasions, the senior inspectors may approve the issue of copies of assignments as a guide to teachers new to their subject.

The Advanced Studies for Teachers Division of the correspondence school has a dual role. It is used to help teachers become qualified to teach and to improve the teaching qualifications of already practicing teachers. The school's program includes assistance to individuals who have not been fully qualified but who have undertaken some teaching in an uncertified capacity. In certain circumstances, they may follow a course conducted by the correspondence school, the completion of which qualifies them for a full teaching certificate.

Teachers who undertake these courses are in three main categories: (1) members of religious orders who teach in church schools and are unable to attend the normal teacher training colleges; (2) teachers in the very small schools in the country; and (3) secondary school teachers who are university graduates and therefore qualify to teach in the secondary service, but who wish to gain certification that they have qualified pedagogically to teach.

Teachers who have not taught for three years are required to undertake a retraining course before their teachers' certificates are reissued to them. This includes teachers who have gone overseas for lengthy periods and wish to return to the New Zealand teaching service. A large proportion are married women who have been out of teaching while raising a family but wish to return to the profession. The correspondence school conducts certain retraining courses through its Advanced Studies for Teachers Division. The remainder of the training must be done in a practical situation in the classroom.

The diploma in teaching is available to teachers who wish to improve their professional background. These courses are not only of practical value in the professional advancement of the teachers; they also certify them for a higher teaching level and a higher salary. The subjects for the diploma in teaching may be taken through the correspondence school. In addition, teachers may take alternative subjects at a university and build up credits toward the diploma in teaching. The Advanced Studies for Teachers Division also conducts certain courses for specialist teachers, for example, teachers of handicapped children and of very young children.

The Advanced Studies for Teachers Division works somewhat differently from the remainder of the school. It is controlled dually by the principal of the correspondence school and the director of teacher education in the head office of the education department. The major portion of the tutoring is done through the lecturing staff of the teachers' colleges. The planning, course production, and overall coordination is done through the correspondence school.

Parental Supervision of Correspondence Students

One of the distinguishing features of correspondence education, particularly with young children, is that in a very real sense parents must be prepared and assisted to be direct and active "teaching partners" of the school's professional staff. In the correspondence school context parental involvement is not a luxury; it is a necessity. Consequently, any discussion of teacher issues here cannot afford to overlook the role of the actual "classroom supervisors."

When the schoolroom is in the home and family life carries on around it, there will be many diversions and distractions. Even the area where the child studies can create a problem. A recent school questionnaire revealed that 36 percent of the pupils did their schoolwork in the kitchen; 11 percent did it in the bedroom; and 53 percent worked elsewhere in the house or beyond (one family said their child studied in a caravan [trailer], and another indicated that a bus was the regular work area for their child).[2]

This survey pointed out that although most children (80 percent) worked on a regular schedule, farming families often needed to make adjustments (or even briefly put aside the schoolwork) during peak periods of farm activity. This, of course, has its effect on supervision of lessons, and it is to the credit of 38 percent of the mothers that they were able to say that outside responsibilities never interfered with their supervising duties. Other mothers reported difficulty in concentrating on schoolwork because of the need to do other jobs in the home. As many as 62 percent of mothers stated that supervision sometimes suffered. But in spite of these difficulties, 98 percent of the mothers managed to read over their children's completed work.

The survey also confirmed the assumption that mothers rather than fathers were the primary supervisors for the children's school activities. However, one parent took umbrage at the presumption of "mother's" involvement and argued, "The School should not be fostering archaic principles by its insistence that Mother be helping all the time. I see no reason for the School's assumption that I should be female. Nor can my wife!"

How does an untrained mother cope with the duties of a teacher (which are complicated by the fact that she is supervising her own children)? Does she feel the inadequacy of her own education? Does she have to spend inordinate time on preparation? Has she received much support from her husband? How real are her fears that her own inadequacies are holding up her children's progress? Does she feel harassed when new work arrives? These are some of the questions this survey sought to answer.

Of course the pressures vary from one mother to another. For example, 47 percent of the mothers surveyed had only one child, whereas 16 percent had to cope with four or more children. Differences also existed in the amount of supervision time actually spent. Some mothers reported spending more than three times as many hours on supervisory activities as other mothers of correspondence school pupils. The amount of time spent is not necessarily an indicator of the quality of supervision provided, nor of the hardship imposed on each family. Fifteen percent of the respondents spent less than ten hours supervising their child's work, while 16 percent spent more than thirty hours.

Fortunately, 76 percent of the mothers felt they were able to give their children adequate supervision, but 32 percent felt the need of some further education themselves; 29 percent were concerned they were unable to spend enough time; and 14 percent found difficulties in coping with subject content. (Mathematics seemed to be the prime culprit. One mother stated she had difficulty with metrics, but hadn't time to learn.) Thirty-five percent lacked confidence. In spite of the difficulties, only 40 percent felt their children would make better progress if they had had more supervision. One parent was convinced she had given an older child too much help and ruined his ability to work alone. She wrote, "It is necessary to ensure that the pupil does not become completely dependent on the supervisor—self-help must be encouraged."

It was pleasing to note that 68 percent of the mothers actively enjoyed supervising their children's work and only 6 percent felt harassed by the arrival of more work to be done. When asked which subjects were most interesting, dozens of respondents replied "everything." Library books also proved popular, with 73 percent of mothers reading them too.

The results of the survey, as well as years of observation, support the conclusion that the most important and most exacting period in which supervision is required is through the first three years of the children's schooling. This is also the period in which the parents show the most uncertainty and anxiety. To help the parent-supervisors, the junior school courses provide assignments for the mothers to parallel those sent to the pupils. There is a "mother's booklet" explaining what the children should be learning and giving general information to assist the supervision. In addition, the school broadcasts regularly feature advice to mothers on the teaching of the younger children.

The resident and visiting teachers give a special emphasis to assisting mothers of young children. When school camps are arranged, it is common for mothers to come and stay, and special programs are arranged, involving evening discussions with educational advisors on different aspects of learning and teaching.

The correspondence school publishes a newsletter once a term, called "Mailbag," which is sent to every home with children on the roll. "Mailbag" gives school news, reports on the latest developments in education, and advises parents on educational problems and how best to solve them. Future plans to help parents include weekend seminars for mother-supervisors, which will be held in various regions and conducted by the senior teachers of the infant and junior schools.

Problems and Performance of the Correspondence School

The Dropout Rate

All distance education systems have a regular dropout rate. The New Zealand Correspondence School is no exception. For teachers and other adult students, there is a regular falling off of about 30 percent of the roll.

This is to be expected, although every effort is made to encourage adult students to continue.

For children of compulsory school age (ages six through fifteen inclusive) there is a legal obligation on the parents to ensure that work is returned regularly. If it is not, then the matter is handed over to the attendance officer of the local education board. It is comparatively rare for parents not to cooperate. A particular feature of correspondence education is that any default in performing the required work is very apparent. The work is written down and mailed back to the school, and this constitutes tangible evidence. The lack of returned assignment lessons makes any default very obvious. Failure to complete work in an ordinary day school is often not so obvious. Where there are problems, the teachers contact the resident or visiting teacher and ask him to pay a special visit to try to solve any problems on the spot and report back on any further action that needs to be taken.

Prompt Return of Work

Good organization of a large correspondence teaching establishment requires the prompt turnaround of all schoolwork. A student may easily become discouraged if his lessons are out of his hands too long. He needs the reinforcement of the teacher's comments and encouraging remarks. A rule within this school is that all lessons must be returned in the week they arrive. This deadline is sometimes hard to achieve, but it is nevertheless conscientiously pursued.

Short-Term Enrollments and Late Starters

The large turnover in the school's roll is caused mainly by children who come and go because of illness and recovery or because they have moved from one place to another. Other secondary schools sometimes place pupils on the school's roll at short notice, when they suddenly suffer the loss of a teacher. Short-term enrollments are always a problem, as different schools do not always cover their syllabus topics in the same order.

At present, most of the school's courses consist of fifteen lessons in sequential order. As plans are made for new courses, the aim is to have some of them on a modular system. Each topic will be covered by two or three modules which can be done in any order. Thus students will be able to move more easily into the assignment pattern.

Practical Subjects

Subjects which require practical work bring some problems. As mentioned earlier, the school has specially designed kits for practical work in subjects such as art, woodwork, and the sciences. At the highest levels in the specialized sciences, equipment is too sophisticated and expensive to provide to every student. In these cases, the correspondence school concentrates practical work into a one-week or two-week course and arranges for students to be accommodated at the nearest secondary school. In the new correspondence school facility, opened in 1978, there is a fully equipped laboratory for practical science work, and students are brought in to complete this work under the guidance of their own teachers.

Provision of Textbooks and Other Materials

As mentioned earlier, the correspondence school issues textbooks on loan free to all school-age pupils. This is required by law. The school also issues tape recordings, practical kits, and art materials. These services bring problems of both distribution and collection. The correspondence school maintains its own textbook store, manned by administrative personnel on the staff who mail and receive back all the necessary materials. Among the most difficult recent items are the cassette tape recorders, which are awkward to store and to mail and which require servicing. At present, the solution is to have the resident and visiting teachers issue cassette recorders to the students, and when necessary, retrieve them from the students. But this is not a complete solution, as the resident teachers do not cover the whole country. Pupils in areas outside the jurisdiction of the resident teachers have their recorders mailed to them from the main store in Wellington. There is some concern that the current solution may overburden the already very busy resident teachers, and the school is seeking other alternatives. One possible arrangement is to make the issue and recovery of tape recorders the function of the district stores officer of the education boards scattered throughout the country.

The production of cassette tapes also brings problems of volume. When tape recordings were confined to courses in language and music, the school could handle them. But as more subjects and teachers become involved, the problems of recording, sending, and receiving back the cassettes are growing. Very careful planning needs to be carried out to ensure that the system does not become overburdened and can cope with the ever-increasing demand.

Adequate Staffing and Facilities

The correspondence school has had some problems in obtaining adequate administrative staffing. It is most essential that the school has not only good teachers, as discussed elsewhere in this paper, but that it has an adequate administrative staff to back up teaching services.

The whole staff of the school must work as one team devoted to the same objective, and that is a good and swift service to the students. The school must therefore have an efficient system. At present, a new physical plant for the school has just been completed. It is an unusual building designed to carry out an unusual task. In the words of the architect who designed it in consultation with the school staff, it needs to be "something of a school, something of an office and something of a warehouse. It is all three things; it is none of them; but it is the sum of them."

Costs

The New Zealand Correspondence School is not designed as a cost-saving institution. Its particular task is to give as full and complete an education as is possible at a distance. The aim is to provide the students with teaching, resources, and opportunities that approximate as closely as possible daily attendance at a conventional school. Obviously there are some expensive items of equipment, such as film projectors, which cannot be issued on an individual basis. But it is intended to make the students of the correspondence school feel equal to those children who are able to attend school.

The staffing of the correspondence school is on approximately the same ratio as that of ordinary schools. Because teachers' salaries are one of the major costs in education, there is no saving in this sector. Nevertheless, education by correspondence in New Zealand is slightly cheaper than the cost of educating children in ordinary day schools. A precise figure is difficult to arrive at, as there are many hidden factors in the costing of the correspondence school services. As far as it is possible to estimate, the per-pupil cost is about 15 percent below the average per-pupil costs in normal New Zealand schools. It would be possible to make correspondence education much cheaper than conventional education. This, however, is not the aim in New Zealand. The aim is to give equal opportunity to all.

Effectiveness

Correspondence school students take the usual New Zealand public examinations for school certificate, university entrance, and university bursaries (scholarships). These examinations correspond approximately with the British general certificates of education at the O and A levels, although there is no exact equivalent. Like all major schools, the correspondence school is an accrediting school, entitled to accredit its students for university entrance. It may also award its students two important internally assessed certificates, the sixth form certificate and the higher school certificate.

The school keeps complete records of examination results, which reveal that its pupils perform as well as students studying by conventional methods. But bare results from examinations do not show a complete picture, and in the case of the correspondence school the situation is confused by the large number of students who come on the roll during the year. Some of them are transferred quite late and join the corresondence school just before examination time. Comparisons are very difficult to make. What can be confidently stated is that the examination results of correspondence school pupils are well up to the national standard. Correspondence school students cover the same syllabuses as students at other New Zealand schools. Whenever they transfer from the correspondence school to a conventional school they have no difficulty in taking their place in the equivalent classes.

In conclusion, the New Zealand correspondence school can properly be regarded as an innovation in rural education which has proved its merit and thereby become a well-established, permanent feature of the national education system.[3] Problems and challenges continue to arise, of course, but innovative strategies to successfully meet them are continually being developed and incorporated in the correspondence school structure. Perhaps the comment which sums up best of all the hoped-for response was from a young pupil whose mother writes, "Our little five year old is usually asking by 7 a.m. 'When are we going to start?'"

Notes

1. Some of the Introduction is taken from E. E. Henry, *Aspects of Pre-School, Primary and Secondary Education in Sparsely-Populated Areas of New Zealand* (Paris: OECD/CERI, 1978).

2. Survey data was extracted from a November 1977 correspondence school report entitled *Schoolroom in the Home.*

3. For further information on the New Zealand Correspondence School, see Hector E. McVeagh, *Mass Delivery Systems. New Zealand's Experience with Correspondence Education,* Report of the Commonwealth Conference on Materials for Learning and Teaching, September 22–October 3, 1975 (London: Commonwealth Secretariat, 1976), pp. 81–87; McVeagh, "The New Zealand Correspondence School and its Use of Media," *Educational Broadcasting International,* Vol. 6, No. 4 (December 1973), pp. 175–179, republished in *Epistolo Didaktika* 1974, Vol. 1, pp. 69–74; McVeagh, "Pregnant Schoolgirls and their Continuing Education," *New Zealand Medical Journal,* Vol. 83 (May 26, 1976), pp. 354–357. See also the following, published by the New Zealand Correspondence School, Wellington: Albert E. Kaye, *The Uses of Correspondence Education in Developing Countries,* a report on establishing correspondence systems in Malawi and Uganda (1976); Hector E. McVeagh, *Correspondence Education in New Zealand* (1976); McVeagh, *The Development of Open Learning for Adults* (1977); and McVeagh, *Some Aspects of the New Zealand Correspondence School,* paper presented to the Australasian Conference on the Changing Role of the Correspondence School, Raywood, South Australia (November 1976).

IN-SCHOOL INNOVATIONS

8

Sea Change in the Western Isles of Scotland: The Rise of Locally Relevant Bilingual Education

John Murray and Finlay MacLeod

EDITOR'S INTRODUCTION

In recent years, government reorganization has inspired far more cynicism than hope. Although promoted as a method for better problem solving, it has often been used as a technique for delaying the solution of any problem. Instead of increasing the government's effectiveness and inspiring needed reforms, reorganization has commonly had the demoralizing effect of increasing confusion and reducing the potential for reform. Given this record, it was perhaps to be expected that throughout the OECD nations, government reorganization has fallen into some disrepute and has come to be viewed as something to be endured rather than embraced.

Therefore, it is perhaps all the more surprising that the spur to a series of reforms and the catalyst for a rejuvenation of social, educational, and cultural life in the Western Isles of Scotland was the government reorganization of 1975. Prior to 1975, the islands' affairs had not only been administered from the mainland but also had been divided between two separate mainland authorities. Many residents of the Western Isles felt that their concerns got lost in the shuffle under this arrangement. So, when the Western Isles Islands Council was born in 1975, it became the focal point for encouraging (and asserting) the local people's emerging sense of solidarity, pride, and common purpose.

A cluster of new educational and culturally oriented initiatives has been

This chapter describes events through the end of 1978. For more recent (and detailed) information, see John Murray et al., *Bilingual Primary Education in the Western Isles* (Stornoway, Scotland: Western Isles Islands Council, 1980).

inaugurated since the reorganization took effect. Their overriding purpose
has been to serve as forums for people to gain a deeper understanding of
their cultural identity and then use that increased awareness to improve
the cohesiveness and quality of their own communities and of the
Western Isles as a whole. This report is an attempt to describe one of
these innovations and to explore its meaning and value within the context of the Western Isles.

First, however, it might prove useful to understand a bit more about
the Western Isles themselves.[1] Otherwise known as the Outer Hebrides,
five major islands (Lewis, Harris, North Uist, South Uist, and Barra) compose the Western Isles. The largest and most northerly is Lewis, whose
principal town of Stornoway is the headquarters for the new Western Isles
Islands Council.

The Western Isles lie off the northwest coast of Scotland. Their total
area is 1,119 square miles and the total population is some 30,000, of
whom 5,500 live in Stornoway, Lewis. Apart from Stornoway there is no
sizable township, with most of the population living in villages situated
mainly near the coast.

Over the past sixty years there has been a steady decline in population,
as shown in Table 1. The number of deaths has exceeded the number of
births, and migration outflow has exceeded inflow, though at a much
reduced rate in recent years. In fact, there is speculation that one important consequence of the initiatives started after 1975 will be a stabiliza-
tion of the population (or even a small return migration).

Crofting (farming) is the traditional way of life. Manufacturing
employment, dominated by the textile industry, particularly the making
of Harris tweed, has leveled out after a decline. One of the primary occupations is fishing, in which there has been reasonable stability. There is

Table 1

POPULATION OF THE WESTERN ISLES, 1911–1974

Year	Population
1911	46,732
1921	44,177
1931	38,986
1951	35,591
1961	32,609
1973	30,141
1974	30,060

a substantial and increasing service sector, particularly in education, health, and local government. In this sector female employment has increased while male employment has declined. Employment in the construction industry, mainly male, declined substantially between 1969 and 1971 but has increased somewhat since. A significant number of the working population is self-employed. The rate of unemployment, at 14 to 15 percent, is high but has been improving. Oil-related developments have so far had only a slight impact on the economy, resulting from the establishment of a construction unit near Stornoway. A military base has developed on the island of Benbecula, where the military population, including families, outnumbers the local indigenous population.

Communications have improved in recent years. Main roads are of good quality, and subsidiary roads, though often narrow, are well maintained. Ferry and air services, both interisland and to the mainland, are reasonably regular. The geography of the islands, however, means that relatively few areas are readily accessible to Stornoway, so far to the north. The outlying areas of Lewis and Harris can be up to two hours' road distance from the town. The Uists, although linked together through Benbecula by a good road, can be reached from Harris only by ferry. The island of Barra, in the south, is in a particularly isolated position despite being on the air route. Smaller islands, such as Eriskay and Vatersay, are served only by very small craft. In winter, communications, both internal and external, can pose real problems.

Gaelic is the spoken language of a high proportion of the population. It is frequently the language of the home, the neighborhood, and the church. The 1971 census showed a total of 23,205 Gaelic-speakers. The Western Isles Islands Council has adopted a policy of positive support for the bilingualism characteristic of the area. Table 2 indicates the percentage of the population, by area, which is bilingual (in Gaelic and English), and Table 3 shows the age distribution of bilingualism.

Table 2

PERCENTAGE OF GAELIC-ENGLISH SPEAKERS IN THE
WESTERN ISLES, BY AREA

Area	Percentage of Population
Lewis (landward)	89.5
Lewis (Stornoway)	53.7
Harris	88.8
North Uist	89.2
South Uist	77.2
Barra	87.3

Table 3

AGE DISTRIBUTION OF GAELIC-ENGLISH SPEAKERS
IN THE WESTERN ISLES

Age	Percentage of Gaelic-English Speakers
3 - 4	42
5 - 9	66
10 - 14	74
15 - 24	76
25 - 44	79
45 - 64	90
65 +	94

The Education System

The people of the Western Isles have traditionally placed a high value on academic achievement, and a large number of young people have always sought to enter the professions. Teaching has been particularly attractive, and as a result the region is largely self-supporting in its teacher supply. An important factor has been the desire of many young teachers to return to the Western Isles after completing their training, or following a short period of service elsewhere.

At present about 90 percent of the total teaching staff in primary schools are natives of the Western Isles. The overall pupil-to-teacher ratio, 18.7:1, compared with the national level of 22.4, is favorable, and there is a great deal of stability in staffing. Most primary schools in the Western Isles provide a house for the head teacher. Such provision has in the past acted as a considerable incentive to recruitment of head teachers. This is perhaps less so now, when home ownership is economically more attractive, but the majority of school houses are still occupied by head teachers. Recognizing that the small primary schools cannot be expected to have specialists on their own staffs, the education authority deploys itinerant teachers of music, art, physical education, dancing, and piping.

Staffing standards in secondary schools are on the whole satisfactory. The pupil-to-teacher ratio is 12.4:1. There are shortages in certain subjects. Remoteness of schools, and to some extent lack of housing, cause difficulty in recruitment of staff. There is considerable use of itinerant teachers; however, the bad weather occasionally restricts their travel from school to school.

As is true for most of rural Scotland, small schools are the norm rather than the exception. Given the long-standing policy that no primary school student should be required to live away from home, there have been situations of schools in the Western Isles having only one or two students, as well as exceptional arrangements in which a teacher is provided at a very remote location even in the absence of a school. Table 4 indicates the range of school sizes at the primary level; Table 5 illustrates the range among secondary schools. It should be noted that of the fifty-nine primary schools all but three are in sparsely populated areas; eleven have a single teacher, nineteen have two teachers, and thirteen have three teachers.

Table 4

ENROLLMENT DISTRIBUTION OF PRIMARY SCHOOLS
IN THE WESTERN ISLES

Enrollment	Number of Schools
1 - 19	11
20 - 49	22
50 - 75	14
76 - 100	3
101 - 125	5
126 - 150	1
151 - 180	1
181 - 210	1
700 +	1
Total primary enrollment: 3865	Total primary schools: 59

Table 5

ENROLLMENT DISTRIBUTION OF SECONDARY SCHOOLS
IN THE WESTERN ISLES

Enrollment	Number of Schools
1 - 19	2
20 - 49	2
50 - 75	4
76 - 100	2
101 - 125	-
126 - 150	1
151 - 180	2
181 - 210	-
211 - 240	1
1200 +	1
Total secondary enrollment: 2410	Total secondary schools: 15

It is also the policy of the education authority that primary school pupils should be able to attend without the need for undue daily travel from home. For a journey of over two miles, school transport is provided free. Twenty percent of primary pupils are transported to and from school daily. In the secondary sector, 38 percent of pupils are transported daily. In Harris, the Uists, and Barra, journeys from home to school are seldom in excess of one hour. Not surprisingly, many pupils who have to travel daily find difficulty in taking part in recreational activities or other extracurricular pursuits.

Innovations in Community and Cultural Education

As noted earlier, the creation of the Western Isles Islands Council has been the catalyst for a variety of "locally relevant" development activities. The Bilingual Education Project (BEP) is the focal point of this chapter not only because it is the most school-related initiative, but also because it serves as a prime example of the direction and effects of current innovations in the Western Isles.

It should be noted that the full burden of innovation—of saving the language and culture—did not fall exclusively upon the Bilingual Education Project. BEP's role was (and is) a crucial one, but it can properly be viewed as one of a series of related innovations sponsored by the Western Isles Islands Council, the Highlands and Islands Development Board, philanthropic organizations, and the national government.

From the community and cultural education perspective, the most important complements to BEP are the following:

1. *The Community Education Project* (Proisect Muinntir nan Eilean). With funding from the Bernard van Leer Foundation, this project has been working since 1977 to organize community-based, community-run initiatives in villages of the Western Isles. In essence, the Community Education Project (CEP) provides an education/training dimension to local community action efforts. For example, in Ness (the first project site) CEP played a central role in organizing play groups for young children without access to organized preschool activities; aided a group of local adults seeking to improve the production of vegetables on their crofts (farms); established a major local history group; helped renovate and revive the community center; and was a key agent in the creation of a multifunction community cooperative for the Ness area. In 1978, two other CEP sites were added, one in Harris and the other in Iochdar (South Uist).

2. *The Community Cinema and Video Project* (Cinema Sgire). Since the only cinema in the Western Isles is located on a military base in

Benbecula, and since the national media rarely broadcast either in Gaelic or on subjects of special interest to Western Isles residents, the need for Cinema Sgire was obvious. One major service rendered by this project is to travel around the Western Isles showing films in remote rural villages having no other access to them. Yet the more innovative part of Cinema Sgire's work involves videotaping a wide variety of locally relevant programs in Gaelic which are entertaining and/or instructional—and which, in any case, are designed to reinforce local traditions, local pride, and local development. For example, videotapes have been made on everything from traditional songs of Western Isles weavers to new commercial fishing opportunities and processes. In addition to their intrinsic worth, the materials produced through this effort serve not only as an educational tool but also as a springboard for community discussions and community action on common problems.

3. *The Gaelic Theatre Company* (Fir Chlis). In July 1977, the first professional Gaelic-language live theater group was formed in the Western Isles, with grant aid from the Scottish Arts Council and the Islands Council. The group tours extensively in the Western Isles and Western Scotland, performing for adult audiences and for schools. The company aims to present new work as far as possible, and by adopting a flexible format it encourages active participation by the audience in Gaelic drama. In schools, the company uses specially written material to stimulate children to explore through drama the potential of themes of particular relevance, such as "the sea." The actors also take part in drama workshops in schools, and the company intends to become involved in training amateur groups throughout the Western Isles.

Of course, it should be remembered that the Bilingual Education Project and the other efforts described above represent a significant departure from past practice and a new direction for the development of the Western Isles' human resources. Thus, these innovations are very much in a state of evolution themselves. Modifications of present practice will inevitably occur with further experience. However, the underlying strategy of community self-reliance and a style of development which is respectful of and responsive to local concerns will doubtless remain intact.

The Bilingual Education Project

In the Western Isles, where there is no varied network of institutions, the school exerts a particularly powerful influence on the attitudes and perceptions of the population as a whole. To a great extent, the school defines for pupils and the community what experience is valuable and what knowledge is important. Gaelic, which is the everyday language of eight out of every ten people in the islands, was not deemed suitable for inclusion in the state school curriculum until this century, and although for many years Gaelic has been taught as a *subject* in primary and secondary schools, only in the past two decades has serious consideration been given to its use as a teaching and learning medium. In recent years, the Scottish education department and local authorities in Gaelic areas have encouraged and assisted schools to adopt a mode which would develop the capabilities of the bilingual child. However, in the absence of any structure through which resources could be channeled and directed, progress toward a bilingual program and a minimal provision of supportive teaching materials was spasmodic and haphazard.

As a result of negotiations involving the Scottish education department and the local education authority during the transitional period of local government reorganization, a three-year research and development project in English/Gaelic bilingual education in primary schools was established in the Western Isles in September 1975. At the completion of this initial period, a second three-year component was approved and funded by the Western Isles Islands Council and the Scottish education department. These new resources are being used both to consolidate all the gains made thus far and to spread the project's work even more extensively throughout the Western Isles.

The general aim of the Bilingual Education Project is to introduce and develop for children from a Gaelic-speaking background a primary school curriculum which will enable them to learn through Gaelic as well as through English. Two experienced primary school teachers, one from North Uist and one from Lewis, were sent by the Western Isles education department to work full time on the project team with the director, a native of Lewis with experience in both teaching and Gaelic publishing. Several weeks later, a secretary was appointed. In August 1976, a teacher of art joined the project two days per week to assist the team with illustrations and graphic work.

The principal tasks set out for the project team in cooperation with teachers and others are

1. to devise situations and activities which will encourage children to use Gaelic in school as a natural language for exploration and description of experience;
2. to devise and evaluate a wide range of relevant materials, both printed and audiovisual;
3. to provide in-service courses for teachers;
4. to make materials and findings emanating from the project available to all schools in the Western Isles;

5. to inform parents and the community and seek to involve them in the project; and
6. to develop and maintain connections with similar projects elsewhere and with other interested agencies.

In its first year the project concentrated on primary classes 1 through 3. The following year classes 4 and 5 were included, and in the third year, with the inclusion of classes 6 and 7, the project was in operation throughout the primary school. It was acknowledged at the outset that this rate of growth would place severe strains upon the team and the schools, but it was agreed that the necessity to make some impact throughout the primary school curriculum was of paramount importance.

Of the fifty-nine primary schools in the area, twenty were invited to become "trial schools" (see Figure 1). The letter of invitation stated that acceptance would involve the staff and pupils actively in changing the balance of language use in school and in effecting a fundamental and far-reaching alteration in primary school education as a whole. All twenty schools accepted the invitation. The total enrollment of these schools is about 1,100, amounting to 28 percent of the total primary school population of the Western Isles; 90 percent of the children and fifty-two out of the fifty-four teachers involved have a knowledge of Gaelic. The schools range in size from the five-teacher school at Back, Lewis, with one hundred and thirty pupils, to the one-teacher, fifteen-pupil school at Kallin, North Uist; and geographically they are spread throughout the hundred-mile-long island chain. As soon as the letters of acceptance were received, the team visited the twenty schools and discussed the aims of the project with head teachers and staff.

The early months of the project were fraught with practical difficulties, but these shared vicissitudes helped to bring the team—who were virtual strangers to each other—together. Much time was spent in discovering mutual and individual interests, strengths, and predilections through extensive open discussion of all aspects of the project. This period of intensive assimilation of ideas and information from a variety of sources was crucially important in developing solidarity within the team as well as in establishing the main thrusts, the pace, method, and style of operation of the project.

It was decided that the team member from Uist should work from a base at Claddach Kirkibost, North Uist, and be principally concerned on a day-to-day basis with the ten schools in Uist and Barra, while the Lewis team member should work with the ten schools in Lewis and Harris. The project director agreed to be based in Stornoway. The greatest disadvantage of operating the project from two centers has been the separation of the team; on the other hand, it brought the project into closer contact with individual schools and teachers throughout the area than would have been possible

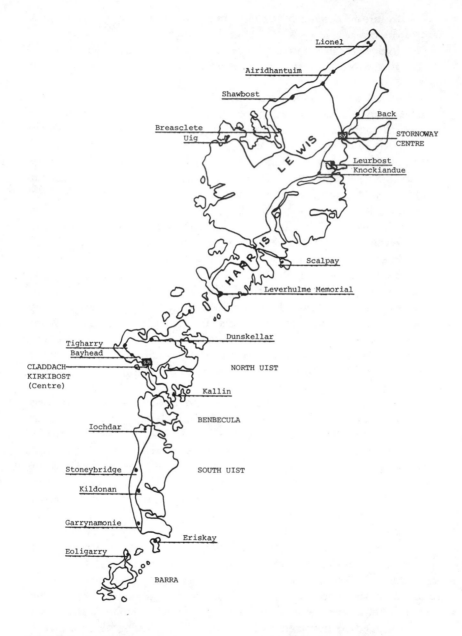

FIGURE 1   Bilingual Education Project: Project Schools and Project Centers.

otherwise. Thus, although the team—particularly the person working in Uist—has undoubtedly suffered in some respects, the schools have undoubtedly benefited.

Underlying all the project's activities is the attempt to discover and to fulfill the special needs of the bilingual child in terms of the local and national communities to which that child naturally belongs. Since the team's access to the children is indirectly through teachers, it was necessary to discover first the way in which teachers perceived the children's needs, as well as the teachers' perception of their role in the school and in the community. Subsequently, the team had to be ready to persuade or convince teachers, if necessary, that changes had to be made; that they could be done; and that teachers were the right people to plan and to put into effect these fundamental changes.

It became evident to the team at an early stage that a school's acceptance of the original invitation to participate in the project did not necessarily mean that the school would welcome change, nor that individual teachers were prepared or even willing to become agents of change. The project works in an area involving complex and emotionally charged attitudes—toward language, toward schooling, toward cultural traditions, and toward the local community. It was evident that one of the greatest services the team could perform would be to bring latent attitudes of all kinds to the surface by encouraging, provoking, and facilitating open discussion and debate of issues and questions concerning bilingualism and bilingual education.

The project's attempts to do this were assisted by statements issued by the Western Isles Islands Council concerning its overall bilingual policy, statements in which the project was proclaimed to be the most significant and important venture undertaken so far in the direction of bilingualism. A number of public statements have been made since about bilingualism in general and the project in particular by political parties, community groups, agencies, institutions, and individuals. Undoubtedly, these circumstances placed some strain on the team, which had to continue its work with unmitigated energy and conduct its affairs with the utmost discretion.

Encouragement of fresh thinking by the teachers themselves together with a readiness to appraise the thinking and practice of others is essential for curricular review and development. Accordingly, it was arranged that the team should work with teachers individually and in groups, and that *all* teachers should be involved in groups which would meet as often as possible. The project has organized more than one hundred meetings of such groups since January 1976. Groups meet in project centers, or, if the focus is on the work of one teacher, in school classrooms.

In these groups, teachers are involved in planning and in carrying out tasks as a group and as individuals. They bring valuable information and acquire valuable information; they review activity and progress; they devise materials based upon the immediate needs of their own classes as they see them; and above all, they are encouraged to discuss their work in an informal but purposeful manner. The blend of open discussion and practical involvement in mutually agreed-upon tasks has helped to counter the isolation suffered by many rural school teachers and the general lack of discussion of the curriculum within schools.

Teachers became better acquainted with the experiences, environments, and interests of island children, as well as the outlook and skills of their colleagues. At early meetings, teachers looked to the project team member to do the talking, seeing themselves as customers, the project as a product, and the team as the sales staff. At a later stage, the project team was seen by some — and still is by a few — as not knowing what it was doing because it was not handing out cut-and-dried solutions to difficulties. Gradually, most teachers saw that their own role should not be one of either passive acquiescence or resistance.

In these meetings the team member present tries to guide the group to a clearer view of the tasks to be done and to help in arriving at informed decisions by a sensitive, positive participation in discussion. Groups have become more able to sustain pointed discussions; more tolerant; more willing to learn from each other; more resourceful; and better equipped to make and implement decisions effectively. The BEP team has shared in the benefits, as well as the frustrations, of this process and has gained a great deal in terms of personal and professional growth.

Thus the project is providing a level of in-service training and support of a continuity and relevance impossible for colleges of education to achieve at present. Its influence on preservice training of teachers, though in itself slight so far, points the way to a more adequate and relevant preservice training for teachers who hope to work in bilingual communities. Student teachers from Jordanhill College of Education in Glasgow have carried out part of their teaching practice in project schools each year, maintaining a close contact with the team during the three-week period. It should be possible to build this up into a course component based upon and contributing to the continuing bilingual education provision in the Western Isles with close liaison between the college and the local area.

In the first year, 1975-76, the project concentrated on primary class levels 1 through 3. It was agreed by the team and teachers that the work done in school through the medium of Gaelic should make a positive and enriching contribution to the primary school curriculum as a whole; that the use of Gaelic in school should be closely engaged with the children's experience; that the emphasis should initially be on development of oral spontaneity and proficiency; and that a greater direct use be made of the resources of the immediate environment as raw material for a wide range of developmental work in language and other fields.

Teachers agreed to pursue themes which would sustain the interest of the children over a long period, and further agreed that direct investigations outside the school should be an integral part of the work on any theme. Suggested lines of development were provided by the project team, but it was emphasized that teachers should develop themes in ways best suited to their own particular circumstances. Gradually, teachers began to do this more and more, and now most individual teachers, after group discussion of ideas, select and plan their own program of work.

Linking Bilingualism and
Rural Curriculum Development

From the beginning of the project, the use of Gaelic was linked with broad-based curriculum development. At first, some teachers found this exciting, while others were daunted by it. Some schools accepted only selected aspects of the program, while other schools underwent a dramatic change. However, no school was totally unchanged.

The adoption of a direct, "hands-on" involvement with the local environment was crucially important. Excursions outside the school provided the teacher with a new ambience which made it easier for those who had not done so previously to use Gaelic as a teaching medium. Similarly, for the children this field-based approach provided a learning milieu in which they were naturally more confident in seeking and exploiting fresh experiences than had been the case in formal classroom work. Teachers and their classes also came into contact—as part of school work—with local people, so the community's activities began to impinge upon the curriculum. In the long term this will profoundly affect the interaction of school, home, and community in the Western Isles.

Initial reactions revealed the occasional awkwardness encountered in implementing such innovations. For example, one teacher took her pupils aged between five and seven, across the moor to watch a group of local men at work cutting peat. On the way, the teacher and pupils spoke easily about their surroundings in Gaelic (as the project intended). And the men, as they worked, conversed in Gaelic as usual. When the teacher and her pupils arrived, however, the men greeted them in English, and continued to talk in English until the teacher intervened to ask them to speak in Gaelic, as they would normally have done outside the school context to the local children and local teacher.

In the course of the project, most teachers have undertaken numerous themes and a wide range of related expeditions have been made. Classes planted potatoes and vegetables, interviewed crofters and other local workers, adopted lambs, carried out simple experiments, watched birds' eggs hatching — the variety of work and the excitement injected into schools was remarkable. These shared experiences were recorded and built upon through the use of still and motion picture cameras, drawing, modelmaking, and craftwork as well as through tape recordings, stories, plays, and some writing. At the end of the first year and in each year since, the project has organized "open days" in Lewis and in Uist. These enable all primary school teachers to view exhibitions of work emanating from the project and provide an opportunity for informal discussion about the materials and activities generated.

Transforming Gaelic from a subject to a normal part of school life had beneficial effects on the curriculum as a whole. The development of classroom materials is now based directly upon known needs, and teachers' groups have taken major responsibility for creating new materials. Perhaps the most important spin-off effect was that the local community surrounding the school had become the "classroom," and the whole local environment had become integrated with the school curriculum.

This joint thrust on bilingualism and on locally relevant curriculum was maintained as the project moved up into higher levels of the primary school. In 1976-77, classes 4 and 5 were engaged in a more structured approach to their environment than classes 1 through 3. For example, through making models and plans of small objects in the classroom the children progressed to making a plan, first, of the room itself; next, of the school; and then, of their school precinct. Eventually, they were able to compile their own large-scale maps of the surrounding area. With this behind them, they were able to use official Ordnance Survey maps very skillfully. Again, Gaelic was extended into new areas of the curriculum and at the same time the approach and the content of the teaching of mapping was improved. This process also involved excursions from school and brought pupils and teachers out to work in the villages. Classes supplemented the program by the use of a relevant English novel, both as a stimulus for environmental work and for various kinds of imaginative development.

Mapping and surveying of the locality inevitably led classes to a consideration of social and economic aspects of their own environment, to comparisons with other areas, and so on. In the 1977-78 session, classes 6 and 7 were engaged in social studies in a bilingual mode. Two excellent series of BBC programs for schools — one on archaeological and historial sites, the other an adaptation of a historical novel — were used as the springboards for an appraisal of aspects of the history of their own community, as well as for seeking out information both locally and further afield. In the absence of adequate and appropriate reference works in Gaelic or in English, schools have had to use the physical and human resources of the area as their "reference work." This has proved mutually beneficial to the school and the community.

Teachers are helped in various ways to develop materials for their own use, based on the language use, interests, and current activities of the children. This has resulted in a massive accumulation of excellent tailor-made tapes, tape-slide combinations, photographic sequences, models, drawings, stories, and poems. This material, as well as the comments of teachers upon it, provided a sound basis for the preparation of handbooks and other published materials for schools.

The way in which the provision of early reading material is being tackled typifies the carefully planned approach of the project. A group of beginning classes (1 through 3) adopted the theme "Sinn Fhein" (Ourselves). The children produced stories and drawings about themselves, their families, their domestic animals, their pursuits and interests. Teachers recorded these stories in various ways, and, in workshop sessions with the project team, fitted them to a standard format: sixteen-page booklets with two or three lines of large type per page, the rest of each page being blank. These were printed and returned to the schools for the children to illustrate, while the teacher monitored content and language suitability. The books were then collected and revised by teacher groups. Finally, a selection of the books were printed, using the children's drawings wherever possible, and distributed.

This is a continuing process and is thought preferable in every way to the devising of a single, standard reading scheme. In their position, it is inconceivable that the teachers will be offered a choice of reading schemes from rival publishers, as is the case in English; and no single scheme would be sufficient. So circumstances and circumspection favor the adoption of an approach which is universally agreed to be desirable, but which in majority languages is difficult to attain.

Bilingual Publications:
The Creation of Acair Ltd.

It is necessary also to produce published materials of a high standard which, as well as being attractive and lively, are in accord with the aims of the project itself. Publishing books in Gaelic is a daunting task, and the project does not have the resources to publish extensive, professional-quality materials. However, by joining forces with other agencies, BEP has been instrumental in ensuring an unprecedented flow of Gaelic books for young children. Between November 1976, when the first book edited by the project team was published, and September, 1978, twenty-four books were published. All were edited by the team (who had also written over half of them). In the early summer of 1977, the project was cooperating with An

Comunn Gaidhealach (a Gaelic-language promotion agency) and the Highlands and Islands Development Board (HIDB) in the publication of six books; with the University of Stirling in the preparation of a series of video cassettes on environmental studies as pursued by children in project schools in Uist; and with the Western Isles Islands Council (WIIC) and Longman Group Ltd. in London in the publication of a series of twelve books.

The pace and scale of these ad hoc publishing ventures were new in Gaelic. They attracted considerable publicity as well as affecting people's attitudes significantly. Such ventures could not provide a secure basis for long-term sustained production of books. They indicated the possibility of developing a more permanent structure, however, and the project initiated informal and formal discussions which culminated in the establishment of Acair Ltd.

Acair Ltd. is a new Gaelic and English traditional publishing company based in the Western Isles. The company was registered in December 1977, and the principal shareholders are WIIC, HIDB, and An Comunn Gaidhealach. In addition to shared capital contributions, WIIC and HIDB have made substantial contributions to assist with the setting up and operation of the company for its first three years. The Scottish Arts Council has also made a general grant to the company, and Grampian TV, an independent broadcasting company, has given financial assistance as a prelude, it is hoped, to a fuller participation in Acair Ltd. The board of directors reflects the input of shareholders; each director has a considerable and specific skill which will be at the company's disposal. The presence of the director of BEP on the board is an interesting departure from the norm, reflecting the fact that Acair Ltd. is a direct result of the cooperative networks investigated and utilized by BEP. (Originally BEP was to be a shareholder, but this was found to be impossible to arrange.) In April 1978, a full-time manager and secretary were appointed and offices were obtained.

The choice of a commercial company structure indicates the flexibility of approach which initiators must adopt to the formulation of relevant and efficient structures for development. Acair Ltd. is not simply another Gaelic and English educational publishing company: it is the first and only one.

Gaelic publishing as a whole is largely a part-time activity by altruistic persons whose efforts have maintained a valuable, albeit erratic, flow of books over the years. None of these companies is capable of providing the range and number of titles needed by schools as a result of the work of BEP, for instance. Furthermore, the function of Acair Ltd. is essentially similar to that of the other projects (BEP, the Community Education Project, Cinema Sgire) and is seen as such by its shareholders. Each shareholding body is interested in maintaining a confident, open-minded, and well-informed population in the Western Isles, each has cooperated with the other in specific ways previously, and each has promoted or undertaken publication of educational books in Gaelic. By pooling their resources in an area of common interest, each will go a longer way toward achieving its goal than it could alone.

Acair Ltd. is the outcome of careful planning to satisfy known needs. It fills a serious gap which would inhibit the development of a relevant education. It provides a resource to which the community has access, and its own activity should stimulate and enable the community to make greater use of that access. And it will work along with other innovations in community and cultural education in a mutually supportive and coordinated organization.

As soon as Acair Ltd. was announced in the press, offers of cooperation of various kinds came from well-known publishers in various parts of Britain, and manuscripts began to arrive from Gaelic and from English writers. Evidently Acair provides a framework which encourages them to contribute, and a facilitative structure where none existed before.

Getting Started:
The Routine Side of Innovation

One characteristic of rural areas in the Western Isles (and, one suspects, nearly everywhere else) is an absence of many human, material, and institutional resources which are often taken for granted in metropolitan areas. This means that rural projects must cope with a whole range of very pragmatic (even mundane) side issues in addition to carrying out their basic mission. Efforts like BEP, CEP, Acair Ltd., Cinema Sgire, and Fir Chlis do not just spring into action. They must first contend with difficult (and sometimes delicate) problems both within the communities being served and in relation to their respective sponsors.

For example, in setting up these initiatives in a group of scattered islands considerable attention had to be devoted to the problem of where each project was to be located. It was essential to have adequate coverage throughout the area, but dissipation through excessive scatter had to be avoided. With BEP, it was decided to place the first phase in twenty of the fifty-nine schools. Of these twenty, ten were chosen in Lewis and Harris and ten in the Uists and Barra. A project center was set up in Lewis and in Uist. The project director was based in the Lewis center. The Uist fieldworker has worked by herself during the first three years and has been joined by another fieldworker only recently.

There is no better illustration of the practical problems posed than a brief review of the facility arrangements which had to be worked out in launching these projects. Office space is a problem throughout the area. The Stornoway office of BEP is a converted tailor's shop. When the project team moved in, they had to shift large sewing machines to one end of the main room and then dismantle intricate steam piping which was suspended from the ceiling. The Uist office of BEP is an old school which had been closed. It is cold and uncomfortable, and only the most assiduous of project staff would have continued working there. The CEP fieldworker in Ness also works from a room in an abandoned schoolhouse. The Harris fieldworker lives and works in a youth hostel in Tarbert which recently closed. The Uist fieldworker cannot be based in the right community because no usable space has yet been found in the Iochdar area. The Acair Ltd. offices are a converted mortuary (which fortunately had been renovated before Acair obtained it).

On the human level as well, finding necessary resources is a very time-consuming task. In setting up the project network in an isolated rural area, the problem had to be faced of how those involved were to be kept in touch with scholars in related academic fields as well as with those working in similar research and development projects elsewhere. There are no university field stations or teacher training outposts in the area: the presence of higher education and the influence of educational research is minimal.

The proposals for each of the projects outlined the need for a consultative committee whose members would be drawn from the Scottish education department, the sponsoring bodies, and individual academics as well as local staff directly involved in the projects. This has proved to be most successful, not merely in terms of the consultative meetings but in the way in which channels of information between the projects and outside agencies and individuals have developed. The education department through its inspectorate has been interested in these developments from the beginning and has given continued meaningful support. Stirling University has been involved with BEP in the production of video programs. The professor of education at Aberdeen University is involved directly with BEP and CEP. Jordanhill College of Education is administratively and nominally involved in BEP.

Sponsoring bodies vary in the degree of contact they wish to retain with the projects. The Scottish Film Council has a keen interest in Cinema Sgire, and its staff keep in contact with the project team and attend consultative meetings. The council has also provided training facilities for project staff. HIDB is a shareholder in Acair Ltd., with appropriate representation on the board of the company. The Scottish Arts Council is also represented on this board and on that of Fir Chlis.

The Bernard van Leer Foundation is in close contact with those involved in CEP. Some of their staff have visited the Western Isles, and project members have been to the foundation's home city, The Hague. The foundation provides the CEP staff with information from a worldwide network of projects in which it is involved, and links have built up between CEP staff and members of projects in a number of other countries. Meetings have been held with project leaders from Colombia, Israel, Zimbabwe, and South Africa. Project workers from Malaysia and Nigeria have visited CEP. Other Bernard van Leer projects in the United Kingdom (Coventry, Liverpool, and Birmingham) are in contact with CEP.

It is not necessary to list the many visitors and academic tourists who have visited the projects. Nor is it feasible even to outline the amount of correspondence the projects have generated, especially the extent to which BEP has caught the interest of people engaged in bilingual education programs throughout the world. Project staff have been involved in various conferences as well as specific training courses and study tours. As the staff has increased, it has become possible to set up local seminars and discussion groups.

All these meetings, trips, and contacts, in addition to an extensive recording program, have meant that the members of the projects are able to renew themselves through exchange with new people and new thinking. Discussion, criticism, and new information are crucial to creative development: the projects' network highlights how this is being achieved in one isolated rural area.

Of Relevance Elsewhere?

The kind of development dealt with in this chapter is rooted in the community in which it takes place. The exact form it takes will be unique to that community. In an area such as the Western Isles, united physically, culturally, and linguistically, it is easier to conceive of such development as a unity, and this may well be one of the main reasons why such development is taking place there. Uniqueness is in no way related to, or synonymous with, parochialism or insularity. On the contrary, such development encourages the widest contacts and exchange of experience.

Although people in minority cultures may tend to have more need for new structures to compensate for the lack of adequate provisions in the past, it is likely that the approach being adopted here will be of relevance to rural communities generally. In the Western Isles, the essential first step was making a firm commitment to the value and importance of the local community as the foundation upon which all development work in education, or elsewhere, must be built. As one group of scholars has noted,

> If development is the development of man, as an individual and as a social being, aiming at his liberation and his fulfillment, it cannot but stem from the inner core of each society. It relies on what a human group has; its natural en-

vironment, its cultural heritage, the creativity of the men and women who constitute it, becoming richer through exchange between them and with other
groups. It entails the autonomous definition of development styles and of life
styles. This is the meaning of endogenous and self-reliant development.[2]

From the juxtaposition of this emerging philosophy of self-reliance, the
support of external agencies, and the reality of a governmental reorganization, a series of rural education and development innovations have begun in
the Western Isles. Although not without its growing pains, the Bilingual
Education Project and all the other manifestations of the Western Isles rejuvenation appear to be maturing in ways which bode well for the future.
Initiating rural innovations can be a risky business, but at least in the
Western Isles, the risk has been well worth taking.

Notes

1. Most of the statistical (and other background) information in the introduction
has been taken from R. S. Johnston et al., *Basic Education and Teacher Support in
Sparsely Populated Areas: United Kingdom Country Paper (Scotland)* (Paris: OECD,
1977).

2. The Dag Hammarskjold Foundation, *Development Dialogue,* No. 1/2 (1975),
p. 34.

9

Finland's Small Schools
and Combined Grades:
An Overview with Special Reference
to the Kuusamo District

Reijo Laukkanen and Lauri Muhonen

There is growing recognition in Finland that small rural schools have special needs and require special attention. This increasingly positive attitude toward small rural schools, evidenced by politicians and professional educators alike, is a clear departure from past attitudes and action in this area. The benefits of this policy shift are now beginning to be felt in the nation's rural districts. This chapter will describe the current status of Finland's small rural schools. Particular emphasis will be given to recent innovations such as the reform of combined grade instruction in primary schools.

To facilitate an understanding of both the national context and the way in which rural schools actually operate, the chapter uses a joint local-national format. Each aspect of rural education will be viewed from the vantage point of the Kuusamo district as well as Finland as a whole. The Kuusamo area was selected not only for its geographic isolation (it lies just below the Arctic Circle near the Russian border), but also because it is in many ways a microcosm of education in rural Finland. In addition, Kuusamo served as the site for a small, sixteen-nation conference on rural education and development held in September 1979 under the joint sponsorship of the Finnish Ministry of Education and OECD's Centre for Educational Research and Innovation.

The municipality of Kuusamo, situated in the province of Oulu on the eastern border of northeastern Finland, is by its population and area one of the largest in the nation, having an area of 5,701 square kilometers. The area has heavy winter snowfall; on an average, the snow cover varies from 40 to 70 centimeters. The altitude variation is more than 200 meters. In the northernmost part of the area there are several mountains 300 meters above sea level. A large proportion of the area (13.7 percent) is covered by marshes.

In the 1979 budget of the district of Kuusamo, 45 percent of the total public expenditure was allocated to culture. Of the cultural expenditure a major proportion (about 62 percent) goes to the comprehensive school, which comprises the lower level (grades 1–6) and the upper level (grades 7–9). The next largest amount is allocated to secondary-level vocational education, the upper secondary school (grades 10 and 11), and the library. As usual, staff salaries are the largest single expenditure item.

The major proportion of the costs of education is paid by the state; i.e., the national government. For instance, the 1978 state subsidies covered 90 percent of the salaries of the comprehensive school teachers, 93 percent of the transportation and accommodation costs, and 65 percent of the maintenance of buildings, rents, and school operating capital. The organization of the public education system in Kuusamo is presented in Figure 1.

Population Trends

With a total area of 337,037 square kilometers, Finland is one of the largest European countries in physical terms. However, as far as its number of inhabitants is concerned, Finland is among the smallest. Although the overall population density is rather low, there are great regional differences (e.g., Uusimaa province has 113 inhabitants per square kilometer, while Lapland province has only 2 inhabitants per square kilometer). The southern and southwestern parts of Finland, with the exception of the archipelago, are densely populated; in the northern parts of the country there are vast areas which remain nearly unpopulated. According to recent projections, the population will become more and more concentrated in southern and southwestern Finland. Thus, population migration is likely to continue to flow from sparsely populated areas to established population centers. Table 1 shows recent population trends.

The so-called large age groups were born in 1946 through 1949, when more than 100,000 children were born annually. In the 1960s the birth rate dropped to slightly more than half that rate. In 1976 the age group of seven-year-olds consisted of 64,631 children. In 1980 this age group will reach a new low (56,005 children). The size of this age group is then expected to increase during the 1980s.

Kuusamo

There are slightly over 17,000 people in Kuusamo, of whom about 52 percent are male. In 1960 the majority of the population in the municipality

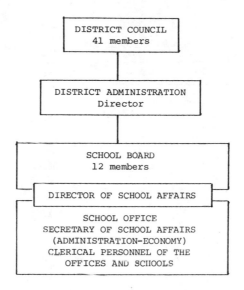

```
┌─────────────────────────┐
│   DISTRICT COUNCIL      │
│      41 members         │
└─────────────────────────┘

┌─────────────────────────┐
│  DISTRICT ADMINISTRATION│
│       Director          │
└─────────────────────────┘

┌─────────────────────────┐
│     SCHOOL BOARD        │
│      12 members         │
└─────────────────────────┘

┌─────────────────────────┐
│ DIRECTOR OF SCHOOL AFFAIRS│
└─────────────────────────┘

      SCHOOL OFFICE
  SECRETARY OF SCHOOL AFFAIRS
  (ADMINISTRATION-ECONOMY)
  CLERICAL PERSONNEL OF THE
    OFFICES AND SCHOOLS
```

The Public School System in the Kuusamo District

Comprehensive Schools

44 Lower level schools, of which:	2 Upper level School Districts:	2 Special Schools
31 2-teacher schools	Stem-Kuusamo's	
11 3-teacher schools	Upper Level	
2 4-teacher schools	Northern Kuusamo's Upper Level	11 Special teachers

Upper Secondary School

The Kuusamo Upper Secondary School Board of Trustees

Vocational Schools

The Kuusamo Vocational School Board of Directors	The Kuusamo Business School and College Board of Trustees

FIGURE 1   Organization of the Public School System in Kuusamo, 1979-80.

TABLE 1

POPULATION DISTRIBUTION AND DENSITY, FINLAND, 1950-1978

	1950	1960	1970	1977	1978
Total number of inhabitants (1,000 persons)	4,030	4,446	4,598	4,738	4,757
Number of inhabitants in cities and towns (1,000 persons) and percentage out of the whole population	2,302 (32.8)	2,707 (38.4)	2,340 (50.9)	2,826 (59.6)	2,840 (59.7)
Inhabitants/sq. km. (entire country)	13.2	14.6	15.1	15.5	15.6

earned its living from agriculture and forestry (68 percent). By 1970 the share of these occupations had diminished to 45 percent. It is estimated that in 1980, 28 percent of the population will be engaged in agriculture and forestry, and only 24 percent in 1985. The trade, traffic, and service industries are developing into the largest economic sectors in Kuusamo. In 1980, 46 percent of the population is estimated to earn its living from these sources.

The change in the industrial structure is clearly reflected in migration within the district. While 80 percent of the population lived in sparsely populated areas in 1960, only 57 percent of the population lived outside the densely populated Kuusamo center in 1976. In sixteen years the population of the center doubled. The development of Kuusamo's population is presented in Table 2.

The figures in Table 2 show that the total population has remained relatively stable in the area. However, the actual figures are somewhat more negative than is reflected by the numerical analysis, because those who emigrated from the district (to Sweden) between 1960 and 1970 remain in the population register of the municipality until, after returning from Sweden, they have settled down permanently in another district, or until they have been granted Swedish citizenship. During this period, about 2,500 persons emigrated to Sweden from Kuusamo.

From 1960 to 1970 the total number of children under fourteen diminished by nearly 21 percent. From 1970 to 1980 the reduction was 38 percent. Simultaneously, the percentage of old people is increasing. The change in the population structure is also reflected in the numbers of students. While the number of children of comprehensive school age was about 4,500 in 1966, it was less than 3,900 in 1975. In 1979-80 the number of children

TABLE 2

POPULATION DISTRIBUTION AND DENSITY, KUUSAMO, 1950-1978

	1959	1960	1970	1977	1978
Population in the entire municipality	15,198	18,639	18,204	17,186	17,263
Population in the Kuusamo centre and their percentage share of the entire population		3,751 (20.1)	5,317 (29.2)	7,298 (42.5)	7,458 (43.2)
Population in the district's sparsely populated areas and their percentage share of the entire population		14,888 (79.9)	12,887 (70.8)	9,888 (57.5)	9,805 (56.8)
Inhabitants per land sq. km.	3.8	3.9	3.8	3.6	3.6

attending comprehensive school was only 2,833. Table 3 shows the most recent projections for the number of pupils in the local comprehensive school and in two-year secondary-level institutions.

These declining enrollments have been caused both by a reduction in the birth rate typical of the whole country in the 1970s and by certain other factors which have changed the population structure. The number of upper-level pupils in the sparsely populated northern Kuusamo area will diminish to one-half its present level until 1985, largely because of migration within the municipality and the higher average age of the Kuusamo farmers (compared to the average age of the whole population).

Although a substantial upward trend in the number of pupils is unlikely, it appears that the number will stabilize by the late 1980s. Therefore, it is projected that Kuusamo will need approximately 400 to 500 permanent two-year vocational and secondary-level student places. At present, the arrangement of two-year vocational education for those who leave comprehensive school is problematic. It has been possible, however, to compensate for the lack of permanent student places with temporary arrangements in the form of vocational courses.

Lower-Level Small Schools

The most important goal of education policy is to fill the educational and cultural needs of the population living in the sparsely populated areas and to

TABLE 3

ENROLLMENT PROJECTIONS, KUUSAMO, 1979-1989

School Year	Lower Levels, Total	Kuusamo's Upper Level (densely populated)	Northern Kuusamo's Upper Level (sparsely populated)	Comprehensive School Pupils, Total	Secondary Level Education (16- to 17-yr.-olds)
1979-80	1,618	881	334	2,833	900
1980-81	1,511	833	286	2,630	909
1981-82	1,455	741	279	2,475	983
1982-83	1,433	641	251	2,325	825
1983-84	1,480	606	216	2,302	789
1984-85	1,465	568	182	2,215	732
1985-86	1,511	561	167	2,239	637
1986-87					566
1987-88					502
1988-89					487

diminish regional inequality. The Finnish comprehensive school system, based on uniform education, gives better opportunities than before for the implementation of an egalitarian policy.

The predominance of small schools has always been characteristic of Finland's educational system. This has resulted from geographical factors, settlement patterns, and the nation's economic structure, as well as such pragmatic considerations as road and weather conditions. In the 1950s, there were still more than 1,000 one-teacher schools. The majority of the lower-level schools have always been two-teacher schools. The distribution of lower-level small schools in the 1970s is presented in Table 4.

In all subjects the small schools have curricula similar to those found throughout the nation. Consequently, in terms of the weekly or even daily course offerings there are no major differences among Finnish schools, irrespective of size or geographic circumstances. In the development of Finland's educational system the dominant principal has been one of individual and regional equality. Hence the population structure of a community does not substantially affect the quality of the educational services. However, the character of the district (such as low population density) does affect means and arrangements.

A small school is especially sensitive to reductions in numbers of students, which produce pressure to close the school. About 2,300 schools have been closed in the post–World War II era, and most of these were lower-level one- and two-teacher schools in sparsely populated areas. The principal reasons for the closings have been the reduced birth rate, migration, factors internal to the school system, the availability of building funds, and the improve-

TABLE 4

NUMBER OF LOWER-LEVEL SMALL SCHOOLS, FINLAND, 1970-1978

School Year	One-Teacher Schools		Two-Teacher Schools		Three-Teacher Schools		Four- or More Teacher Schools		Total	
	n	%	n	%	n	%	n	%	n	%
1970-71	118	2.6	2,351	52.6	1,009	22.6	992	22.2	4,470	100
1971-72	87	2.1	2,173	51.1	979	23.0	1,012	23.8	4,251	100
1972-73	63	1.5	1,984	47.5	1,063	25.5	1,062	25.5	4,172	100
1973-74	54	1.3	1,865	45.3	1,092	26.5	1,106	26.9	4,117	100
1974-75	46	1.1	1,774	43.7	1,098	27.0	1,145	28.2	4,063	100
1975-76	42	1.0	1,715	42.7	1,090	27.2	1,169	29.1	4,016	100
1976-77	33	0.8	1,682	42.1	1,094	27.4	1,187	29.7	3,996	100
1977-78	34	0.8	1,667	42.0	1,079	27.1	1,198	30.1	3,978	100
1978-79	39	1.0	1,678	42.2	1,047	26.4	1,208	30.4	3,972	100

ment of rural road conditions. At its height, the annual school closure rate was almost 300 (for example, 296 were closed in 1970), but it has diminished in the past few years, thanks to the changeover to the comprehensive school system and the lowered minimum requirements for state aid (in 1972 and 1977, respectively). During the past few years 20 to 50 schools have been closed annually.

The combination of lower birth rates and steady outmigration has served to diminish the effectiveness of new measures aimed at preventing school closures. A new wave of closures is expected despite policies which increasingly support small schools. According to an estimate made in 1977, 700 schools are threatened with closure in the 1980s. The enrollment declines are most severe in the eastern and northern parts of the country where the smallest schools are situated.

As the number of students continues to fall, retaining all the schools which are in operation is not feasible. On the basis of the 1976 report of the national working group on small schools, the decree on the comprehensive schools was amended so that in a sparsely populated municipality (i.e., with a population density of less than ten inhabitants per square kilometer), the student minimum entitling the municipality to a state subsidy was reduced from sixteen to twelve. The reduced student minimum may also be applied to remotely situated schools in densely populated municipalities, if the distance to the nearest school is more than ten kilometers (measured directly). Still, even this concession will not be adequate to preserve all of the two-teacher schools under the threat of closure.

At the same time, the municipalities were given the possibility of maintaining one-teacher schools in cases where the school closure would unreasonably lengthen school journeys. The regulations were revised so that the student minimum for this type of school was reduced from thirteen to six.

Kuusamo

In 1956 there were a total of sixty-seven lower-level schools in Kuusamo. This number dropped to fifty-seven in 1966 and to forty-eight in 1975. The changes in the number of lower-level schools in Kuusamo during the 1970s are shown in Table 5. In the school year 1978-79, twenty-seven (60 percent) of the schools were two-teacher schools, fifteen (33 percent) were three-teacher schools, one was a four-teacher school, and two were larger than four-teacher schools. Two-teacher and three-teacher schools are small. They range from three schools with a total enrollment of ten students each to the five schools having thirty pupils each. On average two-teacher schools in the Kuusamo area have between fifteen and nineteen students, while the

TABLE 5

NUMBER OF LOWER-LEVEL SCHOOLS, KUUSAMO, 1970-1980

School Year	Two-Teacher Schools *		Three-Teacher Schools		Four- or More Teacher Schools		Total	
	n	%	n	%	n	%	n	%
1970-71	37	74	10	20	3	6	50	100
1971-72	36	72	11	22	3	6	50	100
1972-73	27	56	18	38	3	6	48	100
1973-74	23	48	22	46	3	6	48	100
1974-75	25	52	20	42	3	6	48	100
1975-76	24	51	20	43	3	6	47	100
1976-77	24	52	19	41	3	7	46	100
1977-78	25	54	18	39	3	7	46	100
1978-79	27	60	15	33	3	7	45	100
1979-80	31	70	11	25	2	5	44	100

three-teacher schools have an average enrollment of between twenty-five and twenty-nine.

The trend toward school closings can be seen in Kuusamo. For example, one of the two-teacher schools was closed on July 31, 1979. At the same time, six three-teacher schools were converted to two-teacher schools, and the only four-teacher school in the district was turned into a three-teacher school. Closure of a school presupposes the potential for combining that school's human and material resources with another school. This increases the demand on school transportation but improves the operating potential of the school to which the pupils are transferred. Most centralization has taken place in the Vuotunki area (a subdistrict of Kuusamo). Whereas five separate catchment areas existed there in the 1960s, they have been combined into one unit today.

In the national comprehensive school decree it has been prescribed that the state subsidy for a teacher's post will not be canceled unless the number of pupils has fallen below the minimum for three consecutive years. In the case of the Kärppä school it will be possible to apply the 1977 regulation concerning rural two-teacher schools, according to which the minimum pupil number of the school must be twelve. In 1983-84 the three years of grace allowed by the regulation will be over and the school will have to be closed or changed into a two-teacher school. Similarly, the Määttälä school will be changed into a two-teacher school. The Vuotunki school has already been changed into a three-teacher school because of low pupil numbers. Although the district would be entitled to a state subsidy for maintenance of a one-teacher school, this alternative has not yet been utilized in Kuusamo.

Traditionally the lower-level schools have served as institutions supporting the cultural life of the community as well as providing instruction for the pupils. In recent times this community role has waned noticeably. Mass communication media (radio and television) have had a paralyzing effect on the cultural activities of the villages. Since many village school teachers now live outside the local area and the age structure of the population has grown older, the intensity of the school-community interaction has dropped.

The present level of social interaction at the village schools does not fulfill the cultural needs of the community. During the school year 1978-79 there were fifty-six pupils' clubs in Kuusamo's comprehensive schools which held a total of 1,269 meetings with an average attendance of ten. Correspondingly there were fifteen clubs for youth who had completed their schooling, with 250 meetings and, on an average, fifteen participants.

By a resolution of the local school board, school premises may be used by nonschool groups. Adult education institutions are granted the right to use the premises during the school year. Upon application, different kinds of local organizations may be granted the premises for their use, either permanently or for special occasions. During 1978 school premises were used by these community groups 117 times.

Transportation

About 173,000 children (28 percent of all students) at the compulsory education level utilized school transportation. In the school year 1977-78, the total number of children transported was 184,000 (the number of schoolchildren in the whole country was 659,848). Two-thirds of these children were transported by bus and one-third by taxis. The number of transported students has increased following the changeover to the comprehensive school system. The reason for this is that all students now continue their studies at the upper level. The closing of small schools has also contributed to an increase in the number of transported students.

Research on student transportation patterns indicates (not surprisingly) that the distance traveled to upper-level schools by rural students was significantly greater than the length of journeys to school by urban students. In another study, in which pupils born in the same community in 1940, 1947, and 1955 were compared, it was found that in the 1960s the pupils with short journeys continued their studies in upper secondary school or vocational school more frequently than pupils with long journeys. The pupils with long journeys had poorer achievement and more absenteeism. Similarly, the attitude of the students' guardians toward continuation of the studies was more negative among the pupils with long school journeys.

Kuusamo

In the Kuusamo district, the distances to school are long and the pupil

TABLE 6

PUPIL TRANSPORTATION DATA, KUUSAMO, 1977-78

Length of the Pupils' School Journeys, One-Way, in Kilometers	Number of Pupils (Total of 3,371)
2.9	1,651
3.0 - 4.9	275
5.0 - 9.9	396
10.0 - 19.9	263
20.0 -	786
Time Spent on the Pupils' Transportation, Including Waiting Time, in Hours	
2.0	2,658
2.1 - 2.5	633
2.6 - 3.0	78
3.1 -	3
The Pupils' Principal Means of Transportation	
Public Transportation (school buses and municipal buses)	1,070
Subscribed Private Transportation (taxis and boats)	541
Other (by foot, bicycle, etc.)	1,760

transportation costs remarkably high. According to the 1977 financial report, the cost of basic pupil transportation and accommodation was about 11 percent of total comprehensive school expenditures. A significant proportion of the Kuusamo area pupils use school transportation daily. Table 6 shows the length of the pupils' journeys and means of transportation.

Teacher Support in Small Schools

Language instruction in the small lower-level schools has often been arranged through the deployment of traveling teachers. Similarly, the instruction of pupils with difficulties in reading, writing, and speech has, to a large extent, been handled by circulating teachers. This is a common practice in rural as well as urban schools. To some extent, instruction in handicrafts has been given by circulating teachers or by one of the other teachers in the school.

In Finland, a branch of the municipal library often operates within the school building. If this is not the case, the municipalities strive to meet the requirements of the schools for literature with the aid of library buses. In many municipalities the library bus or some other school service vehicle (for instance, the one in charge of catering) brings audiovisual equipment (e.g., records and tapes) to the school. In many cases, the municipal audiovisual center assumes responsibility for mimeographing and delivering examination papers which are to be given throughout the schools of the municipality.

In terms of in-service teacher training, the special skills needed for combined grade instruction are considered to be an important element in the basic as well as the supplementary training of teachers. Hence three-day supplementary education courses related to combined grade instruction have been arranged for teachers working in teacher practice schools. During 1979-80 a five-day supplementary education course was arranged for 600 Finnish teachers working in combined grade situations.

An advisory education system was established at the beginning of the 1970s. Since then, the system has been expanded to cover most subjects. Experienced active teachers are appointed as advisers to their colleagues. For educational purposes, the provincial government excuses the adviser from regular teaching work for a period of one month yearly. The adviser receives his or her salary for that period from the state. So-called guidance teachers are also active in the municipalities. Since 1977, nearly every province has had an adviser of its own specializing in combined grade instruction. The adviser's duty has been to support the teachers of small schools through consultation and by arranging training for them.

Kuusamo

At the lower level, language instruction is given by the regular classroom teachers of the schools as well as by other teachers within the Kuusamo district. Altogether, there are seven traveling teachers of English. They use their own cars to go from one school to another. There are four special education teachers in the district; two of them teach pupils who have difficulties in reading and writing and two work with children having speech difficulties.

The Kuusamo municipal library has two library buses, which stop weekly at the lower-level schools according to a set timetable. The pupils are given an hour to visit the library. At the same time other activities, such as individual tutoring, are arranged for those who do not use the library. The pupils also have access to the school's own library, which contains basic manuals and reference books. The library bus brings a range of general literature offerings to supplement those books specifically intended for use at school. A large proportion of the loans are books taken by the pupils for their own use at home and for use by their parents.

All the books, audiovisual materials, and other resources of the library are cataloged, and these catalogs are made available to all Kuusamo schools. The collection includes eighty-three different book series (each containing twenty to thirty-two copies of the same book). Additionally, the schools may order records or tapes in languages, literature, physical education, music, etc. The collection includes slide series on a wide range of subjects, complete with teacher manuals. The library buses also deliver books and audiovisual resources from the central library of the province.

Favorable experience has been gained from the library bus system. For example, Kuusamo now has a clinic bus for medical examinations of the pupils at the small schools. Reception hours are also reserved for adults in sparsely populated areas. A maternity and child care center in one of the small villages had to be closed because of its poor condition and small number of visitors. The clinic bus now takes care of these services in the village. Some of the other maternity and child care centers are also in a poor condition and their needs could be met by using the clinic bus, but some conflict arises from the fact that many village residents do not wish the maternity care centers to be closed, and insist that the local facilities should be maintained.

Boarding Schools

During the past few years the number of pupils living in dormitories and with other families has diminished considerably throughout Finland. Changes can also be observed in the age and level of schooling of the boarding pupils. The number of boarding pupils has diminished most markedly in lower-level comprehensive schools. Of all boarding pupils, only 6 percent were lower-level pupils in the school year 1977-78. Boarding in connection with the comprehensive school primarily concerned the pupils of the upper level as well as the pupils of special schools and grades. A total of 3,000 pupils were living in dormitories in 1972-73 (including 300 living with other families), but in 1978-79 there were no more than 1,334 boarding pupils.

A gradual phasing out of the boarding activities is, of course, partially a function of improved local services and road conditions. However, it also clearly reflects the demand of rural parents for schools which are close enough to allow their children to continue living at home.

Kuusamo

As recently as the 1950s, boarding pupils were common in Kuusamo. For example, the largest number of pupils ever accommodated in the Kärppä lower-level school (38) occurred in 1958. In the same year a total of 451 pupils were accommodated in the municipal lodging houses. Yet, in the mid-1960s to early 1970s a gradual shift had taken place toward increased use of school transportation. At present there are only about thirty pupils using boarding facilities in the Kuusamo district. No boarding accommodation is used by the lower-level pupils except at times when the roads are in very bad condition.

Combined Grade Instruction

In Finland, the term *combined grade* refers to basic classroom units in the lower-level comprehensive school which include pupils from more than one grade. Not surprisingly, the majority of Finland's combined grade classrooms are in the small rural schools. In 1977-78, 88 percent of all combined grades were in the one- to three-teacher schools. The most common combined grade types are presented in Table 7. However, very different kinds of combined grades (e.g., 4-5, 1-3, 4-6, 2-6, etc.) can also be found in Finland.

The fact that in 1977-78 about 40 percent of all lower-level classrooms brought together children from more than one grade reflects the widespread acceptance of combined grade teaching in Finland. As Figure 2 shows, more than half the provinces had more than half their lower-level classrooms in combined grade arrangements. In one province, combined grade units made up 60 percent of the total *classrooms* but only 27 percent of all the lower-level *pupils*. This, of course, is due to lower pupil-to-teacher ratios in combined grade situations. In the same school year, the average size of a lower-level class unit was 21.3 pupils. However, the average size of combined grade units in the one- to three-teacher schools was only 13.4 pupils.

In the fundamental subjects (mathematics, mother tongue, and foreign language) combined grade teaching is implemented so that the pupils of each age group are taught separately. Thus, for instance, the third-grade pupils of a combined grade 3-4 class are taught mathematics in a way which

TABLE 7

DISTRIBUTION OF COMBINED GRADE TYPES, FINLAND, 1977-78

Grade Combinations	Percentage of Classes
1 -2	38
3 -4	23
5 -6	18
3 -6	14
1 -6	0.3
Others	7

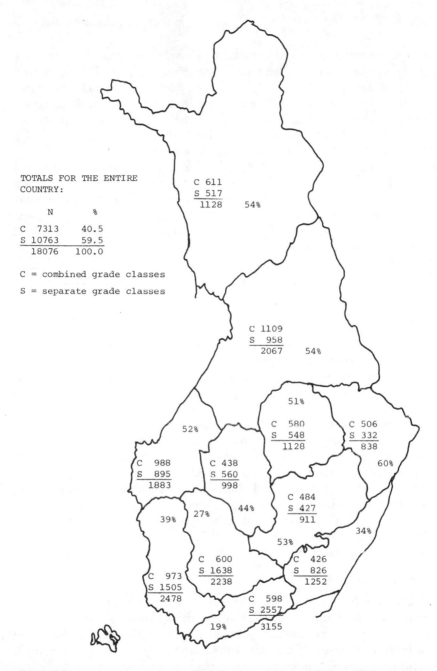

TOTALS FOR THE ENTIRE COUNTRY:

	N	%
C	7313	40.5
S	10763	59.5
	18076	100.0

C = combined grade classes

S = separate grade classes

C 611
S 517
1128   54%

C 1109
S 958
2067   54%

51%

C 580
S 548
1128

C 506
S 332
838

52%

60%

C 988
S 895
1883

C 438
S 560
998

C 484
S 427
911

39%   27%   44%

34%

53%

C 600
S 1638
2238

C 426
S 826
1252

C 973
S 1505
2478

C 598
S 2557
3155

19%

FIGURE 2 The Number and Percentage of Combined Grade Classes in Lower-Level Schools in Each Province of Finland, 1978.

completely corresponds to the instruction given to third-graders in a separate grade situation. On the other hand, in the historical and scientific subjects (religion, biology, geography, civics, environmental studies, history) teaching is implemented on a combined basis in the small rural schools. These are referred to as period instruction courses. Teaching takes place in one or two study groups, with pupils of two grade levels in the group. The entire study group studies the same curriculum during a school year.

The combined grades 1-2, 3-4, and 5-6 form study groups of their own. The combined grade 3-6 is divided up into study groups 3-4 and 5-6. When the study group 3-4, for instance, is taught geography, the 5-6 pupils study independently. In a combined grade 3-4 the pupils study the third-grade-level course one year (i.e., first period instruction course) and the fourth-grade-level course the next year (i.e., second period instruction course) in the historical and scientific subjects.

Certain problems arise when period instruction is used, including the following:

1. Every second age group studies subjects in the wrong order.
2. A pupil transferred from a combined grade to a separate grade may completely miss the studies of certain grade levels.
3. Period course instruction in the historical and scientific subjects is not suited for use in all combined grade structures.

In order to eliminate such drawbacks an experiment has been carried out for several years under the direction of the National Board of General Education. At first an attempt was made to balance the instruction period courses by combining curricula of two grade levels and preparing new period instruction courses. In the second phase of the experiment, special attention was paid to helping the teacher of the combined grade 3-6. In the experiment, four period instruction courses were prepared instead of two. It was, however, considered impossible to unify lower-level instruction like this as a whole, and therefore the experiment had to be revised.

Annual Courses

Since the beginning of the school year 1975-76, instruction by annual courses has been done experimentally in the scientific and historical subjects. When the experiment ended in spring 1979, teachers from five municipalities were participating. The experiment has covered instruction in religion, geography, biology, environmental studies, and civics.

A separate curriculum will not be prepared for the combined grades. Instead, the curriculum of the comprehensive school will be adapted so that it will be better suited for combined grades. In the annual course instruction, the comprehensive school curriculum is used to make the study materials of the grade levels in the historical and scientific subjects parallel. The study material of each grade level forms an annual course of its own. In other words, during the same lesson the different grade levels are taught different subject matter within the scope of the same general topic. Progress takes place from the known to the unknown, from individual pieces of information and skills to general laws.

It is hoped that as a result of this developmental work, study material suited especially for the combined grades will be attained. It is intended that the same study materials could be used in both combined and separate grades. Three combined grade experiments are being carried out in support of the developmental work.

On the basis of the feedback received from the annual course experiment, the National Board of General Education confirmed, in March 1979, the new curricula and simultaneously offered recommendations about teaching in combined grade classrooms and the breakdown of lessons in environmental studies, civics, and educational guidance. According to these recommendations, the lessons in these subjects should use the principles of annual course instruction.

Other Experimental Activities

An attempt has also been made through experiments to develop individual and group work, as well as the flexible use of time, as a remedy for the problems of combined teaching. Flexible formation of the study groups is one of the most recently tested and generally recommended innovations. The intention is to make instruction more efficient by forming groups, both small and large, which differ from the normal basic grade breakdown.

It has been possible through these arrangements to place pupils under the supervision of any teacher in the school. The responsibility of the teachers for all the pupils in a school is thus stressed. Likewise the activities of the schools are freed for pedagogically appropriate measures. In order to implement these arrangements the schools are encouraged to use senior pupils as tutors of junior pupils.

Flexible formation of study groups was tried out during two school years in a municipality in southeastern Finland. On the basis of the experience gained, the National Board of General Education gave permission for all two- to three-teacher schools to use the arrangement for one school year. Only 18 percent of the schools entitled to it applied for permission to use the system from the provincial governments. However, the feedback obtained was so positive that at present the arrangement can be used in all two- to six-teacher lower-level schools until the end of the school year 1981-82.

Large and small group instruction based on the flexible formation of study groups requires only very simple arrangements. However, its implementation in practice depends to a large extent on the willingness of the teachers to cooperate with each other.

Experimental Activities in Kuusamo

The lower-level schools in Kuusamo are, with two exceptions, two-teacher and three-teacher schools. In all these schools there are combined grades. This is why the district has been interested in developing instruction methods in these grades. The district has participated in national experimental activities under the supervision of the National Board of General Education.

In the school year 1974-75 an experiment was started in Kuusamo concerning four-cycle course instruction for the combined grades in geography and biology. From the beginning of the following year the experiment was revised so that annual course instruction was tested. The experiment was carried out in three schools and terminated at the end of the school year 1978-79. Today the study material used during the official experiment has been adopted by many of the Kuusamo schools and annual course instruction has been started in the subjects included in the experiment.

Upper-Level Schools in Sparsely Populated Areas

In Finland's 380 rural municipalities there is, as a rule, only one upper-level school. In the nation's 84 cities and towns there are usually more upper-level units. When the municipalities cannot maintain upper-level schools of their own, they have formed common upper-level school districts.

According to the national regulations on comprehensive schools, an upper-level school district may be formed if each grade has at least ninety pupils speaking the same language. A permanent upper-level school may be established in a sparsely populated area if each grade has at least forty pupils with the same mother tongue. The Council of State may, however, grant permission for ten years for the formation and maintenance of a temporary upper-level school even if the student numbers are smaller.

Ninety-one (mostly rural) municipalities are currently entitled to establish a temporary upper-level program. In response to recent enrollment forecasts, twenty-five upper-level programs in Finland will operate with enrollments of thirty-three to fifty pupils. Of these, ten schools have been given a time limit for their operation. There are fifty-five temporary upper-level units which have (or are projected to soon have) thirty-two or fewer students. No time limit has been set for the operation of more than half of these schools.

A negative attitude has developed toward the closing of upper-level schools because of the following factors:

1. Closing an upper-level school usually means significantly lengthening the school journey of the pupils and causing the number of transported pupils to increase substantially. Combining the upper levels would apparently increase the boarding costs, as well.
2. Closing upper levels would cause problems in the form of underuse of school premises. The premises of the majority of the current upper-level institutions are at least satisfactory. On the other hand, problems would also arise in the receiving schools in the form of a lack of adequate facilities.
3. Closing an upper-level school would weaken the availability of services in the municipality much more than closing a lower-level one. An upper-level school is able to offer multiple cultural services. Closure would also greatly increase unemployment among the teachers.

In many cases, the closure of the upper-level school would also lead to closure of the upper secondary school in the municipality. Practical experience has shown that one of the criteria for the location of industrial and other enterprises in an area is the level of educational services. Undoubtedly the disappearance of the upper-level school would cause economic life in the community to deteriorate and would accelerate migration of the population from the municipality.

As a facet of labor policy, an experiment has been carried out since 1977-78 concerning arrangement of additional education within the comprehensive school. The training has been intended for those young people who have completed the ninth grade of the comprehensive school and have been left outside the secondary education system. The training lasts one year. This educational scheme has been expanded year by year. During the first school year the scheme was implemented in the two northernmost provinces. In the subsequent year three more provinces were added and in 1979-80 it was implemented in eight provinces.

Kuusamo

In the municipality there are two upper-level schools: Kuusamo's school in the village and Northern Kuusamo's school at Rukatunturi. The school in Kuusamo village belongs both to the district of central Kuusamo and to the southern, sparsely populated area of the district. The district of Northern Kuusamo is also sparsely populated (for instance, no single lower-level school there has more than three teachers). The upper-level school in Northern Kuusamo has about one-third of the total number of upper-level pupils in Kuusamo village. The relative size of this school will diminish according to the pupil enrollment projections noted earlier.

Typically, the upper-level pupils must make long journeys to school. All except two pupils of Northern Kuusamo's upper-level school used school transportation in the year 1978-79. This factor makes school attendance heavy (and costly) in the Rukatunturi school.

In the upper-level schools of sparsely populated areas pupils usually come from the small lower-level schools. Since the number of pupils there is usually very small (for instance, only one pupil transferred from the Kärppä lower level to an upper level at the beginning of the school year 1979-80), this tends to increase the heterogeneity of the basic instruction groups at the upper level.

Upper Secondary Schools in Sparsely Populated Areas

The network of upper secondary schools covers by and large the whole of Finland. Owing to the good coverage of the upper secondary school network, regional differences in terms of education evened out during the 1970s. The upper schools have also become smaller as a result of falling birth rates throughout Finland. The importance of the preservation of the upper level and the upper secondary school has already been noted.

During the next few years the upper secondary school network will remain more or less unchanged. The arrangement of instruction in the small upper secondary schools will emerge as the most acute problem. The number of students will be reduced from its present level, in the small rural upper secondary schools in particular.

It seems clear that by the middle of the 1980s the most common form of upper secondary school education will be the school with one or two grades. A small upper secondary school cannot offer the same kind of selectivity or choice of syllabi as a large one. This must be taken into account in developing the curriculum of the upper secondary school in sparsely populated areas.

Kuusamo

Kuusamo's upper secondary school is an administratively independent, municipally owned and operated school. The target attendance of the school is about 40 percent of an age group in the Kuusamo area. As the district has only one upper secondary school, which is situated in the village of Kuusamo, it is rather large. According to the most recent estimates, the number of pupils attending this school will be at its highest during the school year 1979-80 (a total of 556 pupils). As the number of new entrants decreases, enrollment will be reduced to 315 in the school year 1986-87.

Students enter the upper secondary school from the ninth grade. Generally about 45 percent of the pupils of central Kuusamo's ninth grade go to the upper secondary school, while the corresponding figure from the Northern Kuusamo school is 25 to 35 percent. Some of the reasons for this difference are:

1. Upper secondary school education causes substantial costs for parents living in remote areas (lodging, food, journeys).
2. Motivation toward and active interest in upper secondary education increases (for reasons which are not entirely clear) as the size and density of population increases.
3. Boys in the sparsely populated areas are the group with the least motivation to attend upper secondary school.

The Kuusamo district has attempted to partly eliminate the problems referred to in the first item by granting progressive financial assistance for school journeys and lodging, but items 2 and 3 are less amenable to solution.

Conclusions

Many problems in Finland's educational system are caused by the settlement patterns of the country. In the planning of the nation's school network the Finnish authorities have had to choose between two alternatives: to take rural pupils long distances to large schools (where the organization of schooling would perhaps be easier and more economical), or to keep the schools as near as possible to the pupils' homes and have many small schools. The latter strategy has been adopted as fully as possible in recent years. Until just ten years ago this alternative was the only practical one because of inadequate road conditions.

With the improvement of the road system, it would have been possible to centralize schooling and greatly decrease the number of schools. However, the Finnish authorities believe that maintaining as many schools as possible will promote equal opportunities for education in all parts of the country—even though many schools must remain rather small. Long trips to school are too arduous for the young pupils at the lower level of the comprehensive school. In addition, schooling at faraway locations tends to break natural ties between the school and the pupils' homes. The parents wish to keep their children at home at least during the period of basic schooling. For this reason boarding schools have been avoided as much as possible.

An important reason for the policy favoring small rural schools has been the recognition of a school's effect (both actual and potential) on the rural community. The task of the school in the sparsely populated areas is not restricted to its educational function. It is an important factor in the community's cultural and social life, and the services offered to, and by, the community decrease considerably with the closure of a small village school. For this reason, the local population in Finland wants to maintain its own schools and the activities relating to their educational function for as long as possible.

10

Foxfire:
Experiential Education
in Rural America

Gail Armstrong Parks

It took Foxfire twelve years to make that name worth wanting.
— Mary Ann Martin

Foxfire is, fourteen years after its almost accidental inception, the name of an educational concept, a magazine, a series of books, a learning center, and a way of life for a small staff and group of students in one corner of rural America. Located in Rabun County, Georgia (a typically mountainous area at the southern end of the Appalachian region), Foxfire began when a young high school English teacher decided, with equal amounts of anxiety and courage, to confront the discrepancy between traditional teaching and the kind of real learning a good teacher would like to see.

When a disruptive student whom this teacher had moved to the front of the classroom forced the situation by setting fire to the lectern — "a protective device a teacher cowers behind while giving a lecture nobody's listening to" (Wigginton 1975, p. 112) — the seeds for Foxfire were planted. After some soul-searching the teacher decided he would not be yet another one who compulsively (and desperately) repeats the bad lessons of his own schooling. He decided to try something different to break the circle of repressive responses that were provoking escalations into increasingly disruptive counterresponses. The next day he came into class and asked his students how they would like to throw out the textbooks and publish a national magazine. This was the beginning of Foxfire.

The teacher was Brooks Eliot Wigginton, who had been reared in Athens, Georgia, where his father was a professor of landscape architecture at the University of Georgia. Having spent his summers in the mountains of Rabun County, Wigginton knew that when he finished his education he wanted to go back to teach in the mountains, because "as a child I had been happy there" (Wigginton 1978, p. 1). He is there today, living in a log house that students helped him build and continuing to play a major role in the myriad Foxfire activities that have sprouted from the initial student magazine.

There is an astonishing fact about Foxfire. It may be the one curricular idea in American rural secondary education that has the unique distinction of having spread to more than two-thirds of the fifty states, Canada, Australia, Guam, Puerto Rico, the Dominican Republic, and American Samoa, but has received little recognition in the country's professional education journals (Sitton 1978, pp. 5–6). With this discrepancy in mind, four major questions will be addressed in this chapter: What is the essential Foxfire process? What accounts for Foxfire's popularity and success among teachers, students, and communities? Why is it ignored in the professional literature but recognized in some leading art and literary publications? What are the essential problems in replicating and disseminating the Foxfire concept?

Foxfire can be described in a number of ways: as cultural journalism, as compassionate anthropology, as ethnography, as folklore, and as oral history. By this time, it is also a story, one that began in 1966 when Wigginton threw out the texts, sat down on the floor with his students, and began to plan a magazine. No one in the room knew anything about publishing, marketing, or distributing. No one knew what might sell or what a single issue would cost to produce and print. The result of that initial economic innocence was that the magazine was losing money after one issue and on the edge of bankruptcy throughout the first year, even though every issue sold out rapidly.

After some tentative issues featuring a combination of Appalachian folklore and student poetry, the magazine staff decided to concentrate on articles about life in the mountains. They had learned that it was the pieces about mountain people and mountain life that appealed most to their readers, both locally and elsewhere. Once the magazine began to succeed commercially, Wigginton was approached about gathering some of the articles together for a book to be put out by a major American commercial publisher. *The Foxfire Book,* published in 1972, was the result. By October 1979, it had sold 4,184,856 copies, and was followed by *Foxfire 2* (1973), *Foxfire 3* (1975), *Foxfire 4* (1977), and *Foxfire 5* (1979). Today, a sixth book is being prepared.

Once the substantial royalties from these books began arriving, it was possible for Wigginton and his "Foxfire kids" to expand their operation by hiring more staff and buying some needed equipment. As a teacher of English and journalism, Wigginton had taught students to conduct and transcribe interviews and use a camera. Assisted by Margie Bennett and

Suzanne Angier, he continues the journalistic activities, but two photography courses, introductory and advanced, are now taught by Paul Gillespie, a former Foxfire student who returned to the mountains as a Foxfire advisor after he finished college. Mike Cook, another former Foxfire student, teaches video recording and helps students create programs for the local cable television system. George Reynolds teaches classes in traditional music, folklore, and record publication. These classes have produced two albums, and others are planned. Bob Bennett teaches a science class in environmental awareness, and Sherrod Reynolds produces *Hands On,* an information-sharing newsletter for Foxfire teachers and students, and has completed the archiving of Foxfire materials.

Foxfire classes are taught in Rabun County High School, a relatively new "fortress-like structure of poured concrete and brick that keeps vigil atop a hill" (Thomas 1978, p. 15). Wigginton moved them there in 1977 from the semiprivate school, Rabun Gap–Nacoochee, where it had all begun.

> "It was a hard decision to make. We saw it coming as early as 1975, when the bond issue passed for the new school," explained Wigginton. "I was committed to keeping the program in the community. I didn't want to teach all dormitory kids who would go home to Florida or Alabama or wherever. The main thrust of our project had been to help those community students see who they were and where they came from. Without them, the project rings false." (Thomas 1978, p. 2)

That move led to, or conveniently coincided with, the building of several structures on mountain land that Foxfire (now officially known as The Foxfire Fund, Inc.) had bought in 1974. When the fund purchased the land, Wigginton and his students scouted the countryside for abandoned log cabins, dismantled them, and hauled the logs up the mountain. Having lost its office space in the private school, Foxfire set about constructing a learning community of offices, staff housing with dormitory space for visiting students and teachers, and replicas of old local structures: a smokehouse, a springhouse, a blacksmith shop, a mountain home, and a special cabin for a loom that women in the community who remember traditional crafts can use as a classroom for teaching students. "We started collecting the log cabins just like they were spinning wheels, so they wouldn't pass out of existence," a Foxfire staffer has said (Thomas 1978, p. 28).

The Foxfire staff has an unusual affiliation with Rabun County High School, an arrangement that was worked out among the district, the state, and Foxfire. Foxfire teachers hold classes at the school in the afternoon so that in the mornings they are free to work with students individually and attend to the many administrative details of running a substantial enterprise.

(As they "run" it, the staff members simultaneously teach students how to do everything they can do, and students in turn teach other students.) The Foxfire Fund pays staff salaries, so that in return for classroom space, the high school gains several teachers at no cost and several elective courses in the departments of English, history, fine arts, and science. Foxfire teachers abide by all school rules and regulations except that they are on a first-name basis with their students.

In the eyes of the high school principal, Leland Dishman, the arrangement is mutually beneficial. Foxfire staff, he explains, contribute to the instructional program in important ways by sharing their activities with the entire school, as when they arrange a folk music concert for the student assembly. Their dedication, to the non-college-bound students in particular, has won his respect. Dishman alludes proudly to the fact that the Foxfire kids, who do astonishing things with magazines, books, photography, and video, are not predominantly from the top academic group. In fact, the reverse is true, for only a few students at top academic levels believe that their college preparation schedule gives them the flexibility to choose Foxfire electives (Dishman 1978).

This enrollment pattern is in keeping with the origins of the project. It did not evolve as a result of disruptive activities by the academically talented. Those students who were not seen as talented, who had simply been passed along or ignored throughout their schooling, were the ones who sent signals of distress to Wigginton. It is those students in particular who are the concern of the Foxfire staff. Wigginton has expressed some of his thoughts on the "lower-track" students as follows:

> A Foxfire activity is ideally suited for those poor kids who have gotten stimulation, reward and a sense of achievement nowhere else. Kids that can't write well (yet) can conduct magical interviews or take brilliant photographs—and later find themselves writing captions and descriptions to go with them. Kids that don't read well (yet) can make wonderful videotapes and films and slide shows—and later find themselves reading and writing scripts. . . . I've watched it happen for nine years. (Wigginton 1975, p. 10)

Many of these students are now going to local community and state colleges, some of them because of Foxfire, according to John Singleton, an eleventh-grader who worked for Foxfire during the summer of 1978 (Foxfire students 1978).

Foxfire students tend to talk about their experience in terms of gaining competence, being needed to do important work, and acquiring adult knowledge. "What Foxfire does," Mary Ann Martin has said, "is make you aware." John Singleton has expressed it thus: "It makes you feel like you're needed, like you're doing something that's . . . contributing to something.

Because Wig could have easily . . . made some phone calls [in response to Gail Parks's letter asking Foxfire to set up appointments for her with local people] and that would have been that. But instead he handed it to me and made me sweat for about four or five hours. And all the same I feel like I accomplished something" (Foxfire students 1978).

Foxfire people and the Rabun County community are the larger part of the story but not the whole. Luck, chance, and the subsequent development of a far-flung network are also important in the chronology. In 1970, when the magazine was young and Wigginton was in Washington "begging for money," he ran into Junius Eddy of the U.S. Office of Education. Eddy arranged a meeting with Herb McArthur at the National Endowment for the Humanities, and the first "significant" grant to Foxfire came shortly thereafter. It happened that Wigginton's college fraternity brother, Mike Kinney, who had a job with Anchor Books, persuaded Wigginton to compile the articles for a book and then persuaded Anchor to publish it.

One of the most significant relationships developed between Foxfire and the Institutional Development and Economic Affairs Service (IDEAS). The director of IDEAS, Brian Beun, saw the Foxfire magazine at the Smithsonian Institution in 1970: "A quick perusal of its pages made me intuitively aware that Foxfire represented a prototype learning experience which, with further refinement, had the potential to benefit large numbers of young people" (Beun 1975, p. vi). Beun made contact with Wigginton, and a close affiliation developed between the two leading to Wigginton's becoming an associate of IDEAS and the development of "a conceptual framework for extending Foxfire to cultures beyond its origin in the Southern Appalachian mountains" (Beun 1975, p. vi). By 1971, IDEAS had begun working with several schools to establish Foxfire demonstration projects. By 1974, IDEAS had helped "more than a dozen schools initiate such projects, helping them to 'tailor the concept to meet existing educational needs as determined by their particular schools, districts, and state systems'" (Beun 1975, p. vii).

That arrangement also enabled some of Wigginton's students to experience "a whole new series of educational opportunities" as they were "invited by new projects to spend a summer on location helping get their first issue of a magazine together" (Wigginton 1977, p. 9). For former Foxfire students Gary Warfield and Claude Rickman, those were transforming experiences that gave them, at an early age, adult insights and responsibilities as they confronted racial prejudice, miles of red tape, students who had been defeated by negative schooling experiences, and grinding poverty. Having known and loved their part of the world, Warfield and Rickman became more cosmopolitan, expansive, and universal as they worked in other cultural settings. Wigginton has written about the need for this broader awareness:

I have learned through bitter experience . . . that it is not enough for my kids to have an intimate understanding of their own past, roots, and heritage. That is immensely important, but to be truly effective citizens, they must next acquire an equally sophisticated knowledge of their culture's relationship to others. We are a multicultural world, and we are all linked one to another, for better or worse. (Wigginton 1977, p. 10)

The Foxfire Program and Pedagogy

I discovered that I was in the middle of a community filled with older peo- ple who had once been totally self-sufficient human beings. They had built their own log homes completely by hand, raised sheep and carded and spun and woven the wool into cloth using looms they had made themselves, they had made their own shoes, their tools, their pottery, their musical instru- ments, their guns, raised and preserved their own meat and vegetables, healed their sick, buried their dead. And staggeringly, almost none of their grandchil- dren — my students — knew it. The gap between what these living pre-flight, pre-automobile, pre-communication individuals had had to do, and what their grandchildren now knew how to do, was complete.

— Eliot Wigginton (1978, p. 3)

When Eliot Wigginton, as a first-year teacher, was experiencing his crisis in the classroom, he utilized two resources in resolving the crisis: the mem- ories of his own education, in particular those experiences that "stuck," and the values inherent in the community where he was living. On the subject of the former, he has said this: "Visitors from the community, visits into the community, times when we were trusted with responsibility, and moments when things we were allowed to create or do were given an audience beyond our classroom teacher — those were the things that stuck. As a new teacher, my task and my challenge became to somehow create a curriculum around those core elements." (Wigginton, 1978, p. 3)

The good fortune of being in a "community filled with older people who had once been totally self-sufficient human beings" was perhaps — and perhaps not — a dollop of serendipity. The community as it exists and as it is preserved in the living memories of its older inhabitants has become the basis for the content of the Foxfire curriculum. Wigginton maintains that the *process* stands apart, that while a "Foxfire project" need not feature the past, it must utilize the community. As he has pointed out,

As you look at the moments, you will see that folklore *per se* (or local history or oral history or whatever) does not have to be the vehicle you use to make these things happen. A perfectly good project utilizing all the following activities might be a community magazine that talked not about the past but about the present. . . .

I'm simply saying that if you can put your kids in a position where they can experience many of the following moments (no matter what the end product or the vehicle or your style of teaching), they will have a choice of coming far closer than the average high school student to being sensitive and whole as human beings. (Wigginton 1975, pp. 16–17)

Perceptions about the degree to which one can create a successful Foxfire-type activity without drawing heavily upon the local community's past as well as its present may vary somewhat. Unfortunately, there is only one extensive study of the Foxfire projects, and even that relied on survey instruments rather than site studies to obtain the needed information. However, this study does indicate, first, that Foxfire projects outside small towns and rural areas tend not to last, and second, that the vast majority of successful projects focus on the past (Sitton 1978). These facts might be explained by the general condition of metropolitan schools, which do not permit as much student freedom (because of urban dangers) or as much institutional flexibility (because of greater size and bureaucratization) as their rural counterparts. Still, the facts might also reflect a greater difficulty in discovering and celebrating the local traditions and culture in very large communities of essentially rootless transients. It is at least interesting that the one suburban project that has endured is located in an area serving many students of displaced Appalachian families. With the consideration that rurality may be significant, the words of an early and consistent Foxfire supporter are worth noting:

Foxfire is a learning process possessing a demonstrated capability to use creatively the talents of high school aged youth within a reality structure. It can serve a subject matter purpose while simultaneously providing opportunity by which young people may better sense and develop their own identities. The concept involves students in the establishment of new or renewed relationships by conducting extensive interviews with members of a fast vanishing oldest generation. Out of those relationships the participating youth document the wisdom and capture the essence of their own, immediate, cultural heritage while developing a wide range of academic and practical skills. The result is that schoolwork becomes applicable to the everyday life of their community.

From the outset, the central thrust of Foxfire programs lies in a focus on cultural heritage as a motivational force for learning. This positive effect is reinforced by the initiative and collaboration of students working together in the planning and production of a marketable publication. When the resulting publication succeeds in attracting wide public interest there is further reinforcement made the more meaningful by the approving judgment of a real world. Thus, the major objective of Foxfire is to serve cultural pride through engagement of the student's own skills in its discovery. At no stage in life is this more important than in the mid teens, when young people think most deeply about their lives, their futures, and the relevance of their surroundings to both. (Beun 1975, p. vii)

When *The Foxfire Book* was published in 1972, David Shapiro reviewed it for *Saturday Review,* describing it as "a fine example of Emersonian self-reliance and compassionate anthropology that would have charmed James Agee and Oscar Lewis" (Shapiro 1972, p. 36). Shapiro went on to make a point of great subtlety, one that is often missed in descriptions of Foxfire: "The book is paradoxically as immersed in the future as in the past, for it does not merely lament loss of knowledge, but maintains a sinuous strategy to recover some of the "lost worlds" and "lost words" of Appalachia" (Shapiro 1972, p. 36).

Being "immersed in the future" renders Foxfire simultaneously a brilliant pedagogy and an elusive model; one that probably cannot be replicated in the usual systemic or mechanistic sense but rather must grow, as did the original, from the center outward. Each individual initiator must use his or her particular setting and geopolitical circumstances to fashion a "curriculum " that links past, present, and future.

The Foxfire process links students to their own past and encourages their active involvement in shaping their own futures. It relies on a theory of adolescent development that goes hand in hand with "steps" or "movements" toward a developmental ideal, which Wigginton calls "beyond self." It seems to grow from a belief that what counts, in the end, is to "have on your hands a strong, warm, whole human being who has done a rare and beautiful thing; he has demonstrated choice. Self-determination. Responsible, positive direction. A kid who is beginning to influence his fate as he sees it" (Wigginton 1975, p. 94).

There are two strands in this part of the Foxfire concept—concern for the freedom and autonomy of the student and concern for social justice and the preservation of the community:

> High school is not too early a place to begin the testing that will help a student define the boundaries of tolerance of human behavior. I'm not saying that our project seeks to radicalize our kids and send them out sniffing into and protesting loudly—and perhaps irresponsibly—about conditions that may exist in the school or community. But I *do* like to feel that our project here has the sort of atmosphere surrounding it that will allow a student to express his opinions or voice his gripes without being mocked . . . or bring up points of concern to him and not be ignored or have them passed off as irrelevant. (Wigginton 1975, pp. 85–87)

David Shapiro has labeled the educational process that supports the development of a passion for justice and an accompanying sense of autonomy "a radical empiricism" and has commented on its pedagogical usefulness:

> The artist or teacher may do well to follow the example of Foxfire. . . . For example, just as utopian fantasies teach much to children, so video taping, tape recording, and, in general, Margaret Mead's classic field techniques of contact, cooperation, and analysis are particularly suitable and inspiring tools for use in and out of the classroom. Foxfire points the way toward a true sense of place, and it is a pity that we do not have more examples of "field work" in the schools. . . . The anthropological field trip, which salvages life stories, catalogues, details, analyzes speech, is a fine form for reaching out and touching today's student. (Shapiro 1972, p. 37)

What is it, precisely, that Foxfire students learn to do, and how do they learn it? These are the essential questions for teachers. It is not difficult to answer the first question, at least minimally. Foxfire students learn, as a basic minimum, to conduct and transcribe interviews, write articles for publication, operate a reasonably sophisticated camera, develop film, and participate in the governance of Foxfire (each Foxfire person has one vote). Ideally, they learn an expansive range of skills, perspectives, and values, including:

- acquisition of vocational skills which are transferrable, marketable, and can be useful for a lifetime, i.e., editing and writing, photography, darkroom technique, marketing, bookkeeping, printing, typing, filing, transcribing, design, organization and management, circulation, advertising, public relations, public speaking, museum curatorship, community leadership, and banking.
- acquisition of a discipline for learning, demanding of both individual initiative and communal responsibility.
- acquisition of respect for and pride in their communities, their elders, and the human values which sustain them; and the development of a sense of place and belonging among their own people.
- acquisition of an interdisciplinary perspective toward learning and the interrelationship of subject studies.
- acquisition of an awareness of and appreciation for the visual and literary arts as they are applied to enhance the process of communication.
- acquisition of an inquiring sense of direction from which to explore new subjects, develop new relationships, and enter new experiences. (Beun 1975, pp. vii–viii)

How they learn these things is a far more complex matter. In *Moments,* Eliot Wigginton has tried to explain how one translates his theory into operational terms; he gives numerous examples of activities and even appropriate words to use with students. Fundamentally, Wigginton believes that teachers who operate within traditional role definitions cannot work in the most effective way with adolescents. Thad Sitton, who has closely examined Wigginton's writings, believes that the idea of rejecting the conventional teacher-student relationship is the most central tenet of Wigginton's thoughts: "Wigginton's purpose . . . was to use the magazine project as a vehicle to effect a basic change between himself and his students—a traditional role relationship that he saw as essentially destructive" (Sitton 1978, pp. 21–22). He appears to believe that teachers must learn to do something most educators would probably consider a difficult feat—behave toward students in a nonformal, egalitarian manner while accepting full adult responsibilities for student growth and never allowing one's own ego needs to intrude. With Wigginton, that approach, at least as an ideal, has apparently succeeded in virtually eliminating serious disciplinary problems. One of several examples he has given will probably illustrate the style he uses:

> Even though the main thrust here is to begin to satisfy each student's ego and sense of self-esteem, my personal approach is to downplay that goal verbally and concentrate on achieving it quietly. I may say to a student, "Look, this camera looks like a Chinese puzzle, but it's really not so bad. Come on outside with me and I'll show you how it works, and then you can fire off a couple of shots yourself and we'll print them and see what happens. Right?" But I do not say to a student, "The main purpose of this exercise is to prove to you that you can operate a camera and thereby add to your sense of self-esteem and satisfy your ego." Much of the work I do in this direction I never verbalize at all. I simply watch, work behind the scenes to make things happen, and constantly ask myself if each kid is coming along, and if not, where I am going wrong? I want to give him a deep, firm, unselfish sense of worth—not turn him into a self-indulgent egomaniac. (Wigginton 1975, p. 18)

From this base, Wigginton moves students along to the development of highly skilled interview and transcription techniques. He has taken pains in *Moments* to describe various activities that can lead high school students to become skillful ethnographers. It seems doubtful, however, that most teachers could quickly replicate what he can do at this stage, even with the guidance of *Moments*. In fact, there seems to be general agreement that only a few of the student magazines can match or surpass Foxfire sophistication. The instructions in *Moments*, nevertheless, are highly informative. For example:

> At this point I also like the students to be involved in exercises that begin to

get their eyes open to the world around them. I ask each, when in an interview situation, to look closely at the room/environment of the contact, list all the things he notes there, and the same day write a full description of the setting using that list. He should create a photograph in words so that the audience that couldn't be with him will be able to see and feel the person and the room, and share the moment with him as fully as possible. The idea here is not only to get the student watching the world he encounters, but also to prove to him that he has power over words and can use them as tools rather than the reverse. He should be able to make words paint pictures for him and know that because he opened his eyes he was able to create something special. (Wigginton 1975, p. 32)

Can any school have a Foxfire? Is the essential process transferable across demographic and cultural differences? Eliot Wigginton maintains that the answer is yes and that, given a principal who will "let it happen," success depends on a teacher's desire for change, willingness to change, and ability to invest "a tremendous expenditure of energy and ingenuity" along with "hours and hours of time for which (he or she) will never be reimbursed monetarily" (Wigginton 1975, p. 5). The existence of 150 Foxfire projects (primarily teacher-inspired) scattered throughout the United States and elsewhere lends substance to the idea of transferability but does not suggest much about necessary and sufficient conditions—except, as was noted earlier, that there are far more rural than metropolitan projects.

Certainly, the uniquely Appalachian personalities and the special times that are evoked in the various Foxfire books are what has appealed most to its massive audience—which largely consists of suburbanites jaded by humdrum affluence and old-timers who "remember when" (and who often become the subject of new articles after they write to amend or add to information in Foxfire articles). Financially, Foxfire is far more successful than its imitators, only two of which (Salt in Maine and Bittersweet in Missouri) have produced widely selling books.

Yet what has happened after the magazine began may indeed be serendipity. Without the land, the recording company, the royalties, or the cabins, there would still be Foxfire, an essential learning process emanating from "a remarkable venture in homespun high-school journalism" (Maxwell n.d., p. 1). Teachers, Wigginton warns, should avoid the temptation of "focusing on the end product so intensely that the process is forgotten or downplayed." The product, he observes, is necessary for giving students the motivation to "work their material into communicable form." Moreover, the publishing of student work gives it importance in adult eyes: "It matters. It is going to be used. But far too often . . . in the desire to create a superlative product, the teacher hand picks those few superior students who can produce and doesn't allow the others to get involved. . . . The kids that would have benefitted the most from this kind of activity were ignored (as usual) and lost" (Wigginton 1975, p. 10).

To the principal and counselor of Rabun County High School, the quality that shines through in the work of Foxfire staff is devotion to and respect for students. "The most impressive thing about Wigginton," a Rabun County High School counselor commented, "is that he really loves kids." Bob Bennett, teacher of the class in environmental science, likes "to go hiking with some high school kids for weekend relaxation." Asked whether he would continue to live and work on the Foxfire land if there were no students, musician and folklorist George Reynolds replied, "If there were no kids, Sherrod (my wife) and I would go find other jobs for ourselves."

Dissemination and Institutionalization of the Foxfire Concept

There are two facts of fundamental significance about the dissemination of Foxfire projects. Within a relatively short time, extensive dissemination has occurred, and it has occurred outside regular channels. Projects in approximately 150 schools have now become institutionalized. That they occasionally exist on marginal financial terms and with tentative, year-by-year commitments from some school administrators or school boards is also significant. Fortunately, there is empirical documentation on the dissemination process and enough material to enable several informed speculations about the current status of the Foxfire concept in American secondary schools (Sitton 1978, pp. 58–78).

Both dissemination and diffusion are involved in spreading Foxfire projects. As noted earlier, IDEAS was the enabler in the formal dissemination process, securing funding for a dissemination project that it undertook with Foxfire in 1971-72 and has since expanded. Thad Sitton has described the initial IDEAS strategy as follows: "(1) To locate likely schools within rural areas of distinctive regional culture; (2) to approach these schools with the idea of initiating a Foxfire-concept publication while offering both advice and limited financial support should the idea be adopted; and (3) to follow a school's acceptance with a variety of such support" (Sitton 1978, p. 61). After identifying the schools in 1971, IDEAS provided initial financial support for staff workshops and some minimal equipment. The first step was to bring students and teachers to Rabun Gap for training in process theory and methods. After these workshops, which were conducted by Foxfire staff, "student-staff members from Foxfire were paid by IDEAS to accompany these groups to their home schools and help them make preparations for beginning a publication in the next school year" (Sitton 1978, p. 61).

By 1972 there were twelve operating Foxfire-type projects in U.S. schools, most if not all in that group resulting from the formal dissemination effort (Sitton 1978, p. 59). There was to be, however, a "second wave" that consisted of teachers who approached either IDEAS, Foxfire, or both. One might characterize this process as diffusion, since "publication of *The Foxfire Book* in 1972 stimulated a wave of teacher interest in Foxfire"; thus "these 'second-wave projects' were self-initiated" (Sitton 1978, p. 62). By the spring of 1975, twenty-seven projects had been created; this number increased to thirty-four by that summer, to forty-three in February 1976, and to "at least eighty" in the summer of 1977 (Sitton 1978, p. 59).

The result today is an extensive network of people, institutions, and publications. In 1973, IDEAS expanded its scope of workshop activities to include on-site activities in the participating schools. One state (Alaska) has made a statewide commitment to disseminating and enabling the concept. *Exchange,* a project newsletter, was first funded by IDEAS in 1973, at the request of the projects themselves. In 1975, two books intended as practical guides were published by IDEAS: *Moments,* a guide for teachers by Eliot Wigginton; and *You and Aunt Arie: A Guide to Cultural Journalism,* by Pam Wood, advisor to Salt in Maine. The latter is written specifically for students.

What initially intrigued the teachers who sought out Foxfire and IDEAS, or simply started out alone? And what has motivated teachers throughout the years to continue their projects, which involve so much additional time and energy that it would be a great deal easier to abandon them? Sitton's landmark study once more provides answers that, if not definitive, seem very convincing.

It appears that many teachers choose to initiate and continue (even fight for) their projects in large part because of the different relationships with students that the activities facilitate (and may, indeed, dictate). The need to alter existing student-teacher relationships is, of course, central in Wigginton's thought. The teachers who responded to Sitton's questionnaire, particularly those who answered the "discussion" section, provided strong support for the premise that more egalitarian relationships are both pedagogically helpful and personally satisfying: "The teachers who responded . . . stressed this matter of altered role relations under question two, 'particular advantages of their project.' . . . They stressed that student-teacher relationships were much closer and more relaxed" (Sitton 1978, p. 87). Within that general context, many teachers also emphasized that "the project effectively increased student esteem and confidence" (Sitton, 1978, p. 87).

Sitton's data suggested further that teachers enjoyed the esteem of the community as a result of their magazines, that they liked the stimulation of work having intrinsic interest (i.e., teaching cultural journalism and field interviewing), and that the satisfaction derived from having a role in producing a quality product was not inconsiderable.

The fact that teachers gain status in the community as a result of project magazines and the work they do with students can bring problems as well as blessings. Responses to Sitton's questionnaire indicated substantial problems with administrators in a number of situations. He noted the existence of strong community support for magazines: "In general, . . . project-community relations seem to be excellent. It is difficult to avoid the judgment that the projects are selling something that the local community really wishes to buy—fulfilling some very real need. Perhaps they give voice to a "sense of community" at a deeper level than the local newspaper can afford to reach" (Sitton 1978, p. 99). Taking into account teacher comments on administrative support (ranging from minimal to tolerable to adequate), Sitton's assessment of what might be true was as follows: "The Foxfire-concept publications open new channels between the school and community. The 'control of channels,' however, is normally the province of the administrative arm of the school, not the classroom teacher. The very success of a project can lead to jealousy and trouble in situations where the administrator is still described as basically favorable, and there are several descriptions of this sort in the questionnaire data" (Sitton 1978, p. 95).

Community support for projects, however, can make them "untouchable" administratively. In at least one known case, a school administration planning to terminate a project was persuaded instead to include a cultural journalism class in the school curriculum because of community support and a teacher's willingness to fight for it (Gjelten 1979).

An exciting thing happens in small towns and rural places when the first issue of a Foxfire-concept magazine appears in grocery stores and on local lunch counters. It sells out the first day. Most projects underestimate the public response and have to reprint. The vast majority of projects, in fact, support themselves locally. As a result, project students and advisors gain a lively sense of self-esteem from community people, who seem to feel greater self-esteem as a result of the magazines. It is almost a magic formula, given honest work.

Something should be said for those administrators who have had Foxfire-type projects in their schools for several years. It is no mean feat for an individual with the ascribed status of leader to continue support for a teacher whose activities may outshine his or hers in the community—surely it is a manifestation of considerable graciousness. Even the ones who "let it happen," which Wigginton claims is all that is really necessary, may be due some praise and may well be a necessary ingredient in the magic formula. As Gjelten (1979) has noted,

This effort to improve education in a rural community comes down to what seems to be the same old story. The teacher who is willing, in his own words, "to play the game" in his school to insure that his project survives. The superintendent with sufficient generosity and flexibilty to tolerate and support the development of a new activity which was, at various times, embarrassing, disruptive, and uncontrollable. (p. 39)

There is yet another sense in which Foxfire dissemination has not occurred through channels:

For whatever . . . reasons, Foxfire and IDEAS . . . went directly to teachers, students and administrators in "hand-picked" schools, and later other teachers, students and administrators went directly to them. When it was necessary, Foxfire and IDEAS opened direct negotiations with state educational agencies, and with philanthropic foundations, public and private. What they did *not* do was to associate themselves with, or have themselves "authenticated by," the university educational community in this country, as embodied in such organizations as the National Council for the Social Studies. (Sitton 1978, p. 77).

Have there been and are there likely to be consequences resulting from such neglect? Would dissemination have occurred on a grander scale if "regular channels" had been used? These questions will be addressed more fully in the concluding section.

However, it is perhaps neither overly dramatic nor overly suspicious to suggest that there is a causal relationship between the fact that Foxfire and IDEAS ignored universities and their affiliated channels and that the professional education journals and periodicals of universities and their affiliates have ignored the Foxfire concept for thirteen years. Since Foxfire has been written about in such places as the *New York Times Book Review, Saturday Review of Literature, Natural History, Audubon, Time, Life, Oral History Association Newsletter, Seventeen,* and *The New Republic,* it strains credibility to accept that the professional educators who write for the journals, and the journals' staffs themselves, have not heard that a significant success story has taken place in American secondary schools (primarily those in rural areas and small towns) over the past thirteen years.

Why the wall of virtual silence? As pure exercise of prerogative? As a stark (and scary) message about "legitimate" control? As a "lesson" to "outsiders"? As a reflection of indifference? As an inability to perceive something significant happening in American education? As a way of avoiding the issue? These questions may well be related to a far more comprehensive matter, which is the philosophy of education, humanity, and society that underlies the Foxfire concept. That is the next matter for discussion.

Reflections on the Value of
the Foxfire Concept

In 1966, Eliot Wigginton was thinking seriously about both individual student learning and the significance of a community. In 1972 he had written about both. By 1977, he had come to link together kids, their school, their community, their region, and their world. He has thus in theory linked the individual, the local, and the universal. The pedagogically sophisticated thinking that is embedded in Wigginton's writings deserves special consideration from educators because it is based on many years of "laboratory" experimentation, i.e., direct involvement with students engaged in community fieldwork.

Wigginton's activities in Rabun County (as Thad Sitton has asserted) are simultaneously preservationist, practical, and utopian. He has recognized that the "salvage ethnography" of his students will not, in and of itself, preserve the Appalachian culture of the north Georgia mountains, which is being eroded by tourism and exploitation from the outside. And since Wigginton transmits what he understands to students in terms *they* can understand, he has showed them how to research current problems of land use, commercial exploitation, and environmental disruption.

The concern with preserving the natural world and making it more habitable is strongly preservationist, as is the concern with Appalachian culture. The activities that students undertake in their fieldwork and research on local problems have a practical focus and teach practical skills. The result, should efforts like Wigginton's succeed, will be to reconstruct conditions in communities and societies, for people will be living in a world where values will have changed. The vision is utopian.

So perhaps Sitton's thesis is correct: Wigginton's Foxfire concept is "a functional attempt at reconciliation of the individualist and social schools of progressivism within a single curricular formula" (Sitton 1978, p. 125). Foxfire began with a concern for the individual student's need to acquire a sense of self-worth and with a set of activities intended to make it happen. That concern was linked to a passionate sense that a beautiful culture with admirable traditions and values was disappearing without a trace. It made sense to link those concerns by having students interview the older people in the community and record their personal histories, folklore, and folkways. It has made further sense for students to use similar research methods to investigate their community's present problems, learn to participate in running a business enterprise (The Foxfire Fund, Inc.), and return the profits of their work to the community. And finally, it has become apparent that no culture is an island and that it is not enough to care about only one's own community or region. Wigginton now talks about creating "islands of decency" throughout the continent, islands that are linked by networks of people who are concerned about both individual and social decency.

"At Foxfire," Thad Sitton has written, "study of the 'old mountain culture' has generated both the *motivation* to reform the present-day community of Rabun Gap and some of the means to do it" (1978, p. 124). In one respect, possibly the most important one, the Foxfire concept has gone a major step beyond Counts, Dewey, Brameld, and the other progressives: it has involved students directly in social change by giving them disciplinary skills (fieldwork, interviewing, research, writing) and vocational skills (transcribing, editing, photography, videotaping, accounting, interpreting contracts) and by putting those skills to work. Foxfire students have that "firsthand contact with actualities" that John Dewey recommended; they *do* adult work, and apparently many of them, especially in later adolescence, do it well.

The fact that these young students, who are not primarily from the top group in school, can do adult work competently, can even produce work considered to have outstanding literary merit, may be for the education profession as a whole the worst pill to swallow. If it is true that "average" students, nonacademic students, students in the "probable drop-out" category can do these things, what does that mean? Does it mean that the education system has all along not been doing something it could have done, had it gone about things differently? Does it mean, possibly, that society as it is now structured does not need, or could not use, the talents that would appear with a different kind of education? Does it mean that it would be harder to justify great discrepancies in wealth, discrepancies that assign significant numbers of persons to a poverty status, if it turns out that most people are more talented and able than we have thought? A U.S. government official has offered an interesting interpretation for the education profession's apparent unwillingness to acknowledge the Foxfire concept. "Foxfire is a solution," he has observed, "and people who work in government bureaucracies and who get grants from bureaucracies don't want solutions." Solutions make their jobs unimportant or unnecessary.

One need not look for evidence of conspiracies and unenlightened self-interest to understand some of the reasons that the Foxfire concept has not been promoted officially. It may have been, and it may yet be, necessary for these projects to begin as purely individual and/or local efforts. One suspects that a massive government effort to disseminate the concept would, in the process, do things that violate the essential process. Curriculum intended for mass use has tended to be "packaged" in materials that reflect a reductionist attempt at condensing realities to "core concepts" and that eliminate much of the teacher's creative work.

Eliot Wigginton insists, however, that teachers *must* work, and that if they are serious about having Foxfire projects, they must be willing to work longer and harder with no additional pay. With the rise of collective bargaining by teachers in recent years, this requirement might create problems with dissemination. It may have been for the best, therefore, that Foxfire projects came about voluntarily, as they did. Their chances for success and continuation may be strengthened by this fact.

The most frequent criticisms that one hears about Foxfire are that it is too local and insular (as opposed to cosmopolitan and expansive) and too "commercial." Both those criticisms appear to arise from valid concerns and should be addressed.

By Wigginton's own admission, Foxfire once adopted an isolationist policy because it seemed the only way, at the time, to keep the project's integrity in the face of so much national attention. That policy has changed, as Wigginton has noted. The isolationism was a stage, and it might be helpful for burgeoning "Foxfires" to keep in mind that what exists today is the result of a long evolution that has had "bitter experience" and some mistakes in its progression.

The accusation that Foxfire is too commercial is a puzzle for two reasons. First, schools throughout U.S. society carry on numerous commercial enterprises, including selling student work. The *scale* of Foxfire's financial success is different; but the impossible barrier for some critics to cross may be that the enterprise was created and is handled by students and teachers, is outside institutional jurisdiction, and has nevertheless succeeded. Second, unlike the university professors who pocket, with no apparent sense of guilt, the royalties from the books they write, Foxfire staff and students return the profits from their books to the community. It seems a curious definition of "commercial"—a term that carries at least a hint of materialism and greed—to so label the activities of a group that appears to operate in the tradition of Christian socialism known in the United States as "utopianism" or "communalism." Witness, for example, the words of one Foxfire staff member:

> With the money earned from *The Foxfire Book*, 50 acres of mountain land were purchased. That land has become the headquarters for the Foxfire Organization—we call it "the land", but its official title is the Foxfire Learning Center. Our offices are located here, several staff members live in the reconstructed log houses, and there are plans to set up various shops for the kids to use. We have a blacksmith shop, weaving shed, woodworking shop, two museum buildings, and a mill. We have gotten some criticism from tourists for not being more accessible and "commercial"; that is not our purpose. The

learning center will never be a tourist attraction—it is for our kids and our community. And that's really what Foxfire is all about. (Bennett 1977, p. 8)

Appendix 1: Active Foxfire-Type Projects

Alabama

GOOD MORNING, YESTERDAY
Alabaster, AL 35007

MORNIN' DEW
Clio, AL 36017

SPARROW HAWK
Centerville, AL 35042

RAVEN
Aniston, AL 36201

YESTERYEAR
Montgomery, AL 35130

Alaska

CHAMAI
Kodiak, AK 99615

ELWANI
Kodiak, AK 99615

KALIIKAQ YUGNEK
Beth, AK 99559

FORGET ME NOT
Anchorage, AK 99504

KIL-KAAS-GIT
Craig, AK 99921

KWIKPUGMUIT
Emmonak, AK 99581

TUNDRA MARSH
Nunapitchuk, AK 99614

UUTUGTWA
Naknek, AK 99633

Arizona

SADDLEBAG
Wickenburg, AZ 85358

California

GOLDEN HINDSIGHT
San Anselmo, CA 94960

LONG, LONG AGO
Bell Garden, CA 90201

OUT-N-ABOUT
Salinas, CA 93908

THE TRI-COUNTY INDIAN
DEVELOPMENT COUNCIL
Yreka, CA 96097

Colorado

MONTANE
Basalt, CO 81621

PTARMIGAN
Montrose, CO 81401

THREE WIRE WINTER
Steamboat Springs, CO 80477

WHISTLEWIND
Sterling, CO 80751

This list was current when the chapter was written. New projects may have been initiated since then. *Source:* Sherrod Reynolds, the Foxfire Fund, Rabun Gap, Georgia.

District of Columbia

CITYSCAPE
Washington, DC 20007

Florida

LET THE CHILDREN SPEAK
TEACHER EDUCATION PROJECTS
Tallahassee, FL 32301

Georgia

CHICKYPIN
Statenville, GA 31648

FOLK AND KINFOLK
Hamilton, GA 31811

FOXFIRE
Rabun Gap, GA 30568

EBB TIDE
St. Simons Island, GA 31522

Hawaii

LAULIMA
Honaka'a, HI 96727

MO'OLELO
Kaumakani, HI 96747

Bob Palmateer
Kapaa, Kauai, HI 96746

NA LEO O LANAI
Lanai City, HI 96743

NA KUPUNA
Molokai, HI 96748

MANAO O WAIANAE
Waianae, HI 96792

Leslie Lauro
Pahala, HI 96777

Kauai High School
Lihue, HI 96766

Illinois

REDLETTER
Chicago, IL 60626

STREETLIGHT
Chicago, IL 60601

Indiana

FLATROCK
Connersville, IN 47331

Iowa

ROOT PROJECT
Remsen, IA 51050

WILDROWS
Adel, IA 50003

Kentucky

MOUNTAIN REVIEW
Whitesburg, KY 41858

RECOLLECTIONS
Jackson, KY 41339

Louisiana

LAGNIAPPE
Baton Rouge, LA 70815

Maine

ROOTS
Calais, ME 04619

SALT
Kennebunkport, ME 04046

SILVER BIRCHES
Stockholm, ME 04783

HOMEGROWN
Ellsworth, ME 04605

TERRA
Presque Isle, ME 04769

Maryland

SKIPJACK
Cambridge, MD 21613

Massachusetts

INNER HARBOR
Gloucester, MA 01930

PROJECT BLUEBERRY
Wilbraham, MA 01095

Sean Kennan, Coordinator
Andover, MA 01810

Michigan

LOOKING GLASS
Portland, MI 48875

PROJECT SNAP
Flint, MI 48505

WOODEN SNEAKERS
Holland, MI 49423

Minnesota

PATCHWORK
St. Paul, MN 55101

COMPAS
St. Paul, MN 55102

Mississippi

NANIH WAYIH
Philadelphia, MS 39350

Missouri

BITTERSWEET
Lebanon, MO 65536

IN RETROSPECT
Webster Groves, MO 63119

Montana

DOVETAIL
Ronan, MT 59864

New Hampshire

FULCRUM
Hanover, NH 03755

BACKLOG
Nottingham, NH 03290

SPILE
Hollia, NH 03049

New Jersey

ARMADA
Highway 36
West Long Branch, NJ 07764

PROJECT USE
Longbranch, NJ 07740

New Mexico

TSA' ASZI
Ramah, NM 87321

Ms. Beverly McCrary
Santa Fe, NM 87501

New York

EIDOS MAGAZINE
Cazenovia, NY 13151

WILD APPLE PRESS
Friendship, NY 14739

PAUMANOK
Shoreham, NY 11786

North Carolina

APPLE CORPS
Flat Rock, NC 28731

COTTONSEED ANTHOLOGY
Charlotte, NC 28216

KIN'LIN'
Hallsboro, NC 28442

SEA CHEST
Buxton, NC 27920

SOUTHERN LIVES
Hillsboro, NC 27278

HOMESPUN
Lexington, NC 27292

Ohio

Garnet Byrne, Advisor
Stowe, OH 44224

THISTLEDOWN
Pataskala, OH 45750

TWENTY MILE MAGAZINE
Marietta, OH 45750

Oregon

JR. BUFF
Madras, OR 97741

CLOUDBURST
Beaverton, OR 97005

RAINBARREL
Hillsboro, OR 97229

VALLEY LOG
Halsey, OR 97348

Pennsylvania

CHELTENHAM LOOK AROUND
Wyncote, PA 19095

Upattinas School
Malvern, PA 19355

OUT OF THE DARK: MINING FOLK
Barnesboro, PA 15714

South Carolina

REFLECTIONS
Seneca, SC 29678

South Dakota

Tom Casey
Pine Ridge, SD 57770

Texas

BIG COUNTRY, PLACES, EVENTS
& PEOPLE
Abilene, TX 79601

BLACK GOLD
Carthage, TX 75633

CHINQUAPIN
Douglass School
Douglass, TX 75943

FIRE WHEEL
Texas City, TX 77590

LOBLOLLY
Box 88
Gary, TX 75643

OLD TIMER
Albany, TX 76430

SALT GRASS
Alvin, TX 77511

Groesbeck Ind. School District
Groesbeck, TX 76642

THOSE COMFORTING HILLS
Comfort, TX 78013

Utah

TAMARAK
Vernal, UT 84078

Vermont

STOWE'S MORE THAN SNOW
Stowe, VT 05672

Brooksie Stanton
Barnet, VT 05821

Virginia

SNAKE HILL TO SPRING BANK
Alexandria, VA 22307

Washington

CROSSCUT
Port Townsend, WA 98368

West Virginia

HICKORY AND LADYSLIPPERS—
LIFE AND LEGEND OF CLAY
CO. PEOPLE
Clay, WV 25043

MOUNTAIN TRACE
Parkersburg, WV 26101

American Samoa

FAASOMOA PEA
Pago Pago, American Samoa 96799

Australia

ASCOLTA
Victoria, Australia

John White
Western Australia

Canada

Harrow Smith
Ontario, Canada

Dominican Republic

GUARIQUEN
Santo Domingo, Dominican Republic

Guam

Lucy San Nicolas
Agana, Guam 96910

Puerto Rico

GUAJANA
Las Lomas Puerto Rico

References

Bennett, Margie. 1977. "Focus: Foxfire," *Nameless Newsletter* I, 1. (September and November), pp. 6–8. Rabun Gap, Georgia: The Foxfire Fund, Inc.

Beun, Brian. 1975. "Introduction," in Eliot Wigginton, *Moments*. Kennebunk, Maine: Star Press.

Dishman, Leland. 1978 (August). Interview by Gail Parks. Rabun County, Georgia.

Martin, Mary Ann; Raimey, Tom; Singleton, John; and Welch, Ronnie (Foxfire students). 1978. Interview by Gail Parks. Rabun Gap, Georgia.

Gjelten, Thomas. 1979. "LOBLOLLY: Curriculum Enrichment in Gary, Texas." Unpublished paper. Education Commission of the States, Denver, Colorado.

Maxwell, Neil. n.d. "High-School Journal Spawns Small Empire and Host of Imitators." *New York Times*.

Shapiro, David. 1972. "Recovering a Sense of Past and Place." *Saturday Review of Literature* (April 29), pp. 36–38.

Sitton, Thad Edward, Jr. 1978. *The Foxfire Concept Publications: A First Appraisal.* Ph.D. dissertation, University of Texas, Austin.

Thomas, Diane C. 1978. "The Foxfire Empire: Eliot Wigginton's Complex Battle to Preserve a Simple Way of Life." *Atlanta Journal and Constitution Magazine* (April 9).

Wigginton, Eliot. 1978. "Foxfire." Unpublished paper. 9 pp.

Wigginton, Eliot. 1977. "Introduction," *Foxfire 4*. Garden City, New York: Anchor Press, Doubleday. Pp. 7–13.

Wigginton, Eliot. 1975. *Moments*. Kennebunk, Maine: Star Press.

11
Locally Relevant Curricula in Rural Norway: The Lofoten Islands Example

Karl Jan Solstad

Introduction

For a five-year period from 1973 through 1978, a group of researchers from the University of Tromsø carried out a program of "action research" in cooperation with local teachers and regional authorities in the Lofoten Islands of northern Norway. The basic purpose of the Lofoten project was to make the education system in this "remote" and sparsely populated region more locally relevant. Seven comprehensive schools, comprising the lower level (grades 1–6) and the upper level (grades 7–9) were selected for inclusion in the project; they were helped by the research team to initiate a set of significant curricular and operational reforms during the life of this effort.

The specific accomplishments and effects of the Lofoten project will be dealt with later in the chapter. The important point for the moment is that the assumption underlying the Lofoten effort – that rural communities can be strengthened by an educational system which is both reflective of and responsive to local realities – is gaining considerable support in Norway today. For example, similar innovations have gotten under way in Rødøy (a sparsely populated island community in Nordland County) and in the county of Finnmark. In addition, several regional colleges were created during the middle to late 1970s in Norway which include locally relevant curricula and direct involvement in regional affairs as an important part of their overall mission.

While it would be an exaggeration to state that locally and regionally oriented education innovations are becoming the norm in Norwegian rural education, the fact remains that this movement is an increasingly influential one. In order to better understand the context in which the Lofoten project and the other related innovations have occurred, and to understand why they are considered innovations at all, a bit of background information is required.

Sparsely Populated Areas in a National Context

In 1979, Norway had approximately four million inhabitants spread over an area of 308,000 square kilometers (km²). Therefore, the population distribution for the country as a whole is around 13 people per km². Thus, compared to other European nations (for instance, the Netherlands with 320 residents per km²), Norway can accurately be described as a sparsely populated country.

This description can be somewhat misleading, of course, for the population distribution is not the same throughout Norway. For example, the region which includes Oslo has more than 1,000 inhabitants per km², while the nation's northernmost county, Finnmark, contains fewer than 2 residents per km². Even the population distribution within rural areas is uneven. Finnmark's residents tend to cluster into small or medium-size towns. Only 35 percent of the population of Finnmark lives in the open countryside. The remaining 65 percent lives in settlements having 200 or more residents.

The most rural part of Norway is the region of North Norway, most of which lies above the Arctic Circle. This large area (which includes the Lofoten Islands and the University of Tromsø) accounts for more than one-third of the land in Norway and includes many remote islands and mountainous areas. The economic base here is still heavily dependent upon primary-sector activities; i.e., fishing, forestry, and agriculture. Industrial development remains scarce, but recent years have witnessed a rise in the importance of the service sector.

For more than twenty years, the national government's focus has not been on rural development per se but rather on slowing the tide of rural out-migration and on aiding "underdeveloped" or "poorly developed" regions of the country. Many government publications contain descriptions similar to the following: "Poorly developed districts tend to be larger geographic areas marked by a weak or one-sided occupational structure, poor job opportunities and insufficient private and public services. Usually these districts experience migration to other areas, and a lower income per inhabitant than other areas."[1]

To counteract the "imbalance" in national patterns of economic development, Norway has implemented a series of political, economic, and social policies designed to strengthen the peripheral areas of the country. As noted above, the aim of government policy for more than two decades has been to stop the migration from "underdeveloped" areas and to preserve (insofar as possible) the existing pattern of settlement.

Obviously, achieving this goal implies that existing occupational opportunities must be safeguarded and that new economic opportunities must be created. National policy has addressed these issues both by restricting economic activity in the already developed areas and concomitantly stimulating investment and other forms of economic activity in the "poorly developed" regions. In addition, there has been a very active effort to enhance the infrastructure of rural regions, in both physical and human terms. Among other initiatives, this has included major investments in education at every level.

It is not the purpose of this chapter to discuss the merits of Norwegian economic and social policy in these areas nor to analyze their intended (and unintended) effects. It should suffice to say that if halting rural outmigration and redistributing economic opportunities in favor of "poorly developed" areas are the criteria, then national policy has only been a partial success.

Compulsory Schooling in Sparsely Populated Areas

The primary school in Norway is a nine-year compulsory school starting at the age of seven and divided into two levels: the lower (child) level—usually the first six years—and the upper (youth) level—the last three years. This system, replacing the traditional seven years of compulsory schooling, was put into effect by the 1969 Education Act. The new nine-year primary schools include the first two years of what was formerly secondary education. The school is a public responsibility, regulated by school laws decided by the Parliament. There is currently one curriculum for the whole country.

Until 1959, there were two separate school laws; one for schools in towns and one for schools in rural areas. During the past century, however, the urban schools have been regarded as the norm for the development of the nation's school systems. Each successive school law has tried to make the rural schools more like the urban ones by narrowing the gap between them. More specifically, the school laws made rural schools more like their urban counterparts by discouraging combined grade classes (i.e., classes serving more than one age group); by lengthening the school year in rural areas to make it comparable to the urban school calendar; and by expanding the curriculum of rural schools to include subjects (like English) previously found only in metropolitan schools.

The impetus for these legislative reforms was the struggle for equality of educational opportunity. The struggle itself is hardly a new one. Indeed, equality has been the underlying goal of all major school reforms in Norway since before the turn of the century. Over time, however, the interpretation of equality has altered. In the modern era, the favorite yardstick for measuring equality has been access to the gymnasium, the most highly academic form of secondary education in Norway. Thus, the gymnasium, with its highly standardized curriculum and operational style firmly rooted in the urban middle- and upper-class culture, has been the model which rural schools have been encouraged to emulate.

From a legislative viewpoint, the process of urbanizing rural education was completed in 1959 with the passage of a uniform national school law which treated all schools, urban and rural, exactly alike. Since that date, every Norwegian school (at least in principle) has been operated according to the same curriculum and the same school calendar.

The third "improvement" sought by the reformers — the elimination of small rural schools with multiage, combined grade classes — has proven much harder to achieve. Sparsely populated regions with children widely dispersed over the countryside or clustered in very small settlements remain a fact of life in much of Norway. Accordingly, the sheer physical difficulties of bringing large numbers of children together on a daily basis has meant that the school size desired by many educational reformers has simply not been possible.

However, a significant amount of school closures or reorganizations have occurred. Since the end of World War II, an extensive governmental program of road and bridge construction, coupled with the availability of school buses, enabled a network of larger rural schools to be established. The pace of school reorganization has slowed considerably in recent years as obvious candidates for merger become harder to find.

Thus, as Table 1 indicates,[2] relatively small rural schools with combined grade classes continue to be the norm. Even today, more than 25 percent of Norway's rural primary schools have only one or two classes, and the survival of many of these seems assured by their physical isolation and by a topography and climate which discourage long-distance daily commuting. So, other than schools which "close themselves" because of declining enrollments, the current stock of rural schools is likely to remain fairly stable.

TABLE 1

DISTRIBUTION OF LOWER PRIMARY SCHOOLS (GRADES 1-6)
IN NORWAY, BY TOTAL NUMBER OF SEPARATE CLASSES IN EACH SCHOOL
1978

Number of Classes	Schools					
	Urban		Rural		Total	
	N	%	N	%	N	%
One	16	1	78	5	94	4
Two	79	7	285	20	364	14
Three	85	8	239	16	324	13
Four	95	9	225	15	320	13
Five	36	3	86	6	122	5
Six or More	789	72	543	37	1,332	52

The Lofoten Project: Initial Stages

As noted earlier, the Lofoten project was a five-year program carried out in seven schools in the Lofoten region of northern Norway. Many factors made this project an innovation in the context of Norwegian rural education. Not the least of these was the composition of the full research team, a group which brought together social scientists (including the author) from the University of Tromsø, teachers from the participating schools, and local and regional school officials.

Another innovation can be found in the questions posed by the research team in approaching this effort. Issues were repeatedly raised which traditionally are overlooked in Norwegian educational research, including such topics as What is "local knowledge"? How can local knowledge be effectively incorporated into the school curriculum? What are the consequences of a more locally relevant education for the students, the community, and the education system as a whole? The ways in which these concerns were dealt with will be an underlying theme of this chapter. First, the Lofoten project's initial stages will be described. Then the project's concrete achievements will be examined in more detail.

Choosing the School Level

Prior to launching the Lofoten project, the author took part in an extensive research program on the functioning of the recently implemented grade 7 through 9 comprehensive school (youth school) in areas of scattered population. The research work was initiated by the Forsoksradet (National Council for Innovation in Education) in response to heavy criticism of the national policy of centralization (i.e., the reorganization of small rural schools into larger units).

The investigations, mainly of the survey type, covered such aspects as recruitment of teachers, educational achievement in large and small schools, effects of school transportation, and school-home relationships. A follow-up data collection included pupils from fifty-five schools throughout the country. The author visited most of these schools (including all of those located in northern Norway).

It became increasingly clear from numerous discussions with teachers and school authorities that the problems of education in rural areas far from the urban centers were not merely the result of rapid centralization and a high turnover of staff. In many places, the main problem was felt to be that education was detached from the community it served, in terms of both the syllabus and the timing of the school terms. This complaint was most frequently met in the fishing districts of northern Norway. The evidence supporting this diagnosis was low school attendance and low motivation for schoolwork, especially during the main fishing season.

Such problems did not seem to be equally important at the lower stage of compulsory schooling. At this stage, the generally accepted task of mastering the three R's constitutes the bulk of the curriculum, and schooling does not interfere with what has traditionally been thought of as the age of work. A project designed to tailor education to local needs seemed to be most urgent at the upper stage of compulsory schooling (the youth school).

Choosing the Region

One of the most important seasonal "industries" in Norway is cod fishing in the Lofoten region. This normally starts in January when the North Atlantic cod approach Lofoten to spawn, and the fishing season lasts for about three months. Despite some annual variations in the time of the cod's arrival and the amount of fish available, the regularity and dependability of the cod fishing season throughout the centuries is striking. Because of its predictability and the amount of the catch, seasonal cod fishing is a very important factor in the economy of the area, and it has had a decisive influence on the type of settlements and communities developed.

During the season, a large number of fishermen and fish workers from other parts of the Norwegian coast, especially from elsewhere in northern Norway, gather in Lofoten; some of the typical fishing villages (*vær*) may have their adult population doubled or tripled. Even taking into consideration that there is good farming in some areas of Lofoten and that the tertiary sector of the economy is important in centers of population such as Kabelvåg/Svolvær and Leknes, it is fair to say that the prosperity of the region is heavily dependent on the winter cod catch.

Traditionally, any human resources available during the season were in some way involved in activities related to fishing. This applied equally to youngsters who had just left compulsory school at the age of fourteen (and in some cases to schoolchildren as well). In Lofoten before 1960, a postelementary year of schooling was organized in two separate phases: an academic semester during the autumn term and a period devoted to practical studies from April until June. The months between these two phases were left free to allow the youngsters to work during the cod season. Prior to the 1936 Education Act, special arrangements also applied in some areas of Lofoten to allow pupils in the upper class of the elementary school to take part in a range of helpful activities in the community during the fishing season.

With the introduction of another two years of compulsory schooling, as required by law in 1969, many people in Lofoten felt that education interfered with the interests of the local economy and was making a negative impact on the community. Important human resources were not available at the time they were needed most. In addition, the youngsters (especially those who were most likely to go on to further schooling) were prevented from acquiring firsthand knowledge of the economic activity on which the whole community was based.

Such considerations explain why one of the Lofoten youth schools (Værøy) sought the municipal school council's permission to change its time schedule so that the pupils from grades 7 through 9 could take part in work related to the cod fishery during the height of the season. This application for a reorganization of the school year received some public attention and was followed by a discussion in the local newspaper early in 1972. When the author visited this school in April 1972 some kind of research involvement was also discussed with the headmaster.

In conclusion, when the first plans for a project with the aim of adjusting education to the local situation vaguely emerged during 1972-73, the region of Lofoten appeared to be a good choice. As has been pointed out above, the conflict between an important aspect of the local and regional economy and the recent expansion of compulsory education seemed to be more apparent than in most other areas in Norway. The choice was also facilitated by the fact that members of the university research group had firsthand knowledge of the region, including a number of personal contacts.

Choosing the Participating Schools

During spring 1973, the youth schools and the municipal school councils in the Lofoten region were visited to find out whether the schools actually wanted (and would be allowed) to take part in an innovation project. These initial visits also included discussion, in general terms, of several types of possible action. At this stage, the school director of the county of Nordland had already approved the general idea proposed.

It was considered important to include schools of varying sizes, from different types of settlements, and of different degrees of centralization. It was also deemed vital to include a sufficient number of schools in order to allow for variations in school leadership and teacher characteristics. For instance, there were substantial differences between schools within the area regarding turnover rate and degree of local recruitment of teachers.

The most enthusiastic backing for the idea of new strategies to counteract the dysfunction of standardized schooling was found in the municipalities of Røst, Værøy, and Moskenes (and Flakstad), the communities most highly dependent on fishing. However, the preliminary choice of schools included, in addition to the four existing youth schools in these municipalities, one school in Vestvagoy and two in Vagan (see Table 2 and Figure 1). In a meeting with representatives from all these seven schools their participation was confirmed, but, as will be shown, participation turned out to mean everything from passive acceptance of some proposals to active engagement in developmental work.

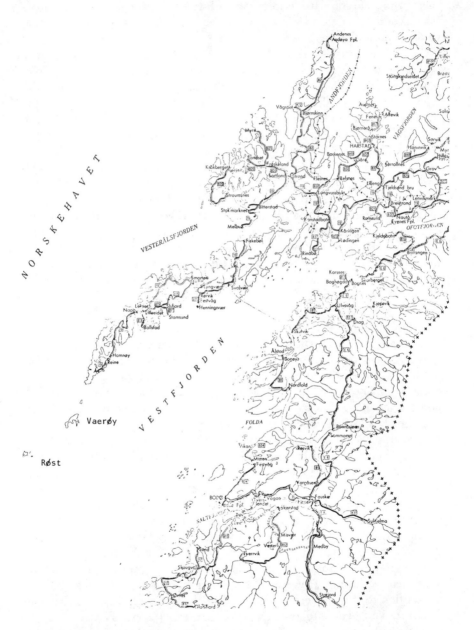

FIGURE 1 Map of the Lofoten Islands.

TABLE 2

PARTICIPATING SCHOOLS.   TYPE OF SCHOOL* AND NUMBER OF
CLASSES, PUPILS, AND TEACHERS IN GRADES 7-9 IN 1973/74

Name of School	Type of School	No. of Classes	No. of Pupils	No. of Teachers
Røst	Combined	3	50	11
Vaerøy	Combined	3	56	12
Moskenes	Combined	4	85	12
Flakstad	Combined	6	140	15
Bøstad	Combined	6	168	16
Henningsvaer	Combined	3	38	8
Kabelvåg	Pure	7	148	13

*'Combined' schools are 1- through 9-grade schools. 'Pure' schools are exclusively 7- to 9-grade schools (= youth schools).

The Lofoten Project: Implementation Stage

The project was approved by school authorities at the regional and national level on the condition that all innovations had to be carried out within the general framework established by the 1960 Education Act and the prevailing national curriculum plan (the "Mønsterplanen"). The latter, fortunately, did state explicitly, "Education ought to keep in touch with the local community. The pupils should be given the opportunity to learn by means of information and from their own experiences how the community functions and how it is governed."[3] Regarding the teaching of individual subjects, the plan emphasizes that "on many occasions the local environment favours one syllabus rather than another." It is fair to say that the Mønsterplanen, more than the earlier curriculum plans, is open to local variation in education. This was an important precondition for the project, in which the following two general approaches were proposed in order to develop a more locally relevant education:

1. All the pupils should be allowed to take part in the economic activity on which the community is founded; i.e., seasonal cod fishing.
2. Local and regional matters should be made a more important part of the curriculum for all pupils.

When negotiations began with the schools about their participation in an innovation program, questions concerning leadership, strategy, or benefits were often asked in one way or another: Who is going to plan for whom? Who is going to profit from this work—the community, the school, the teachers, or the social scientists? Is it going to be some kind of a prepackaged experiment, or are the teachers allowed to take part in developing the curriculum? Such questions were asked both directly and indirectly by teachers, thus indicating a need to clarify the role of the researchers and to establish some form of contract between the schools and the university research group. The resolution of these issues will be described next.

From the beginning, it was obvious that the communities of the region shared many common features, such as their ecology, history, labor market, and culture. Consequently, there were good reasons for making educational materials similar for all the schools in the region. This implied that it was necessary to build up planning groups both within the teaching staffs of the respective schools and between the participating schools.

Negotiations with the teachers and parents of the selected schools took place in the autumn of 1973, during which it was made clear that a meeting was to be arranged where representatives from the respective schools could gather and plan the first step of the program. The teaching staff at each school elected a representative who, to a certain extent, was to be in charge of the innovation at that school.

The first meeting with the headmasters concerned and the elected teachers was also held in the autumn of 1973. At this meeting the roles of the research group and the schools in the project were discussed. As in the meetings already mentioned, questions arose concerning leadership, strategies, and benefits.

The negotiations resulted in a two-pronged agreement between the schools and the research group. First, there had to be reciprocity as to the benefits. The main goal was to make a curriculum useful for the schools. Second, as a result, the enterprise was defined as a cooperative project in which the schools and the university research group planned and carried out the different parts of the program together. By these formulations the role of the research group was principally settled. Of course, the status of being university-based social scientists legitimated the presence of the "outside" researchers in the community. No special privileges accrued to the researchers, and they were expected to actively participate in all aspects of the ongoing work.

Introductory working seminars at the respective schools and between the schools were also arranged. These seminars focused on two main problems: developing a regional educational syllabus and identifying educational topics from the respective local communities.

It was decided that a textbook on regional topics had to be written. This decision was followed by a preliminary plan concerning topics to be covered. Some twenty people, either living in the region or by origin or work closely related to it, were asked to write on the various topics according to their specialties. About two months later the first version of the textbook was available, and the schools started using the new syllabus.

When the schools had been using the textbooks for six months, an evaluation seminar was arranged. Teachers from the schools, the authors of the textbooks, and the university researchers participated in this seminar. On the basis of fieldwork (consisting of meetings, talks with the teachers, interviews, and a questionnaire), the research group presented a summary of the teachers' experiences with the textbooks. This summary focused on the texts' geographical and thematic representativeness and their usefulness in teaching. The discussions which followed resulted in agreement on a detailed outline of a more permanent version, including principles for modifying the already existing articles, plans for new topics, and proposals for illustrations and format.

Thus, this seminar guided the work of completing the textbooks. The regionally based series of textbooks has now been completed, and consists of four volumes covering the following topics:

Volume 1: The Physical Environment
1. Land and Sea
2. Weather and Climate
3. Plants and Animals in the Sea
4. Plants in the Tidal Area
5. Animals in the Tidal Area
6. Plants and Animals on Land

Volume 2: History
1. The Early History
2. Lofoten in the Middle Ages
3. The Bergen Merchant, the Væreir ["owner" of the fishing village] and the Fisherman
4. The History of Fishing, Whaling, and Hunting

Volume 3: Economy
1. The Region of Lofoten: Population, Economy, and Communication
2. Agriculture and the Mixed Economy of the Area
3. The Fish from the Sea to the Table [including fish processing technology]
4. Important Issues in the Fishing Industry

5. Fishing and the Future
6. The Rost Innovation Company

Volume 4: Culture
1. Local Customs
2. The Dialect of the Lofoten Region
3. Humor
4. Lofoten in Norwegian Literature
5. Lofoten in Pictorial Art
6. Songs and Musical Traditions of the Region—Past and Present

Although the various topics are based on the Lofoten region, much of the content is so general that the books may also be used in other areas of the country. The books have also been used successfully at a number of upper secondary schools.

Evaluation of the teaching used in the project was carried out. After all the topics had been used in teaching, a new working seminar on teaching local and regional topics was arranged, consisting of teachers from all the schools. Results of the fieldwork were presented as an introduction to the subject. The discussion that followed resulted in a decision that some kind of teachers' handbook had to be developed which could link the educational content with the most appropriate teaching methods. A committee, consisting of three teachers and the research group was later assigned to this project. A preliminary version of the book has been finished and has been used for some time by the schools.

The handbook first outlines the ideas on which the innovation was based, as well as the experiences gained in the developmental work. The main part consists of proposals for topic projects and teaching methods. A number of audiovisual materials have been produced by several teachers, and a compilation of these and other available resources relevant to local teaching has been made.

In the spring of 1976 a new working seminar was arranged, in which the teachers were expected to contribute to the evaluation of both the teachers' handbook and the innovation program as a whole. It was decided that the new materials had to be tried out for one more year before any further changes could be made.

During the whole innovation period, a conscious effort was made to establish a permanent planning group at each participating school. When this work began, the head of each group was paid from the research grant. Working as a project member is now regarded as part of the teacher's normal duties, and teaching loads have been reduced accordingly. To the extent that effective local project teams have emerged, the innovation at the school concerned may be judged to be successful.

At most of the participating schools the teaching staff has a fairly rapid turnover rate. At one of the schools about 50 to 70 percent of the personnel leave each year. Not surprisingly, this has created great problems in maintaining a measure of continuity and long-term commitment within the local schools.

Locally administered training courses have, as a consequence, become another feature of the innovation. In the early stages, these courses were arranged by the research group, but currently this responsibility has been taken over by the local administration. At one of the project schools, the local board of education has intentionally hired teachers having specific qualifications and experience related to the new curriculum. But this healthy step toward institutionalizing the innovations has not yet been adopted everywhere.

The emerging pattern of the innovation has now been described. The word *emerging* should emphasize that the pattern was *not* planned beforehand, but has been the result of the researchers' initial assumptions, the subsequent decisions made, and the experiences gained during the developmental process.

A major part of the work has been devoted to building a body of teaching materials which can facilitate the teaching of local knowledge. They include (1) four textbooks on topics such as science, history, economy, and culture; (2) the preliminary teachers' manual; (3) seven slide series on various regionally relevant topics; and (4) tape recordings of radio programs on Lofoten broadcast by the Norwegian Broadcasting Corporation from 1950 onward. Apart from possible modifications of these teaching materials (especially the teachers' manual), the curricular aspect of the project is considered to be complete.

The project as a formal operation ended by 1979. However, the work itself continues in the Lofoten schools. As might be expected, the aftereffects vary greatly. Two schools were still very actively engaged in the work in 1980; two others evidenced only sporadic implementation; and the remaining three sites continued the work, but at a reduced level of activity.

Participation in Work Related to the Local Economy

As part of the general national curriculum, all Norwegian pupils in eighth and ninth grade are given a week out of school to get some firsthand experience of economic life. In the Lofoten schools this out-of-school week was sometimes taken in autumn or spring, i.e., outside the fishing season. In Værøy, for instance, the pupils were often sent away to larger towns where they could more easily be provided with work.

As part of the project, it was decided to expand this period of practical work from one to three weeks *and* to schedule it in the fishing season. The only practical way to arrange this was to close the youth school for these weeks. The school days lost had to be compensated for by starting the school year earlier in the autumn, continuing longer into the summer holidays, and expanding the school week to include a number of Saturdays. Four out of the seven schools took part in this reorganization of the school year in 1973-74, whereas only two schools participated the year afterward. All the participating schools were located in the western municipalities, where the cod fishery played an especially important part in the local economy.

Given that the project had to operate within the national guidelines and regulations, a number of circumstances complicated this experiment:

1. The timing of the following school year had to be fixed before the summer holiday. Yet, it was obviously impossible to predict when the peak of the cod season would come.
2. It was hard to find suitable work for all the sixth- through ninth-graders simultaneously.
3. In the small combined primary and secondary schools many of the teachers were teaching at both levels. A period of partial free time for the teachers when the sixth- through ninth-grade pupils were out working, and partial work time when the lost school days had to be made up, was a distinctly unpopular arrangement.
4. The experiment resulted in increased expenses for school transportation, heating, and cleaning. To avoid this problem one of the school boards decided to close the primary level as well for three weeks.
5. This, in turn, provoked negative reactions among parents who saw no reason why the small primary school children should be given holidays in the middle of the winter term.

The experiences gained during the first two years of the project strongly indicated that providing a better knowledge of the predominant feature of the local economy by means of direct participation in work related to the seasonal cod fishery was not possible within the limits set by school regulations and available economic resources.

One School's Experience

An interesting feature of this project has been the diversity which has occurred in implementing the Lofoten effort. Each of the seven schools has had different, and sometimes startlingly different, experiences during the course of the project, and none can really claim to be typical or representative of all the others. Nevertheless, teachers at one of the project schools developed some interesting ideas as to both the nature of locally relevant curricula and new strategies for teaching these curricula.

The teachers at this school have found that teaching local knowledge can best be organized through a larger project. This has meant that each class, or a smaller group within the class, has worked on a topic from the local community, the municipality, or the region of Lofoten. The project was organized in such a way that the various classes collected information about the region in general all through the year, yet at the same time prepared themselves to work on a specific topic concerning the local community. These subproject activities culminated in a week in the middle of the winter during which the normal schoolwork was abandoned and the various student groups concentrated on preparing a presentation of their work.

Each group presented its work by making an exhibit of illustrations and written materials. The whole display was arranged in the school hall, and on the last evening of the week members of the local community were invited to look at the work done at the school. A local pictorial artist was also invited to give an exhibition of his work. In addition, different kinds of entertainment (music and sketches) by "actors" from the school or from the local community were provided. This annual open night is becoming a tradition at the school, and the presentations have been met with great interest by the local people, a situation that is encouraging both for the pupils and the teachers.

A description of the projects the students have been working on during the previous year is set out below.

Three old farms. This is the story of three old farms on the outskirts of the local community and how they were the starting point for the three neighborhoods now in existence. The students and the teacher visited these neighborhoods several times, interviewed and talked with people, took pictures, and then presented their work, consisting of written compositions, maps, and a series of slides.

The wildlife of Lofoten. The students drew the various animals and birds found in Lofoten. They also took impressions of different animal tracks found locally. In addition, they wrote descriptions of the area's animals and their habitats.

The local church. One group of students defined church architecture as their object of study. They gathered written material about the church, talked with the clergyman and the parish clerk, and wrote a composition about it. They also took several pictures both from outside and inside and presented a series of slides.

A display of old pictures. The previous year a group of students had collected old pictures from the community. This year another group arranged an exhibition and made notes on the various pictures.

A small fishing village. A small fishing village was about to be sold to a person who was supposed to restore it as a tourist center. A group of pupils visited this village, took pictures of it, and interviewed people about their way of life. Later they made a series of slides and wrote a number of small reports about their visit.

The "Lofoten wall." A class made a large map of the Lofoten region. The different fishing villages in the region were marked and a picture from each of them was put on the map. The class gave a description of the regional economy with particular reference to fishing. They presented texts, tables, and diagrams of the changes in Lofoten cod fishing, including the amount of fish caught, the types of equipment used, and the number of people participating.

Making a curtain. By applying a special technique, one group of students made a woolen curtain utilizing motifs from the region.

Making a fishing cottage. A miniature fishing cottage with drawings and diagrams of its use was made as a part of one group's contribution. The same group did a project on the Arctic cod. A map was drawn of fishing areas and the global wanderings of the cod. There was also an article on spawning locations. This group had been taken to sea on a research ship and had been allowed to do some simple observations. The same pupils made splices and different kinds of rope knots as another part of their contribution.

All these projects are good examples of integrated group activities. The projects were structured to a considerable extent by the teachers, but the different facets of the projects and the progression of the work were decided to a large extent by the students themselves. The projects were also designed so that they consisted of different activities matching the abilities and interests of the various pupils. Thus students with different abilities and interests could work together as a team. The teachers at this school plan to develop this way of working further. At present, an integrated school project is being planned in which the different classes will cooperate schoolwide.

Teacher Perceptions and Problems

Although the progress of the project described above was both substantial and fairly smooth, it should not be inferred that this was characteristic of the project as a whole. The local teachers were the key to the eventual success of the Lofoten project. The fact that they also were the group which had the most problems and experienced the conflicts most keenly should not come as a surprise.

As alluded to earlier, the problem of teacher turnover was (and is) both persistent and debilitating, even in project schools. The shortage of qualified teachers has plagued school authorities in rural Norway for many years, and while the situation is improving, it seems unlikely that the problem will be eliminated in the foreseeable future. The northern and western parts of Norway are, as always, the hardest hit by high teacher turnover rates.

In many cases pupils and parents have had to adjust to at least as many teachers as school years. In schools having one or two teachers only, this situation obviously has resulted in an extreme discontinuity regarding educational planning and community-school relations.

Yet, beyond the issue of a given teacher's knowledge of and commitment to the local community (factors which obviously are called into question in schools with high teacher turnover), the teachers themselves expressed some reservations about locally relevant education. Most of the illustrations of teachers' perspectives used below are the product of research conducted by one member of the research group, Tom Tiller.[4]

It should be noted that within this project the teachers came to realize that the teaching situation with a locally relevant curriculum had to be based on new "rules" for defining knowledge and for performing the roles of teacher and student. The teachers indicated that local knowledge had to be taught through methods different from those applied to the traditional school program. The students should have the opportunity to benefit from their local status by discovering or creating knowledge about the local community.

This definition of the educational situation would imply that for many of the topics concerned, the students would have as good a grasp (or even better) of the situation as their teachers. Such circumstances would again have consequences for defining the teacher-student relationship. The feeling quickly arose that implementing a locally relevant curriculum would only be successful if accompanied by a more interactive, student-centered teaching method than was normally employed.

For example, in this new context a detailed and rigid lesson plan prepared in advance by the teacher may prove more of a hindrance than a help. The Lofoten project teachers came to believe that teaching in a locally relevant framework essentially becomes a question of planning an encounter in which the teacher and the student jointly steer the learning process. In this context, the aim of the work of the research group has not been to produce a fixed teaching syllabus on local knowledge, but rather to give resources to the schools which would enable them to plan their own teaching.

Tom Tiller has, within this project, written a thesis, "Working with Local Content in the Upper Stage of the Compulsory School." As a part of his data collection the teachers were asked about the desirability of developing more detailed courses within the project. Most of the answers he got were negative, and the following reply is characteristic: "It will not be possible to completely plan the teaching in advance. A teacher may make a detailed plan of his teaching beforehand, but one must not expect that his program will be followed in any detail. Instead one must be prepared to change it during the lesson. The teaching plan must always be open, especially when one is dealing with content of which the students have some knowledge."[5] Summarizing the results of this questioning, Tiller said, "Having made several visits to the schools, one developed the impression that it was neither possible nor desirable to programme teaching on local topics in advance."[6]

"We have the ghost of a compulsory curriculum hanging over us." Despite the fact that the new national curriculum plan (the Mønsterplanen) has no compulsory teaching plans in the traditional sense, many teachers felt bound by that concept. Consequently, they found themselves facing the dilemma of deciding whether to direct their effort toward local knowledge or to give the students a "safe" education through the school's ordinary curriculum. Tiller gave an excerpt from his talk with a teacher who tried to explain one side of the dilemma but initially was unable to express himself adequately. Tiller said, "Two days after my visit I got a postcard from the same teacher who had written: Now I have found the right phrase for what I wanted to express: It is not the compulsory curriculum, but the ghost of a compulsory curriculum that is the biggest problem."[7] When the teachers tried to change their teaching methods, many of them found it difficult for reasons which can be explained in terms of the school as a social system.

"My timetable is a great nuisance." Owing to the fact that the national curriculum is subject-oriented rather than student-oriented, the teachers' timetables at most schools, especially in the upper stage of compulsory schooling, are arranged in a subject-teacher system. Teaching local knowledge implies an interdisciplinary effort cutting across the boundaries of several traditional subjects. Thus, teaching local curriculum in a subject-teacher system is difficult, and some teachers felt unable to reconcile these conflicts.

At smaller schools where a class-teacher system was operating (one teacher had the class for most of the subjects), reorganizing the syllabus was easier. The students could then stay on a task over a longer period and did not have to break every three-quarters of an hour. At one school the teachers had changed from planning a yearly timetable to planning for shorter periods (one month or two months). If a subject or a group of subjects was given too much emphasis during one period, this could be compensated for in the next period. At this school, the headmaster insisted that the teachers had to take part in planning the timetable.

"A rigid budget makes it difficult to work with local content." At most of the schools the annual budget did not allow for "unpredictable" expenses during the year, such as arranging short excursions or buying unforeseen teaching materials. The schools found they needed to have a more flexible budget or to devise other ways of meeting expenditures resulting from the new curriculum. In many cases the research group had to contribute "research money" to solve acute problems faced by teachers trying to carry

out certain plans. The local school authorities have now become aware of this problem and are working toward long-term solutions.

"We do not want it because we do not know the outcome." In a school where the timetable has been given to the teachers at the start of a year and the teachers have planned their lessons individually, it may be difficult to switch to other working routines. Many of the teachers have emphasized that developing a locally relevant curriculum implies that the teachers will cooperate in building up a library of literature and other teaching materials, and in planning and carrying out the teaching. One teacher made the following comment on the situation: "As you understand it is not difficult for me as a teacher to produce a good excuse not to cooperate. And in fact we may have such good excuses. However, we must not be blind to the fact that the teachers themselves can solve these problems if they want to. But maybe we do not want to solve them, and that is the greatest problem. We do not want it because we do not know the outcome."[8]

Implications of the Lofoten Project

The aim of the Lofoten project has been to achieve an education relevant to the local community. Educationally, this approach to schooling may be equally strongly defended whether it involves urban or rural settings. The choice of a rural region partly reflects the judgment that traditional education in particular has been irrelevant to the rural situation, and partly the belief that economically weak communities need any support that might contribute to the maintenance of their social and cultural integrity.

Accepting the idea of an education adjusted to local needs implies that as a matter of principle any viable community should be allowed to create and be served by an education system which bolsters rather than undermines its existence and further development. The whole concept of "remote" areas and "remote" schools should be abandoned altogether. The point of departure for education in and education for rural areas far from the national center(s) should be these rural areas themselves, not the urban center which is so "remote" from them and their concerns.

Uniformity of educational provision in a country where there are great variations in life-style is certain to lead to an education irrelevant and remote from reality for many of the people it ostensibly serves. Compulsory education in Norway, as in most OECD countries, has developed into a highly urban, middle-class, institutionalized system. Therefore, the school is particularly in disharmony with communities that by virtue of tradition, culture, communications, and economy are most distant from the urbanized, industrialized (i.e., powerful) parts of the country.

What then is the impact in rural areas of an education largely removed from the realities of everyday community life? We believe that the educational system in operation today directs young people away from their own communities, and that this in turn has an adverse effect on these areas. The school curriculum defines for the children what is important knowledge and what is not. This results in irrelevant learning for those who do not move to more urban areas. Because of the time and effort put into school, it also prevents children from experiences that might have been important for a future life in the community. Perhaps even more important, the exclusion of locally relevant problems and knowledge is likely to influence the pupils' attitudes and feelings toward their home environment. The pupil is neither qualified nor motivated for the type of opportunities and employment his own community offers.

Unpublished data from "Grissgrendtprosjektet," a large-scale three-year followup study of about 4,000 pupils from fifty-five youth schools throughout the country, may partly substantiate the statement above. The issue of the relevance of education was presented as follows to ninth-grade pupils as part of an extensive group-administered questionnaire:

> We do not know if the youth school as it is today is equally suitable for all pupils. It is important to know how you, as a pupil, feel about this. It is, of course, difficult to really *know* what school is like for pupils who have a different background from yours and who have different plans for the future. Therefore we only expect you to say something about the group *you think* gains most from attending school, or if you believe that schooling is equally suitable for both groups mentioned.

The actual questions used and the distribution of the replies are given in Table 3. The findings strongly support the view that the upper stage of compulsory schooling is biased toward urban life and predominantly urban occupations. For instance, the children claim three times more often that the school prepares them for an urban life than for a rural one (question 6). When considering the large percentage of pupils opting for the third alternative ("equally suitable") on questions 1 and 6, it is probably right to point out that it is a strange idea indeed that the only school we have should not be suitable for people living, or planning to live, in certain types of area.

As regards the questions that are more indirectly related to the rural-urban dimensions, i.e., questions 2 through 5, the manifestation of an urban bias is even clearer, particularly for the pupils of higher ability, who are the most likely ones to grasp the meaning of the questions and to be aware of the influence of education.

It may also be pointed out that bright, resourceful pupils are likely to be the ones most influenced by this orientation away from their home milieu,

TABLE 3

ANSWERS TO THE QUESTION: "FOR WHOM IS THE YOUTH SCHOOL MOST SUITABLE?" (PERCENTAGE DISTRIBUTION, BY ABILITY LEVEL.)

	Ability Level			All Pupils
	Low	Medium	High	
The school is more suitable for:				
1 Pupils living in towns or large villages	15.3	19.5	18.7	18.4
Pupils living in small places	1.9	7.9	8.5	8.9
Equally suitable for both groups	72.8	72.6	72.8	72.7
2 Pupils who intend to go on to vocational training	14.8	6.9	4.5	8.0
Pupils who intend to go on to the 'gymnasium'	26.5	35.3	45.1	36.0
Equally suitable for both groups	58.7	57.8	50.4	56.0
3 Those who want to be farmers, fishermen, or general workers	9.7	4.8	1.8	5.1
Those who want to work in an office	46.2	53.9	61.4	54.2
Equally suitable for both groups	44.1	41.3	36.8	40.7
4 Pupils mainly having theoretical abilities	29.4	47.9	67.8	49.1
Pupils mainly having practical abilities	17.8	7.3	3.1	8.5
Equally suitable for both groups	52.7	44.8	29.1	42.4
5 Pupils who want to continue their education	55.9	62.2	65.6	61.9
Pupils who want to start working immediately after leaving school	12.5	5.1	1.7	5.8
Equally suitable for both groups	31.7	32.7	32.7	32.3
6 Those who want to go on living in rural areas	13.3	5.8	4.0	7.0
Those who want to go on living in towns and populous areas or want to move to such places	22.8	20.8	17.9	20.5
Equally suitable for both groups	63.9	73.5	78.1	72.5
Number	645	1,515	774	2,934
Percent	22.0	51.6	26.4	100.0

even if this cannot be directly inferred from Table 3. However, since these children acquire more from the urban-biased educational syllabus, experience more success during school life, and achieve better relationships with their teachers, they will probably also more often internalize the attitudes and values on which education is based, and develop more urban attitudes regarding work and spare time activities.

The value orientation and the natural priorities which have dominated the school system may be very well illustrated by the following statement made by a former school counselor in a discussion on the Lofoten project:

> Whenever a ninth-grade pupil asked me what to do after completing school, and I didn't know him personally, I went to the pupil files. If it turned out to be a fairly clever pupil obtaining good marks in the main subjects, I advised him to opt for the gymnasium. If he was an average pupil, I suggested that he might go to the vocational school for commerce. If it was a really low-achieving boy, I might ask whether or not his father had a fishing boat or a farm. If so, I suggested to him to join his father in the first place.[9]

The audience, headmasters and municipality school inspectors from the country of Nordland, generally agreed with this description.

Of course no one believes that every clever child accepts the standards set by the educational system, that every resourceful pupil does well at school, and that no one receiving a post-compulsory "academic" type of education returns to his home village (e.g., as a teacher). However, even if these effects are limited, they may have a decisive impact on the future of already small and weak communities.

An education that ignores local values and local knowledge may not just disqualify young people for adult life in typical rural areas, it may also create dependency and feelings of inferiority. Education is most likely to have this effect when a national system is imposed on ethnic minority groups. However, it is also reasonable to argue that even when the culture gap is less obvious, the school may (particularly among those not belonging to the "dominant" culture) produce attitudes such as "What is considered worthwhile in school has nothing to do with us," "We can't get important jobs in our village," or "It is not nice to talk in the way we do."

Conclusions[10]

If we want to enable people to stay in small settlements and in remote areas and encourage others to move into such communities, at least two conditions have to be met. First, the economy and labor market must allow people to make a living. Second, people (especially the young) must judge the way of life in remote areas and small settlements to be at least as attractive as the urban life. The important thing, however, is not the comparison between rural and urban life, nor the contrast between life in a political, economic, and/or cultural center and life in more peripheral areas. The main aim of the school should be to treat the home environment, the locality, and the region as a foundation of common experience from which to expand. Such an education will not only work to provide individual equality, but it will also further local, regional, and national equality.

In this context, it is also important to stress that every community should have its own school—but not just any school. Rather, the need is for a school that does not ignore problems relevant to the people it serves; that stresses the relationships between the local area and the regional and national level; and that shows how the local dialect has its grammatical rules and special concepts (i.e., its own values). If schools choose to embrace the challenge, they can be effective in imparting a sense that the student's own community has a history and tradition that is valid and important. Such schools will enable their students to develop the feeling of being members of a fully respected community. This feeling is probably a precondition for developing the self-confidence that is necessary for later success in life, be it in the home community or in the "outside world."

The Lofoten project was a modest first step in the direction of locally relevant rural education. To fully appreciate the project, one must view it not as an isolated innovation but rather as a manifestation of a larger movement in Norway and much of the rest of the world—a movement away from standardization and toward diversity; away from urbanization and toward a fuller appreciation of rural qualities; away from paying lip service to the importance of community and toward actively using the community as the foundation on which to build young people's understanding of themselves and the world in which they live.

Notes

1. St. meld. nr. 13, *Om mal og midler i distriktsutbyggingen.* [Parliamentary report No. 13: On the aims and means of district development] (Oslo, 1972-73).

2. In addition to the schools mentioned in Table 1, there are 325 schools in Norway with some sort of cross-age grouping, but without pupils at all six grade levels. Among these, there are 158 schools with pupils in grades 1 to 3 only, and 43 schools with pupils in grades 1 to 4. Most of these schools are located in the pupils' local environment, and were established to avoid long-distance transportation or boarding for such young children (aged seven to ten).

3. *Mønsterplanen for grunnskolen.* En foreløpig utgave. (Oslo: Aschehoug, 1973.)

4. Tiller, T. *Arbeidet med lokalt laerestoff: grunnskolen.* Thesis. (Tromsø:

University of Tromsø, 1976.)
5. Ibid., p. 24.
6. Ibid., p. 24.
7. Ibid., p. 139.
8. Ibid., p. 150.
9. Statement made at a meeting in September 1973 arranged by the school director of Nordland for municipal school inspectors.
10. For further information on the Lofoten project, see:

Høgmo, A. and Solstad, K. J. (1977): Lofotprosjektet. En skole ogsa for det lokale samfunn. *Forskningsnytt*, 22, no. 3-4.

Høgmo, A. and Solstad, K. J. (1977): Lofotprosjektet. Videreforing og oppfølging. 1 *Skolens arbok*. Oslo: Tanum - Norli.

Solberg, B. (1977): Sosialisering og tilhørighet. En litteraturstudie med utgangspunkt i Lofotprosjektet. Thesis. Oslo: University of Oslo.

Tiller, T., Solstad, K. J., Høgmo, A., Solberg, B., red. (1976): *Idehefter til Lofoten - i gar - i dag - i morgen.* Tromsø: University of Tromsø.

Solberg, B., Solstad, K. J., Høgmo, A., Tiller, T., red. (1975/76): *Lofoten - i gar - i dag - i morgen* / I–IV. Bodø. Nordland Boktrykkeri.

Høgmo, A. and Solstad, K. J. (1974): Lofotprosjektet. Et opplegg for en skole tilpasset lokalsamfunnet. 1 *Skolens arbok*. Oslo: Tanum.

12

Reform and Resistance: Rural School Improvement Projects in the United States

Faith Dunne

There is a quiet war in Iowa. On one side is assembled the professional education establishment of the state: the Department of Public Instruction (DPI), the state board of education, and legislators with significant influence over the committees that affect distribution of state aid to local school districts. Opposing them is an assortment of small-town citizens, farmers, and a few rural school people pulled together by two housewives into a grass-roots political organization called People United for Rural Education (PURE).[1]

The central issue in the war is the fate of this prosperous farm state's smallest school districts. Forty-five of Iowa's most rural schools have enrollments under 300, kindergarten through twelfth grade. Another 135 have fewer than 500 students enrolled. In the eyes of the DPI, these schools have no reason to exist. There is no rational impediment to consolidation of school districts in Iowa. The state is culturally homogeneous; there is little apparent difference between one small farm town and the next. The terrain is essentially flat and the climate reasonable, so that there would be little difficulty in busing students five miles (or fifteen) to schools in larger communities.

Therefore, the DPI has conceived a simple plan for the wholesale improvement of education in rural Iowa. Small districts would merge, or join with larger town schools, to form thousand-pupil units. This simple maneuver would provide an adequate student base for the provision of varied academic, vocational, and sports programs of a quality competitive with metropolitan Des Moines and Cedar Rapids. Without such programs, the DPI argues, students in the rural communities are deprived of a range of resources that would allow them to lead richer, more productive lives. Without such programs, they say, students will not be adequately prepared for future schooling or for employment outside their home communities.

Unfortunately, the education establishment's conception of sweet reason does not persuade all the residents of the small rural communities. PURE members and their allies argue that the school is the center of the rural community, its source of identity, its rallying point, its central concern. Businessmen feel that towns that lose their schools dry up as families begin to go to church where their children go to school, and then to shop and bank where the schools and churches are. School people point out that the winning basketball team or the state champion drill team engender great community pride and support; again and again, they tell stories of $7,000 raised for band uniforms in a single week, or of fathers who brought their heavy equipment down to the school and created a first-rate baseball diamond in a single weekend. Parents say that local schools permit them to keep track of what is happening to their children during and after school, attributing the low level of juvenile delinquency in rural Iowa to a high level of parental and community monitoring of the young. These are desirable outcomes too, PURE members argue, even if they can't be measured.

The battle rages back and forth. The DPI points out that good education cannot come out of a school where a teacher has five different preparations a day, where the college-bound student has insufficient competition to motivate excellence, where adequate facilities for science and foreign language study cannot be maintained. The PURE membership argues that students can get an equally good grounding in the basics in a small rural school, and can learn more about "communication . . . cooperation . . . and compassion" in the smaller setting.[2]

The most recent round of the conflict began in 1976 and was still raging in 1979. Arguments were rebutted and refined; battle lines drawn and fortified. And yet, the conflict remained remarkably free of any taint of evidence. DPI statisticians rejected the value of the "unmeasurable outcomes" so cherished by small-school proponents on the grounds that it was impossible to weigh the impact of variables that cannot be quantified. And yet, they have never compared the measurable outcomes of the smallest schools in the state with larger schools, even though they have the data and the capacity to control for socioeconomic status (a necessity to make such a comparison meaningful). The PURE organization, on the other hand, fills its newsletters primarily with personal testimonials ("One-Room Schoolhouse Had Virtues") and discussions of ways in which rural schools can wring more money from the state in a period of rising costs and declining enrollment ("Rethinking Iowa's State School Finance Plan"). Like the DPI, PURE's concern seems less with analysis of evidence than with defending an ideology. Evidence, on both sides, is used less as a means of testing hypotheses than as a bludgeon to keep an enemy at bay.

Two Models of Educational Reform

The Iowa situation is instructive not because it is unique, but because it is so typical of U.S. rural education reform conflicts over the last century. As in Iowa, rural education reform has traditionally pitted the professional educators (and, often, the university establishment) against the citizens of small communities. As in Iowa, both sides have generally believed that they were fighting for "quality education" in rural areas, and against people whose basic interests were not the same as those of rural students. And, as in Iowa, the battles have focused more on ideology than on data; they have been fought under the flags of differing clusters of assumptions about what constitutes "equal educational opportunity" and "adequate general education."[3]

Strategies for reform (and resistance to reform) have varied over the years, as have the techniques for implementing particular changes in rural schools. But the basic reform models, the clusters of assumptions which underlie the strategies, have remained remarkably constant. As Table 1 suggests, there are two primary models for rural school reform, one which can be labeled "Import and Improve," and one which can be called "Community-Based Reform." The differences between these models are at the root of the Iowa battle, and of hundreds of other fights presently erupting in rural America.

The Import and Improve model begins with the assumption that there is a single system of education which would benefit all children, if only it could be delivered to them in some consistent manner. "Equal educational opportunity" would thus require the provision of similar programs, facilities, and teachers to all children — or at least come as close as possible to this ideal condition.

Adherents of this model also tend to believe that the primary function of education is to increase the range of options for individuals. Therefore, they tend to define educational quality in terms of quantity of inputs. The best programs are those which provide the most opportunities — the widest variety of courses, the teachers with the most credentials, the broadest range of physical facilities. As the Iowa DPI will assert, a school's academic quality can thus be meaningfully measured by a simple count of its course offerings.

In rural areas, young people can have a maximum range of options only if they are prepared to cope with an urbanized society that is quite different from their home communities. Rural youngsters need to be trained to compete with one another if they are to be able to compete successfully in the urban labor market. They need to learn to deal with strangers in impersonal settings if they are to be able to live and work happily in metropolitan places. They need to learn job skills which will be marketable in the cities. Import and Improve advocates believe that this kind of preparation should

TABLE 1

CONTRASTING MODELS OF RURAL EDUCATION REFORM

Import and Improve	Community-Based Reform
1. Equality defined as similarity of services.	1. Equality defined as equally suited to different needs of different places.
2. Quality defined in terms of desirable inputs.	2. Quality defined in terms of desired outcomes.
3. Preparation for the future requires learning to deal with strangers, institutional policies, impersonality.	3. Preparation for the future requires a firm grounding in community values and a trained appreciation of the values of community life.
4. The appropriate primary locus of educational control is the professional establishment.	4. The appropriate primary locus of educational control is the community.
5. The primary function of schooling is to increase the range of individual options.	5. The primary function of schooling is to maintain and nurture the life of the community.

be a primary function of the schools, that the schools should serve as the bridge from the home communities to the larger world.

Finally, those who subscribe to the Import and Improve model believe that control over educational policy and practice is appropriately held by professionals, not community members. Professionals, they argue, spend a lifetime learning what is best for schooling young people. They have links with a national network which brings them new ideas for teaching and fresh information about the demands the culture is likely to make on the next generation. They can push schools to maintain minimum standards, so that a child in one school will have the same basic exposure to knowledge as a child in another. Further, professionals have the advantage of detachment: their job is to keep the best interests of schoolchildren at the center of their minds. They do not need to worry about tax burdens, or community stability, or the individually pressing problems of individual towns.

It is easy to see how acceptance of the Import and Improve cluster of assumptions leads to the conclusion that larger schools (within limits) are better ones. It is difficult to offer a varied program without large numbers of students to take advantage of the different courses. It is hard to build specialized, modern facilities or to hire highly trained (and expensive) teachers without a broad tax base. It is virtually impossible to train young people to compete in a depersonalized metropolitan setting if they are kept in small, community-based schools with peers they have known all their lives. Thus, proponents of the Import and Improve model tend to see educational reform in terms of consolidation of small schools, establishment of regional high schools, and the creation of large administrative units within the states.

The opposing cluster of assumptions, the Community-Based Reform model, orders its educational priorities quite differently. Adherents of this model define equality not as similarity, but as "equally responsive to the differing needs and desires of different communities." Equality is thus achieved when each community has (within very general constraints) the kind of schooling it wants for its children. Those who maintain the Community-Based cluster of assumptions believe that the ideal school system would provide multiple kinds of settings, each tailored to the specific needs of different communities.

Community-Based Reform proponents see the rural school as the heart of rural community life and want to enhance its capacity to maintain that function. Thus, they are ready to sacrifice breadth of program and specialization of facilities to keep schools local and responsive to the perceived needs of the community. Since they reject quantity and diversity of offerings as a first priority value, they tend to want to assess program quality in terms of outcomes rather than inputs, and to define those desired outcomes in a necessarily limited way. From their point of view, rural school reform must be approached carefully. It should grow out of the self-identified needs of a community and must be carried out by known and trusted leaders. Their emphasis is on continuity rather than change, so they tend to be less relentlessly progressive than the Import and Improve advocates. In short, they are *conservative* in the most fundamental sense of that abused term.

Like those who accept the Import and Improve model, Community-Based Reform adherents recognize that rural children face an uncertain future. However, they do not believe that young people must be prepared in school to fit easily into urban settings, preferring to look to the strengths inherent in rural community life to support young people through such transitions as they find it necessary to make.

Finally, those who believe in Community-Based Reform feel that the appropriate locus of educational control is in the community itself. Only a community can determine what it needs from the school to allow it to survive and flourish. Only a community is likely to have a genuine long-term stake in the development of its young people. Some advocates of Community-Based Reform do believe that local people lack the broad view and specialized expertise of the professionals, and they want to engage professional assistance in determining educational needs and in program design. But all feel that the important choices should be made by the local citizens in a rather unregulated fashion.

For obvious reasons, those who believe in Community-Based Reform reject the notion that size is associated with quality. Instead, they want to found rural school improvement plans on local values, on the inherent qualities of smallness, and on the kinds of cooperative network building that has served small-scale rural economic interests well in the past.

Early Rural School Reform: Implementing Importation

From the beginning of the rural school reform movement in the mid-1800s, the Import and Improve model has been strongly promoted by the professional educators. The concept of a single, unified system of schooling seems to have emerged as part of the movement toward free, universal, compulsory education. David Tyack, in *Turning Points in American Educational History,* quoted conservative Massachusetts governor Edward Everett (who appointed Horace Mann as the first secretary of the Massachusetts State Board of Education) on the function of schooling in a democracy: "We must establish such a system of general education as will furnish a supply of well-informed, intelligent, and respectable citizens, in every part of the country and in every walk of life, capable of discharging the trusts which the people may devolve upon them."[4]

It seems clear that Everett, and those who agreed with him that a common education was a necessary precondition for a stable democracy, wanted to be sure that the well-informed citizens had access to the same body of information, and that they were capable of discharging trust in similar ways. From the conception that schools were to prepare people to take equivalent shares in the democratic process came (at least in part) the sense that their education should be equivalent as well.

If one kind of educational system was to be spread through the nation, it was clear to the professional educators of the late nineteenth century that it should be the new, modern, urban model of schooling. Ellwood Cubberley, a professor at Stanford University and a leading rural school reformer at the turn of the century, stated the common position flatly: "Compared with a good town or city school the country school is poor, often miserably poor, and the numerous classes, overburdened programme, absence of equipment and lack of ideas and impulses to action offer odds against which the best of teachers can make but little headway."[5] The answer, Cubberley went on to say, lies in school reorganization, which will centralize, consolidate, and standardize the rural school so that it can more closely resemble the "good town or city school to which it compares so poorly." He promised much: "With about twenty such schools to a county, instead of a hundred and fifty little ones . . . the whole nature of rural life and education could be redirected and revitalized in a decade, and life on the farm could be given a new meaning."[6]

It is easy to see how Cubberley, and the vast majority of other professional reformers, came to this position. Unquestionably, the rural schools varied widely, according to the wealth of the community and its conception of adequate education. When Cubberley described the typical rural school as a "miserable, unsanitary box," lacking all but the most primitive equipment and the most poorly trained teachers, he reflected accurately the condition of many rural schools. Schools in newer, more prosperous urban areas were often far superior in both program and personnel to most rural schools. Cubberley, like many of his contemporaries, made the leap from correlation to causation, reasoning that size was the key to adequate funding, and that standardization was the key to an adequate curriculum. Thus, consolidation and objective standards became (and remain to this day) the professionally acceptable mode for rural school reform.

Other factors bolstered these lines of reasoning. The period of industrialization in the United States brought with it a near worship of factory modes of efficient production. And, as Tyack pointed out, the factory model was soon applied to conceptions of schooling.[7] If one believed in a single appropriate system of education that "should be a model of bureaucratic punctuality and precision,"[8] the rag-tag assortment of rural schools, locally controlled and as varied as the communities they served, could not provide quality education under any circumstances. The salvation of rural schooling had to lie in the elimination of traditional rural schools.

Finally, there was a rising sense among Americans, both rural and urban, that the future was in the cities. Outmigration from rural to urban areas rose steadily through the end of the nineteenth century and the beginning of the twentieth. Cubberley bewailed the desertion of country life by yeomen farmers who left their lands in the hands of tenants with no strong sense of civic responsibility and who were (at least in his view) incapable of adequately managing their schools. Larger administrative units were recommended as a means of keeping control of the schools out of the hands of incompetents (and in the hands of professionals). And consolidated schools were the only way to recruit and hold "town-sick" teachers, who would be easily lured to the metropolitan areas if they could not teach standardized materials to single-grade classes in the country.

Against the logic and experience of the professionals stood the rural communities, armed only with an ill-defined, ill-defended version of the Community-Based Reform model. Consolidators like Cubberley had elaborate plans for the "new rural school," detailed down to the floor plan of the concrete-and-porous-tile basement.[9] Rural lay people rarely had a coherent counterplan for improving their schools; all they knew was what they did not want to relinquish. They were thus readily dismissed by the education establishment as backward folk who did not have the best interests of their own children at heart. Cubberley described them thus: "extremely conservative, unprogressive, jealous, penny-wise, and lacking in any proper conception of the value of good educational conditions. Any progressive proposal is usually met by determined and often unreasoning opposition, and progress by consent of the voters is a slow and arduous undertaking."[10]

There was little sense in this period that the rural citizenry had an alternative model of appropriate education, much less that their model had merit. They were perceived simply as roadblocks to progress, impediments to the quick and fruitful implementation of the "one best system" which would provide America with an effectively educated electorate and a skilled and tractable work force.

Import and Improve: Contemporary Variations

Since the inception of the idea that free, compulsory public schools could prepare individuals for participation in a common governmental process, Import and Improve has been the persistent model of rural education reform. Its most obvious manifestation is the school reorganization movement, which began its most recent and most effective effort immediately after World War II, and which is still alive and well today in Iowa and elsewhere. Between 1950 and 1970, the number of one-teacher schools in the United States dropped from 60,000 to 2,000. The number of elementary schools dropped from 128,000 to 66,000 in the same period, despite the postwar "baby boom" and major building programs in cities and suburbs.[11] The drive to consolidate rural schools has slowed considerably in the last few years, primarily because most of the schools that were amenable to consolidation have been reorganized. However, the cluster of assumptions that supports the Import and Improve model has not vanished with the one-room school.

Today, the Import and Improve model informs a variety of rural school improvement programs. First, it is the basis of programs that attempt to simulate the virtues of consolidated schools in schools where actual reorganization is impossible. The Rocky Mountain Area Project for Small High Schools (RMAP) and its successor, the Western States Small Schools Project (WSSSP), were designed as this kind of conscious complement. Their originators believed that consolidation and standardization provided the best kind of education, especially at the secondary level, but recognized that terrain, climate, and sparse population prohibited school closures in many parts of the mountainous and rangeland West. Therefore, they tried to adapt the programs and methods of the metropolitan schools to the "necessarily existent" small school. RMAP started in 1958, at the beginning of the wave of technological and instructional innovations typifying the 1960s. WSSSP, which expanded the work of RMAP using Ford Foundation funds, focused on fashionable metropolitan innovations, bringing to remote, tiny rural schools computerized scheduling, team teaching, programmed instruction, and the like. This "innovations assembly," clearly based on the Import and Improve assumptions, attempted to produce the advantages of size, specialization, and breadth in schools unable to provide such advantages for themselves.

A second kind of Import and Improve program involves the use of technological equipment to provide rural areas with resources that are readily available in metropolitan contexts. The most spectacular example of this kind of program is the satellite jointly sponsored by the National Institute of Education and the National Aeronautics and Space Administration. In the early 1970s it beamed teacher education films to school personnel in remote areas of Alaska, the Rocky Mountains, and Appalachia, where in-service education was not available through the customary, urbanized system of universities, teacher centers, and workshops.

Other, less far-flung programs provide a broader range of resources to more limited areas. Several states maintain "intermediate service units,"

agents of the state departments of education whose purpose it is to provide
rural schools with access to materials, equipment, and educational
specialists. Expensively equipped vans bring museum exhibits, environmental studies laboratories, multimedia curricula, and film libraries to rural
schoolchildren in states from Maine to Texas.

The National Diffusion Network (NDN) focuses on the innovations adoption process, and has made that a national effort.[12] Begun in 1974, NDN
supports a dissemination effort that relies on "state facilitators," whose job it
is to introduce school people to tested, "proven effective" materials and
practices developed by education professionals from all over the country.
The success of a "state facilitator" is gauged by the number of "adoptions"
that take place in that state and the rate at which new programs are introduced into the schools.

Although the programs offered by the NDN developers are rarely tailored
to the specific needs of rural schools, many facilitators see the rural districts
as their primary target group. They reason that the smaller, more isolated
districts need NDN most, since they have less ready access to the professional
and university networks serving large school systems and are thus less likely
to encounter new, up-to-date materials on their own.

A final contemporary Import and Improve program variant comes out of
efforts to provide standardized services to highly unstandardized schools in
rural areas. For example, the state of Vermont preceded its legislation to integrate handicapped students into regular classrooms with an offer to pay 75
percent of the salary for a trained consulting teacher, who would set up appropriate programs for handicapped children and assist teachers with
classroom problems. To qualify for state salary support, however, the consulting teachers had to be trained by a specific program at the University of
Vermont that focuses on behavior modification techniques. This program
has been in operation since 1968; thus, the vast majority of handicapped
children in Vermont public schools now work with a highly homogeneous
group of consulting teachers who provide similar services in very similar
ways. Other states take comparable measures to insure standardization and
quality control, particularly in the provision of services outside of the
classroom routines.[13]

As these examples should make clear, the Import and Improve model is
neither the answer nor the devil, although it has been called both by different rural reformers. Where importation is the only way to get important
educational and cultural resources to students, it is obviously necessary to
import. When standardization can be proved to be the best way to ensure
quality of service, it is clearly important to standardize. The primary problem with Import and Improve as a model of educational reform is not that it
is ineffective nor even that it is wholly inappropriate, but rather that it has

been promoted as the *only* accurate set of assumptions from which productive rural reform could possibly stem. This monolithic viewpoint has limited the capacities of rural communities to develop solutions that rely on local resources, and it has often engendered unnecessary antagonism between reformers and the rural school districts they are trying to help. Unfortunately, this antagonism has developed even in situations where local citizens might have willingly adopted proposed reforms if they had not had to simultaneously abandon their sense that their community is unique and thus in need of specially tailored improvements.

Community-Based Rural School Reform:
An Alternative Strategy

An alternative view of rural school improvement needed to emerge — a view that would allow rural communities to build reforms from their own strengths, and would seek improvements based upon the real and perceived differences among them. Over the past twenty-five years, this alternative view has gradually taken hold. Beginning in the 1950s, at the same time as the last great push for rural school consolidation, the Community-Based model of reform has gained gradual credibility among professionals, thus augmenting its traditional support among rural residents. At first conceived as a means of improving schooling in places too small to consolidate — a kind of Community-Based companion piece to Import and Improve projects like WSSSP — this cluster of assumptions has gained considerable power as a competing mode of rural school reform. Between 1950 and 1978, more and more rural educational reformers and their financial supporters came to see the Community-Based model as a legitimate way to attack some of the important problems of rural education.

An originator of this new professional view of rural education was Frank Cyr, a professor at Columbia University's Teachers' College in the 1950s. Cyr suggested that small rural schools were different in kind, not simply in quality, from large schools. He compared the urban school to a train, made up of specialized cars, hooked together and proceeding at a great rate along a given track. The rural district, Cyr suggested, needs an educational vehicle that resembles an automobile, "designed as a self-contained unit. It should not be designed as a series of specialized units, as is the railroad train. Like the automobile, the small school should be designed to serve the varied needs and interests of small groups of students. This means there is need for a new design of small schools, a design that will replace the rigidity of the specialized big-school pattern with a more flexible pattern."[14]

In 1957, the Ford Foundation funded an experimental program under Cyr's leadership in a three-county region in rural New York State. The Catskill Area Project in Small School Design (CAPSSD) included some elements—an emphasis on technology and on special programs for gifted students—associated with the Import and Improve programs of the same period. Cyr's basic disposition, however, was to build programs that would exploit the strengths of smallness—flexibility, strong personal relationships between staff and students, articulated organization, and the integration of the school with the local community. Specific innovations were tied to these perceived strengths. CAPSSD experimented with multiple classes under a single teacher's supervision, with the use of community aides, with shared services among schools, and with supervised correspondence study. The practices themselves were not unique, but the attitudes that informed them were unusual in a professionally inspired program.

Another important program of that decade, the Berea College Rural School Improvement Project, which ran from 1953 to 1957, attacked the educational problems of poverty-stricken, mountainous eastern Kentucky. The originators of the Berea project described the rural mountain schools in terms almost identical to those used by Cubberley fifty years earlier: "drab, uncomfortable, run-down and shabby quarters, where many children of the mountains went to classes. The weed-grown paths; grassless and muddy playgrounds; faded paint; dirt-smeared weatherboarding; cracked window glass; rutted and untidy yards; ill-lighted interiors; stiff-backed desks; potbellied stoves; dim blackboards; corner water buckets; dusty pictures hung too high—all these things and more made many elementary schools in the mountains dismal and uninteresting."[15] Their proposed remedy, however, was not identical to Cubberley's. Perhaps the program initiators did not see consolidation as a realistic possibility for the mountains, where roads routinely run directly through brooks, and often vanish without a trace into muddy trenches during rainy seasons. The Berea project was conceived as a locally oriented improvement program that would send specially trained teachers into individual communities to improve the quality of education in the elementary schools, engaging local support and utilizing local resources.

Like CAPSSD, the Berea project was based on a combination of Import and Improve and Community-Based assumptions. The program assumed that the way to improve poor rural schools was to send in highly trained teachers and to provide those teachers with a support network based in a central location (in this case, Berea College). The program originators assumed that they could meet the needs of these teachers for more specialized training with college institutes on subjects such as remedial reading, use of audiovisual materials, and other currently topical educational subjects. Field trips and traveling resources (such as bookmobiles and foreign visitors) were provided to children who often had no other kind of contact with the world beyond their home communities.

At the same time, however, the Berea project deliberately set out to facilitate Community-Based efforts at school improvement in community-identified areas. The teaching fellows in each community formed groups with local leaders and children to establish goals and objectives for the improvement of the school. These aims were to stem from the specific qualities of the communities; evidently, they did. The Berea project report said that the "number and variety of goals and objectives [in the thirty-eight communities where there were teaching fellows] were so great that they defy explanation of each."[16] Many of the goals concerned the improvement of the school building itself, and the report notes as one of the major successes that local people contributed both their labor and their money to school improvements in virtually all of the project communities.

This kind of community-based school improvement activity suggests an entirely different attitude toward rural people and their concern for their children's education than one finds in Cubberley or his colleagues. The Berea project assumption is that local communities care deeply about their children's schooling, that they will be willing to contribute to the improvement of the local school, and that a community stake in rural school improvement is crucial, since the ultimate fate of such projects will be in its hands once external funding is gone.

Ironically, in the years since the Berea project, the counties served by it have been the target of an intensive consolidation drive. Few of the schools to which the project sent teaching fellows still exist. The primary legacy of the Berea project seems to be its sense that rural communities must be involved in school reform and the concept that, in some ways at least, each rural community must be treated as a separate entity, with individual problems requiring unique solutions.

Projects of the 1960s and 1970s:
New Approaches

The 1960s and 1970s saw a rise in the number and variety of rural school improvement programs founded on Community-Based assumptions. There seem to have been three reasons for this. First, consolidation (the primary manifestation of the Import and Improve philosophy) had to pay the price of its own success. Thousands of communities had agreed to consolidate their schools on the grounds that it would be cheaper, or that their children would get a vaguely defined "better" curriculum, or that new facilities would improve both teacher and student performance. By the mid-1960s, it was clear to both the consolidated districts and their unconsolidated neighbors that the advantages of reorganization did not come without costs. When the education establishment (the universities and the state departments of education) began to push for second-generation reorganization of rural schools, community people who had allowed their one-room schools to be consolidated began to balk. In rural places across the country, people began to ask for alternative plans that might permit them to keep their schools within their self-defined communities.

Second, the late 1960s provided a national climate hospitable to pluralism. The sense that there had to be a "one best system" for universal education began to erode under the pressure of a hundred years of failure to find such a system and a rising sense that it was legitimate for communities, like individuals, to "do their own thing." U.S. rural communities, long bastions of political conservatism and staunch localism, were able to translate this shift in national attitude into a reassertion of their right to local self-determination.

Finally, social and technological changes had made unnecessary some of the reforms the Import and Improve model is best suited to carry out. Television, the interstate highway system, and the increasing homogenization of the United States (a McDonald's hamburger stand on every highway and a shopping mall in every third town) have produced a relatively sophisticated rural population. Familiarity with the national culture, easy access to general information, awareness that there exist groups of people unlike themselves, are all available to rural young people without consolidated schools — indeed, without schools at all. Thus, the need for importing urban resources to the country school has become less important to rural parents than the need to keep the less attractive urban influences at bay.

It would be erroneous to suggest that these conditions caused an upsurge of Community-Based rural school improvement projects that eclipsed the Import and Improve model. Import and Improve remains the basic mode of rural school reform. But new, innovative projects, especially those funded at the national level, began more and more to use the language of local determination, of community identification of problems, and of solutions unique to specific localities.

Programs built on the Community-Based assumption cluster took a number of forms. One of the earliest was the small-scale educational cooperative, funded by a combination of district contributions and grant money. Many of these "regional centers" still exist. Some are prospering; some barely make it from budget year to budget year. Centers provide their constituent districts with a variety of services, which differ from center to center and have changed over time. One such cooperative, the Regional Center for Educational Training in Hanover, New Hampshire, offers among other things a purchasing service (providing small member districts with discounts on large joint orders), a variety of in-service training experiences, and an array of specially tailored "Move Kits" (multimedia curriculum packages that are constantly on loan to local schools). These relatively informal local cooperatives are limited by low funding levels and by their general mandate to respond to the perceived needs of districts rather than to initiate innovative rural programs. But, at their best, they provide some of the benefits of consolidation without many of the costs, and they can serve as resources for the identification and development of programs designed around the special qualities of smallness and ruralness.

Regional cooperatives developed as one major kind of Community-Based school reform in the early 1960s. In the middle of that decade, a second important form emerged: the Leadership Development Program. In 1966, program officers at the Ford Foundation reviewed several past rural school improvement projects and came to two conclusions. First, rural school improvement, no matter how brilliantly conceived or lavishly funded, cannot work if there is no local leadership to implement it. The innovation will dry up as soon as the outside funding and guidance departs. Second, the natural leadership in rural communities has been weakened over the years by a combination of the migration of bright young people to metropolitan areas and the increasing dominance of outside control over the lives of those who remain. The Ford Foundation decided to approach this problem by funding a program to identify potential local leaders in rural communities and provide them with financial and technical support that would allow them to develop their skills and expertise. These leaders, it was assumed, would then be able to bridge the gap between the needs of their home areas and the resources available at the state and national level for rural improvement.

The Leadership Development Program was a deliberately high-risk venture. The project specialists who chose the fellows were not given a fixed definition of leadership to guide their selection process; instead, it was assumed that there were nearly as many kinds of local leaders as there were kinds of communities. This led to a very broad assortment of fellows, ranging from a Blackfoot Indian teacher from a Montana reservation who spent his fellowship year developing curriculum materials reflecting the culture of his people, to an Appalachian coal miner who used his fellowship money to gather data on black lung disease, to an urban transplant from California who spent her time trying to act as an "undercover change agent" in a rural New England school.

The Leadership Development Program had distinct limitations. The high-risk nature of the selection process produced some startling successes, but also some startling failures. Further, it was very expensive; over a ten-year period, the Ford Foundation spent approximately $10 million on 700 fellowships. As Paul Nachtigal points out in his case study of the program, it "has not at this point been successful in attracting funds from other sources to continue in its original form. All four programs have been closed out in spite of fairly intense efforts in both the Northeast and the Southeast to attract new funding, the high cost likely being the primary reason."[17] Finally, and perhaps most significant, the determination of who was a potential community leader remained in the hands of a Ford Foundation "specialist," whose own predispositions and assumptions shaped the nature of the fellowship group. In the Northeast, for example, the project specialists tended to select highly educated, articulate young people whose leadership potential seemed more likely to find its appropriate outlet at the state or national level than in the local community. In Appalachia and the deep South, on the other hand, fellowships tended to go to potential leaders from traditionally disenfranchised minority groups, who were likely to remain tied to their communities of origin. In neither case, however, did the communities have a free hand in selecting their own leaders for the fellowships. There were built-in problems in the Leadership Development Program; nevertheless, it was clearly a beacon rural improvement project of the Community-Based variety.

Throughout the late 1960s and early 1970s, variations on the basic themes of leadership training and small school networks continued to emerge. The Southern Appalachian Leadership Training Program (SALT) was directly inspired by the larger, richer, Ford program. It has a narrower focus, both geographic and philosophic, but it works, as did the earlier program, to prepare community people to put pressure on schools that do not meet the needs of their children. In another kind of adaptation, the Northwest Regional Educational Laboratory recast the rural school network idea in the form of their *Promising Practices* series.[18] In this series of softcover books on rural program and curriculum innovations, the Northwest Laboratory described original, tested programs primarily from rural school districts in the western part of the United States, and made these descriptions available to rural schools across the country. SALT took a national program and focused it on a smaller set of people and issues; the Northwest Laboratory took a model developed by small local district cooperatives and enlarged it for national use. But, in both instances, the related assumptions and the general strategies remained constant.

The 1970s: Community-Based Programs
as High Fashion

The Community-Based programs of the 1960s tended to be structural; they focused on developing rural means of achieving cosmopolitan ends. The Leadership Development Program was intended to create a group of rural community people who could obtain and manage outside resources in a sophisticated fashion. The small school cooperatives were expected to provide metropolitan-type services to nonmetropolitan districts. The initiators of these programs assumed that uniquely rural structures were needed to achieve these desired ends. However, the expectation that rural communities could define the *content* of reform did not emerge in a full-blown, self-conscious form until the 1970s.

The Northwest Laboratory's Rural Futures Development Program (RFD) was perhaps the first manifestation of this new vision of rural school improvement.[19] Begun in 1971, the RFD program was a comprehensive effort to train whole rural communities in decision-making processes leading to educational reform. "Process facilitators" from the local community were trained by the Northwest Laboratory to help form local "school-community groups" and to train those groups in a complex but clearly defined way of resolving conflict and making decisions about educational improvement. The Northwest Laboratory produced a series of "how-to" manuals on the change process, but made no effort to define what would be changed or who ought to benefit from the change process.

Like any model of educational reform, the RFD strategy is not without flaws. School-community groups are easy to form when there are major issues to resolve; they tend to atrophy when things are running smoothly. Further, when the process facilitators are paid by the school district (as they must inevitably be if the program is to exist without outside funding), they come under continuous pressure to act as agents of the administration and school board rather than as organizers for the community at large. Some can withstand such pressure, but it is difficult for most people to avoid responding to the needs of those who pay their salaries. Nevertheless, RFD has trained cadres of rural community people in a planning and decision-making process that may enable them to develop unique and self-sustaining reforms for their own schools. This was certainly the intent of the Northwest Laboratory program developers.

In the seven years following the implementation of the RFD strategy, most of the educational programs funded by foundations or federal agencies have at least attempted to appear Community-Based. The federal Experimental Schools Program, whose rural initiative began in 1972, offered direct funding to small school districts that wanted to carry out locally constructed plans for comprehensive school reform.[20] When the National Institute of Education decided to fund a major study of rural school improvement projects over the past twenty-five years, a basic evaluation criterion was the extent to which the projects enhanced a community's capacity to solve its own problems.[21]

The recent large-scale program with the greatest potential impact on rural school reform is probably the teachers' center movement. Originally an urban, teacher-initiated strategy for school reform, the teachers' center concept is more readily adaptable to rural needs than many earlier models. Teachers' centers are deliberately small-scale, locally oriented organizations whose primary function is to provide resources appropriate to teachers in a limited number of schools. Like the small school cooperative organizations of the 1960s, the teachers' centers are oriented toward local service. However, they focus on classroom and schoolwide program issues rather than on administrative needs. Thus rural teachers' centers have the opportunity to fulfill some of rural education's least met and most pressing needs: the need for curricula designed around rural community life and resources; the need for professional enrichment among teachers who live very isolated work lives; the need for a local organization staffed by known and trusted people who, nevertheless, have access to the resources of a national network.

It is not yet clear that rural teachers' centers will fulfill their promise. While there is increasing rural consciousness among nonmetropolitan teachers' center staff members, there is still some tendency for the movement to show its urban roots. Many teachers' centers are located in population centers (particularly in towns large enough to support a university or college) and tend to offer their most intensive services to the schools within that district. Teachers from outlying very small districts are welcome to come in to the town centers, to borrow materials and make use of resources, but they tend to get little of the direct classroom program assistance so badly needed in rural schools. Furthermore, some of the pioneer organizations, such as Vermont's Mountain Towns Teachers' Center, received no money in the late 1970s federal funding cycle, apparently because their rural orientation kept them from offering services to a large enough number of teachers and children.[22]

It is too early to tell what direction rural teachers' centers will take. Perhaps they will become indirect vehicles for Import and Improve school reforms; it is equally possible that they will be innovative forces on behalf of Community-Based interventions. Their ultimate direction will depend on the philosophic orientation of their leadership and the practical costs of genuinely rural ventures.

More promising than the national efforts at Community-Based rural school reform are the scores of small-scale projects springing up all over the United States. They are less restricted by guidelines and external supervision than the larger programs, and they do not depend on the whims of federal policy and state funding patterns. A good example is the proliferation of Foxfire-type oral history projects in rural communities from Maine to Hawaii. The organization of Iowa's PURE as a formal political action group advocating the positive qualities of small schools is another. The reestablishment of a fine, tiny school in Big Laurel, West Virginia, is a third. The list could go on and on, citing programs and projects entirely different from one another, which have in common only their intensely local orientation and their fundamentally rural bias.

These small-scale projects seem to have been accelerated by two general trends in the culture at large. First, there has been, over the past decade, an increasing sense of rural self-worth. The popularization of Schumacher's "small is beautiful" philosophy, a general disenchantment with the fragmenting, alienating quality of urban life, and the concomitant pattern of outmigration from metropolitan to rural areas have all contributed to a growing sense that country life has many positive attributes, and that a commitment to rural citizenship does not necessarily make one a hick.

Second, there is a growing communications network among rural educators, facilitated by the increasing popularity of pluralistic approaches to school reform. Tom Gjelten, principal of a tiny school on a remote Maine island, worked with teachers to design and test a career education program for his extremely isolated community. In the spring of 1978, he published a small book on that experience and made it available, with minimal publicity, to other rural educators.[23] Within six months the entire first printing was gone, and requests for more copies have not diminished. It is unlikely that this kind of demand for descriptions of small-scale rural programs would have existed ten years ago, but it will probably increase over the next decade. It is interesting to note that Gjelten's program is not, as the federal jargon would put it, "transportable"—that is, the North Haven Island curriculum could not simply be installed "as is" in another rural community. Thus, the people who request his book are less likely to try to replicate his curriculum than to use it as a source of ideas on the basis of which they can make their own design.

Balance and Fashion:
The Future of Rural Educational Reform

The growing numbers of small-scale rural school improvement projects and the rising popularity of the Community-Based model among policymakers and funding sources appears to bode well for the future of rural educational reform. But there are still risks. At best, the new trend will provide those who want to improve rural education with a new array of flexible and effective strategies with which to attack the enduring problems of country schooling. At worst, it will provoke a pitched battle among professionals about the appropriate way to improve country schools, a battle which rural people can only lose.

The most serious potential problem is that the Community-Based model will replace Import and Improve as the latest version of the One True Way. There is a tendency in American education to rush wholeheartedly from one panacea to another, to embrace the newest fashion as the answer to all possible problems, and to reject the last mode as hopelessly flawed and therefore useless. This tendency has two unfortunate effects. First, it does not permit the identification and retention of the best aspects of the earlier mode which might still be useful in creating constructive change. Second, it creates the expectation that the new model will be flawless, which leads inevitably to disappointment and, ultimately, to a new round of wholesale rejection and subsequent adoption of a new True Way. In any setting, this process is wasteful and distracts reformers from the difficult business of designing appropriate educational improvements. In rural areas, where innovation is regarded with (often legitimate) suspicion, the swiftly changing tides of fashion can destroy future chances for any kind of productive reform.

Genuine productive reform must be hybrid. It is not built from single-minded ideology, but from the requirements of a particular situation in a particular setting. It combines the most suitable elements from a range of strategies and puts them together in a way not amenable to labels. When Vito Perrone went to the University of North Dakota in 1968, his mandate was to Import and Improve. The New School program, which he directed, was intended to upgrade teacher training in a state where 59 percent of the teachers lacked a college degree and, simultaneously, to convert all North Dakota elementary schools to open classroom practices. But Perrone's administrative style was not characteristic of the centralized, standardized Import and Improve reforms. He recognized that rural community differences interfere with comprehensive program implementation, but instead of fighting that interference, he incorporated it into the New School program. The non-degree teachers who were the target of the program were experienced practitioners, most with deep roots in their local schools and communities. The New School program taught them a uniform philosophy of education and a group of techniques stemming from that philosophy; dissemination of these practices was left primarily in the hands of the teachers, who were expected to interpret informal education in ways that would be acceptable to the local community and the local school. The wide variation in the results was considered a sign of adaptation, not of failure.[24]

The New School program is a model, not of teacher retraining, not of open classroom practice, but of how to create a hybrid educational reform. The New School educational improvement effort is informed by experience broader than an individual community could produce, but it is structured to be adapted to local needs by someone likely to know what those needs are.

The trouble back in Iowa—the trouble, in fact, with all the American communities currently engaged in destructive battles over the future of their rural schools—is an overdose of ideology. So much energy is lost arguing over who holds the right view of "equal education" that no one has the time or the energy to construct a hybrid approach. Rural schools should keep their children from provincial narrowness; this requires an Import and Improve approach. At the same time, it is critical that rural communities be able to convey their own identities and their own values to their children through the educational system; this calls for a Community-Based point of view. There is no Higher Good in an educational situation like this. The aim must be to adapt, to combine, to create a hybrid from outside ideas and local needs which will suit a particular community at a particular time. Such a notion has no conceptual elegance; its only redeeming quality is that it is likely to work.

Notes

The unpublished case studies noted below were produced by the National Institute of Education–funded project "Improving Education in Rural America: Past Efforts, Future Opportunities," directed by Paul Nachtigal. They were revised and published in book form in 1981. Anyone who would like information about this book should address inquiries to Thomas Schultz, Program Officer, National Institute of Education, 1200 19th Street, N. W., Washington, D. C. 20208.

1. Faith Dunne, "Have You Considered Reorganization? Iowa's People United for Rural Education" (Unpublished case study, 1979).

2. *PURE Newsletter*, Volume 2, Number 3 (March 1978), Alden, Iowa.

3. Faith Dunne, "Iowa's Small Rural Schools: Rejecting the Inevitable," *PURE Newsletter*, Volume 3, Number 3 (March 1979).

4. David Tyack, *Turning Points in American Education* (Lexington, Mass.: Xerox College Publishing, 1967), p. 122.

5. Ellwood Cubberley, *The Improvement of Rural Schools* (Boston: Houghton Mifflin Company, 1912), p. 14.

6. Ellwood Cubberley, *Rural Life and Education* (Cambridge, Mass.: The Riverside Press, 1914), p. 255.

7. David Tyack, *The One Best System* (Cambridge, Mass.: Harvard University Press, 1974), pp. 39–59.

8. Ibid., p. 43.

9. Cubberley, *Rural Life and Education*.

10. Cubberley, *The Improvement of Rural Schools*, p. 12.

11. Jonathan Sher, ed., *Education in Rural America* (Boulder, Colo.: Westview Press, 1977).

12. Dan Cromer and Thomas Gjelten, "The National Diffusion Network" (Unpublished case study, 1979).

13. *1968–1969 Yearly Report of the Consulting Teacher Program, Volume 1* (Washington, D.C.: Bureau of Education for the Handicapped, 1969).

14. Frank Cyr, *Catskill Area Project in Small School Design* (Oneonta, N.Y.:

State University Teacher's College, 1959).

15. Roscoe E. Buckland, ed., *Rural School Improvement Project: Final Report* (Lexington, Ky.: Transylvania Printing Company, 1958), p. 15.

16. Ibid., p. 87.

17. Paul Nachtigal, "Ford Leadership Development Program" (Unpublished case study, 1978).

18. *Promising Practices in Small High Schools* (Portland, Ore.: Northwest Regional Education Laboratory, 1970).

19. James Branscome, "Rural Futures Program: San Juan County, Utah" (Unpublished case study, 1978).

20. Lawrence Hennigh, "Cooperation and Conflict in Long-Term Educational Change: South Umpqua, Oregon" (draft) (Cambridge, Mass.: Abt Associates, 1978).

21. Paul Nachtigal, "Improving Education in Rural America: Past Efforts, Future Opportunities" (Response to the National Institute of Education's Request for Proposals, Number NIE-R-77-0011, 1977).

22. Faith Dunne, "Mountain Towns Teachers' Center Case" (Unpublished case study, 1979).

23. Thomas Gjelten, *Schooling in Isolated Communities* (Portland, Me.: Maine Department of Education and Cultural Studies, 1978).

24. Faith Dunne, "'Going Open' in North Dakota: The New School for Behavioral Studies in Education" (Unpublished case study, 1979).